Lecture Notes in Computer Science 15376

Founding Editors

Gerhard Goos
Juris Hartmanis

The series Lecture Notes in Computer Science (LNCS), including its subseries Lecture Notes in Artificial Intelligence (LNAI) and Lecture Notes in Bioinformatics (LNBI), has established itself as a medium for the publication of new developments in computer science and information technology research, teaching, and education.

LNCS enjoys close cooperation with the computer science R & D community, the series counts many renowned academics among its volume editors and paper authors, and collaborates with prestigious societies. Its mission is to serve this international community by providing an invaluable service, mainly focused on the publication of conference and workshop proceedings and postproceedings. LNCS commenced publication in 1973.

Vincent G. Duffy
Editor

HCI International 2024 – Late Breaking Papers

26th International Conference on
Human-Computer Interaction, HCII 2024
Washington, DC, USA, June 29 – July 4, 2024
Proceedings, Part III

 Springer

Editor
Vincent G. Duffy
Purdue University
West Lafayette, IN, USA

ISSN 0302-9743   ISSN 1611-3349 (electronic)
Lecture Notes in Computer Science
ISBN 978-3-031-76808-8   ISBN 978-3-031-76809-5 (eBook)
https://doi.org/10.1007/978-3-031-76809-5

This Springer imprint is published by the registered company Springer Nature Switzerland AG
The registered company address is: Gewerbestrasse 11, 6330 Cham, Switzerland

If disposing of this product, please recycle the paper.

Foreword

This year we celebrate 40 years since the establishment of the HCI International (HCII) Conference, which has been a hub for presenting groundbreaking research and novel ideas and collaboration for people from all over the world.

The HCII conference was founded in 1984 by Prof. Gavriel Salvendy (Purdue University, USA, Tsinghua University, P.R. China, and University of Central Florida, USA) and the first event of the series, "1st USA-Japan Conference on Human-Computer Interaction", was held in Honolulu, Hawaii, USA, 18–20 August. Since then, HCI International is held jointly with several Thematic Areas and Affiliated Conferences, with each one under the auspices of a distinguished international Program Board and under one management and one registration. Twenty-six HCI International Conferences have been organized so far (every two years until 2013, and annually thereafter).

Over the years, this conference has served as a platform for scholars, researchers, industry experts and students to exchange ideas, connect, and address challenges in the ever-evolving HCI field. Throughout these 40 years, the conference has evolved itself, adapting to new technologies and emerging trends, while staying committed to its core mission of advancing knowledge and driving change.

As we celebrate this milestone anniversary, we reflect on the contributions of its founding members and appreciate the commitment of its current and past Affiliated Conference Program Board Chairs and members. We are also thankful to all past conference attendees who have shaped this community into what it is today.

The 26th International Conference on Human-Computer Interaction, HCI International 2024 (HCII 2024), was held as a 'hybrid' event at the Washington Hilton Hotel, Washington, DC, USA, during 29 June – 4 July 2024. It incorporated the 21 thematic areas and affiliated conferences listed below.

A total of 5108 individuals from academia, research institutes, industry, and government agencies from 85 countries submitted contributions, and 1271 papers and 309 posters were included in the volumes of the proceedings that were published just before the start of the conference. Additionally, 222 papers and 104 posters were included in the volumes of the proceedings published after the conference, as "Late Breaking Work". The contributions thoroughly cover the entire field of human-computer interaction, addressing major advances in knowledge and effective use of computers in a variety of application areas. These papers provide academics, researchers, engineers, scientists, practitioners and students with state-of-the-art information on the most recent advances in HCI. The volumes constituting the full set of the HCII 2024 conference proceedings are listed on the following pages.

I would like to thank the Program Board Chairs and the members of the Program Boards of all thematic areas and affiliated conferences for their contribution towards the high scientific quality and overall success of the HCI International 2024 conference. Their manifold support in terms of paper reviewing (single-blind review process, with a minimum of two reviews per submission), session organization and their willingness to act as goodwill ambassadors for the conference is most highly appreciated.

This conference would not have been possible without the continuous and unwavering support and advice of Gavriel Salvendy, founder, General Chair Emeritus, and Scientific Advisor. For his outstanding efforts, I would like to express my sincere appreciation to Abbas Moallem, Communications Chair and Editor of HCI International News.

September 2024   Constantine Stephanidis

HCI International 2024 Thematic Areas and Affiliated Conferences

- HCI: Human-Computer Interaction Thematic Area
- HIMI: Human Interface and the Management of Information Thematic Area
- EPCE: 21st International Conference on Engineering Psychology and Cognitive Ergonomics
- AC: 18th International Conference on Augmented Cognition
- UAHCI: 18th International Conference on Universal Access in Human-Computer Interaction
- CCD: 16th International Conference on Cross-Cultural Design
- SCSM: 16th International Conference on Social Computing and Social Media
- VAMR: 16th International Conference on Virtual, Augmented and Mixed Reality
- DHM: 15th International Conference on Digital Human Modeling & Applications in Health, Safety, Ergonomics & Risk Management
- DUXU: 13th International Conference on Design, User Experience and Usability
- C&C: 12th International Conference on Culture and Computing
- DAPI: 12th International Conference on Distributed, Ambient and Pervasive Interactions
- HCIBGO: 11th International Conference on HCI in Business, Government and Organizations
- LCT: 11th International Conference on Learning and Collaboration Technologies
- ITAP: 10th International Conference on Human Aspects of IT for the Aged Population
- AIS: 6th International Conference on Adaptive Instructional Systems
- HCI-CPT: 6th International Conference on HCI for Cybersecurity, Privacy and Trust
- HCI-Games: 6th International Conference on HCI in Games
- MobiTAS: 6th International Conference on HCI in Mobility, Transport and Automotive Systems
- AI-HCI: 5th International Conference on Artificial Intelligence in HCI
- MOBILE: 5th International Conference on Human-Centered Design, Operation and Evaluation of Mobile Communications

Conference Proceedings – Full List of Volumes

1. LNCS 14684, Human-Computer Interaction: Part I, edited by Masaaki Kurosu and Ayako Hashizume
2. LNCS 14685, Human-Computer Interaction: Part II, edited by Masaaki Kurosu and Ayako Hashizume
3. LNCS 14686, Human-Computer Interaction: Part III, edited by Masaaki Kurosu and Ayako Hashizume
4. LNCS 14687, Human-Computer Interaction: Part IV, edited by Masaaki Kurosu and Ayako Hashizume
5. LNCS 14688, Human-Computer Interaction: Part V, edited by Masaaki Kurosu and Ayako Hashizume
6. LNCS 14689, Human Interface and the Management of Information: Part I, edited by Hirohiko Mori and Yumi Asahi
7. LNCS 14690, Human Interface and the Management of Information: Part II, edited by Hirohiko Mori and Yumi Asahi
8. LNCS 14691, Human Interface and the Management of Information: Part III, edited by Hirohiko Mori and Yumi Asahi
9. LNAI 14692, Engineering Psychology and Cognitive Ergonomics: Part I, edited by Don Harris and Wen-Chin Li
10. LNAI 14693, Engineering Psychology and Cognitive Ergonomics: Part II, edited by Don Harris and Wen-Chin Li
11. LNAI 14694, Augmented Cognition: Part I, edited by Dylan D. Schmorrow and Cali M. Fidopiastis
12. LNAI 14695, Augmented Cognition: Part II, edited by Dylan D. Schmorrow and Cali M. Fidopiastis
13. LNCS 14696, Universal Access in Human-Computer Interaction: Part I, edited by Margherita Antona and Constantine Stephanidis
14. LNCS 14697, Universal Access in Human-Computer Interaction: Part II, edited by Margherita Antona and Constantine Stephanidis
15. LNCS 14698, Universal Access in Human-Computer Interaction: Part III, edited by Margherita Antona and Constantine Stephanidis
16. LNCS 14699, Cross-Cultural Design: Part I, edited by Pei-Luen Patrick Rau
17. LNCS 14700, Cross-Cultural Design: Part II, edited by Pei-Luen Patrick Rau
18. LNCS 14701, Cross-Cultural Design: Part III, edited by Pei-Luen Patrick Rau
19. LNCS 14702, Cross-Cultural Design: Part IV, edited by Pei-Luen Patrick Rau
20. LNCS 14703, Social Computing and Social Media: Part I, edited by Adela Coman and Simona Vasilache
21. LNCS 14704, Social Computing and Social Media: Part II, edited by Adela Coman and Simona Vasilache
22. LNCS 14705, Social Computing and Social Media: Part III, edited by Adela Coman and Simona Vasilache

69. LNCS 15380, HCI International 2024 - Late Breaking Papers: Part VII, edited by Aaron Marcus, Elizabeth Rosenzweig, Marcelo M. Soares, Pei-Luen Patrick Rau and Abbas Moallem
70. LNCS 15381, HCI International 2024 - Late Breaking Papers: Part VIII, edited by Don Harris, Wen-Chin Li and Heidi Krömker
71. LNCS 15382, HCI International 2024 - Late Breaking Papers: Part IX, edited by Helmut Degen and Stavroula Ntoa
72. CCIS 2319, HCI International 2024 - Late Breaking Posters: Part I, edited by Constantine Stephanidis, Margherita Antona, Stavroula Ntoa and Gavriel Salvendy
73. CCIS 2320, HCI International 2024 - Late Breaking Posters: Part II, edited by Constantine Stephanidis, Margherita Antona, Stavroula Ntoa and Gavriel Salvendy
74. CCIS 2321, HCI International 2024 - Late Breaking Posters: Part III, edited by Constantine Stephanidis, Margherita Antona, Stavroula Ntoa and Gavriel Salvendy

https://2024.hci.international/proceedings

26th International Conference on Human-Computer Interaction (HCII 2024)

The full list with the Program Board Chairs and the members of the Program Boards of all thematic areas and affiliated conferences of HCII2024 is available online at:

http://www.hci.international/board-members-2024.php

HCI International 2025 Conference

The 27th International Conference on Human-Computer Interaction, HCI International 2025, will be held jointly with the affiliated conferences at the Swedish Exhibition & Congress Centre and Gothia Towers Hotel, Gothenburg, Sweden, June 22–27, 2025. It will cover a broad spectrum of themes related to Human-Computer Interaction, including theoretical issues, methods, tools, processes, and case studies in HCI design, as well as novel interaction techniques, interfaces, and applications. The proceedings will be published by Springer. More information is available on the conference website: https://2025.hci.international/.

General Chair
Prof. Constantine Stephanidis
University of Crete and ICS-FORTH
Heraklion, Crete, Greece
Email: general_chair@2025.hci.international

https://2025.hci.international/

Contents – Part III

Ergonomics and Digital Human Modelling

Design for Health and Wellbeing

Perceptions of Pregnant Women on Mobile App Design and Information Credibility

Olubukola Akanbi[✉]

University of Baltimore, Baltimore, MD 21201, USA
bmakanbi@gmail.com

Abstract. This aim of this study was to explore the perceptions of American pregnant women on mobile app design and information credibility and what features they look for in pregnancy apps.

To achieve this, explanatory sequential mixed methods research was used. Fifty-nine pregnant women participated in the quantitative phase using anonymous web surveys while multiple-case studies involving remote co-designing was used to gather the qualitative data from four pregnant women and one gynecologist.

Findings revealed that majority of the women used pregnancy apps during their current pregnancy. More than a fourth-fifth agree that the apps they used were applicable, related, pertinent and relevant to their health needs. Women said that they experience poorly designed health apps, and this experiences often frustrate their app use and information search. Participants favor evidenced-based contents and desire app information from health professionals and institutions. Reliable information based on gestational week and fetal development tracker were the most important features women want in their app(s).

Keywords: Health apps · Mobile app design · Pregnant women

1 Introduction

Pregnancy is a common health condition that requires access to health care and health information for better outcomes [1–3]. Accessing information is one of the activities pregnant women engage in to navigate and make sense of the new changes experienced during pregnancy. Women typically use variety of information sources to meet their information needs. These sources comprised of primary health care providers, internet, family members, traditional and social media but more recently mobile apps have been the most preferred source for pregnant women [4, 5].

Advancement in mobile and internet technology has changed the ways people search and seek information. More than ever, there is more reliance on internet information and health apps for dealing with everyday life activities, including managing health. One of the most sought out information on the internet is health information [6].

Pregnant women are more reliant on newer technology for going through pregnancy as well as coping with developmental changes associated with pregnancy. Mobile apps are advantageous to women for accessing health information and dealing with all the changes that occur during pregnancy. Despite the comfort and convenience of mobile apps, several pregnancy apps have raised safety concerns as many lack evidence-based content and are poorly designed [7].

The aim of this paper is to investigate how American pregnant women perceive mobile app design and information credibility of the health apps used during current pregnancy.

1.1 Background

A recent study reported increased adoption of health apps in the United States, with approximately three-in-ten adults reported using at least one health on their smartphones [8]. Beyond the United States, health app usage increased three-fold from 2016 to 2018 [9]. Studies found that app users are using this technology for tracking diet, sleep, exercise, weight, and managing diabetes, blood pressure, and other diseases [8–10]. The impact of mobile apps is evident in the delivery of health behavior interventions, remote patient monitoring and self-management of chronic health conditions [11, 12]. Health apps have a positive effect on patients' satisfaction and knowledge [13].

Within the pregnancy domain, more women use health apps for early detection of abnormality and obstetric danger signals, deal with gestational weight gain, track pregnancy and fetal movement, receive and share information [14–19]. An average of three pregnancy apps are downloaded by women during their pregnancy and they use about half-hour daily on at least one to two apps [4, 20].

Health apps serve as a self-care tool for many pregnant women. They use this technology for telemedicine, setting health goals and reminders, self-diagnosis, recording and receiving behavioral and physiological data, accessing emergency health responses and health literacy [7, 21]. Additionally, it is an excellent communication modality that could increase activation and engagement levels of pregnant women with health care providers thereby promoting patient-physician communication and interaction [22].

Conversely, design and safety concerns of health apps have been noted in literature and it is gradually becoming a public health issue [7, 23, 24]. For example, a study investigated the quality of top 10 freely available pregnancy apps in Australia and found that all 10 apps were less than optimal in quality, practicality, and functionality [25]. Also, Lee & Moon's [26] review on the characteristics, contents, and credibility of mobile apps used for pregnancy, birth and childcare found that apps are effective for providing answers to women's questions on health and accessing physician quick opinions. However, more than a third of the respondents reported that the apps they used lacked credibility.

Mehralizade et al. [27] stressed the significant dearth on research and evidence concerning the use of mobile apps to improve maternal health in the United States as well as underrepresentation of pregnant women in research. This might be limiting the extent of studies done with pregnant women [28].

Since maternal health is one of the key pointers to a nation's reproductive health and more women consume health information through health apps, this study contributes to knowledge by exploring the perceptions of women on mobile app design and information credibility.

2 Related Work

Studies in Human-Computer Interaction (HCI) have stressed the need for more studies focused on women's health [29, 30]. Interestingly, maternal health and pregnancy have found expressions in HCI [30, 31]. This section provides a brief on women's health in HCI and pregnancy and HCI.

2.1 Women's Health in HCI

Women's health refers to any health concerns that affects women [29]. Past studies in HCI have explored women's health particularly in the areas of chronic health conditions [32], menstruation [33], intimate care [29], breastfeeding [30], menopause [34], mental health, [35], support from online health communities [36], women general wellbeing [37] and pregnancy [36].

Mobile technology is breaching the gaps in informational and medical resources, healthcare, and location-based resources [30, 38]. For example, Balaam et al. [30] study researched the design of mobile applications for helping women find, review, and share public spaces for breastfeeding purposes. Similarly, Barry et al. [35] explored the utility of mobile apps for dealing with psychological well-being during pregnancy while Smith et al. [21], Hiyama et al. [39] and Ballegaard et al. [40] explored how patients use mobile apps to manage chronic health conditions, track physical activities, connect with physicians, and integrate technology into their everyday life.

Furthermore, HCI women-centered studies have considered the design implications of mobile technology with capability of improving and supporting menopausal experience and contraceptive use [34], maternal behavioral changes [19], keeping track of pregnancy [39], maternal mental health [35], and record management [41].

2.2 Pregnancy and HCI

Pregnancy is an important phase in the life of any woman as women undergo different changes in physiological, immunological, developmental and hormonal changes. Women experience these changes to accommodate the new life within her [1, 36]. Women consume information from the internet, social support groups, health care centers, family members, text messages and health apps [42, 43]. Access to quality medical information and timely health care remain a challenge for women in the many societies. This could possibly be due to systemic and economic barriers to quality and timely healthcare. Healthcare affects women's health, and overall wellbeing [29, 44].

At the intersection of HCI and pregnancy, more studies have centered on designing technology that improves pregnancy experience and support [19, 43]. Pregnancy in relation to information seeking and retrieval [13], health services [21], communication [45], wearables [39], mental wellbeing and weight control [19, 35] have been well-documented in literature.

Relatedly, HCI studies have explored the use of app technology for maternal mental wellbeing and tracking pregnancy. Women use mobile apps for self-reporting gestational depression symptoms and seeking reassurance and comfort [1, 35]. These studies suggest that mobile apps are advantageous for meeting both psychological and physiological needs of pregnant women.

Pregnancy comes with new experiences and triggers the need for information. Peyton et al. [19] describes pregnancy period as teachable moments where women use different information sources to meet their growing information needs. HCI studies have explored a variety of means of supporting pregnancy. For example, Vaira et al. [23] study assessed the use of AI-based chatbot to understand and respond to needs of pregnant women and family members while Kaur, Singh and Wani [45] explored WhatsApp for delivering health information. Similarly, MomLink app was designed to meet the needs of pregnant women in low-resource settings [46] and Wierckx, Shahid and Mahmud [13] developed a mobile app with functionalities which supports answering pregnancy-related questions. Hiyama et al., [39] designed Babybumper, a wearable device with sensor designed to relieve pregnancy-induced stress, monitors fetal kicking activity. These apps were designed for offering education, information, support, and self-care technology to women.

Beyond wearables and mobile apps, existing HCI literatures have explored the usefulness of online health communities among pregnant women. Gui et al. [36] and Poetri et al. [6] confirmed the efficacy of web-based platform and online health communities for supporting pregnant women.

3 Methodology

This study seeks to understand the perceptions of pregnant women on mobile app design and information credibility. Thus, the research question was studied: How does app design interface help with quality health information for pregnant women?

3.1 Research Design

Explanatory sequential mixed methods were used to investigate the perceptions of pregnant women on mobile app design. This study used mixed methods research approach because it offers the strengths of both quantitative and qualitative in answering the research questions. Explanatory sequential mixed methods involve the collection and analyzing of the quantitative data first, and then followed by collection of the qualitative data. The quantitative results are better understood with insights from the qualitative analysis [47].

Anonymous web surveys were used to gather quantitative data while qualitative data were gathered using online case studies involving co-designing. Case study is a research strategy which "investigates a contemporary phenomenon within its real-life context, especially when the boundaries between phenomenon and context are not clearly evident" [48]. It could be single-case or multiple-case studies. Multiple-case studies were used because of its ability to provide more robust and compelling findings on the topic being studied. Yin [49] notes the value embedded in two or more cases in comparison to single-case study, particularly regarding the analytical conclusion.

3.2   Data Collection and Participants

Data was collected between March and June 2021 from pregnant women resident in the United States. A total of 89 women showed interest but only 59 of them completed the surveys. The survey consisted of three parts focusing on profile of participants, information-related to pregnancy and app health information quality with items. Part of the items were measured on a seven-point Likert scale where 1 means 1 'strongly disagree' and 7 means 'strongly agree'.

The researcher first conducted quantitative research using anonymous surveys through SurveyMonkey software to gather responses from research participants. This was achieved by posting the survey link on different social media platforms, particularly WhatsApp, Twitter and Facebook pregnancy groups used by pregnant women resident in the United States. Social media groups were used because the study was carried out during the covid-19 pandemic and many people especially pregnant women were hesitant to interact with anyone. After collecting the quantitative data, online case studies using co-designing techniques were used to gather the qualitative data.

The qualitative phase was initiated by reaching out to women on the same social media platforms to sign-up for online case study research involving co-design. The researcher uploaded invitation links on social media platforms for interested women to register. Then, interested women were emailed to schedule suitable days and dates. A total of five participants who consist of four pregnant women and one gynecologist responded and were included in the qualitative phase.

The qualitative phase was done with Zoom software. Each of the design sessions with the pregnant women lasted about 30 min while the session with the gynecologist lasted 45 min. The study awarded an incentive $50 to each pregnant woman and $100 to the gynecologist for participating in the study. All the participants signed a copy of the informed consent form approved by the IRB of the University prior to the design sessions. Video recordings, audio recordings, notes and screen shots of ideas created by the participants were collected during the design sessions.

4   Findings

This section highlights findings and analysis from the web survey.

4.1   Survey Findings

Demographic Characteristics. The demographic characteristics of the respondents are presented in the table below. Based on data in the table, many of the respondents were aged 25 and 44. About a half identify as White or Caucasian and two-fifths identify as Black or African American. Nearly four-fifths self-reported to be married and three-quarters have completed at least a university degree. Two-thirds of the respondents indicated to be employed, working full-time while one-in-ten were working part-time. No incentives or financial rewards were offered to women who completed the survey (Table 1).

Table 1. Sample demographics

Demographic Characteristics	n%
Age	**n = 57**
18–24	5(8.77%)
25–34	37(64.91%)
35–44	14(24.56%)
45–54	1(1.75%)
55 +	0(0%)
Ethnic Backgrounds	**n = 58**
White or Caucasian	29(50.00%)
Black or African American	24(41.38%)
Hispanic or Latino	2(3.45%)
Asian or Asia American	2(3.45%)
American Indian or Alaska Native	0(0%)
Other	1(1.72%)
Marital Status	**n = 58**
Married	46(79.31%)
Not married	8(13.79%)
Other	4(6.90%)
Education (highest level)	**n = 58**
Have not completed high school	2(3.45%)
Completed high school	5(8.62%)
Associate degree	6(10.34%)
Bachelor's degree	14(24.14%)
Master's degree	19(32.76%)
Doctoral degree	11(18.97%)
Other	1(1.72%)
Employment Status	**n = 59**
Employed, working full-time	39(66.10%)
Employed, working part-time	6(10.17%)
Not employed, looking for work	5(8.47%)
Not employed, NOT looking for work	7(11.86%)
Retired	0(0%)
Disabled, not able to work	2(3.39%)

Information Sources Used During Current Pregnancy. This question was asked to understand the various information sources used by respondents during their current pregnancy. The most sought health information sources were websites 49 (85%), followed by physicians 43 (74%), pregnancy applications (apps) 42 (72%) and friends 36 (62%).

The least sought out health information sources were magazines 3 (5.17%), electronic newsletter 4 (6.90%), brochures 4 (6.90%) and nine-month calendars 4 (6.90%). This question asked the respondents to specify 'other' information sources used but not mentioned in the survey. Three participants responded, and their responses were doulas, Reddit, the app The Bump, and YouTube (Fig. 1).

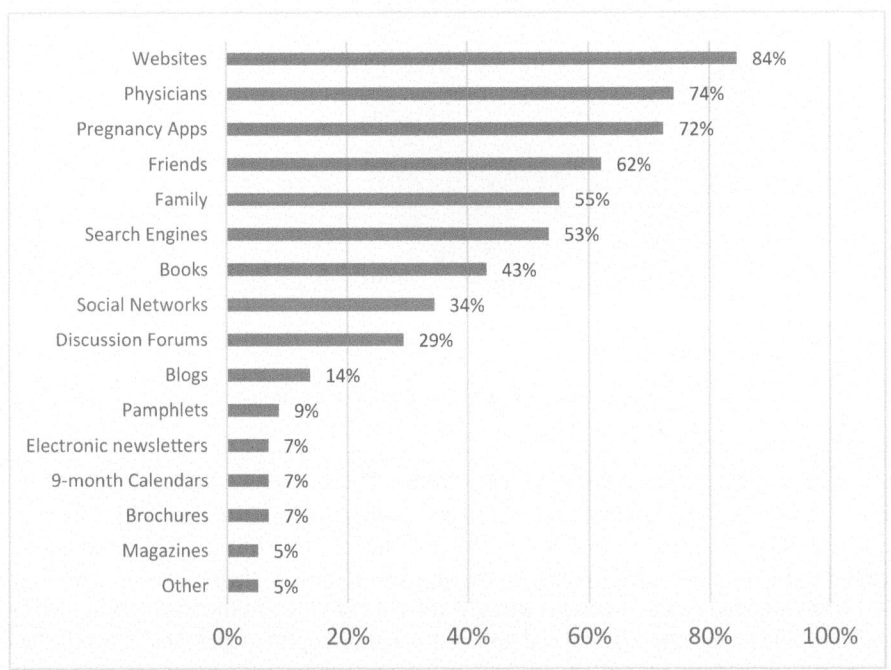

Fig. 1. Sources used for health information

Use of Pregnancy Apps. This question asked respondents about their use of pregnancy or health-related app during their current pregnancy. More than four-fifths (86%) said that they had used a pregnancy app while less than one-sixth had not used any pregnancy apps (14%). The question also provided open ended questions to specific health-related apps used by the respondents. 36 women provided answers to listing specific apps, indicating 16 apps. The most listed apps include Baby center, What to expect, Ovia, Pregnancy + and Flo apps (Fig. 2).

Relevance of App Health Information Quality. This section covers questions on perceptions of pregnant women on the relevance of app health quality.

Applicability of Pregnancy Apps to Health Needs. Of the 59 respondents who provided answer to this question on applicability of pregnancy apps to health needs in current pregnancy, 8 (13.6%) and 24(40.7%) indicated strongly agree and agree respectively followed by 20(33.9%) who indicated 'somewhat agree'. A total of 52(88.1%) showed agreement with applicability of pregnancy apps to health needs. However, 5 (8.5%) were neutral and 2 (3.4%) somewhat disagreed with the applicability of pregnancy app to meeting their health needs.

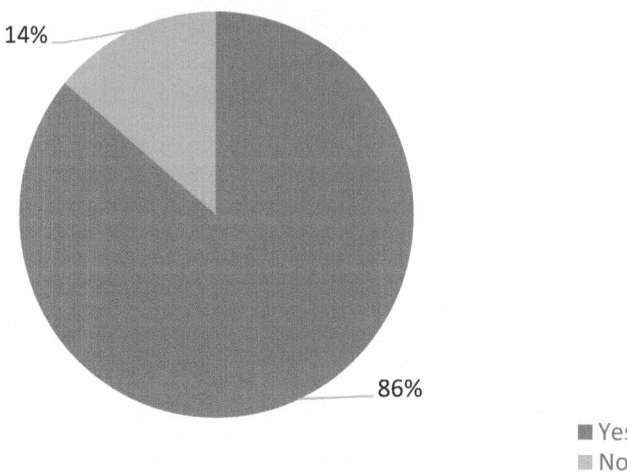

14%

86%

■ Yes
■ No

Fig. 2. Sources used for health information

Relatedness of Pregnancy Apps to Health Needs. This question addressed the related-ness of pregnancy apps to health needs of pregnant women (n = 59). 8(13.6%) indi-cated strongly agree and nearly half of the respondents 28(47.5%) agree that internet health information provided by pregnancy apps was related to their needs, followed by 14(23.7%) who indicated somewhat agree. A total of 50(84.8%) either strongly agreed or agreed or somewhat agreed to relatedness of pregnancy app(s) to their health needs dur-ing their current pregnancy. Conversely, a few women indicated neutral 4(6.8%) while 5(8.5%) showed some degrees of disagreement with the relatedness of pregnancy apps to health needs during their current pregnancy.

Pertinence of Pregnancy Apps to Health Needs. This question assessed the pertinency of the app information to the health needs of the pregnant women (n = 58). 10 (17.24%) and 25 (43.1%) indicated strongly agree and agree respectively, followed by 'somewhat agree' 14 (24.1%). A total of 49(84.5%) showed agreement that app information was pertinent to their health needs during their current pregnancy. On the other hand, 5 (8.6%) were neutral, 4 (6.9%) indicated some degrees of disagreement.

Relevance of Pregnancy Apps to Health Needs. For this question on relevance of preg-nancy apps to health needs of pregnant women (n = 59), 10 (17.0%) and 26 (44.1%) indicated 'strongly agree' and 'agree' followed by those who indicated 'somewhat agree' 14 (23.7%). 50 (84.8%) of the respondents had some level of agreement on the rele-vance of pregnancy app(s) to their health needs during their current pregnancy. Only a few women indicated 'neutral' 5 (8.5%) while 4 (6.8%) indicated some levels of disagreement.

Figure 3 highlights the level of agreement of the respondents with the relevance of app health information. As it shows, the majority of the responded had high levels of agreement with the relevance of app health information used during current pregnancy.

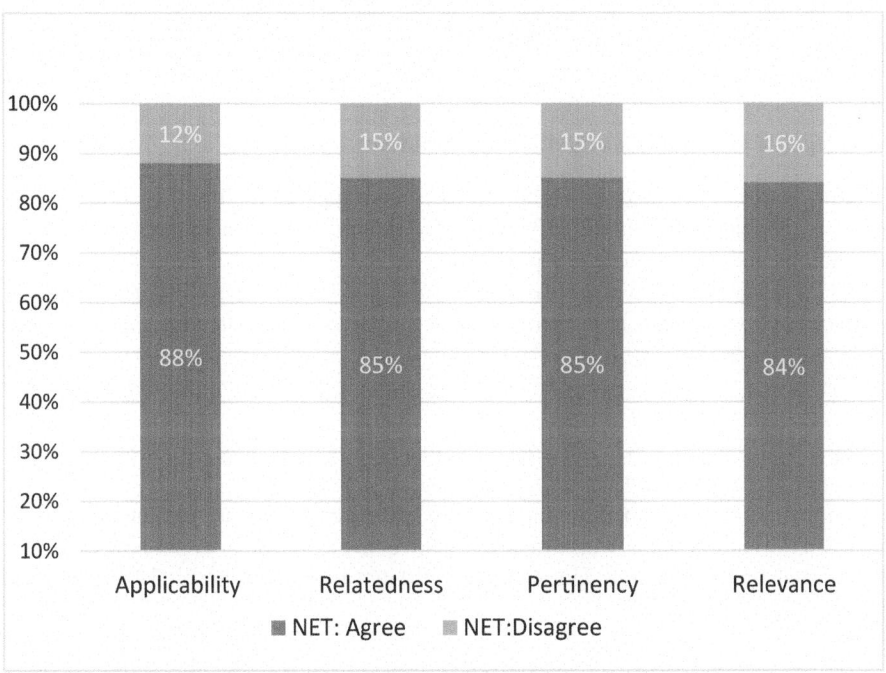

Fig. 3. Relevance of app health information

4.2   Online Case Studies Using Co-design Findings (Pregnant Women)

Mobile App Design. As revealed in literature, health apps are popular source of information among pregnant women, and they use these apps with some expectations of features and functionalities in mind. In this study, respondents revealed mobile app features they look for in health apps. This section discusses features the respondents look for in pregnancy and health apps to meet their pregnancy needs.

Features Pregnant Women Would Like to Have on a Pregnancy App. The participants expressed the need for features that track baby's growth and development, fetal size as well as provide information on gestational week of pregnancy.

a. Baby tracker/baby size tracker/Pregnancy tracker

P1: *"It tells the approximate, like how much longer you have to go in your pregnancy, really like that it tells you about the size of your baby, which is just fine."*
P1: *"It tells like how big your baby is in comparison to other stuff."*
P2: *"I know what's going on in my baby's growth and development."*
P2: *"So things like, I can track my pregnancy, I know what is going on in my body."*
P1: *"…has a common symptoms section, and it tells you, like, at this point your baby will be moving more, expect this, and while you're thinking about it you should count how many kicks the baby is doing."*

P1 and P2 want features that track fetal movements and pregnancy. Fetal growth and development have been documented in literature to be important to pregnant women [5, 16].

b. Snippet of information/organized information

One of the usefulness of mobile devices and apps is for relaying information. Wierckx, Shahid and Mahmud [13] confirmed the use of pregnancy apps for offering information and education during pregnancy.

P1: "*I really like it has a list of articles on the homepage. It has a list of articles, like maybe five or six articles that's related to, say, your third trimester, and it's just it has like a short little snippet.*"

P1: "*…what to pack in your hospital bag and if you want to click on it, you can; if you don't want to, that's fine, too.*"

P4: "*Again, there's like just little facts and information. And [What to Expect] is really like organized. That's what I really liked about it.*"

These participants expressed the need for a feature that lists articles on pregnancy-related information in a well-organized and concise form, and possibly in other audiovisual formats such as video explaining what to pack in hospital bag for child delivery.

c. Mobile design elements: user-friendly/intuitive menu, visual appealing layout

P3: "*Just make sure it's user-friendly, that there's a menu so you can go flip back and forth.*"

P3: "*…want the notifications from the app to remind you to take your prenatal vitamins, that's helpful, send you some emails, those kinds of notifications. But have a way to make sure you can opt out of it so it's not too much.*"

P4: "*It's color-coded for the most part, but it's not like, making your eyes go, you know, crazy because there's so many colors.*".

P3 and P4 expressed a need for a feature that offers seamless interaction, promotes findability of information contents and controlled notification that can prompt or remind users of pregnancy-related tasks. Mao, Wang, Liu and Xiao [24] confirmed that pregnant women paid attention to app's interface, layout, font size, and app function such as monitoring and reminders.

d. Reliable information

P4: "*They post articles from professional websites. So, that was also helpful.*"

P4 mentioned feature or functionality that provides reliable information from professional sources, evidence-based information from medical professionals. Mao et al. [24] reiterated the value of reliable and accurate information in pregnancy apps and one of the requirements sought out by women before using pregnancy app.

e. Specific information e.g. nutritional recommendations and baby names

P2: "*…know what nutrition to give and at what point.*"

P4: "*Like a flashcard of names.*"

f. Chat feature

P2: *"I can chat with other mamas, of course."*
Studies have shown that pregnant women use different online health communities and social media to connect with other mothers to learn from their experiences [36, 45].

Ideal Features in Pregnancy Apps. The participants were asked to use the blackboard feature on the Zoom software to write down three things that are important to them when they download an app.

a. **Information architecture:** clear organized information. Clearly organized information comprising of video category and textual information like articles.
b. **Information from medical professionals:** reliable information from doctors and nurses
c. **Timeline:** pregnancy-information based on week/stage of pregnancy and weekly updates.

P1: *"So I'm not getting irrelevant stuff like, oh you might have morning sickness while I'm in third trimester, not relevant."*

d. **Chat feature:** to communicate with other mothers.
e. **Fetal/Mother development tracker:** Weekly updates on the size of the baby
f. **Pregnancy topics:** particularly on food recommendations, checklists, and exercise restrictions/recommendation

Most Important Feature. The participants were asked to use the blackboard feature on the Zoom software to write down one most important feature to them on a pregnancy app.

a. Reliable/Relevant information

P1: *"I think reliable information has to be the top of it. Like, for me, I love that it's sorted, organized, but if it's not relevant or if it's not reliable, if it's not accurate information, that would really frustrate me.*

I appreciate it, going in the app, reading an article and they say according to, you know, the Pediatric Society or whatever, like this is a thing you should look into, it makes it valuable. Like if the information isn't correct, I'm not going to waste my time."

b. Baby development tracker

P2: *"A feature that tells you about how your baby is growing."*

c. Timeline

P3: *"I guess I just I like to know what's happening, what to expect, what's normal, all at the appropriate time."*

d. Weekly updates

P4: *"Weekly updates on how the baby's doing in there."*
A pregnancy app that provides reliable information, baby development tracking, gestational week-based information and updates were the most important features and

functionality to the participants. The study also sought information from a medical practitioner for the purpose of gathering robust information that would benefit pregnant women. Only one medical practitioner was included in the study.

4.3 Online Case Studies Using Co-design Findings (Gynecologist)

Mobile App Design. The participant was asked to mention features that would benefit pregnant women.
  Features recommended for pregnant women.

a. Information about different stages of pregnancy
b. Commonly asked questions
c. Feature that integrates vitals into patient's medical records

  P5: "*It also should be integrated with your OB labs, so that if you had to go to a different hospital, different from your hospital, you can show them your app and the doctor who's taking care of you, who may not have seen you before, can have a very quick summary of your pregnancy.*"

d. Encouraging and controllable notifications

  P5: "*I also would like an app that is not overwhelming to a patient and sending notifications like five times a day, so perhaps an app that a patient can control how often she receives those notifications.*"

a. Nutritional recommendations

  P5: "*…go over like nutrition if you're breastfeeding while you're pregnant, or if you have twins, something that was, you know, or you had diabetes, you know, an app that can give you recommendations on what you can do to modify your diet for the different comorbidities you may have.*"

b. Prenatal details

  P5: "*…so it tells you your height, your weight for each appointment, you're able to document any concerns that you may have so that you can bring it to your OBGYN to discuss*".

Ideal Features in a Pregnancy App. The participant was asked to mention features she would recommend in a pregnancy app. The participant recommended feature that provided the following:

a. Nutrition information
b. Updates on Covid-19 [the research was done during the covid-19 pandemic]
c. Weekly updates on fetal development

Most Important Feature. The participant was asked to mention the most important feature of a pregnancy app. The participant mentioned:

  Weekly updates on fetal development.

5   Discussion

There is consistency with features recommended by the gynecologist and pregnant women in this study. Both believe provision of information based on gestational week and tracking of fetal development are paramount to pregnant women in apps. Lupton and Pedersen, 2016 [5] confirmed that pregnant women in their study consider feature for monitor fetal development and relevant information significant in pregnancy apps.

Other health app functionalities women look for include reminders and notification features. For example, one participant noted that she would like to have notifications from the app to remind her to take prenatal vitamins, this feature must also be controllable to choose how often she receives such notifications, implying not just a feature but feature with good user experience. This is in accordance with [7, 24].

Literature found increased use of pregnancy apps among women during pregnancy [5, 26]. Majority of the women indicated to have used health and pregnancy apps during their current pregnancy. Interestingly, the participants indicated websites (84%) as the most sought source of health information more than physicians (74%), followed by pregnancy apps (72%). Past studies stress that healthcare providers are still pregnant women most preferred source of health information [50, 51]. Physicians prioritize pregnant women's physiological health needs over the psychological aspect [43]. This might contribute to using other newer information sources for health information.

More than four-fifths of the women who used a pregnancy app rated high on the relevance of app health information quality in terms of its applicability, relatedness, pertinency and relevance to their health needs. This is in line with Lupton and Pedersen [5] findings. Anderson et al. [4] highlighted the relationship between app credibility and referent sources and app developer. However, most women do not bother to check where app developers source for information provided on these apps [5].

A recent study suggest that pregnant women perceive apps recommended by health-care providers or system to be more credible than generic apps [4, 7]. The relevance and accuracy of the information were paramount to all the participants. They expressed that they prefer that the information provided by health app are evidence-based contents from certified health professionals and institutions.

Beyond the informational contents provided on health apps, pregnant women pay attention to app interface, layout, and navigational elements. The participants in this study expressed that they look for apps with intuitive navigation, responsive layouts, simplified information display with good user-friendly design with pleasant color scheme. Poorly designed apps affect the women's perceived information credibility. Previous studies confirmed that design elements affect perceptions of credibility of online information [4, 7].

From health care viewpoint, the medical participant included in this study suggested features that integrates women's medical records, lab results, physiological (such as height, weight) and behavioral data so that if the woman must use a different physician the app can provide a summary. Marko et al. [52] noted the value of remote monitoring of pregnant patients in prenatal care. Health apps can easily help healthcare professionals remotely monitor patients weight gain and blood pressure [53].

Studies have highlighted the value of emotional support to pregnant women [36, 43]. Many women find assurance and comfort connecting with other pregnant women and sharing experiences. One of the participants noted the need for a chat feature to connect with other moms. Women connect with other women going through what they are going through to seek for advice, reassurance, emotional support and to stay abreast of relevant information from experienced mothers.

6   Limitations

A high percentage of the women in study indicated to have completed at least a university degree. This level of education is higher than data provided for American adult population which is less than two-fifths. Also, the study was conducted during the Covid-19 pandemic which was a period of heighten stress for people particularly pregnant women.

Since the study used only pregnant women resident in the United States, perceptions on app technology might be different from women living in other countries. The study was also limited to the reality of the short time associated with pregnancy. One of the participants was a recently new mom.

7   Conclusion

Most pregnant women consider websites, health care providers and health apps as their most sought information sources during pregnancy. In relation to mobile app design, intuitive navigation, responsive layouts, simplified information display based on gestational week of pregnancy, good user-friendly design with pleasant color scheme appeals seems favorable to them. Monitoring pregnancy and fetal development are key features women look to have.

Integration of health apps into prenatal care might be the future of gynecological practices especially in low-resource settings either in terms of access to health information or professionals. Importantly, designers of medical apps must consider the voices of end-users in the design of any technology.

Acknowledgements. I acknowledge the contributions and input of my supervisors/research advisors, Bridget Blodgett and Deborah Kohl of Division of Science, Information Arts and Technologies, University of Baltimore, USA.

References

1. Zakeresfahani, A., et al.: Design implications to support integrative medicine in pregnancy care. Proc. ACM Trans. Comput.-Hum. Interact. **6**(CSCW2), A 439–471 (2022)
2. Ghiasi, A.: Health information needs, sources of information, and barriers to accessing health information among pregnant women: a systematic review of research. J. Matern. Fetal. Neonatal. Med. **34**(8), 1320–1330 (2019)
3. Javanmardi, M., Noroozi, M., Mostafavi, F., Ashrafi-rizi, H.: Challenges to access health information during pregnancy in Iran: a qualitative study from the perspective of pregnant women, midwives and obstetricians. Reprod. Health **16**(1), 128 (2019). https://doi.org/10.1186/s12978-019-0789-3

4. Anderson, L.N., Womack, J.J., Ledford, C.J.W.: Initial development and testing of a measure of credibility of mobile health apps: a clinical study among women seeking prenatal care. Atlantic J. Commun. **31**(2), 144–151 (2023). https://doi.org/10.1080/15456870.2021.2021910

5. Lupton, D., Pedersen, S.: An Australian survey of women's use of pregnancy and parenting apps. Women and Birth **29**(4), 368–375 (2016)

6. Poetri, N.P., Suzianti, A., Pradila, F.: Designing a web-based platform with user experience design method for mothers in their maternity period. In: ICCBN 2017: Proceedings of the 5th International Conference on Communications and Broadband Networking, pp. 65–69, Indonesia (2017). https://doi.org/10.1145/3057109.3057121

7. Akbar, S., Coiera, E., Magrabi, F.: Safety concerns with consumer-facing mobile health applications and their consequences: a scoping review. J. Am. Med. Inform. Assoc. **27**(2), 330–340 (2020). https://doi.org/10.1093/jamia/ocz175

8. Pangarkar, T.: mHealth Apps Statistics 2024 By Technology, Usage, Challenges, Market Scoop. https://scoop.market.us/mhealth-apps-statistics/. Accessed 5 May 2024

9. Khurram, S., Sardar, K.: Patient-centric mobile app solution. In: Proceedings of the Australasian Computer Science Week Multiconference, pp. 1–4, Australia (2020). https://doi.org/10.1145/3373017.3373063

10. Cannon, C.: Telehealth, mobile applications, and wearable devices are expanding cancer care beyond walls. Semin. Oncol. Nurs. **34**(2), 118–125 (2018)

11. Gómez-de-Regil, L., Avila-Nava, A., Gutierrez-Solis, A.L., Lugo, R.: Mobile apps for the management of comorbid overweight/obesity and depression/anxiety: a systematic review. J. Healthc. Eng. **2020**, 1–11 (2020)

12. Nunes, F., Verdezoto, N., Fitzpatrick, G., Kyng, M., Gronvall, E., Storni, C.: Self-care technologies in HCI: Trends, tensions, and opportunities. ACM Trans. Comput.-Hum. Interact. **22**(6), 33 (2015)

13. Wierckx, A., Shahid, S., Al Mahmud, A.: Babywijzer: an application to support women during their pregnancy. In: CHI EA 2014: CHI 2014 Extended Abstracts on Human Factors in Computing Systems, pp. 1333–1338, Canada (2014)

14. van Dijk, M.R., Koster, M.P.H., Oostingh, E.C., Willemsen, S.P., Steegers, E.A.P., Steegers-Theunissen, R.P.M.: A mobile app lifestyle intervention to improve healthy nutrition in women before and during early pregnancy: single-center randomized controlled trial. J. Med. Internet Res. **22**(5), e15773 (2020)

15. Huang, C., Han, W., Fan, Y.: Correlation study between increased fetal movement during the third trimester and neonatal outcome. BMC Pregnancy Childbirth **19**(1), 467 (2019)

16. Skar, J.B., Garnweidner-Holme, L.M., Lukasse, M., Terragni, L.: Women's experiences with using a smartphone app (the Pregnant+ app) to manage gestational diabetes mellitus in a randomised controlled trial. Midwifery **58**, 102–108 (2018)

17. Ginja, S., et al.: Associations between social support, mental wellbeing, self-efficacy and technology use in first-time antenatal women: data from the BaBBLeS cohort study. BMC Pregnancy Childbirth **18**(1), 441 (2018)

18. Sajjad, U.U., Shahid, S.: Baby+: a mobile application to support pregnant women in Pakistan. In: MobileHCI 2016: Proceedings of the 18th International Conference on Human-Computer Interaction with Mobile Devices and Services, pp. 667–674, Italy (2016)

19. Peyton, T., Poole, E., Reddy, M., Kraschnewski, J., Chuang, C.: "Every pregnancy is different": designing mHealth interventions for the pregnancy ecology. In: Proceedings of the 2014 conference on Designing Interactive Systems (DIS 2014), pp. 577–586, Canada (2014)

20. Frazer, C., Hussey, L., Bosch, E., Squire, M.: Pregnancy apps: a closer look at the implications for childbirth educators. Int. J. Childbirth Educ. **30**, 12–16 (2015)

21. Smith, W., et al.: Designing an app for pregnancy care for a culturally and linguistically diverse community. In: Proceedings of the 29th Australian Conference on Human-Computer Interaction, Brisbane, QLD, pp. 10–20, Australia (2017)
22. Ledford, C.J.W., et al.: Unexpected effects of a system-distributed mobile application in maternity care: a randomized controlled trial. Health Educ. Behav. 45(3), 323–330 (2018). https://doi.org/10.1177/1090198117732110
23. Vaira, L., Bochicchio, M.A., Conte, M., Casaluci, M.F., Melpignano, A.: In: Proceedings of 22nd International Database Engineering & Applications Symposium (IDEAS 2018), pp. 18–20, Italy (2018). https://doi.org/10.1145/3216122.3216173
24. Mao, L., Wang, J., Liu, H., Qian, X.: Smartphone apps for pregnant women: the gap between the quality of current apps and patients' needs. Stud. Health Technol. Inform. 250, 197 (2018). https://doi.org/10.3233/978-1-61499-872-3-197
25. Musgrave, L.M., Kizirian, N.V., Homer, C.S.E., Gordon, A.: Mobile phone apps in Australia for improving pregnancy outcomes: systematic search on app stores. JMIR MHealth UHealth 8(11), e22340 (2020). https://doi.org/10.2196/22340
26. Lee, Y., Moon, M.: Utilization and content evaluation of mobile applications for pregnancy, birth, and child care. Healthc. Inform. Res. 22(2), 73–80 (2016). https://doi.org/10.4258/hir.2016.22.2.73
27. Mehralizade, A., et al.: Mobile health apps in OB-GYN-embedded psychiatric care: commentary. JMIR Mhealth Uhealth 5(10), e152 (2017). https://doi.org/10.2196/mhealth.7988
28. Radin, J.M., et al.: The healthy pregnancy research program: transforming pregnancy research through a ResearchKit app. NPJ Digit. Med. 1(1), 1–7 (2018)
29. Almeida, T., Comber, R., Balaam, M.: HCI and Intimate care as an agenda for change in women's health. In: Proceedings of the 2016 CHI Conference on Human Factors in Computing Systems (CHI 2016), pp. 2599–2611, New York (2016). https://doi.org/10.1145/2858036.285818
30. Balaam, M., Comber, R., Jenkins, E., Sutton, S., Garbett, A.: FeedFinder: a location-mapping mobile application for breastfeeding women. In: Proceedings of the SIGCHI Conference on Human Factors in Computing Systems (CHI 2015), pp. 1709–1718 (2015)
31. Haldar, S., Studd, H., Wong, N., Mohr, D.C., Reddy, M., Miller, E.S.: Collaboration challenges and technology opportunities at the intersection of perinatal and mental health journeys. Proc. ACM Hum.-Comput. Interact. 6(CSCW2), 1–28 (2022). https://doi.org/10.1145/3555614
32. Haque, M.M., et al.: Findings of e-ESAS: a mobile based symptom monitoring system for breast cancer patients in rural Bangladesh. In: Proceedings of the SIGCHI Conference on Human Factors in Computing Systems (CHI 2012), pp. 899–908 (2012)
33. Epstein, D.A., et al.: Examining menstrual tracking to inform the design of personal informatics tools. In: Proceedings of CHI 2017, pp. 6876–6888, United States (2017)
34. Lee, M., Koo, B., Jeong, H., Park, J., Cho, J., Cho, J.: Understanding women's needs in menopause for development of mHealth. In: Workshop on Pervasive Wireless Healthcare (MobileHealth 2015), pp. 51–56, United States (2015)
35. Barry, M., Doherty, K., Marcano Belisario, J., Car, J., Morrison, C., Doherty, G.: mHealth for maternal mental health: everyday wisdom in ethical design. In: Proceedings of the 2017 CHI Conference on Human Factors in Computing Systems, pp. 2708–2756, United States (2017). https://doi.org/10.1145/3025453.3025918
36. Gui, X., Chen, Y., Kou, Y., Pine, K., Chen, Y.: Investigating support seeking from peers for pregnancy in online health communities. Proc. ACM Hum.-Comput. Interact. 1(CSCW), 1–19 (2017). https://doi.org/10.1145/3134685
37. Kumar, N., Karusala, N., Ismail, A., Tuli, A.: Taking the long, holistic, and intersectional view to women's wellbeing. ACM Trans. Comput.-Hum. Interact. 27(4), 1–32 (2020). https://doi.org/10.1145/3397159

38. Verdezoto, N., et al.: Indigenous women managing pregnancy complications in rural Ecuador: barriers and opportunities to enhance antenatal care. In: Proceedings of the 11th Nordic Conference on Human-Computer Interaction: Shaping Experiences, Shaping Society (NordiCHI 2020), pp. 1–9, Estonia (2020). https://doi.org/10.1145/3419249.342014

39. Hiyama, R., Saito, M., Nakanishi, Y., Hirose Y., Arisumi, S.: BabyBumper: protector/communication wearable device for pregnant women. In: UbiComp/ISWC 2015 Adjunct: Adjunct Proceedings of the 2015 ACM International Joint Conference on Pervasive and Ubiquitous Computing and Proceedings of the 2015 ACM International Symposium on Wearable Computers, pp. 173–176, Japan (2015). https://doi.org/10.1145/2800835.2800907F

40. Ballegaard, S.T., Hansen, T.R., Kyng, M.: Healthcare in everyday life - designing healthcare services for daily life. In: CHI 2008: Proceedings of the SIGCHI Conference on Human Factors in Computing Systems, pp. 1807–1816, Italy (2008). https://doi.org/10.1145/1357054.1357336

41. Enquist, H., Tollmar, K.: The memory stone – a personal ICT device in health care. In: Proceedings of the 5th Nordic conference on Humancomputer Interaction (NordiCHI 2008), pp. 103–112. ACM Press, Sweden (2008)

42. Nabovati, E., et al.: Pregnant women's use and attitude toward Mobile phone features for self-management. BMC Med. Inform. Decis. Making 23(27), 77 (2023). https://doi.org/10.1186/s12911-023-02172-w

43. Newhouse, N.: Bump2Bump: online peer support in first-time pregnancy. In: CHI 2016 Extended Abstracts, pp. 978-1-4503-4082 (2016). https://doi.org/10.1145/2851581

44. Kamali, S., Ahmadian, L., Khajouei, R., Bahaadinbeigy, K.: Health information needs of pregnant women: information sources, motives and barriers. Health Info. Libr. J. 35(1), 24–37 (2018). https://doi.org/10.1111/hir.12200

45. Kaur, J., Wani, A.S., Singh. P.: Engagement of pregnant women and mothers over whatsapp: challenges and opportunities involved. In: CSCW 2019 Companion: Companion Publication of the 2019 Conference on Computer Supported Cooperative Work and Social Computing, pp. 236–240, United States (2019)

46. Chaudhry, B.M., Faust, L., Chawla, N.V.: From design to development to evaluation of a pregnancy app for low-income women in a community-based setting. In: 21st International Conference on Human-Computer Interaction with Mobile Devices and Services (MobileHCI 2019), pp. 1–11, Taiwan (2019). https://doi.org/10.1145/3338286.3340118

47. Creswell, J.W., Creswell, J.D.: Research Design: Qualitative, Quantitative, and Mixed Methods Approaches, 5th edn., Thousand Oaks (2018)

48. Lazar, J., Feng, J.H., Hochheiser, H.: Research Methods in Human-Computer Interaction, 2nd edn. Elsevier, Amsterdam (2017)

49. Yin, R.K.: Case Study Research: Design and Methods. SAGE, Thousand Oaks (2003)

50. Grimes, H.A., Forster, D.A., Newton, M.S.: Sources of information used by women during pregnancy to meet their information needs. Midwifery 30(1), e26–e33 (2014). https://doi.org/10.1016/j.midw.2013.10.007

51. Laugesen, J., Hassanein, K., Yuan, Y.: The impact of internet health information on patient compliance: a research model and an empirical study. J. Med. Internet Res. 17(6), e143 (2015). https://doi.org/10.2196/jmir.4333

52. Marko, K.I., et al.: A mobile prenatal care app to reduce in-person visits: prospective controlled trial. JMIR MHealth UHealth 7(5), e10520 (2019)

53. Marko, K.I., et al.: Testing the feasibility of remote patient monitoring in prenatal care using a mobile app and connected devices: a prospective observational trial. JMIR Res. Protoc. 5(4), e200 (2016)

Beyond Entertainment: TikTok's Profound Effect on Mental Well-Being

Massimo Cellich, Anai Pučić, and Tihomir Orehovački(✉) [iD]

Faculty of Informatics, Juraj Dobrila University of Pula, Zagrebačka 30, 52100 Pula, Croatia
{massimo.cellich,anai.pucic}@student.unipu.hr,
tihomir.orehovacki@unipu.hr

Abstract. In the rapidly evolving realm of digital communication, TikTok has emerged as a significant player, blending entertainment with social interaction and content creation. This study delves into the effects of TikTok usage on mental well-being, analyzing the roles of platform addiction, content exposure, social engagement, feedback nature, and stress perception. Data from 90 university students were examined using structural equation modeling, revealing that platform addiction and content exposure are closely linked to increased social engagement, but also to heightened stress perception, which adversely affects mental well-being. Importantly, the feedback nature on TikTok serves as a critical mediator, influencing users' emotional and psychological states. These findings underscore the intricate balance digital platforms must navigate between enhancing social connectivity and safeguarding users' mental health. The results have profound implications for researchers, developers, and mental health professionals, emphasizing the need for digital environments that support positive interactions and mental well-being.

Keywords: TikTok · Mental Well-Being · Social Engagement · Platform Addiction · Content Exposure · Feedback Nature · Stress Perception · Digital Communication · Structural Equation Modeling

1 Introduction

In the 21st century, the landscape of digital communication has undergone a significant transformation, profoundly influencing how individuals connect and impacting their socio-cultural contexts and personal well-being. The proliferation of smartphones and the widespread accessibility of mobile internet have thrust social media platforms into a pivotal role within this digital paradigm, altering the nature of interpersonal interactions and self-perception. TikTok, in particular, has emerged as a standout platform, experiencing rapid growth and offering a distinct mix of entertainment, social interaction, and content creation, capturing the attention of a diverse user base [15]. The platform's dynamic content algorithm and interactive features have solidified its position in the digital routines of many [30], yet it has also sparked concerns about its potential impact on mental well-being, particularly in terms of platform addiction, content exposure,

V. G. Duffy (Ed.): HCII 2024, LNCS 15376, pp. 20–31, 2025.
https://doi.org/10.1007/978-3-031-76809-5_2

and the quality of online interactions [28]. The significance of the user experience, encompassing the overall impression and emotional response to platform use, is crucial for understanding the complex relationship between platform engagement and mental health, as it directly influences user retention [20], satisfaction [21], and the platform's growth trajectory [22].

The advent of social networks has revolutionized global communication, providing unparalleled opportunities for connectivity and self-expression. Despite the myriad benefits, these platforms have raised significant concerns regarding their psychological implications. Hossain et al. [6] highlight the profound psychological impact of the COVID-19 pandemic, pointing to an increase in mental health issues such as depression, anxiety, stress, and suicidal tendencies, exacerbated by continuous exposure to pandemic-related news on social media. This relentless stream of often distressing information can heighten feelings of anxiety and helplessness, underscoring the dual-edged nature of information dissemination on these platforms. Furthermore, the rise of live video game streaming platforms like Twitch has introduced new dimensions to social interaction. Li et al. [12] examine the relationship between the use of these platforms and various psychological variables, finding that prolonged engagement can lead to behavioral changes, including signs of addiction and altered social behaviors. Despite fostering a sense of community through real-time interactions between streamers and viewers, these platforms may also pose psychological challenges, highlighting the importance of balance in digital engagement. Verduyn et al. [25] delve into the effects of social networks on mental health, distinguishing between active and passive use. Their research reveals that while social media platforms offer avenues for connection and self-expression, the mode of engagement can have diverse impacts on users' mental well-being. Active use, involving direct interactions, can enhance feelings of social connectedness, whereas passive use, such as merely browsing others' posts, can lead to feelings of social comparison and envy, potentially adversely affecting mental health. Dayson et al. [4] explore the therapeutic potential of social networks, highlighting "social prescribing" within secondary mental health services. Their findings suggest that digital platforms like Facebook groups or online forums can provide essential peer support, aiding the recovery process for individuals facing mental health challenges and demonstrating the positive impact of digital communities.

Building on this foundation, our study turns its focus to TikTok, a platform that has garnered worldwide attention with its unique format and user engagement mechanisms. By investigating the complex interplay of various factors, this research aims to shed light on the specific psychological and behavioral consequences of TikTok use. This endeavor seeks to contribute to the ongoing discussion on the impact of social media on mental health, offering new perspectives on the intricate relationship between digital platform engagement and mental well-being.

2 Methodology

2.1 Research Framework

The research framework, aimed at exploring the influence of TikTok on users' mental health, is composed of the interrelationship among six constructs. Platform Addiction (PAD) refers to the compulsive engagement with TikTok, marked by a persistent need to use the app, extended usage beyond intended time, and its dominance as the primary smartphone application. Content Exposure (CEX) refers to the consistent discovery of thought-provoking and informative content on TikTok, along with regular exposure to akin materials within the user's feed. Social Engagement (SEG) involves collaboration with peers, responding to others' content, and live interaction with the audience on TikTok. Feedback Nature (FBN) is defined by the frequent reception of constructive feedback, the high shareability of posts, and primarily positive comments from the community on TikTok. Stress Perception (STP) captures the distress felt over underperforming posts, the pressure to outdo others' content, and the fear of losing followers over time on TikTok. Mental Well-Being (MWB) encompasses using TikTok as a temporary escape from reality and personal issues, followed by feelings of jealousy and envy post-use.

The design of TikTok, marked by its endless scrolling and personalized content delivery, creates an inherently addictive environment that encourages users to remain engaged for extended periods [29]. This engagement is not passive; the platform's algorithmic personalization, based on user interactions, fosters a cycle of continuous participation, where users actively contribute through likes, comments, and participation in community trends [8]. Consequently, this addictive design premise leads to the following hypothesis:

H1. Platform addiction has a significant positive influence on social engagement in the context of TikTok.

The compulsive use of TikTok, driven by its endless content and fast-paced trend changes, places significant stress on users, particularly those with high levels of platform addiction [14]. This environment, characterized by a constant influx of information and social stimuli, creates a pressure to stay continually updated, leading to heightened stress perception. The phenomenon of "content overload" and the fear of missing out (FOMO) further compound this stress, making it challenging for addicted users to balance their TikTok engagement with other aspects of life [18]. Thus, we propose the following hypothesis:

H2. Platform addiction has a significant positive influence on stress perception in the context of TikTok.

TikTok's algorithm exposes users to a diverse array of content through the "For You Page" (FYP), extending beyond their usual interests [3]. This varied content not only enriches the user experience but also stimulates interactions within the TikTok community. As users encounter and engage with a wider range of topics and ideas, they are more likely to participate in discussions, share content, and connect with others. This increased exposure to diverse content naturally leads to enhanced social engagement on the platform [27]. Therefore, we suggest the following hypothesis:

H3. Content exposure has a significant positive influence on social engagement in the context of TikTok.

On TikTok, the broad spectrum of content ranging from educational to entertainment pieces significantly shapes the nature of feedback users receive [2]. The platform's algorithms and participatory features like comments and duets ensure users encounter and engage with a variety of perspectives, leading to a diverse array of feedback from the global audience. This feedback can span from positive affirmations to constructive critiques, mirroring the eclectic mix of content consumed [11]. Given this dynamic, we posit the following hypothesis:

H4. Content exposure has a significant positive influence on feedback nature in the context of TikTok.

TikTok's interactive ecosystem, designed to foster user engagement through likes, comments, duets, and stitches, plays a pivotal role in determining the visibility and reach of content [7]. As users become more engaged, actively participating in the platform's community-driven activities, their content gains greater exposure. This increased visibility naturally amplifies the volume and diversity of feedback received, as a broader audience interacts with the content, leading to a range of responses from praises to critiques [13]. Therefore, we suggest the following hypothesis:

H5. Social engagement has a significant positive influence on feedback nature in the context of TikTok.

On TikTok, feedback is a powerful mediator of users' emotional and psychological states. Positive interactions, such as likes and supportive comments, can uplift users, bolstering their self-esteem and reinforcing their sense of belonging within the platform's community [16]. Conversely, negative feedback can precipitate feelings of inadequacy and distress, adversely affecting mental health [26]. This dynamic is amplified on TikTok due to its highly interactive nature and the emphasis on user-generated content, making the impact of feedback on well-being particularly significant. Thus, we posit the following hypothesis:

H6. Feedback nature has a significant positive influence on mental well-being of TikTok users.

The pressures of maintaining an engaging presence on TikTok, characterized by the constant need to produce resonant content, keep abreast of fleeting trends, and manage the platform's social dynamics, contribute significantly to user stress [10]. This stress, inherent in the platform's fast-paced and trend-focused environment, can manifest as feelings of burnout, anxiety, and a general decline in life satisfaction, particularly for users deeply embedded in the TikTok community [24]. Over time, such sustained stress can negatively impact mental and emotional health, leading to a reduction in overall well-being. Therefore, we propose the following hypothesis:

H7. Stress perception has a significant positive influence on mental well-being of TikTok users.

Addiction to TikTok, marked by excessive and compulsive engagement with the platform, can significantly encroach upon users' daily lives, disrupting routines, sleep patterns, and real-life social interactions. This overuse can detract from essential real-world activities and responsibilities, leading to a cascade of negative repercussions on an individual's mental and physical well-being [1]. The immersive allure of TikTok, with its constant flow of captivating content, often results in prolonged usage periods, potentially sidelining physical activity, social interactions, and even basic self-care routines.

This neglect can manifest in various adverse outcomes, such as feelings of isolation, diminished physical health, and an overall reduction in well-being [17]. Consequently, we posit the following hypothesis:

H8. Platform addiction has a significant positive influence on mental well-being of TikTok users.

2.2 Apparatus

Data were collected via an online questionnaire disseminated through Google Forms. This questionnaire included three demographic items (gender, age, and level of study) and six measures of TikTok engagement (daily usage time, usage frequency, content posting, commenting, liking, and sharing behaviors). Additionally, the questionnaire contained 19 items designed to explore the dimensions of six constructs within the research framework. Participant responses were collected on a five-point Likert scale, ranging from 1 (strongly disagree) to 5 (strongly agree). To assess the reliability and validity of our research framework and examine the hypothesized relationships, we employed partial least squares structural equation modeling (PLS-SEM) as statistical technique [5].

Adhering to the inverse square root method as proposed by Kock and Hadaya [9], and considering effect size ranges for an 80% power level as well as the minimum path coefficient expected to be significant at the 5% level [5], we determined our minimum required sample size to be 86. With an actual sample size of 90, our study meets the criteria for statistical robustness. The SmartPLS 4.1.0.1 software [23] was utilized to evaluate the psychometric properties of both the measurement and structural models, ensuring the rigor and reliability of our analytical approach.

3 Results

3.1 Study Participants

The participant demographics in the study consisted of 90 students, closely balanced in gender distribution with 48.89% male and 51.11% female, which facilitates a comprehensive analysis of TikTok's impact without gender bias. The age range of participants was from 18 to 40 years, with an average age of 22.07 years (SD = 3.042), and the majority were undergraduate students in computer science (64.4%), indicating a tech-savvy cohort. In terms of TikTok usage, a significant portion of the participants, 33.3%, reported spending over 7 h daily on the platform, highlighting the high engagement level among some users. Furthermore, a substantial 35.6% of participants accessed TikTok more than 9 times a day, indicating frequent interaction with the app throughout the day. When examining content creation behaviors, 30% of participants were highly active, having posted content on TikTok 40 or more times. This suggests a notable inclination towards content generation among a segment of the users. Engagement through commenting and liking on TikTok also revealed substantial activity, with 40% of participants commenting on others' posts 40 or more times, and a remarkable 66.7% liking content at the same high frequency. Additionally, 65.6% of the participants shared others' content more than 40 times, indicating a strong trend of content dissemination within the platform.

3.2 Model Assessment

In the PLS-SEM path analysis process, the algorithm determines the standardized partial regression coefficients within the structural model subsequent to the estimation of the measurement model parameters [5]. This is followed by a detailed two-phase examination of the psychometric attributes of the envisaged conceptual model, focusing on the reliability of indicators, their internal consistency, as well as their convergent and discriminant validity.

The reliability of the indicators was scrutinized by analyzing the standardized loadings associated with items and their respective constructs. Adhering to established purification guidelines [5], only those items whose standardized loadings met or surpassed the threshold of 0.708 were maintained within the measurement model. The outcomes of confirmatory factor analysis (CFA) presented in Table 1 revealed that the standardized loadings for all items exceeded the minimum required threshold, with values ranging from 0.869 to 0.975. This indicates that the constructs accounted for 75.52% to 95.06% of the variance in their respective items.

Table 1. Standardized factor loadings of items.

	CEX	FBN	MWB	PAD	SEG	STP
CEX1	0.903					
CEX2	0.940					
CEX3	0.951					
FBN1		0.874				
FBN2		0.953				
FBN3		0.939				
MWB1			0.874			
MWB2			0.873			
MWB3			0.888			
MWB4			0.869			
PAD1				0.926		
PAD2				0.906		
PAD3				0.929		
SEG1					0.925	
SEG2					0.967	
SEG3					0.944	
STP1						0.975
STP2						0.940
STP3						0.949

Furthermore, the assessment of construct internal consistency was conducted using three metrics: Cronbach's alpha, composite reliability (rho_C), and the consistent reliability coefficient (rho_A). Acceptable values for these metrics are between 0.70 and 0.95, denoting adequate internal consistency, whereas values above 0.95 may indicate an issue with item redundancy or undesirable response patterns that could negatively impact the content validity [5]. As demonstrated in Table 2, the constructs of feedback nature, mental well-being, and platform addiction have met the aforementioned criterion across all three indicators. On the contrary, the composite reliability for the constructs of content exposure and social engagement exceeds the recommended reference value, whereas for the construct of stress perception, this holds true for all three internal consistency indicators. From the definitions of the constructs, which reflect the items measuring them, it is evident that the reason for this is not semantic redundancy among items but rather that they genuinely measure distinct facets of the construct domain. Furthermore, analysis of the collected data has confirmed that undesirable response patterns are not the underlying reason either. Taking this into account, content validity is not compromised, and the constructs forming the research framework exhibit a high level of internal consistency.

Table 2. Convergent validity and internal consistency of constructs

Constructs	Cronbach's Alpha	rho_A	rho_C	AVE
Content Exposure (CEX)	0.924	0.929	0.952	0.868
Feedback Nature (FBN)	0.912	0.913	0.945	0.851
Mental Well-Being (MWB)	0.899	0.899	0.930	0.768
Platform Addiction (PAD)	0.910	0.914	0.943	0.847
Social Engagement (SEG)	0.941	0.944	0.962	0.894
Stress Perception (STP)	0.951	0.956	0.968	0.911

The evaluation of convergent validity was carried out using the Average Variance Extracted (AVE) measure. A benchmark of 0.50 or greater for AVE suggests that the construct captures more variance from its indicators than from measurement error [5]. According to the data presented in the final column of Table 2, every construct in the study's framework successfully met this threshold, thereby confirming the measurement model's strong convergent validity.

For discriminant validity, which measures how distinct a construct is from other constructs in the model, the Heterotrait-Monotrait (HTMT) ratio of correlations was employed [5]. A HTMT value beyond 0.90 for closely related constructs indicates a lack of discriminant validity, whereas a more stringent threshold of 0.85 applies to constructs that are theoretically distinct [5]. According to the findings summarized in Table 3, the HTMT ratios for all constructs in the framework did not exceed these critical values, ensuring that each construct is adequately differentiated from the others. This supports the fulfillment of the discriminant validity criteria within the study's conceptual framework.

Table 3. Heterotrait–Monotrait ratio of correlations (HTMT).

	CEX	FBN	MWB	PAD	SEG	STP
CEX						
FBN	0.770					
MWB	0.678	0.788				
PAD	0.872	0.696	0.713			
SEG	0.687	0.856	0.672	0.737		
STP	0.664	0.864	0.755	0.663	0.884	

Following the confirmation of the measurement model's adequacy, attention was shifted to evaluating the structural model. This involved examining aspects such as collinearity among constructs, the model's explanatory capability, path significance, and the influence of exogenous constructs.

The process entailed computing multiple regression equations to map out the interrelations among the constructs. A concern in this stage is the potential for high collinearity if constructs share too much conceptual overlap, which could distort the estimates for the regression coefficients. The Variance Inflation Factor (VIF) is the standard measure used to detect such collinearity in the structural model, with values above 5 indicating significant collinearity issues [5]. As shown in Table 4, the VIF values ranged from 1.000 to 3.102, indicating an absence of collinearity.

Table 4. Results of testing the collinearity in the structural model.

	CEX	FBN	MWB	PAD	SEG	STP
CEX		1.714			2.742	
FBN			3.102			
MWB						
PAD			1.780		2.742	1.000
SEG		1.714				
STP			3.000			

The explanatory strength of the model is gauged by the coefficient of determination (R^2), which quantifies the variance in the dependent constructs explained by the independent constructs. The benchmark for acceptable R^2 values can vary across different fields of study [5]. For instance, Orehovački [19] posits that in empirical research on software evaluation, R^2 values of 0.15, 0.34, and 0.46 signify weak, moderate, and strong explanatory abilities, respectively. The adjusted R^2, which accounts for the number of predictors in the model, is often preferred for a more accurate assessment [5].

The study findings shown in Table 5 revealed that 68.9% of the variance in the feed-back nature was explained by content exposure and social engagement. Additionally, the feedback nature, stress perception, and platform addiction accounted for 58.0% of the variance in the mental well-being. Content exposure and platform addiction together explained 48.7% of the variance in social engagement, while platform addiction alone was responsible for 37.8% of the variance in stress perception. These results underscore the significant explanatory potential of the model concerning the determinants of feed-back nature, mental well-being, and social engagement, with a moderate explanatory power for stress perception.

Table 5. Results of testing the explanatory power of the research model.

Endogenous Constructs	R^2	R^2 Adjusted
Feedback Nature (FBN)	0.696	0.689
Mental Well-Being (MWB)	0.595	0.580
Social Engagement (SEG)	0.498	0.487
Stress Perception (STP)	0.385	0.378

The validity of the proposed relationships within the research framework was further examined through the analysis of path coefficients, employing a bootstrapping resam-pling method with asymptotic two-tailed t-statistics to evaluate the significance of these coefficients. The bootstrap analysis was conducted with a sample size equivalent to the study's and involved 5000 bootstrap samples. The outcomes of hypotheses testing are detailed in Table 6.

The findings revealed that both platform addiction ($\beta = 0.473$, $p < 0.001$) and content exposure ($\beta = 0.268$, $p < 0.05$) had a significant effect on social engagement, supporting hypotheses H1 and H3. Moreover, platform addiction had a notable effect on stress perception ($\beta = 0.620$, $p < 0.001$), corroborating hypothesis H2. Content exposure and social engagement also significantly influenced the feedback nature ($\beta = 0.337$, $p < 0.001$ and $\beta = 0.576$, $p < 0.001$, respectively), affirming hypotheses H4 and H5. In addition, the feedback nature, stress perception, and platform addiction were found to significantly impact mental well-being ($\beta = 0.321$, $p < 0.05$, $\beta = 0.275$, $p < 0.05$, and $\beta = 0.269$, $p < 0.05$, respectively), lending support to hypotheses H6, H7, and H8.

The effect size (f2) indicates the extent of an exogenous construct's influence on an endogenous one, with thresholds of 0.02, 0.15, and 0.35 denoting small, medium, and large effects, respectively [5]. Based on the f2 values obtained, content exposure was determined to have a moderate influence on the feedback nature (f2 = 0.218) and a minor impact on social engagement (f2 = 0.052). Platform addiction was shown to have a substantial effect on stress perception (f2 = 0.625), a moderate influence on social engagement (f2 = 0.163), and a slight effect on mental well-being (f2 = 0.100). Social engagement significantly affected the feedback nature (f2 = 0.635), which in turn had a small influence on mental well-being (f2 = 0.082). Stress perception was found to have a minor impact on mental well-being (f2 = 0.062), indicating the varied strengths of the

Table 6. Results of hypotheses testing.

Hypotheses	Path Coefficients	T Statistics	p-Value	Supported?
H1. PAD → SEG	0.473	4.040	0.000	Yes
H2. PAD → STP	0.620	10.528	0.000	Yes
H3. CEX → SEG	0.268	2.424	0.015	Yes
H4. CEX → FBN	0.337	3.829	0.000	Yes
H5. SEG → FBN	0.576	6.478	0.000	Yes
H6. FBN → MWB	0.321	2.334	0.020	Yes
H7. STP → MWB	0.275	2.054	0.040	Yes
H8. PAD → MWB	0.269	2.428	0.015	Yes

relationships among the constructs in the study. The results of the effect size evaluation are summarized in Table 7.

Table 7. Results of testing the effect size.

	CEX	FBN	MWB	PAD	SEG	STP
CEX		0.218			0.052	
FBN			0.082			
MWB						
PAD			0.100		0.163	0.625
SEG		0.635				
STP			0.062			

4 Conclusion

This study makes a novel contribution to the growing body of literature on the psychological impacts of social media, with a particular focus on TikTok. By examining the multifaceted relationship between platform usage and mental well-being, this research illuminates how TikTok's unique features—such as its endless scroll, personalized content delivery, and interactive engagement mechanisms—can foster both positive social connections and potentially negative psychological outcomes. The findings reveal a nuanced interplay between platform addiction, content exposure, and social engagement, which, coupled with the nature of feedback received, significantly influences users' stress perceptions and overall mental well-being. These insights underscore the complex, dual-faceted role of digital platforms in contemporary social and personal life, offering a deeper understanding of how such platforms can simultaneously enrich and challenge users' psychological landscapes.

For researchers, this work opens up new avenues for exploration within the domain of digital communication and mental health. It suggests a need for further investigation into the specific features of social media platforms that contribute to addictive behaviors and stress, as well as the protective factors that might mitigate these effects. For practitioners—particularly those in mental health and digital platform design—the study highlights the importance of creating and maintaining online environments that support positive social interactions and mental health. This includes considering how platform algorithms and engagement strategies can be designed to minimize stress and addictive usage patterns while enhancing the overall well-being of users.

However, the study is not without its limitations. The reliance on self-reported data from a predominantly young, tech-savvy demographic may limit the generalizability of the findings. Additionally, the cross-sectional design precludes causal inferences about the relationships observed. Future research should aim to address these limitations by employing longitudinal designs, diversifying participant demographics, and integrating objective usage data. Such studies could further elucidate the complex dynamics at play and inform more nuanced, effective strategies for balancing the benefits and risks of social media engagement in the digital age.

Acknowledgments. This study was funded by Erasmus+ project SPADATAS (grant number 2022-1-ES01-KA220-SCH-000086363).

References

1 Baker, Z.G., Krieger, H., LeRoy, A.S.: Fear of missing out: relationships with depression, mindfulness, and physical symptoms. Transl. Issues Psychol. Sci. **2**(3), 275–282 (2016)
2. Bhandari, A., Bimo, S.: Why's everyone on TikTok now? The algorithmized self and the future of self-making on social media. Soc. Media + Soc. **8**(1), 205630512210862 (2022)
3. Boeker, M., Urman, A.: An empirical investigation of personalization factors on TikTok. In: Proceedings of the ACM Web Conference 2022, pp. 2298–2309. ACM, Lyon (2022)
4. Dayson, C., Painter, J., Bennett, E.: Social prescribing for patients of secondary mental health services: emotional, psychological and social well-being outcomes. J. Public Ment. Health **19**(4), 271–279 (2020)
5. Hair, J.F., Hult, G.T.M., Ringle, C.M., Sarstedt, M.: A Primer on Partial Least Squares Structural Equation Modeling (PLS-SEM), 3rd edn. Sage, Thousand Oaks (2022)
6. Hossain, M.M., et al.: Epidemiology of mental health problems in COVID-19: a review. F1000Res **9**, 636 (2020)
7. Kaye, D.B.V.: JazzTok: creativity, community, and improvisation on TikTok. Jazz Cult. **6**(2), 92–116 (2023)
8. Klug, D., Qin, Y., Evans, M., Kaufman, G.: Trick and please. A mixed-method study on user assumptions about the TikTok algorithm. In: Proceedings of the 13th ACM Web Science Conference, pp. 84–92. ACM, New York (2021)
9. Kock, N., Hadaya, P.: Minimum sample size estimation in PLS-SEM: the inverse square root and gamma-exponential methods. Inf. Syst. J. **28**, 227–261 (2018)
10. Kross, E., Verduyn, P., Sheppes, G., Costello, C.K., Jonides, J., Ybarra, O.: Social media and well-being: pitfalls, progress, and next steps. Trends Cogn. Sci. **25**(1), 55–66 (2021)
11. Li, P., Chang, L., Chua, T.H.H., Loh, R.S.M.: "Likes" as KPI: an examination of teenage girls' perspective on peer feedback on Instagram and its influence on coping response. Telematics Inform. **35**(7), 1994–2005 (2018)

12. Li, Y., Wang, C., Liu, J.: A systematic review of literature on user behavior in video game live streaming. Int. J. Environ. Res. Public Health **17**, 3328 (2020)
13. Ling, C., Blackburn, J., De Cristofaro, E., Stringhini, G.: Slapping cats, bopping heads, and oreo shakes: understanding indicators of Virality in TikTok short videos. In: Proceedings of the 14th ACM Web Science Conference, pp. 164–173. ACM, Barcelona (2022)
14. Montag, C., Lachmann, B., Herrlich, M., Zweig, K.: Addictive features of social media/messenger platforms and freemium games against the background of psychological and economic theories. Int. J. Environ. Res. Public Health **16**(14), 2612 (2019)
15. Montag, C., Yang, H., Elhai, J.D.: On the psychology of TikTok use: a first glimpse from empirical findings. Front. Public Health **9** (2021)
16. Nesi, J., Prinstein, M.J.: Using social media for social comparison and feedback-seeking: gender and popularity moderate associations with depressive symptoms. J. Abnorm. Child Psychol. **43**(8), 1427–1438 (2015)
17. Nienstedt, C., Smith, N., Braithwaite, H., Gilbert, B., Wright, R.R.: Swiping away your well-being? Examining Well-being indicators among TikTok account holders. PsiChiJournal **28**(2), 96–106 (2023)
18. Oberst, U., Wegmann, E., Stodt, B., Brand, M., Chamarro, A.: Negative consequences from heavy social networking in adolescents: the mediating role of fear of missing out. J. Adolesc. **55**(1), 51–60 (2017)
19. Orehovački, T.: Methodology for evaluating the quality in use of Web 2.0 applications. Ph.D. thesis, University of Zagreb, Faculty of Organization and Informatics, Varaždin (2013)
20. Orehovački, T., Babić, S.: Predicting students' continuance intention related to the use of collaborative Web 2.0 applications. In: Proceedings of the 23rd International Conference on Information Systems Development (ISD), pp. 112–122. University of Zagreb, Faculty of Organization and Informatics, Varaždin (2014)
21. Orehovački, T., Babić, S.: Identifying the relevance of quality dimensions contributing to universal access of social Web applications for collaborative writing on mobile devices: an empirical study. Univ. Access Inf. Soc. **17**(3), 453–473 (2018)
22. Orehovački, T., Cappiello, C., Matera, M.: Identifying relevant dimensions for the quality of web mashups: an empirical study. In: Kurosu, M. (ed.) Human-Computer Interaction. Theory, Design, Development and Practice, pp. 396–407. Springer, Cham (2016). https://doi.org/10.1007/978-3-319-39510-4_37
23. Ringle, C.M., Wende, S., Becker, J.-M.: SmartPLS 4. SmartPLS GmbH, Oststeinbek (2022)
24. Sadagheyani, H.E., Tatari, F.: Investigating the role of social media on mental health. Ment. Health Soc. Incl. **25**(1), 41–51 (2020)
25. Verduyn, P., Gugushvili, N., Kross, E.: The impact of social network sites on mental health: distinguishing active from passive use. World Psychiatry **20**(1), 133–134 (2021)
26. Weinstein, E.: The social media see-saw: positive and negative influences on adolescents' affective well-being. New Media Soc. **20**(10), 3597–3623 (2018)
27. Wiguna, C., Mulyana, S., Wardoyo, R.: Selection of TikTok content based on user engagement criteria using the analytic hierarchy process. JUITA **11**(1), 125 (2023)
28. Yao, N., Chen, J., Huang, S., Montag, C., Elhai, J.D.: Depression and social anxiety in relation to problematic TikTok use severity: the mediating role of boredom proneness and distress intolerance. Comput. Hum. Behav. **145**, 107751 (2023)
29. Zhang, X., Wu, Y., Liu, S.: Exploring short-form video application addiction: socio-technical and attachment perspectives. Telematics Inform. **42**, 101243 (2019)
30. Zhao, Y.: Analysis of TikTok's success based on its algorithm mechanism. In: Proceedings of the 2020 International Conference on Big Data and Social Sciences (ICBDSS), pp. 19–23. IEEE, Xi'an (2020)

Building Bonds Through Bytes: The Impact of Communication Styles on Patient-Chatbot Relationships and Treatment Adherence in AI-Driven Healthcare

Zhiyun Chen[1]([message]) [ORCID], Xinyue Zhao[2], Min Hua[1], and Jian Xu[2]([message])

[1] USC-SJTU Institute of Cultural and Creative Industry, Shanghai Jiao Tong University, A7-A8 Building, 155 Tanjiatang Road, Minhang District, Shanghai 200241, China
{czywinnie0515,huamin}@sjtu.edu.cn
[2] School of Media and Communication, Shanghai Jiao Tong University, 800 Dongchuan Road, Minhang District, Shanghai 200240, China
{joeyzhao,xujian}@sjtu.edu.cn

Abstract. The proliferation of AI-driven healthcare chatbots has catalyzed a paradigm shift in the healthcare industry, necessitating a deeper understanding of how their communication styles influence potential health outcomes. Drawing upon the Computers are Social Actors (CASA) framework, this study employs experimental design to interrogate the differential effects of dominant and affiliative communication styles on patients' adherence to health information. The findings reveal that an affiliative communication style, characterized by empathy, warmth, and patient-centered language, significantly augments treatment adherence by fostering patients' perceived involvement in shared decision-making and engendering trust in the chatbot. Notably, the study illuminates the absence of a significant moderating effect of patients' self-construal on the relationship between chatbot communication style and treatment adherence, suggesting the potential for a universally efficacious communication strategy. Moreover, the study corroborates the parallel mediation effects of shared decision-making and patient trust, underscoring their pivotal role in the causal pathway between chatbot communication style and treatment adherence. The study propounds the imperative for adopting an affiliative communication style as a universally applicable strategy to optimize patient engagement and treatment adherence, transcending the boundaries of individual differences. Methodologically, this study pioneers a novel approach to manipulating chatbot communication styles through meticulously crafted prompts, presenting a valuable methodological innovation for future research endeavors. The theoretical and practical implications of this study are far-reaching, informing the development of patient-centered, trust-enhancing, and adherence-promoting AI technologies in healthcare.

Keywords: AI-driven Healthcare Chatbots · Communication Styles · Affiliative Communication · Treatment Adherence · Human-Computer Interaction

V. G. Duffy (Ed.): HCII 2024, LNCS 15376, pp. 32–52, 2025.
https://doi.org/10.1007/978-3-031-76809-5_3

1 Introduction

AI-driven healthcare chatbots, powered by technological advancements in machine learning and natural language processing, have emerged as potent tools poised to reshape the medical landscape [1]. Particularly, the advent of generative AI (GenAI) enables these chatbots to leverage vast medical datasets and develop autonomous responsiveness capabilities, empowering them to provide personalized, context-aware healthcare assistance [2]. GenAI-driven chatbots hold great promise in benefiting patients and providers with a wide range of tasks, from patient triaging, online consulting to lifestyle coaching [3], potentially ushering in a new era of preventive and interactive healthcare. Despite the advantages of high accessibility and cost efficiency, the deployment of this technology still faces multiple barriers, such as public skepticism and distrust caused by inappropriate communication [4, 5], hindering the widespread adoption of healthcare chatbots. Previous research has highlighted the crucial role of doctors' communication styles (or "bedside manner") in shaping doctor-patient relationships [6, 7], which in turn influence patients' trust in physicians and adherence to medical advice [8]. Therefore, the overarching goal of the present study is to investigate a more effective human-AI communication strategy that can fully unleash the potential of AI-driven healthcare chatbots and facilitate their integration into medical service delivery.

The *Computers are Social Actors (CASA)* paradigm proposes that individuals tend to apply social rules and expectations to their interactions with computers, even when they are aware that these entities are inanimate [9, 10]. Consistent with this paradigm, previous human-computer interaction research suggests that anthropomorphic cues, such as visual features, voice, and language, can elicit social responses from users and shape their perceptions of artificial agents [11–13]. Building on the CASA literature, we contend that the communication style of AI-driven healthcare chatbots plays a crucial role in shaping users' perceptions, trust, and adherence to the health information provided. As modern healthcare systems increasingly prioritize patient preferences and autonomy [14], patients expect not only clinical competence but also effective and empathetic communication from their healthcare providers [15]. If these expectations extend to human-computer interactions, then designing healthcare chatbots with affective communication styles may be essential for promoting user engagement and trust. Nevertheless, it is worth noting that some researchers have questioned the necessity and appropriateness of emotional support in AI agents, citing concerns such as the uncanny valley effect [16, 17] and the potential for over-reliance on artificial empathy [18, 19]. Given these competing perspectives, further research is warranted to investigate the impact of different communication styles on users' perceptions and behaviors in the specific context of AI-driven healthcare chatbots.

Drawing upon Street et al.'s framework [7], the objective of our study is to better understand the path through which communication styles employed by AI-driven healthcare chatbots influence users' health outcomes. We also examine how individual differences in self-construals moderate the effects of chatbots' communication styles on users' perceptions and behaviors. To approach our research objective, we conducted a scenario-based experiment in which participants interacted with healthcare chatbots exhibiting either dominant or affective communication styles.

The contribution of our research is threefold. First, we propose a processual and empirically supported model that considers the effects of both interactive and individual factors on the development of trust and adherence in the context of healthcare chatbots. This model advances the understanding of the complex interplay between AI system design and user characteristics in shaping the effectiveness of AI-driven healthcare communication. By incorporating users' self-construals as a moderator, our research highlights the importance of considering individual differences in the design and deployment of healthcare chatbots. Second, by identifying the opportunities and boundaries of anthropomorphism in facilitating patient-centered communication, our findings offer practical insights into the design of healthcare chatbots that can better engage users, build trust, and ultimately improve health outcomes. Third, our study introduces a methodological innovation in experiment design by using carefully crafted prompts as experimental manipulations. In this way, our research contributes to the successful integration of AI technologies into medical service delivery and the development of more effective AI-driven health interventions.

2 Theoretical Background

2.1 AI-Driven Healthcare Chatbot: Empowering Patient-Centered Care

The healthcare industry has witnessed a profound shift towards the digitalization of health services. Worldwide, the digital health revolution is expected to enhance every stage of the patient care continuum, from diagnosis to treatment and follow-up [20]. Consider as invaluable agents to achieve patient-centered care, AI technologies, particularly AI-driven chatbots, are deployed at the core nodes of health communication networks [21]. From highly-sensitive cancer care to daily health improvement, healthcare chatbots could address the triple aim of healthcare by enhancing the patient care experience, optimizing population health, and reducing healthcare costs per capita [22].

Despite the immense potential of healthcare chatbots in promoting patient-centered care, their practical application has been fraught with numerous barriers, as highlighted by early research in this field. These obstacles include concerns about chatbots' professional competence and privacy protection [23], lack of humanization and empathic communication [24], and general distrust in artificial intelligence technology [25, 26]. Moreover, compelling evidence suggests that user engagement tends to decline over time [27], posing a significant challenge to their long-term effectiveness.

However, recent advancements in GenAI technologies have brought new opportunities to overcome these obstacles and further enhance the application potential of healthcare chatbots [28, 29]. Compared to traditional rule-based or retrieval-based dialogue systems, chatbots powered by generative models (such as GPT-4 and PaLM2) can more flexibly understand user needs and generate more contextually relevant and personalized responses, making human-computer interactions more closely resemble natural interpersonal communication [30–32]. As a result, these sophisticated AI-driven chatbot technologies are poised to transform the landscape of patient engagement and health communication.

2.2 Chatbot Communication Style Cues and Treatment Adherence

The doctor-patient interaction is a complex progress [33]. Most patient complaints relate to doctors' communication skills rather than their clinical competency [34]. Doctors have been found to avoid discussing the emotional and societal implications of illnesses with patients [35]. Ignoring the emotional component can undermine the patient experience and evaluation of medical visits. The Social Interaction Model of Physician-Patient Interaction posits that patients limited medical knowledge and prognostic anxiety render the affective dimension of physicians' communication pivotal in shaping patient evaluations [36, 37]. The affective aspect of communication, conceptualized as communication style, dictates the interpretation and understanding of verbal and non-verbal cues within the medical dialogue [38, 39].

Literature on doctor-patient communication indicates that doctors exhibit two typical styles during medical visits [6, 40]. One style, domination, includes behavior that establish and maintain the doctor's control and authority in the medical interaction. This type is akin to what Roter and Hall term "paternalism," a traditional approach in medical practice [6], and is most common in Asian contexts [41]. The other style, affiliation, which is care-oriented, involves behaviors expressing interest, friendliness, empathy, warmth, honesty, compassion, and devotion [40]. This type can be regarded as an embodiment of patient-centered care, requiring doctors to treat patients as unique individuals rather than mere cases. Developed in response to the limitations of the paternalistic model of healthcare, it is now the prevailing model of care globally [42].

A doctor's communication style is associated with positive patient outcomes, including patients' satisfaction and treatment adherence [43]. Doctors adopting a more affiliative communication style tend to achieve higher patient treatment adherence [44]. With technological advancements, chatbots will increasingly assume the role of a doctor in conducting medical interactions with patients. CASA paradigm assumes that individuals apply similar rules from interpersonal inter-actions when engaging with computers [45]. A civil society demands politeness and sensitivity to others' rights [46], which, when applied to the medical context, means that a doctor's high social status and respect are bolstered by adopting a more affiliative style, potentially reducing the psychological distance to patients. If a chatbot exhibits anthropomorphic characteristics, consistent with previous literature, the affiliative communication style of the chatbot will positively impact patient adherence [47]. Therefore, we propose our first hypothesis:

H1: An interact with a healthcare chatbot with affiliative communication style (compared with dominant style) will lead to greater treatment adherence.

2.3 From Communication to Health Outcomes: The Mediating Roles of Shared Decision-Making and Patient Trust

Integrated people-centered health services strive to empower individuals to take control of their own health by providing them with the necessary education and support to make well-informed health decisions [48]. Prior studies have established that a trusting relationship between patients and healthcare providers, along with support for shared decision-making, are key factors that can improve primary adherence to treatment [49, 50].

Street et al. [7] demonstrated that communication between patients and providers influences health outcomes through both direct and indirect pathways. The proximal outcomes of consultations that contribute to these effects include patients' trust in healthcare providers, as well as patients and their families feeling that their concerns and apprehensions are being acknowledged and addressed. These outcomes span a variety of aspects, from patients actively participating in medical consultations and decision-making processes to developing the necessary skills for managing their daily health-related tasks and self-care routines.

Considering the profound impact of shared decision-making and patient trust on shaping treatment adherence, this study hypothesizes:

H2: Shared decision-making, enhanced by the communication style of AI-driven healthcare chatbots, will lead to greater treatment adherence in health information.

H3: Patient trust in AI-driven healthcare chatbots, enhanced by the communication style of AI-driven healthcare chatbots, will result in higher treatment adherence in health information.

2.4   The Moderating Role of Self-constural

The boundary conditions for the CASA effect necessitate consideration of individual attributes [46]. Individual preferences vary in their modalities of environmental interaction. Cultural differences manifest in the predominant self-construal among members of respective societies [51]. Individual values, such as interdependent and independent self-construals, surpass cultural dimensions of individualism and collectivism in forecasting communication styles in diverse cultural settings [52]. These values directly influence how individuals perceive themselves and interact with others, thereby shaping their actual communicative actions.

The interdependent self-construal, most prevalent in non-Western cultures, is a view of the self as part of the community and society, which tends to be more relational and connected [51]. The independent self-construal, by contrast, views the self as a unique entity, existing separately from the social environment, focusing on individual goal achievement [53] and posits that every culture encompasses both self-construal, yet the emphasis and integration of these perspectives within social frameworks differ across cultures, affecting individual cognition and behavior. Consequently, the diversity of self-construals shapes our existential perceptions and anchors our interpretations of communicative behaviors, notably in the realm of medical decision-making [52]. Compared to those with a higher independent self-construal, participants with a higher interdependent self-construal tend to rely more on doctors in medical decision-making and prefer a doctor-centered decision-making model [52].

Cultural collectivism greatly influenced the interdependent self-construal [54]. Conducted in the Chinese context, this study assumes that conducting a friendly interaction and establishing a relationship with healthcare professionals is culturally syntonic for individuals of East Asian descent due to cultural orientations toward interdependent self-construal and proposed our research question:

RQ1: How does the individual's self-construal influence the impact of the healthcare chatbot's communication style on treatment adherence?

3 Method

3.1 Experiment Design

This study employed a single-factor between-subject experimental design (see Fig. 1). The independent variable was the communication style of healthcare chatbots, which was manipulated at two types: Dominant vs. Affiliative. Two different versions of healthcare assistant chatbots were created through the design of different prompts, a technique widely employed in conversational AI to manipulate chatbot behaviors [55, 56]. The dominant style chatbot was designed to communicate in an authoritative, professional, and directive manner, while the affiliative style chatbot was designed to be more supportive, empathetic, and encouraging of patient participation [40].

In addition to the manipulation of communication style, participant self-construal (interdependent vs. independent) was measured as a moderating variable prior to the main experiment. The mediating variables, shared decision-making and perceived trust in the healthcare chatbot, as well as the dependent variable, treatment adherence intention, were measured after the participant's interaction with the assigned chatbot.

The experiment followed a scenario-based approach [57]. After providing informed consent, participants were asked to read a hypothetical scenario in which they were described as suffering from influenza-like symptoms. It was chosen for its commonality, relatability, and it's fit with the experimental task, which involves a complete consultation process and potential discussions on lifestyle and medication treatment plans [58, 59]. After reading the scenario, participants were randomly assigned to interact with one of the two chatbot versions (dominant vs. affiliative). They were instructed to consult the chatbot about their symptoms and go through the medical consultation process, from symptom description to treatment plan discussion [60].

3.2 Participants

A prior power analysis was conducted using G*Power to determine the required sample size for this study. With an expected effect size of 0.5, an alpha value of 0.05, a power of 0.95, and two groups, the analysis indicated that a minimum of 54 participants would be needed.

This study was approved by the Institutional Review Board of Shanghai Jiao Tong University (IRB approval number: LL2024000199). A total of 80 participants were recruited from five Chinese universities and three companies. The majority of participants (n = 68) completed the study offline, while 12 participants, due to geographical constraints, completed the study online. Participants were recruited through university bulletin board systems (BBS), WeChat groups, and company mailing lists.

To be eligible for the study, participants were required to have experienced a common health issue (i.e., influenza) within the past six months and be able to recall their symptoms at the time. They also needed to be proficient in using a computer and able to complete the online consultation task.

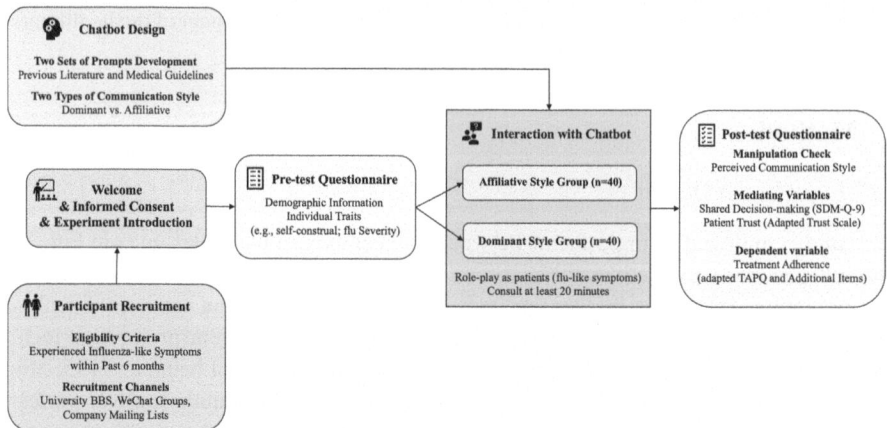

Fig. 1. The flow chat of experiment design

Before taking part in the study, all participants provided informed consent. After data cleaning, a total of 67 valid samples were included in the final analysis. The sample consisted of 27 males and 40 females, with ages ranging from 18 to 32. The majority of participants had completed graduate education or above (56.7%), followed by undergraduate education (37.3%) and below undergraduate education (6%). Table 1 summarizes the participants' demographic characteristics.

3.3 Chatbot Simulus

Based on previous research on physician communication styles [40] and medical communication guidelines [61], two sets of prompts were developed to create GPT-4-driven healthcare chatbots that accentuated affiliative and dominant communication styles respectively.

Both sets of prompts followed a consistent structure: identity statement, action guidelines description, specific key points, and concrete examples. The prompts were designed to differentiate the two communication styles in six key aspects: (1) directness of communication, (2) expression of professional expertise, (3) emotional rapport-building, (4) patient participation in decision-making, (5) informality of language, and (6) use of nonverbal cues. The example set of prompts for both conditions is provided in the following Table 2.

To ensure the validity of the prompts, we invited a panel of experts in artificial intelligence and medical professionals to review the prompts. Based on their feedback, we refined the prompts to better align with the GPT-4 model's capabilities and real-world medical communication practices.

In the affiliative condition, the prompts encouraged the healthcare chatbot to use open-ended questions, empathetic language, and a friendly and informal communication style. The chatbot was instructed to emphasize shared decision-making, provide multiple treatment options, and use positive emojis to add warmth to the conversation. In contrast, the dominant condition prompts directed the chatbot to provide medical

Table 1. Participants' Demographic Characteristics (N = 67)

Variables	Frequency (Percentage)
Gender	
Male	27 (40%)
Female	40 (60%)
Age	
Below 18 years old	0 (0%)
18–25	49 (73.13%)
26–35	18 (26.87%)
Above 35 years old	0 (0%)
Education	
Below undergraduate	4 (5.9%)
Undergraduate	25 (37.3%)
Graduate	38 (56.7%)
Severity of the illness	
Very mild	0 (0%)
mild	0 (0%)
quite mild	3 (4.5%)
moderate	21 (31.3%)
quite serious	25 (37.3%)
serious	15 (22.4%)
Extremely serious	3 (4.5%)
Experience with online medical consultations	
Yes	23 (34.3%)
No	44 (65.7%)
Experience with AI-based diagnostic consultations	
Yes	11 (16.4%)
No	56 (83.6%)

advice assertively, emphasize professional knowledge, limit emotional expressions, and maintain an objective tone. It was prompted to reduce asking for patient opinions, give clear guidance, and use serious emojis to reinforce authority.

3.4 Procedure

After providing informed consent and receiving an instruction manual outlining the study procedure, background information on flu-like symptoms, and sample questions, participants completed a pre-test questionnaire assessing their demographic information

Table 2. Example Prompts for Dominant and Affiliative Communication

Prompt Design [Markdown Syntax]	
Dominant Style	Affiliative Style
You are an AI doctor. When communicating with patients, your communication style should be authoritative. Here are the guidelines you should follow when communicating with patients:	You are an AI doctor. When communicating with patients, your communication style should be negotiative. Here are the guidelines you should follow when communicating with patients:
Emphasize professional knowledge: - Use professional medical terminology when explaining medical conditions. For example: "Your test results show that you have type 2 diabetes, and we need to start insulin treatment immediately." - Use relatively exaggerated expressions to emphasize points and, to a certain extent, exaggerate and emphasize content to deepen understanding. For example: "The flu can also have very serious consequences and, if not intervened in a timely manner, can seriously damage your health."	**Emphasize shared decision-making:** - When providing medical advice, emphasize the patient's right to choose and ability to control. For example: "Here are a few treatment options, and we can discuss which one best meets your needs." - Express respect for the patient's opinions. For example: "Your opinion is crucial for us to develop the best treatment plan."
Use serious and assertive emojis: - When referring to professional knowledge, appropriate emojis can be used to reinforce one's authority and emphasize expertise, such as: "Please make sure to monitor your blood sugar levels daily. 🧘‍♀️"	**Use positive and friendly emojis:** - When appropriate, use emojis to add friendliness to the conversation. For example: "I'm glad to see that you are actively participating in deciding on a treatment plan. 😊"

and individual traits. They were then randomly assigned to one of two experimental conditions, interacting with a healthcare chatbot exhibiting either a dominant (n = 40) or an affiliative (n = 40) communication style. Participants were unaware of which chatbot they were interacting with.

During the experiment, participants were instructed to role-play as patients who had recently experienced flu-like symptoms and to consult the assigned healthcare chatbot for medical advice. They were asked to recall their past experiences with similar symptoms and immerse themselves in the role of a patient seeking medical consultation. All conversations were required to last at least 20 minutes to ensure sufficient interaction. Following the chatbot consultation, participants completed a post-test questionnaire.

3.5 Variable Measurement

Manipulation Check
Communication Style. To assess the perceived communication style of the healthcare chatbot, we adapted 16 items from the Communicator Style Measure based on the study

by Buller and Buller [38]. The current scale included 11 items measuring affiliative style and 5 items measuring dominant style, rated on a 7-point Likert scale. Both subscales showed high internal consistency (Affiliative: $\alpha = 0.972$; Dominant: $\alpha = 0.919$) and construct validity (Affiliative: KMO $= 0.939$; Dominant: KMO $= 0.841$).

Mediating Variables

Shared Decision-Making. To assess patients' perceived involvement in shared decision making during the consultation, we adapted the 9-item Shared Decision Making Questionnaire (SDM-Q-9) developed by Kriston et al. [62].

The SDM-Q-9 has been widely validated across different regions and measures shared decision making from the patient's perspective. Participants rated their agreement with each item on a 7-point Likert scale ranging from 1 (strongly disagree) to 7 (strongly agree). The scale demonstrated good internal consistency (Cronbach's $\alpha = 0.933$) and construct validity (KMO $= 0.895$).

Patient Trust. Patient trust in the healthcare chatbot was measured using an adapted version of the trust scale developed by Dugan, Trachtenberg, and Hall [63]. The original scale was designed to assess patient trust in physicians, health insurers, and the medical profession.

For the purpose of this study, we modified the items to refer specifically to trust in the healthcare chatbot. The adapted scale consisted of 5 items rated on a 7-point Likert scale ranging from 1 (strongly disagree) to 7 (strongly agree) with good internal consistency (Cronbach's $\alpha = 0.933$) and construct validity (KMO $= 0.895$) in the current study.

Moderating Variable

Self-construal Level. We adopted the Self-Construal Scale (SCS) developed by Singelis [64], which was based on the initial conceptualization of self-construals by Markus and Kitayama [51]. The SCS consists of two dimensions: independent self-construal (12 items) and interdependent self-construal (12 items). Participants rated their agreement with each item on a 7-point Likert scale ranging from 1 (strongly disagree) to 7 (strongly agree). The SCS has been widely used in cross-cultural research, including studies on Chinese populations (e.g., Rao et al. [54]). The Cronbach's alphas for the independent and interdependent self-construal subscales were 0.875 and 0.870, respectively, indicating adequate internal consistency.

Dependent Variable

Treatment Adherence. To assess patients' adherence to the treatment recommendations provided by the healthcare chatbot, we used a combination of items from the Treatment Adherence Perception Questionnaire (TAPQ) developed by Sanford and Rivers [65] and two items from Kim and Park [66]. We selected 14 items that were most relevant to our study context and adapted them to refer specifically to adherence to the healthcare chatbot's recommendations.

The adapted scale measured various aspects of adherence, including likelihood of following recommendations, perceived effectiveness, potential barriers, comparison to typical patients, anticipated evaluation by the chatbot, and overall intention to adhere.

Items were rated on 5-point (items 2, 3, 4, 5, 7), 6-point (items 1, 6, 9, 10), or 7-point (items 8, 11, 12, 13, 14) Likert scales. For consistency, all items were converted to a 7-point scale during data analysis with good internal consistency ($\alpha = 0.968$) and construct validity (KMO = 0.937).

4 Result

4.1 Data Analysis

A one-way analysis of variance (ANOVA) was used to examine the between-group differences (H1). To explore the mediating effects of shared - decision making (H2) and trust in healthcare chatbot (H3), as well as to investigate the moderating effects of self-construal (RQ1), we conducted the moderated mediation analysis using model 5 in SPSS PROCESS [67].

In addition to the manipulation of communication style, participant self-construal (interdependent vs. independent) was measured as a moderating variable prior to the main experiment. The mediating variables, shared decision-making and perceived trust in the healthcare chatbot, as well as the dependent variable, treatment adherence intention, were measured after the participant's interaction with the assigned chatbot.

4.2 Manipulation Check

We performed manipulation checks for communication style. The result of a one-way ANOVA revealed that participants in the affiliative conditions perceived significantly more emotion (M = 5.99, SD = 1.66) compared to those in the dominant conditions (M = 3.58, SD = 1.50), $F_{(1, 65)} = 73.217$, $p < .001$. Conversely, participants in the dominant conditions perceived significantly more control (M = 4.03, SD = 0.97) compared to those in the affiliative conditions (M = 2.73, SD = 1.23), $F_{(1, 65)} = 21.941$, $p < .001$.

4.3 Hypotheses and Research Questions

Correlation analysis indicated that among all demographic variables and other factors, only education showed a significant correlation with the dependent variable. However, given that our sample in this study was highly concentrated at the levels of undergraduate and postgraduate education and above (94%), additional variables, including education, were not included as control variables in the subsequent analysis.

A one-way ANOVA was conducted to explore the main effects of two different chatbot communication style on treatment adherence. Results (Table 3) showed that there was a significant main effect of chatbot communication style on treatment adherence ($F_{(1, 65)} = 71.153$, $p < .001$). The results indicated that affiliative communication (M = 5.29, SD = 0.74, $p < .001$) significantly increased treatment adherence compared to dominant communication (M = 3.78, SD = .71, $p < .001$) (Fig. 2). Therefore, H1 was supported (Fig. 3).

Results of one-way ANOVA revealed that affiliative communication style significantly led to higher perceived shared - decision making (M = 4.94, SD = 1.20) than

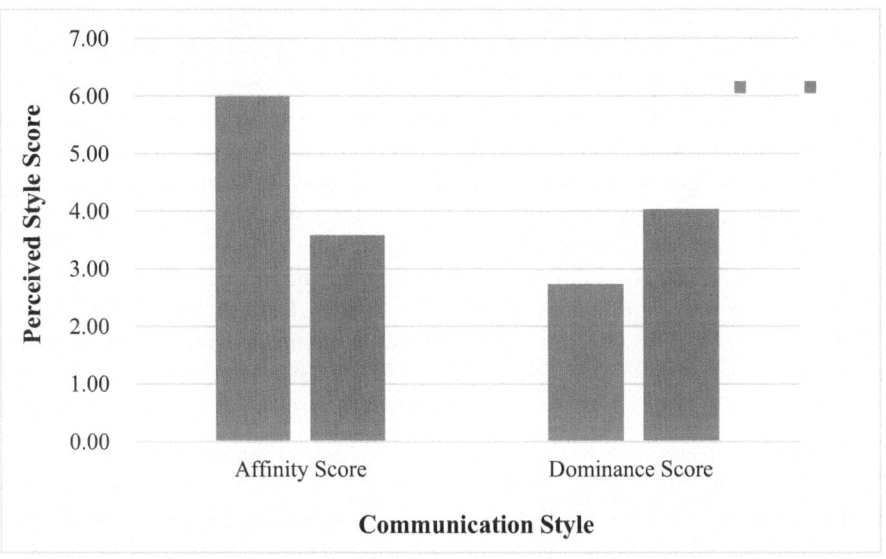

Fig. 2. Mean Scores of Perceived Styles for Chatbots between Two Groups.

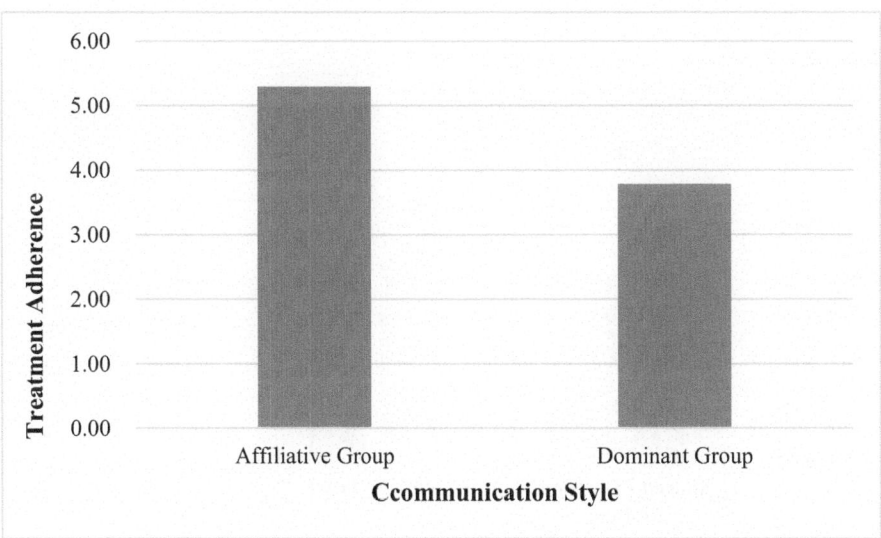

Fig. 3. Mean scores of treatment adherence for chatbots between two groups.

dominant communication style (M = 3.82, SD = 1.12), F (1, 65) = 15.300, p < .001. As shown in Table 3, communication styles significantly predicted shared decision making (a1 = 1.116, p < .001), which in turn had a significant impact on treatment adherence (b1 = 0.201, p < .001). A 95% bias-corrected confidence interval based on 5000 boot-strap samples indicated that the indirect effect through trust (a1b1 = 0.224) was entirely above zero (0.088, 0.400).

Similarly, Results also showed that affiliative communication style significantly led to higher level of trust in chatbot (M = 5.58, SD = .87) than dominant communication style (M = 4.36, SD = 1.01), F (1, 65) = 28.300. As shown in Table 3, communication styles significantly predicted trust (a2 = 1.222, p < .001), which in turn had a significant impact on treatment adherence (b2 = 0.438, p < 0.001). A 95% bias-corrected confidence interval based on 5000 bootstrap samples indicated that the indirect effect through trust (a2b2 = 0.536) was entirely above zero (0.265, 0.865). Besides, including the direct effect (c' = 0.744, p < .001), the total effect of communication styles on treatment adherence was 1.504 (p < .001). Thus, H2 and H3 were supported.

Table 3. Indirect Effect(s) of Communication Style on Treatment Adherence.

Mediation Paths	Effect	BootSE	BootLLCI	BootULCI
Total Effect	0.76	0.183	0.429	1.146
Communication Style -> Shared - Decision Making -> Treatment Adherence	0.224	0.082	0.088	0.4
Communication Style -> Patient Trust -> Treatment Adherence	0.536	0.155	0.265	0.865

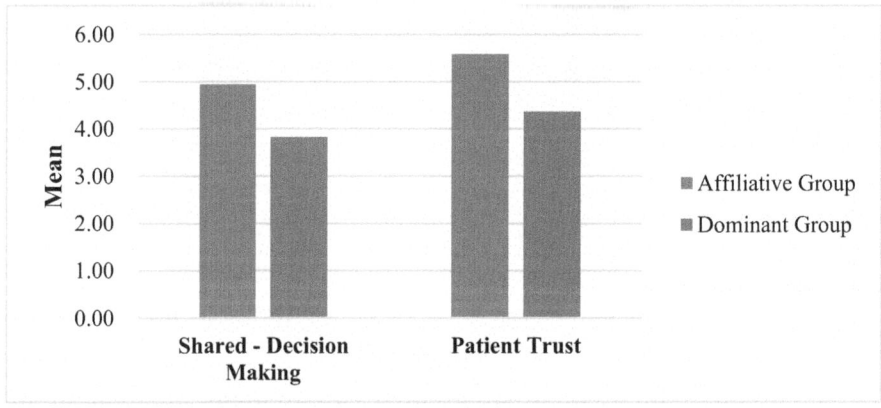

Fig. 4. Mean scores of shared - decision making and patient trust for chatbots between two groups.

No significant moderating effect of self-construal on the relationship between communication style and treatment adherence was found (B = .087, p > .01). RQ1 was rejected (Fig. 4).

5   Discussion

5.1   The Power of Affiliative Communication in Healthcare Chatbots

Drawing upon the literature on doctor-patient communication and the CASA paradigm, this study conducted an experiment to investigate the influence of chatbot communication style design on treatment adherence, through two mediators and considering the conditional effects of communication style across different levels of self-construal during healthcare interactions.

We first found that affiliative communication significantly led to higher treatment adherence compared to dominant communication (H1), consistent with the findings in the literature on interpersonal doctor-patient communication. This underscores the importance of enhancing emotional design in the development of healthcare chatbots.

The HCI literature indicates that enhancing the anthropomorphic design of robots is not always beneficial [17]. The hypothesis of Uncanny valley of mind predicted that perceived affective experience of technological artifacts leads to perceptions of uncanniness [68]. Individuals who attribute feelings to robots perceive the chatbot's display of affective empathy as particularly chilling and intriguing [12]. Previous studies have indicated that the effectiveness of emotional design during interaction may depend on the task type of or the conversation topic. Typically, participants regard medical consultation as a machine-appropriate task, placing greater trust in chatbots that exhibit robot-like design cues over those with layperson-like cues [69]. This reveals the "machine heuristic" effect, where users consider machines to be more accurate, trustworthy, and adept at tasks requiring objective judgment and complex cognitive skills [70]. Therefore, in the context of medical consultation, it seems that the efficiency, accuracy, and objectivity of information quality is more important than the expression of emotions. However, our findings refute this notion and reinforce the CASA paradigm, indicating that users attribute their perceptions and reactions to the healthcare chatbot to cues with relevant social implications. As CASA posits that when a computer displays human-related cues, users impose their preconceived social expectations of humans onto it [9, 10]. Notably, users perceive higher trust and compliance with chatbots that have an affiliative style design cue (compared to those with a dominant style design cue) even though the accuracy and expertness of the health information delivered by chatbots are same. This finding suggests that the communication style of the chatbot, as a design cue, may function as a cognitive heuristic [9].

5.2   The Intrinsic Mechanisms of Human-AI Adherence

Patient adherence to health information is a pivotal factor in achieving optimal health outcomes with individuals' health attitudes and behaviors [71, 72]. Although the deployment of advanced digital devices, such as AI-driven healthcare-chatbot, has become a prerequisite for delivering enhanced customer experiences, monitoring health status, and improving medical adherence [73, 74], the underlying mechanisms warrant further investigation. This study reveals that an affiliative communication style is significantly associated with adherence to treatment recommendations provided by healthcare chatbots, with this effect mediated by two parallel pathways: shared decision-making and patient trust (H2, H3). These findings align with previous research emphasizing patient-centered communication models [8], indicating that healthcare chatbots should adopt a communication style that fosters trust [50] and facilitates shared decision-making [14, 75], akin to interpersonal patient-provider communication, to enhance patient adherence to medical information and treatment plans.

Notably, despite some studies suggesting that emotional expressions may reduce a healthcare agent's credibility [76], our research demonstrates that trust established on the foundation of emotional support and equal treatment provided by affiliative communicative chatbots promotes users' reliance on health chatbots rather than evoking feelings of incredibility due to the uncanny valley effect. This could be attributed to advancements in NLP and LLMs, enabling chatbots to provide appropriate compassionate dialogical functions that better align with human expectations, thus fostering healthcare robot–human healthcare practice [77]. This finding offers new evidence for the technology R & D and real-world application of chatbots, suggesting that we should prioritize shaping chatbots' emotional warmth and empathy to drive the development of human-AI trust, rather than solely focusing on their knowledge and expertise [78].

Shared decision-making also plays an instrumental role in the relationship between affiliative communication and treatment adherence. This finding not only corroborates prior research but also extends its applicability to the realm of human patient-AI health provider interactions. By accentuating the perception of shared decision-making and underscoring patient autonomy, healthcare chatbots can significantly enhance patient buy-in and adherence to treatment regimens [14, 79]. To optimally facilitate shared decision-making, it is imperative for healthcare chatbots to cultivate an environment that encourages patient self-expression and active engagement in dialogues [80, 81]. Affiliative communication serves as a conduit for achieving this objective, empowering AI-driven healthcare chatbot to make patients feel heard, respected, and valued through a combination of targeted inquiries, active listening, and lucid explanations.

5.3   Universality of Patient-Centered Communication

Despite considerable support for the CASA paradigm, recent studies have questioned its universal applicability, highlighting the need to consider boundary conditions and user attributes [46]. This study sought to extend the CASA framework by investigating the moderating role of self-construal on the relationship between chatbot communication style and treatment adherence in the context of AI-driven healthcare. While previous research suggests that an affiliative communication style may be more effective for individuals with higher interdependent self-construal [82], our moderation analysis findings did not support this cultural association.

The absence of a significant moderating effect suggests that the effectiveness of different communication styles in human-computer interaction may not always be contingent upon individual cultural tendencies. Instead, our findings underscore the importance of considering the potential for universally effective communication strategies in the design and development of AI-driven healthcare chatbots. Patient-centered communication, which emphasizes empathy, collaboration, and tailoring to individual needs [83], has been widely recognized as a critical component of effective healthcare communication. Our findings suggest that the principles of patient-centered communication such as empathy, active listening, and shared decision-making, can be successfully translated to AI-driven healthcare chatbots, irrespective of users' self-construal level. This highlights the potential for AI-driven chatbots to deliver high-quality, personalized healthcare communication that mirrors the best practices of human-human interactions.

5.4 Limitation

While this study aimed to enhance participants' sense of presence in medical consultations through recruitment restrictions and experimental guidelines, there remains a gap between the scenario-based experiment and real-world evidence [84]. To further improve the ecological validity of future research, investigators should consider recruiting actual patients experiencing specific health issues, strictly adhering to ethical guidelines. This approach would not only eliminate potential confounding factors such as cognitive load [85] but also provide a more authentic representation of patients' genuine experiences and behaviors when engaging with chatbots for medical consultation.

While this study has, to a certain extent, verified the positive impact of an affiliative communication style on treatment adherence, the longevity of this effect [86] and its tangible influence on patients' actual health outcomes remain unclear. Future research should employ longitudinal designs to examine changes in treatment adherence levels and health status after long-term use of medical AI systems, ultimately evaluating the long-term effectiveness and practical clinical value of the affiliative communication style.

6 Conclusion

As AI-driven chatbots serve as the increasingly ubiquitous conduit for digital health interventions, healthcare providers' success hinges on their ability to effectively design these conversational AI agents. The question of which communication style will facilitate authentic and productive interactions between human patients and intelligent healthcare entities remains open. To this end, our study provides compelling evidence that the communication style employed by AI-driven healthcare chatbots significantly influences patients' adherence to treatment recommendations. The findings underscore the importance of adopting an affiliative communication style, characterized by empathy, emotional support, and encouragement of patient participation, to foster shared decision-making and establish patient trust, ultimately enhancing treatment adherence. The findings offer important implications for the advancement of patient-centered care in the era of artificial intelligence and the development of more effective AI-driven health interventions. Future research should employ longitudinal designs to further investigate changes in treatment adherence levels and health outcomes following long-term use of medical AI systems, ultimately assessing the enduring effectiveness and real-world clinical value of affiliative communication styles.

Acknowledgments. NA.

Disclosure of Interests.   The authors have no competing interests.

References

1. Harrer, S.: Attention is not all you need: the complicated case of ethically using large language models in healthcare and medicine. EBioMedicine **90**, 104512 (2023)
2. Thirunavukarasu, A.J., Ting, D.S.J., Elangovan, K., Gutierrez, L., Tan, T.F., Ting, D.S.W.: Large language models in medicine. Nat. Med. **29**(8), 1930–1940 (2023)
3. Abbasian, M., et al.: Foundation metrics for evaluating effectiveness of healthcare conversations powered by generative AI. NPJ Digit. Med. **7**(1), 82 (2024)
4. Wutz, M., Hermes, M., Winter, V., Köberlein-Neu, J.: Factors influencing the acceptability, acceptance, and adoption of conversational agents in health care: integrative review. J. Med. Internet Res. **25**, e46548 (2023)
5. Kocaballi, A.B., et al.: Design and evaluation challenges of conversational agents in health care and well-being: selective review study. J. Med. Internet Res. **24**(11), e38525 (2022)
6. Ong, L.M.L., de Haes, J.C.J.M., Hoos, A.M., Lammes, F.B.: Doctor-patient communication: a review of the literature. Soc. Sci. Med. **40**(7), 903–918 (1995)
7. Street, R.L., Gordon, H., Haidet, P.: Physicians' communication and perceptions of patients: is it how they look, how they talk, or is it just the doctor? Soc. Sci. Med. **65**(3), 586–598 (2007)
8. Street, R.L., Jr., Makoul, G., Arora, N.K., Epstein, R.M.: How does communication heal? Pathways linking clinician–patient communication to health outcomes. Patient Educ. Couns. **74**(3), 295–301 (2009)
9. Nass, C., Moon, Y.: Machines and mindlessness: social responses to computers. J. Soc. Issues **56**(1), 81–103 (2000)
10. Reeves, B., Nass, C.: The media equation: how people treat computers, television, and new media like real people, vol. 10(10), Cambridge, UK (1996)
11. Partala, T., Surakka, V.: The effects of affective interventions in human–computer interaction. Interact. Comput. **16**(2), 295–309 (2004)
12. Liu, B., Sundar, S.S.: Should machines express sympathy and empathy? Experiments with a health advice chatbot. Cyberpsychol. Behav. Soc. Netw. **21**(10), 625–636 (2018)
13. Jiang, Y., Yang, X., Zheng, T.: Make chatbots more adaptive: dual pathways linking human-like cues and tailored response to trust in interactions with chatbots. Comput. Hum. Behav. **138**, 107485 (2023)
14. Sandman, L., Granger, B.B., Ekman, I., Munthe, C.: Adherence, shared decision-making and patient autonomy. Med. Health Care Philos. **15**, 115–127 (2012)
15. Nembhard, I.M., David, G., Ezzeddine, I., Betts, D., Radin, J.: A systematic review of research on empathy in health care. Health Serv. Res. **58**(2), 250–263 (2023)
16. Song, S.W., Shin, M.: Uncanny valley effects on chatbot trust, purchase intention, and adoption intention in the context of e-commerce: the moderating role of avatar familiarity. Int. J. Hum.-Comput. Interact. **40**(2), 441–456 (2024)
17. Stein, J.P., Ohler, P.: Venturing into the uncanny valley of mind—the influence of mind attribution on the acceptance of human-like characters in a virtual reality setting. Cognition **160**, 43–50 (2017)

18. Singh, G., Mishra, A., Pattanayak, C., Priyadarshini, A., Das, R.C.: Artificial intelligence and the institutional ethics committee: a balanced insight into pros and cons, challenges, and future directions in ethical review of clinical research. J. Integr. Med. Res. **1**(4), 164–168 (2023)
19. Choudhury, A., Shamszare, H.: Investigating the impact of user trust on the adoption and use of ChatGPT: survey analysis. J. Med. Internet Res. **25**, e47184 (2023)
20. Awad, A., et al.: Connected healthcare: improving patient care using digital health technologies. Adv. Drug Delivery Rev. **178**, 113958 (2021)
21. Sarella, P.N.K., Mangam, V.T.: AI-driven natural language processing in healthcare: transforming patient-provider communication. Indian J. Pharm. Pract. **17**(1), 21–26 (2024)
22. Xu, L., Sanders, L., Li, K., Chow, J.C.: Chatbot for health care and oncology applications using artificial intelligence and machine learning: systematic review. JMIR Cancer **7**(4), e27850 (2021)
23. Belen Saglam, R., Nurse, J.R., Hodges, D.: Privacy concerns in chatbot interactions: when to trust and when to worry. In: Stephanidis, C., Antona, M., Ntoa, S. (eds.) HCI International 2021-Posters: 23rd HCI International Conference, HCII 2021, Virtual Event, 24–29 July 2021, Proceedings, Part II 23, pp. 391–399. Springer, Cham (2021). https://doi.org/10.1007/978-3-030-78642-7_53
24. Palanica, A., Flaschner, P., Thommandram, A., Li, M., Fossat, Y.: Physicians' perceptions of chatbots in health care: cross-sectional web-based survey. J. Med. Internet Res. **21**(4), e12887 (2019)
25. Nadarzynski, T., Bayley, J., Llewellyn, C., Kidsley, S., Graham, C.A.: Acceptability of artificial intelligence (AI)-enabled chatbots, video consultations and live webchats as online platforms for sexual health advice. BMJ Sexual Reprod. Health **46**(3), 210–217 (2020)
26. Baldauf, M., Fröehlich, P., Endl, R.: Trust me, I'ma doctor–user perceptions of AI-driven apps for mobile health diagnosis. In: Proceedings of the 19th International Conference on Mobile and Ubiquitous Multimedia, pp. 167–178 (2020)
27. Schachner, T., Keller, R., v Wangenheim, F.: Artificial intelligence-based conversational agents for chronic conditions: systematic literature review. J. Med. Internet Res. **22**(9), e20701 (2020)
28. Moulaei, K., Yadegari, A., Baharestani, M., Farzanbakhsh, S., Sabet, B., Afrash, M.R: Generative artificial intelligence in healthcare: a scoping review on benefits, challenges and applications. Int. J. Med. Inform. **188**, 105474 (2024)
29. Rodriguez, D.V., et al.: Leveraging generative AI tools to support the development of digital solutions in health care research: case study. JMIR Hum. Factors **11**(1), e52885 (2024)
30. Walker, H.L., et al.: Reliability of medical information provided by ChatGPT: assessment against clinical guidelines and patient information quality instrument. J. Med. Internet Res. **25**, e47479 (2023)
31. Song, H., et al.: Evaluating the performance of different large language models on health consultation and patient education in urolithiasis. J. Med. Syst. **47**(1), 125 (2023)
32. Ebrahimian, M., Behnam, B., Ghayebi, N., Sobhrakhshankhah, E.: ChatGPT in Iranian medical licensing examination: evaluating the diagnostic accuracy and decision-making capabilities of an AI-based model. BMJ Health Care Inform. **30**(1), e100815 (2023)
33. Ha, J.F., Longnecker, N.: Doctor-patient communication: a review. Ochsner J. **10**(1), 38–43 (2010)
34. DiMatteo, M.R.: The role of the physician in the emerging health care environment. West. J. Med. **168**(5), 328–333 (1998)
35. Maguire, P., Pitceathly, C.: Key communication skills and how to acquire them. BMJ **325**(7366), 697–700 (2002)
36. Ben-Sira, Z.: The function of the professional's affective behavior in client satisfaction: a revised approach to social interaction theory. J. Health Soc. Behav. **17**, 3–11 (1976)

37. Ben-Sira, Z.: Affective and instrumental components in the physician-patient relationship: an additional dimension of interaction theory. J. Health Soc. Behav. **21**, 170–180 (1980)
38. Norton, R.W.: Foundation of a communicator style construct. Hum. Commun. Res. **4**, 99–112 (1978)
39. Norton, R.W.: Communicator Style: Theory, Applications, and Measures. Sage, Beverly Hills (1983)
40. Buller, M.K., Buller, D.B.: Physicians' communication style and patient satisfaction. J. Health Soc. Behav. **28**(4), 375–388 (1987)
41. Pun, J.K.H., Chan, E.A., Wang, S., Slade, D.: Health professional-patient communication practices in East Asia: an integrative review of an emerging field of research and practice in Hong Kong, South Korea, Japan, Taiwan, and Mainland China. Patient Educ. Couns. **101**(7), 1193–1206 (2018)
42. Sheeran, N., et al.: How culture influences patient preferences for patient-centered care with their doctors. J. Commun. Healthc. **16**(2), 186–196 (2023)
43. Paternotte, E., van Dulmen, S., van der Lee, N., Scherpbier, A.J.J.A., Scheele, F.: Factors influencing intercultural doctor–patient communication: a realist review. Patient Educ. Couns. **98**(4), 420–445 (2015)
44. Pinto, R.Z., et al.: Patient-centred communication is associated with positive therapeutic alliance: a systematic review. J. Physiother. **58**(2), 77–87 (2012)
45. Reeves, B., Nass, C.: The Media Equation: How People Treat Computers, Television, and New Media Like Real People. Cambridge University Press, Cambridge (1996)
46. Mou, Y., Xu, K.: The media inequality: comparing the initial human-human and human-AI social interactions. Comput. Hum. Behav. **72**, 432–440 (2017)
47. Hesse, C., Rauscher, E.A.: The relationships between doctor-patient affectionate communication and patient perceptions and outcomes. Health Commun. **34**(8), 881–891 (2019)
48. World Health Organization: WHO global strategy on people-centred and integrated health services: interim report (No. WHO/HIS/SDS/2015.6). World Health Organization (2015)
49. Polinski, J.M., Kesselheim, A.S., Frolkis, J.P., Wescott, P., Allen-Coleman, C., Fischer, M.A.: A matter of trust: patient barriers to primary medication adherence. Health Educ. Res. **29**(5), 755–763 (2014)
50. Young, H.N., Len-Rios, M.E., Brown, R., Moreno, M.M., Cox, E.: How does patient-provider communication influence adherence to asthma medications? Patient Educ. Couns. **100**(4), 696–702 (2017)
51. Markus, H.R., Kitayama, S.: Cultural variation in the self-concept. In: Strauss, J., Goethals, G.R. (eds.) The Self: Interdisciplinary Approaches, pp. 18–48. Springer, New York (1991). https://doi.org/10.1007/978-1-4684-8264-5_2
52. Kim, M.S., Smith, D.H., Yueguo, G.: Medical decision making and Chinese patients' self-construals. Health Commun. **11**(3), 249–260 (1999)
53. Kitayama, S., et al.: Individual and collective processes in the construction of the self: self-enhancement in the United States and self-criticism in Japan. J. Pers. Soc. Psychol. **72**(6), 1245 (1997)
54. Rao, N., Singhal, A., Ren, L., Zhang, J.: Is the Chinese self-construal in transition? Asian J. Commun. **11**(1), 68–95 (2001)
55. Marvin, G., Hellen, N., Jjingo, D., Nakatumba-Nabende, J.: Prompt engineering in large language models. In: Jacob, I.J., Piramuthu, S., Falkowski-Gilski, P. (eds.) International Conference on Data Intelligence and Cognitive Informatics, pp. 387–402. Springer, Cham (2023). https://doi.org/10.1007/978-981-99-7962-2_30
56. Wang, J., et al.: Prompt engineering for healthcare: methodologies and applications. arXiv preprint arXiv:2304.14670 (2023)
57. Alexander, C.S., Becker, H.J.: The use of vignettes in survey research. Public Opin. Q. **42**(1), 93–104 (1978)

58. Prior, L., Evans, M.R., Prout, H.: Talking about colds and flu: the lay diagnosis of two common illnesses among older British people. Soc. Sci. Med. **73**(6), 922–928 (2011)
59. Eccles, R.: Understanding the symptoms of the common cold and influenza. Lancet. Infect. Dis **5**(11), 718–725 (2005)
60. Manalastas, G., Noble, L.M., Viney, R., Griffin, A.E.: What does the structure of a medical consultation look like? A new method for visualising doctor-patient communication. Patient Educ. Couns. **104**(6), 1387–1397 (2021)
61. Tate, P., Frame, F.: The Doctor's Communication Hand-Book. CRC Press, New York (2019)
62. Kriston, L., Scholl, I., Hölzel, L., Simon, D., Loh, A., Härter, M.: The 9-item shared decision-making questionnaire (SDM-Q-9). Development and psychometric properties in a primary care sample. Patient Educ. Counsel. **80**(1), 94–99 (2010)
63. Dugan, E., Trachtenberg, F., Hall, M.A.: Development of abbreviated measures to assess patient trust in a physician, a health insurer, and the medical profession. BMC Health Serv. Res. **5**(1), 1–7 (2005)
64. Singelis, T.M.: The measurement of independent and interdependent self-construals. Pers. Soc. Psychol. Bull. **20**(5), 580–591 (1994)
65. Sanford, K., Rivers, A.S.: Treatment adherence perception questionnaire: assessing patient perceptions regarding their adherence to medical treatment plans. Psychol. Assess. **32**(3), 227 (2020)
66. Kim, S.S., Park, B.K.: Patient-perceived communication styles of physicians in rehabilitation: the effect on patient satisfaction and compliance in Korea. Am. J. Phys. Med. Rehabil. **87**(12), 998–1005 (2008)
67. Hayes, A.F.: Introduction to Mediation, Moderation, and Conditional Process Analysis: A Regression-Based Approach, 2nd edn. Guilford Press, New York (2018)
68. Gray, K., Wegner, D.M.: Feeling robots and human zombies: mind perception and the uncanny valley. Cognition **125**, 125–130 (2012)
69. Gambino, A., Kim, J., Sundar, S.S.: Digital doctors and robot receptionists: user attributes that predict acceptance of automation in healthcare facilities. In: Extended Abstracts of the 2019 CHI Conference on Human Factors in Computing Systems, pp. 1–6 (2019)
70. Sundar, S.S., Kim, J.: Machine heuristic: when we trust computers more than humans with our personal information. In: Proceedings of the 2019 CHI Conference on Human Factors in Computing Systems (2019)
71. Horwitz, R.I., Horwitz, S.M.: Adherence to treatment and health outcomes. Arch. Intern. Med. **153**(16), 1863–1868 (1993)
72. Fava, G.A., Cosci, F., Sonino, N., Guidi, J.: Understanding health attitudes and behavior. Am. J. Med. **136**(3), 252–259 (2023)
73. Mistry, C., et al.: MedBlock: an AI-enabled and blockchain-driven medical healthcare system for COVID-19. In: ICC 2021-IEEE International Conference on Communications, pp. 1–6. IEEE (2021)
74. Al Kuwaiti, A., et al.: A review of the role of artificial intelligence in healthcare. J. Personalized Med. **13**(6), 951 (2023)
75. Joosten, E.A., DeFuentes-Merillas, L., De Weert, G.H., Sensky, T., Van Der Staak, C.P.F., de Jong, C.A.: Systematic review of the effects of shared decision-making on patient satisfaction, treatment adherence and health status. Psychother. Psychosom. **77**(4), 219–226 (2008)
76. Seitz, L., Bekmeier-Feuerhahn, S., Gohil, K.: Can we trust a chatbot like a physician? A qualitative study on understanding the emergence of trust toward diagnostic chatbots. Int. J. Hum.-Comput. Stud. **165**, Article 102848 (2022)
77. Betriana, F., Osaka, K., Matsumoto, K., Tanioka, T., Locsin, R.C.: Relating Mori's Uncanny Valley in generating conversations with artificial affective communication and natural language processing. Nurs. Philos. **22**(2), e12322 (2021)

78. Goodman, R.S., et al.: Accuracy and reliability of chatbot responses to physician questions. JAMA Netw. Open **6**(10), e2336483–e2336483 (2023)
79. Milky, G., Thomas, J., III.: Shared decision making, satisfaction with care and medication adherence among patients with diabetes. Patient Educ. Couns. **103**(3), 661–669 (2020)
80. Babel, A., Taneja, R., Mondello Malvestiti, F., Monaco, A., Donde, S.: Artificial intelligence solutions to increase medication adherence in patients with non-communicable diseases. Front. Digit. Health **3**, 669869 (2021)
81. Färber, A., Schwabe, C., Stalder, P.H., Dolata, M., Schwabe, G.: Physicians' and patients' expectations from digital agents for consultations: interview study among physicians and patients. JMIR Hum. Factors **11**, e49647 (2024)
82. Gudykunst, W.B., Matsumoto, Y., Ting-Toomey, S., Nishida, T., Kim, K., Heyman, S.: The influence of cultural individualism-collectivism, self construals, and individual values on communication styles across cultures. Hum. Commun. Res. **22**(4), 510–543 (1996)
83. Epstein, R.M., Street Jr, R.L.: Patient-centered communication in cancer care: promoting healing and reducing suffering (2007)
84. Sherman, R.E., et al.: Real-world evidence—what is it and what can it tell us. N. Engl. J. Med. **375**(23), 2293–2297 (2016)
85. Schmidhuber, J., Schlögl, S., Ploder, C.: Cognitive load and productivity implications in human-chatbot interaction. In: 2021 IEEE 2nd International Conference on Human-Machine Systems (ICHMS), pp. 1–6. IEEE (2021)
86. AlHewiti, A. Adherence to long-term therapies and beliefs about medications. Int. J. Family Med. **2014**, 1–8 (2014)

Externalizing Internal Conversations: Toward a New Paradigm of Interacting with Our Internal Voice via an External Technological Interface

Rahul R. Divekar[✉]

Bentley University, Waltham, MA 02452, USA
rdivekar@bentley.edu

Abstract. This paper introduces a theoretical and provocative exploration into the externalization of internal voice through technological means, proposing a novel paradigm in human-computer interaction (HCI). We explore the conceptual underpinnings, technological feasibility, application scenarios, and ethical implications of making internal voice interactable outside the mind. Drawing from psychology, cognitive science, and computer science, this work aims to provoke discussion and encourage further research within the interdisciplinary field of augmented cognition and HCI.

Keywords: Inner Voice · Self Dialogue · Natural Language Interfaces

1 Introduction and Literature

Talking to oneself, as it is colloquially known, is a commonly experienced phenomenon that has invited deep research from philosophy and psychology [30]. Often, talking to oneself involves an imagined world and an internal voice navigating that world. In the world that's in our heads, we recreate or imagine representations of various people, places, and contexts. We use our internal voice to navigate these representations of people, places, and contexts [7].

At least two types of intrapersonal communication (talking to oneself) exist: self-talk and internal dialogue [27]. Hardy [14] and Oleś et al. [27] synthesized definitions of self-talk and internal dialogue from the research community and note that there are variations in the exact definitions. For the sake of simplicity, here we illustrate the concepts with an example of a teenager wanting to go to party. This teenager might imagine anticipated events of the party, the people who might attend, and all the fun to be had. Guiding of this imagination would be an inner voice where the teenager is the only interlocutor and holds various positions e.g., in regard to jumping into the pool, they might hold conflicting positions like "It will be fun. Although, that might be risky," leading to dilemmas. Such a negotiation and self regulation would be called self-talk [27].

Whereas the same teenager might also imagine dialogues that involve others as interlocutors. For example, they may imagine various persuasive arguments they will make to convince their parents to let them go to the party. Here, the teenager might imagine how their parents will respond, thereby adding parents as interlocutors to the inner voice in addition to their own self. When there are two or more interlocutors in intrapersonal communication, the phenomenon is known as internal dialogue [27].

The above examples show a deliberate and strategic use of internal voice to understand, anticipate, and navigate the world. However, there are non deliberate, automatic, and casual or monologic uses of our internal voice too [15]. For example, as one wakes up and sees the sun shining after many days of cold winter, one may verbalize, "what a wonderful day." Like other non-deliberate actions, this voice often can go unnoticed but still have an impact on our lives. In our example, the person starting out by acknowledging the good weather has started their day on a positive note and likely to be in a good mood for a while even if the internal voice was casual, non-deliberate, and mostly went unnoticed.

Overall, we see that self-talk and internal dialogue are crucial to how we make sense of our world, navigate it and keep ourselves engaged, motivated, informed, and focused. The internal voice helps define identities and personalities, manage cognitive disruption, process important life events, solve problems, and improve performance among other things [4,14,16,23,24,28]. Internal dialogue was even key to underpinnings of philosophy and understanding of the world as seen in works of Socrates and Plato that are an written internal dialogues. Yet, by definition, most of the self-talk is rarely externalized.

Through this paper, first, we discussed the concept of inner voice and self dialogue, as to the best of our knowledge, this topic has not been discussed in the context of human-computer interaction. We argue that there is value in externalizing our inner voice and that it is technologically plausible. The definition of externalization of internal voice we are adopting here is the internal voice becoming available to us to interact with outside of our own minds. This externalization is more than just having a one-way access to a record, transcript, or journal of the inner voice. It rather points towards interacting (i.e., a back and forth) with our inner voice via an external interface (e.g., via a text chat window).

In the next few sections, we detail what we mean by externalization and how it might be possible to do so using technology in the near future. We describe the various usecases and a new human-computer interaction paradigm that may evolve as a result of externalizing our internal voices with technology. Then, we discuss the ethical and societal benefits and harms of such a technology. Overall, through this discussion, we present a theoretical contribution at HCII and invite the community to discuss and debate this thought experiment of talking to oneself using an external device.

2 Externalization of Inner Voice and The Role of Technology

The idea of making ones internal voice available through an external interface is novel but not unreasonable, as technology is already being developed that can be used towards this goal. Fernyhough and Borghi [12] have theorized that use of a brain-computer interface and a language model may effectively be able to embody the inner voice. Recent studies in Brain-Computer Interfaces (BCIs) have shown promise in technology being able to sufficiently transcribe one's thoughts [13,21,34,37]. As time goes by, such BCIs might become more ubiquitous. Therefore, a continuous transcription of the inner voice is possible. However, it is yet to be seen if BCIs will able to capture all of the inner voice since the brain activity with certain types of inner voice activity, especially the ones that are non-deliberate, might be low, leading to new research challenges.

Once a transcription of the internal voice is available, we could treat its externalization as a language modeling and generation problem. Large Language Models [9,31,38] have shown great promise in being able to model and generate language that has already been externalized e.g., written and posted on the internet. However, our chaotic stream of consciousness [33] and inner voices may exhibit a different pattern than the typical sources of data input into LLM training leading to new research challenges.

Overall we see that both BCIs and LLMs are not perfect for this scenario yet. However, they are on the trajectory of growth and show promise towards externalizing the inner voice with additional research. Figure 1 illustrates how these two technologies can come together to enable a new type of interface. As seen in the figure, a user wears or carries an implantable Brain Computer Interface (BCI). The BCI transcribes inner monologue, dialogue, and other non-intentional but linguistic activity. The transcriptions are stored. One (or many) Language Models (LMs) capable of modeling linguistic patterns found in inner speech is trained or fine-tuned on the stored data. The LM is then available to generate a response to user's input thereby effectively giving the user access to their own inner voice through an external interface such as a chat window. Each LM can represent a different voice thereby enabling inner-dialogue (i.e., talking to someone else's representation in our minds) or different positions with the same voice (i.e., talking to oneself but while holding different or contradictory positions).

The figure shows two dotted lines. These dotted lines denote that there is a significant design choice to be made. The first dotted line below "train" conveys that the training can be in real time or offline. Given the state of technology, offline training seems more feasible. However, real-time input from the BCI can be passed as the additional and most updated *context* to the language model leading to a better approximation of talking to oneself in real time.

The second dotted line shows the modality of the interface used to interact with the LM-generated responses. Choices made here will provide vastly different experiences. For example, the conversation can get messy if the user's actual inner voice is used to interact with the system given the spontaneity of the inner voice. However, it may also provide an opportunity to hold two positions more easily at the same time, similar to self dialogue discussed in Sect. 1. Another modality pertains to generating responses in a voice similar to the user's perception of their own voice. This choice might also create an interesting interaction paradigm as it might increase the willingness to believe that one is "talking with their own thoughts." On the other hand, using a purely text-based modality might portray a different set of user characteristics as the language and ideas used in typed text can be less spontaneous and more structured than voice alone. We also note that while the figure shows the interface as a text-based chatbox, we must not be limited by it as the choice of embodiment and can be expanded to be humanoid, robotic, animalistic, etc. In addition, there could be several embodiments present at once to reflect different I-positions or other peoples' representations that occur in the inner voice.

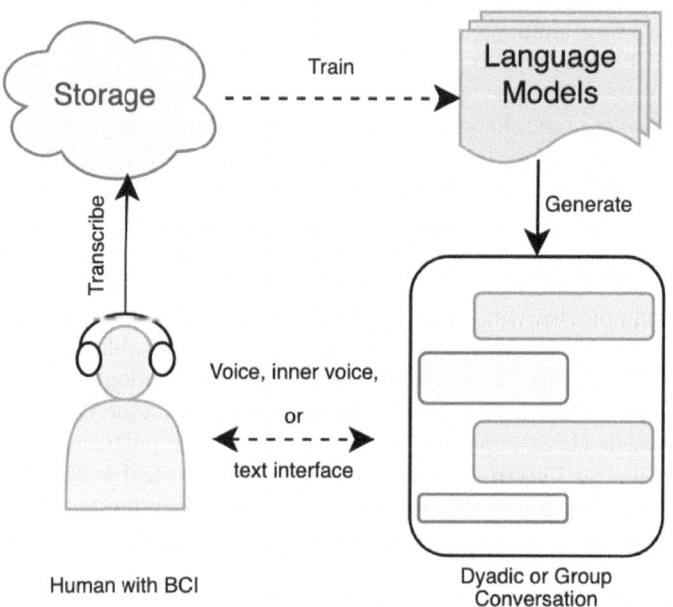

Fig. 1. Flow Diagram of Data and Interaction

Using the above technologies and methods, the inner voice can be made available via an external interface. We note that from a technical standpoint, it is not the inner voice that is being externalized. Rather, it is the representation or model of the inner voice that responds to the user. It is built with an assumption that the model will capture and repeat patterns in a user's inner voice well enough that it will be perceived like one's inner voice itself. It is yet to be seen whether the generated responses from a user's inner voice model will match a user's actual inner voice in real time. Based on our understanding of the technology, it is our opinion that given enough context of a user's current state and environment, it might do a good job. However, providing and processing such extensive state and environment information in real time would be a new research challenge.

Irrespective of the accuracy, it would be interesting to know whether the user believes or feels that a response is their own inner voice. At the surface, expecting a user to believe they are talking to their own voice, i.e., an embodiment of themselves, via an external interface might seem unreasonable. However, research is already underway that indicates people may be willing to accept a technological embodiment of people who have deceased and have a conversation with that embodiment [5]. If people can believe that another person can be embodied by technology, it would be interesting to research whether they may also be willing to believe that their own self can be embodied with technology and that they can effectively converse with their own thoughts.

3   Applications and Impact

Several studies have shown the connection between the inner voice (both self dialogue and internal dialogue) with self awareness, problem solving, cognitive performance, etc. [22,29]. In this section we discuss the possible applications and impact of accessing the inner voice via an external interface.

We base our usecases on the assumption that often our thinking is not linear, we struggle to hold multiple ideas or perspectives at the same time, we are not always mindful of our own thoughts, and we generally do not remember all minor events of our life over longer periods of times. However, achieving these traits might be beneficial for several reasons. We show how recording and externalizing inner voice can help us unlock some the those elusive traits thereby making the case that such an interaction with oneself will be useful.

3.1   Mental Health Resource

Per Cognitive Behavioral Therapy, a key job of a therapist and a patient is to find patterns in thoughts that are negative or destructive and address them [1]. For example, therapy interactions involve finding automatic thought patterns that cause fears or anxieties and asking oneself if they are grounded in any reality [36]. A language model (LM) is great at finding patterns in language. Trained on a person's inner voice that represents thought, a patient could have a conversation with an externalized voice of themselves and address these patterns in second-person. Dolcos and Albarracin [10] have found in a different context that self advice in second person was more effective in behavior regulation. Further, one could even ask their own externalized inner voice whether the fears are substantiated and the language model could bring up instances that may have led to these thought patterns. However, we note that LLMs are designed to reproduce patterns by design rather than break them. Thus the possibility that an LLM can exacerbate a harmful thought pattern seems more likely than breaking it.

3.2   Self Introspection and Reflection

We do not often recognize all of the reasons and motivations of why we are doing something. However, self-understanding is crucial to well-being, motivation, and growth [32]. For example, a student may lose motivation towards the end of the semester. A technique that helps them stay engaged is understanding their values and motivations. Imagine that the said student asks in a chat with themselves, "I don't feel like studying anymore." The student could then chat with their own voice that leads them towards motivation. In addition, the externalized voice might also help the student reflect on all that they have learned so far to boost confidence and increase learning.

3.3   Memory Recall

Our attention span can be thin and memories can be weaker than we expect. As a result, we find ourselves searching for answers like "What was the idea I had when I was in the shower." An LM based on retrieval augmented generation, a technique that combines natural language processing and data stores to generate a fact-based answer in natural language [20], can yield itself well to these types of questions via self dialogue.

In addition to factual memory recall, an LM could also indulge a user in a nostalgic internal dialogue with themselves or the memories of people that existed within the user's inner voice thereby potentially serving emotional and well-being needs.

3.4   Organizing Thoughts

Our thoughts are often scattered across time and in bursts. For example, the writer of a HCII paper has thought about the topic over several weeks, months, or years, often from various angles such as literature, experimentation, synthesis of results, etc. Once they get to writing (or organizing their thoughts), they must digest all of their thinking from the scattered bursts. An externalized inner voice allows us to ask the model "Can you summarize my thoughts on this topic in a 2500-word paper." Further, the thoughts can be connected to external knowledge. For example, "Has anyone else thought of this topic?" and "What is the connection of my thoughts on this topic and the literature." The language model then can connect the synthesized thoughts from the inner voice and make connections to the literature available on the internet, thereby expanding our thinking. Alternatively, a person struggling with articulating themselves could simply tell their external voice to "Make this coherent." However, the act of speaking with an external entity itself is sequential and forces thoughts into a slower stream that might already have benefit on organization.

3.5   Finding Discrepancies Between Actual and Ideal Selves

Higgins [17]'s theory states that discrepancies between the actual self and an ideal or ought version of oneself can lead to emotional discomfort. For example, an *ideal* or *ought* self-representation of a student would possibly be to be in good standing with the university and achieve good grades; however, the *actual* circumstances may present themselves with emotional discomfort. An external conversation with oneself could provide an outlet where such discrepancies can be addressed. A model might even bring in outside information from the web and connect it to one's inner voice to bridge the gap by providing recommendations and action plans.

3.6   Improved Empathy

In a world where technology continues to divide us into filter bubbles [3], an LLM trained on a person's thought who is different from us and holds opposing opinions could create an avenue to bridge the gap with empathy. Of course, one could have such a conversation with a real person but a conversation with an LLM would be more available and of lower stakes possibly inviting more openness.

3.7   Augmenting Decision Making Process

Making big decisions is a complicated process wrought with fears, trust, and anxieties. An external voice that represents one's own voice might be more trustworthy as the conversation and advice is contextualized in your own prior experience.

4   Early Experimentation

In this section, we present our early experiments with a popular language model, ChatGPT 3.5, available via chat.openai.com and accessed on Jan 15, 2024. We presented ChatGPT with several prompts, including short versions of a self-reported and imagined inner voice transcript of two personas. We recognize that there are other models, however, at this time, only ChatGPT is easily interactable and fits well with our intention of doing early work.

   We see that even without any connection to the inner voice, ChatGPT is able to respond coherently. Although, whether this coherent output matches one's inner voice is is yet to be answered. In the spirit of being succinct, we only display two outputs in table 1 and 2. Notice that table 2 explicitly adds a prompt for ChatGPT to be the inner voice. However, the results were not different without that additional prompt. In both cases, we notice that while the response is not completely unhelpful, it does not particularly borrow the tone of an inner voice. Rather, it strikes the tone of an advice blog. This is expected as the model is not trained on any inner speech data, and the prompt/ input is not too deep. However, for the purposes of a late-breaking work, it shows the current state of technology that it is able to model these conversations reasonably well thereby showing promise. More rigorous experiments with LMs and BCIs in the future will tease out specific implementation challenges.

Table 1. Prompting ChatGPT to be the inner voice - a 30 year old professor

User: I am a 30 year old professor and my job involves teaching, research, and service. I was thinking today how nice it would be to go on a walk with my dog. After all it is nice outside. It should be a nice quick walk but I don't want to tire myself out. I want to come back and work on preparing my courses for the upcoming semester. Which reminds me, i probably should even get that started before I take the dog out for a walk. Ugh now the dog seems like a chore - perhaps I shouldn't have had a dog. I wonder what my life would be

ChatGPT: It's completely normal to have moments of reflection about various aspects of your life, including responsibilities and choices like having a dog. Balancing work, personal time, and responsibilities can be challenging, especially when you have a busy schedule as a professor. Taking a break for a walk can be a great way to clear your mind and get some fresh air. It might even help you approach your course preparations with a fresh perspective. As for having a dog, they can bring a lot of joy and companionship, but it's also okay to acknowledge the challenges they present. Maybe consider finding a balance that works for both you and your furry friend. If you have any specific questions or if there's anything specific you'd like to discuss or explore further, feel free to let me know!

5   Ethics and Safety Issues

While several unimagined consequences might exist, we try our best to describe some imaginable ones here.

5.1   Flawed Technology and Intentional Misuse

First, we acknowledge that most technical system are imperfect and it is likely that the system we described (or an iteration of it) will likely be flawed. From a theoretical perspective, such a system cannot be perfect as, much of what we experience remains non-linguistic and does not exist in the inner voice. For example, physical movements that evoke feelings and other body and cognitive processes [26]. However, a flawed system is quickly rejected by users when flaws are apparent. It is only when the flaws are subtle that system acceptability might still be viable. In such a case, subtle flaws could be devastating. For example, when users lean on their own externalized self for advice and conversation, and that externalized self hallucinates or falsifies information as a result of technological limitations, the user might be inclined to still believe the system and take action on those beliefs that might lead to harmful consequences.

Further, the failures of LMs have been extensively documented. LMs have been known to propagate biases [25], spew fake information with confidence [18], generate harmful content [2], among others [35]. In addition to those issues, specific to our topic, we foresee the ethical issue of thought manipulation to arise. For example, a language model could generate a response that relies more on the crowd-sourced or generic data it is trained on rather than reflect the individual person's voice. In this case, if the user believes that the LM is reflecting their

Table 2. Prompting ChatGPT to be the inner voice - a 28 year old student

User: I am a 28 year old PhD student. I had big dreams that I will write an impactful thesis when I got started. But it appears I have no ideas - zero, zilch, nothing. what am i even suppsed to do? Just give up. What would that say about me? Ugh undergrad was so easy - i was a 4 pointer. now look at me. 28 year old with no idea what I am doing. *You are my inner voice. what does my inner voice say about this?*

ChatGPT: I'm sorry to hear that you're feeling this way. It's not uncommon for PhD students to face challenges and uncertainties during their research journey. First and foremost, it's important to recognize that many people go through phases of self-doubt and struggle in academia.

Here are a few suggestions that might help you navigate through this:

1. Talk to your advisor: Schedule a meeting with your advisor to discuss your concerns. They can provide guidance, support, and may help you identify potential research directions.

2. Reflect on your interests: Take some time to reflect on your interests and what motivated you to pursue a PhD in the first place. Consider any specific topics or questions that genuinely intrigue you.

3. Read extensively: Explore literature related to your field of study. Reading widely can often spark new ideas or help you see existing topics from a different perspective.

4. Collaborate with peers: Discuss your concerns with your peers or colleagues. They might offer fresh perspectives or share insights that could stimulate your own ideas.

5. Take a break: Sometimes, stepping back and taking a break can be beneficial. Clearing your mind might allow you to come back with a fresh perspective.

6. Seek support: Don't hesitate to reach out to friends, family, or a mental health professional for support. PhD programs can be challenging, and it's important to prioritize your well-being.

Remember, struggling with ideas doesn't define your worth or intelligence. It's a common part of the research process, and many successful academics have faced similar challenges. Don't be too hard on yourself, and take one step at a time. If you ever need someone to talk to, I'm here to help.

Taking a break for a walk can be a great way to clear your mind and get some fresh air. It might even help you approach your course preparations with a fresh perspective. As for having a dog, they can bring a lot of joy and companionship, but it's also okay to acknowledge the challenges they present. Maybe consider finding a balance that works for both you and your furry friend. If you have any specific questions or if there's anything specific you'd like to discuss or explore further, feel free to let me know!

own thoughts, the LMs mislead a user into believing in a different version of themselves and gradually drift the users' beliefs in a different direction than their own selves.

5.2   Data-Related Ethical Issues

Data-related ethical issues have been widely discussed not only in academic liter-ature but also in common culture. Issues such as who owns the data, how consent is asked before collecting internet data, and how a provider of a technological service can use the data, and more have been debated and even led to legislative action [6,8,11,19].

These issues will further be exacerbated as the provider of the technology we propose will likely have more intrusive access to users' lives by having access to their thoughts. At the simplest form, inner voice data can be used for targeting advertisements e.g., profiting off of a user's mental health conditions without informed consent. However, in more serious forms, it also can lead to judicial injustices via omnipresent surveillance and thought policing. We take the posi-tion of treading cautiously in this direction.

6   Conclusion

We have presented a theoretical concept of a novel interaction paradigm where users interact with their inner voice through an external interface. We have explained the details and definitions of such an interaction, how it might be technologically feasible, the use cases of the interaction paradigm, and the ethical harms that might arise from it. We have provided a high-level system design and shown early experiments to demonstrate the promise of a theory and hereby invite the community to a discussion that teases out more details and opens new research avenues.

References

1. (Jul 2017). https://www.apa.org, https://www.apa.org/ptsd-guideline/patients-and-families/cognitive-behavioral
2. Bender, E.M., Gebru, T., McMillan-Major, A., Shmitchell, S.: On the dangers of stochastic parrots: can language models be too big? In: Proceedings of the 2021 ACM Conference on Fairness, Accountability, and Transparency, pp. 610–623 (2021)
3. Bozdag, E., van den Hoven, J.: Breaking the filter bubble: democracy and design. Ethics Inf. Technol. **17**(4), 249–265 (2015). https://doi.org/10.1007/s10676-015-9380-y
4. Brinthaupt, T.M.: Individual differences in self-talk frequency: social isolation and cognitive disruption. Front. Psychol. **10**, 1088 (2019)
5. Brubaker, J.R., Ringel Morris, M., Thomas Doyle, D., Fiesler, C., Gibbs, M., McGrenere, J.: AI and the afterlife workshop at chi 2024 (2024). https://sites.google.com/view/ai-and-the-afterlife-workshop/ . Accessed 15 Jan 2024
6. Burman, A.: Understanding India's new data protection law (2023). https://carnegieindia.org/2023/10/03/understanding-india-s-new-data-protection-law-pub-90624. Accessed 15 Jan 2024
7. Carruthers, P.: The causes and contents of inner speech. Inner speech New voices 31–52 (2018)

8. Council, E.: The general data protection regulation (2022). https://www.consilium. europa.eu/en/policies/data-protection/data-protection-regulation/. Accessed 15 Jan 2024
9. Devlin, J., Chang, M.W., Lee, K., Toutanova, K.: BERT: pre-training of deep bidirectional transformers for language understanding. arXiv preprint arXiv:1810.04805 (2018)
10. Dolcos, S., Albarracin, D.: The inner speech of behavioral regulation: intentions and task performance strengthen when you talk to yourself as a you. Eur. J. Soc. Psychol. **44**(6), 636–642 (2014)
11. of Ethics, B.O.: China privacy law. https://ethics.berkeley.edu/privacy/ international-privacy-laws/china-privacy-law (2024). Accessed 15 Jan 2024
12. Fernyhough, C., Borghi, A.M.: Inner speech as language process and cognitive tool. Trends cogn. sci. (2023)
13. Hamilton, J.: Brain implants are allowing people to generate speech using thoughts, studies show. https://www.npr.org/2023/08/23/1195542905/brain-implants-are-allowing-people-to-generate-speech-using-thoughts-studies-show (2023. Accessed 15 Jan 2024
14. Hardy, J.: Speaking clearly: a critical review of the self-talk literature. Psychol. Sport Exerc. **7**(1), 81–97 (2006)
15. Hardy, J., Oliver, E., Tod, D.: A framework for the study and application of self-talk within sport. In: Advances in Applied Sport Psychology, pp. 47–84, Routledge (2008)
16. Hatzigeorgiadis, A., Galanis, E.: Self-talk effectiveness and attention. Curr. Opin. Psychol. **16**, 138–142 (2017)
17. Higgins, E.T.: Self-discrepancy: a theory relating self and affect. Psychol. Rev. **94**(3), 319 (1987)
18. Ji, Z., et al.: Survey of hallucination in natural language generation. ACM Comput. Surv. **55**(12), 1–38 (2023)
19. of California Department of Justice, S.: California consumer privacy act (CCPA) (2024). https://oag.ca.gov/privacy/ccpa. Accessed 15 Jan 2024
20. Lewis, P., et al.: Retrieval-augmented generation for knowledge-intensive NLP tasks Adv. Neural. Inf. Process. Syst. **33**, 9459–9474 (2020)
21. Luo, S., Rabbani, Q., Crone, N.E.: Brain-computer interface: applications to speech decoding and synthesis to augment communication. Neurotherapeutics **19**(1), 263–273 (2023)
22. Morin, A.: Possible links between self-awareness and inner speech theoretical background, underlying mechanisms, and empirical evidence. J. Conscious. Stud. **12**(4–5), 115–134 (2005)
23. Morin, A., Duhnych, C., Racy, F.: Self-reported inner speech use in university students. Appl. Cogn. Psychol. **32**(3), 376–382 (2018)
24. Morin, A., Uttl, B., Hamper, B.: Self-reported frequency, content, and functions of inner speech. Procedia. Soc. Behav. Sci. **30**, 1714–1718 (2011)
25. Nadeem, M., Bethke, A., Reddy, S.: StereoSet: measuring stereotypical bias in pretrained language models. arXiv preprint arXiv:2004.09456 (2020)
26. Núñez-Pacheco, C.: Reflection through inner presence: a sensitising concept for design. Multimodal Technol. Interact. **2**(1), 5 (2018)
27. Oleś, P.K., Brinthaupt, T.M., Dier, R., Polak, D.: Types of inner dialogues and functions of self-talk: Comparisons and implications. Front. Psychol. **11**, 227 (2020)
28. Oleś, P.K., Puchalska-Wasyl, M.: Dialogicality and personality traits. In: Hermans, H.J.M., Gieser, T., (eds.) Handbook of Dialogical Self Theory. pp. 241–252. Cambridge University Press (2011). https://doi.org/10.1017/CBO9781139030434.017

29. Perrone-Bertolotti, M., Rapin, L., Lachaux, J.P., Baciu, M., Loevenbruck, H.: What is that little voice inside my head? Inner speech phenomenology, its role in cognitive performance, and its relation to self-monitoring. Behav. Brain Res. **261**, 220–239 (2014)

30. Puchalska-Wasyl, M.M.: Self-talk: conversation with oneself? on the types of internal interlocutors. J. Psychol. **149**(5), 443–460 (2015)

31. Radford, A., Narasimhan, K., Salimans, T., Sutskever, I., et al.: Improving language understanding by generative pre-training (2018)

32. Schön, D.A.: The Reflective Practitioner: How Professionals Think in Action. Routledge (2017)

33. Smallwood, J., Schooler, J.W.: The science of mind wandering: empirically navigating the stream of consciousness. Annu. Rev. Psychol. **66**, 487–518 (2015)

34. University, D.: Brain implant may enable communication from thoughts alone (2023). https://neurosurgery.duke.edu/news/brain-implant-may-enable-communication-thoughts-alone. Accessed 15 Jan 2024

35. Weidinger, L., et al.: Ethical and social risks of harm from language models. arXiv preprint arXiv:2112.04359 (2021)

36. Wenzel, A.: Basic strategies of cognitive behavioral therapy. Psychiatr. Clin. **40**(4), 597–609 (2017)

37. Willett, F.R., Avansino, D.T., Hochberg, L.R., Henderson, J.M., Shenoy, K.V.: High-performance brain-to-text communication via handwriting. Nature **593**(7858), 249–254 (2021)

38. Ye, J., et al.: A comprehensive capability analysis of GPT-3 and GPT-3.5 series models. arXiv preprint arXiv:2303.10420 (2023)

Developing a Theoretical Model for Designing Functional Clothing: Intervening in Behaviors for Weight Loss

Minzi Dong[1,2] (iD), Eunyoung Kim[1](✉) (iD), and Wei Ding[2]

[1] Human Life Design Areas, Japan Advanced Institute of Science and Technology, Nomi City, Japan
1031758804@qq.com, kim@jaist.ac.jp
[2] School of Fashion, Dalian Polytechnic University, Dalian, China

Abstract. Psychological factors play a crucial role in achieving weight loss. However, most studies on clothing design related to weight loss interventions did not focus on psychological factors. This research integrates psychological theories and fashion design to develop the Extended Functional, Expressive and Aesthetic Consumer Needs Model, which encompasses the Functional, Expressive and Aesthetic Consumer Needs Model, the Transtheoretical Model, the Theory of Planned Behavior, Reinforcement Theory, and Body Image. This model is utilized to promote the design of functional clothing, which aims to encourage healthy weight loss behavioral patterns among consumes by influencing various psychological factors, including cognitive, attitudinal, and emotional factors. This study employed a reverse engineering approach to interview 15 overweight or obese participants and propose design strategies for functional weight loss clothing. The survey focused on five dimensions: demographic data, behavior change stages, existing problems, triggers, and demands and preferences for functional weight loss clothing. The findings revealed users' clothing demands and preferences from functional, aesthetic, and expressive perspectives. Attitude, subjective norms, perceived behavioral control, experiential avoidance, and body image influence users' intentions for healthy weight loss. Based on these findings, corresponding design strategy recommendations were derived.

Keywords: The Extended Functional · Expressive and Aesthetic Consumer Needs Model · Behavioral Intervention · Functional Weight Loss Clothing

1 Introduction

1.1 Background

The global burden of obesity constitutes a significant public health challenge that undermines worldwide social and economic development [1]. Two of the most common causes of weight gain and obesity are the promotion of diets high in fat and low levels of physical activity [2]. However, research has shown that psychological factors also significantly

© The Author(s), under exclusive license to Springer Nature Switzerland AG 2025
V. G. Duffy (Ed.): HCII 2024, LNCS 15376, pp. 65–73, 2025.
https://doi.org/10.1007/978-3-031-76809-5_5

and directly impact dietary and exercise behaviors [3]. Therefore, to effectively tackle the issue of obesity, it is imperative to examine these psychological factors and provide interventions.

Although research on fashion design has explored methods of promoting weight loss through functional clothing design, they have primarily focused on physical interventions, with limited attention given to behavioral interventions from a psychological perspective. This study combines psychological theories with fashion design to address this research gap and develop the Extended Functional, Expressive and Aesthetic Consumer Needs Model (EFEACNM).

1.2 Research Objectives

The main research objective (MRO) and secondary research objectives (SRO) of this study are as follows:

MRO: To demonstrate the applicability of EFEACNM in guiding the development of functional weight-loss clothing design strategies.

SRO1: To harness EFEACNM in directing a market survey to develop functional weight-loss clothing.

SRO2: To employ EFEACNM in formulating design strategies for functional weight loss clothing, leveraging market survey insights.

2 Literature Review

2.1 Current Research Status of the Field

Most research on functional clothing for weight loss has predominantly generated patent documentation detailing innovative designs and technological breakthroughs in various aspects, such as compression technology, cutting-edge materials and coatings, biotechnology, and temperature control. However, literature directly addressing the research area of this paper remains scarce.

Binks and Chin [4] delve into how slimming garments motivate obese individuals to engage in physical activity. This review provides a comprehensive theoretical framework incorporating pivotal theories such as the Transtheoretical Model (TTM), Self-Efficacy, Body Image, and Self-perception. These theories guide the theoretical model used in the study.

2.2 Constructing the Extended Functional, Expressive and Aesthetic Consumer Needs Model

The FEA model assesses functional, expressive, and aesthetic considerations, which help designers think beyond commonly accepted definitions of wearer needs and avoid assumptions of client or target market wants [5]. The model resolves design problems, whether predominantly function- or fashion-oriented, to produce a design that meets the needs of the user or is within their cultural context [6]. Therefore, this study adapted the FEACNM as the core theory to specifically investigate the requirements of overweight or obese individuals for functional weight loss clothing. Additionally, it is imperative to integrate these requirements with behavioral change factors pertinent to weight loss as design considerations to propose effective strategies for functional weight loss clothing design. The Extended Transtheoretical Model is employed as a secondary theoretical framework to integrate with the FEACNM to identify the key factors influencing weight loss behaviors.

The TTM offers a promising framework for multiple risk weight management interventions [7]. The TTM posits that behavior alterations result from undergoing through 5 stages of change: pre-contemplation, contemplation, preparation, action, and maintenance [8]. The 10 relevant change processes include consciousness-raising, dramatic relief, environmental reevaluation, self-reevaluation, social liberation, counterconditioning, helping relationships, reinforcement management, self-liberation, and stimulus control, corresponding to the five stages of change [9]. Psychologists have used the TTM to design interventions that align with an individual's motivational state [10]. Since each stage comprises specific and well-researched strategies, appropriately matching the intervention with the stage is relatively straightforward [11]. However, the definition of the model's concepts lacks clarity; it is unclear if individuals must undergo all stages to realize a sustainable change, how individuals change, and why some change more than others [12, 13].

The Theory of Planned Behavior (TPB) addresses the limitations of the TTM by identifying influences on behavior that could undergo change [13]. It postulates three independent factors as the determinants of behavioral intention: attitudes, subjective norms, and perceived behavioral control [14]. The TPB helps analyze many health-related behaviors and is frequently used in studies on weight-reduction behavior [16] to predict exercise and healthy eating habits.

While the TPB focuses on behavior as an external expression of internal beliefs and attitudes [15], Skinner's focus is mostly on the external aspect of behavior [17, 18]. Skinner maintains that behavior is determined by the consequences of a person's actions [18, 19]. Luthans and Kreitner revealed four results or strategies for applying reinforcement theory: positive reinforcement, negative reinforcement, punishment, and extinction [18]. They can enhance or reduce the probability of behavior by providing pleasant stimulation, eliminating aversive stimulation, giving aversive stimulation, and withdrawing reinforcement, respectively [18].

Body image is a unique sociocultural psychological factor associated with positive and negative weight loss reinforcement behaviors. The term "body image" has been used to describe various body-related phenomena, including perceptions, cognitions, affects, and awareness concerning the body [19–21]. Along with the numerous medical problems associated with excess weight, body image dissatisfaction (BID) has been identified as "the most consistent psychosocial consequence of obesity" [22, 23]. Skinner noted that the same behavior may be associated with different emotional states, depending on whether it is a function of negative or positive reinforcement [24]. Regarding weight loss behavior, body-image concerns can be strong motivators of dieting and exercise behaviors [25–27]. However, positive body image enables high body appreciation, resulting in a body-protective behavior [28]. Hence, positive body image prevents the development of unhealthy behaviors linked to obesity [29], promoting sustainable weight management. Therefore, it is imperative to help individuals foster a positive body image to motivate them toward healthy weight management.

3 Method

3.1 Data Collection

This study employed the snowball sampling method and selected 15 overweight (7 participants) and obese (8 participants) Chinese adults, including men and women, to participate in an email interview survey. The participants' ages ranged from 18–44 (3 men and 3 women), 45–59 (2 men and 4 women), and ≥60 (1 man and 2 women). The interview lasted from 50 to 70 min.

3.2 Reverse-Engineering Approach to Survey and Design Strategy

We utilized a reverse-engineering approach in surveying and designing strategies, implying a bidirectional logical sequence between interviewing and design derivation (Fig. 1). The interview questions comprise five dimensions: demographic data, behavior change stages, existing problems, triggers for those problems, and the sample's demands and preferences for functional weight loss clothing. The design was derived from the sample's needs and preferences, orientated toward problem-solving. Through a comprehensive analysis of the factors contributing to current weight loss problems, design strategy recommendations were formulated.

4 Results and Discussions

Three of the participants are in the contemplation stage, four are in the preparation stage, five are in the action stage, and three are in the maintenance stage. The participant's intention to lose weight healthily was positively correlated with their stage. All participants evaluated their body shape unfavorably. Furthermore, 10 participants mentioned that a good body shape would make them feel happy, confident, or healthier.

Participants' attitudes toward and ability to manage healthy weight loss and support and attention from significant others were positively correlated with their intention to lose weight. Participants who believed that "healthy weight loss may not be very effective," "my family and friends think I cannot continue," and "I also think I cannot continue," had "hesitated for a long time." Conversely, those who firmly believed that "healthy weight loss is extremely effective," "my family and friends are supporting and encouraging me," and "I am excellent at controlling myself in this aspect" exhibited a "very determined" intention to lose weight.

The descriptions of the participants indicated that experiential avoidance impacts weight loss intentions. Seven participants in the contemplation or preparation stage explicitly stated a lack of control over diet or avoidance of exercise. Eight participants in the action and maintenance stages reported occasional occurrences of similar problems or attempts to avoid these tendencies. This suggest that these issues remain partly latent.

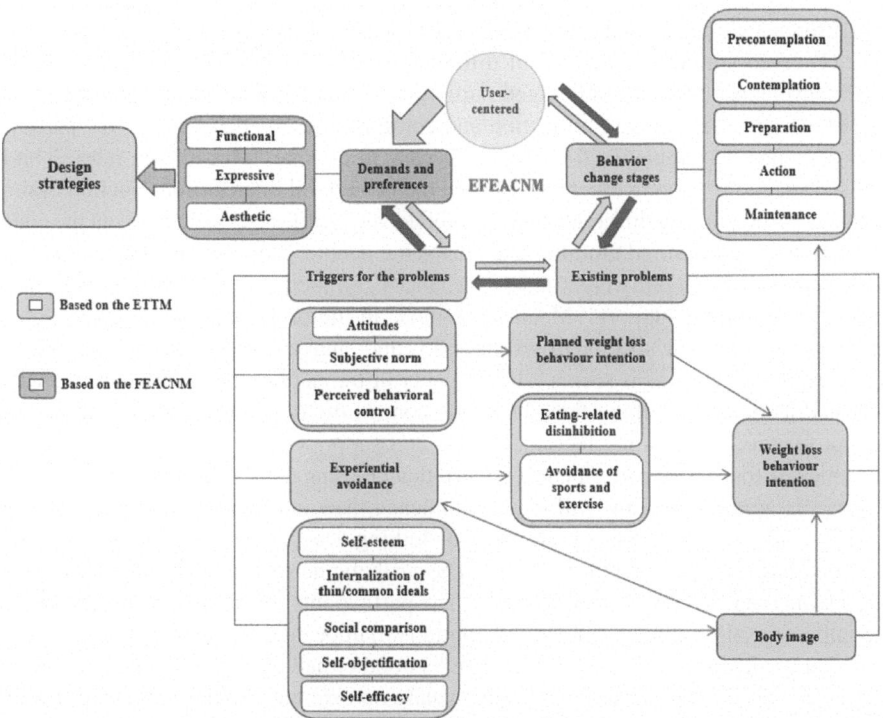

Fig. 1. A Reverse-Engineering Approach to Survey and Design Strategy.

However, 5 participants in the action and maintenance stages indicated that, if they fail to lose weight through exercise, they will not hesitate to try again, as they do not fear the experience of failure. A total of 10 participants (composed of young women, young men, or middle-aged women) believed that negative emotions stemming from a negative body image might lead to poor dietary control or avoidance of exercise. Notably, this impact was less significant among the 4 participants in the action and maintenance stages.

A total of 10 participants, including young men and women and middle-aged women, acknowledged that their body image perception is influenced by factors including self-esteem, societal expectations of thinness, comparing themselves to thinner individuals, others' views on their body, and their belief in their ability to manage healthy weight loss. Moreover, they stated that their body image significantly impacts their intention to pursue healthy weight loss. Middle-aged men and older adults believe that comparing themselves to thinner peers from a health perspective, alongside their perception of control over healthy weight loss, impacts their body image. A total of 6 participants in the contemplation and preparation stages indicated that negative body image acts as a barrier to healthy weight loss. Among the 8 participants in the action and maintenance stages, 6 mentioned that the positive emotions generated from healthy weight loss would enhance their motivation for weight loss. Additionally, 5 participants noted that changing their negative body image was the driving force behind their weight loss efforts.

Differences in the primary functional preferences for functional weight loss clothing were observed among participants of different age groups. Young participants prioritized convenience, while middle-aged participants valued both convenience and comfort. Older adults prioritized protection and comfort. Specific demands by the participants included "convenience for exercise," "easy to operate," "breathable fabric," and "waist protection," among others. Regarding the behavioral intervention function of the clothing, participants at different stages exhibited varying needs. Participants in the contemplation stage preferred clothing that "helps me decide," "encourages me and makes me feel passionate about weight loss," "enhances confidence in my body image," and "provides emotional support." Meanwhile, those in the preparation stage favor clothing that "lets me know specifically what to do" and "makes me feel that losing weight is not as challenging as it seems." Participants in the action and maintenance stages indicated a need for clothing that "helps me control my desire for snacks," "monitors prompt feature," "makes me feel understood and supported," and "continuously motivates me." A total of 10 participants believed that clothing that could shape and tone the body as an aesthetic feature will mainly influence their intention to purchase and use it. Meanwhile, 11 participants preferred the clothing to resemble sportswear, with 7 of them emphasizing fashionability as well. The aesthetic needs of the participants exhibited a wide range of personal preferences. The participants' expressive needs primarily encompassed self-confidence, positivity, optimism, hope, and unique personality.

Eight participants indicated that they understood or had used functional clothing for weight loss. They commented that relying solely on external clothing intervention was insufficient to address the underlying issue. Regardless, all participants believed that this study's functional weight-loss clothing met their needs.

5   Design Strategy Recommendations

Based on the survey results and discussions, this study proposes the following design strategy recommendations for functional weight-loss clothing:

1. Functional weight-loss clothing must include essential functions based on the different preferences across age groups, such as convenience, comfort, and protection.
2. It should utilize wearable sensors, mobile applications, and user manuals to expand the scope of the physical garment and achieve behavioral intervention.
3. The clothing design should be based on the behavior change process described by the TTM to facilitate healthy weight loss. As behavioral relapse is possible, it is recommended that all services be accessible to users at all stages, with personalized support provided by dedicated coaches or customer service. These services should:

   3a: Influence users' cognitive attitudes through informing them about the harms of overweight or obesity and the benefits of healthy weight loss. Services must also motivate users by sharing successful restorative weight loss cases.

   3b: Shape users' subjective norms by establishing helpful and interactive relationships through online communities, personal coaches, or customer service.

   3c: Enhance users' perceived behavioral control by assisting with goal-setting, providing technical guidance, offering alternative healthy behaviors, and monitoring progress.

3d: Incentivize users through rewards and punishments for achieving or missing milestones, combined with emotional regulation to help them overcome experiential avoidance and strengthen their motivation for healthy weight loss.

3e: Address users' negative body image issues by delivering targeted positive messages and perspectives through various media such as app push notifications, online communities, personal coaches or customer service, and manuals.

4. The clothing design should adopt a fashionable, sporty style and utilize the principles of visual illusion to design graphic elements that enhance the wearer's body image.

5. The visual language of the clothing should convey positive psychological messages, including feelings of confidence and happiness, among others.

6 Conclusion

This study argues that functional weight loss clothing must intervene with users' related behaviors by influencing their psychological factors such as cognition, attitude, and emotion to achieve healthy weight loss. To achieve this, we have constructed the EFEACNM, centered on the FEACNM, and integrated with the TTM, the TPB, reinforcement theory, and body image to develop design strategies for functional weight loss clothing.

Based on this theoretical model, a reverse-engineering approach was employed to conduct an interview and propose design strategies. The results support our hypotheses, which comprehensively evaluates users' demands and preferences for weight loss clothing from three dimensions: functionality, aesthetics, and expression. Simultaneously, attitude, subjective norms, perceived behavioral control, experiential avoidance, and body image influence users' intentions for healthy weight loss. Specific factors influencing body image include self-esteem, internalization of the thin or common ideal, social comparison, self-objectification, and self-efficacy. Corresponding design strategy suggestions were derived and designed based on these findings.

Overall, this study validates the applicability of the EFEACNM in guiding the development of design strategies for functional weight loss clothing, providing new perspectives and insights into the theoretical and practical research in this field. However, due to the limitations of snowball sampling and sample size, the generalizability of the findings is limited. Future research could expand the sample range and employ a more diverse sampling approach for quantitative research to further validate our findings' universality. Additionally, further verification of the feasibility of these design strategies through the development of specific products and effectiveness assessments is necessary.

Acknowledgments. The authors extend their heartfelt gratitude to the fifteen participants who kindly offered invaluable insights for this interview. Given that all the participants have chosen to remain anonymous, their names will not be listed here.

Disclosure of Interests.   The authors have no competing interests to declare that are relevant to the content of this article.

References

1. WHO. https://www.who.int/news/item/17-05-2023-new-WHO-framework-available-for-pre vention-and-management-of-obesity. Accessed 05 Feb 2024
2. Drummond, S.: Obesity in the UK. J. Health Visitors' Assoc. **76**(3), 79–80 (2003)
3. Wang, Y.Y., Sun, M.X., Yang, Y.X. (eds.): China Blue Paper of Obesity Prevention and Control, 2nd edn. Peking University Medical Press, Beijing (2021)
4. Binks, M., Chin, S.H.: Theoretical rationale for how slimming garments may motivate physical activity in people with obesity. Progr. Prevent. Med. **3**(4), e0017 (2018)
5. Chae, M.: A needs analysis approach: an investigation of clothing for women with chronic neurological disorders. Int. J. Fashion Des. Technol. Educ. **13**(2), 213–220 (2020)
6. Orzada, B.T., Kallal, M.J.: FEA consumer needs model: 25 years later. Cloth. Text. Res. J. **39**(1), 24–38 (2021)
7. Johnson, S.S., Paiva, A.L., Cummins, C.O., et al.: Transtheoretical model-based multiple behavior intervention for weight management: effectiveness on a population basis. Prev. Med. **46**(3), 238–246 (2008)
8. O'Hea, E.L., Wood, K.B., Brantley, P.J.: The transtheoretical model: gender differences across 3 health behaviors. Am. J. Health Behav. **27**(6), 645–656 (2003)
9. Pekmezi, D., Barbera, B., Marcus, B.H.: Using the transtheoretical model to promote physical activity. ACSMs Health Fit J **14**(4), 8–13 (2010)
10. Ludden, G.D.S., Hekkert, P.: Design for healthy behavior: design interventions and stages of change. In: 9th International Conference on Design and Emotion, pp. 482–488. Ediciones Uniandes, Bogotá (2014)
11. Cowan, R., Britton, P.J., Logue, E., Smucker, W., Milo, L.: The relationship among the transtheoretical model of behavioral change, psychological distress, and diet attitudes in obesity: implications for primary care intervention. J. Clin. Psychol. Med. Settings **2**, 249–267 (1995)
12. Littell, J.H., Girvin, H.: Stages of change: a critique. Behav. Modif. **26**(2), 223–273 (2002)
13. Niedderer, K., Mackrill, J., Clune, S., et al.: Creating sustainable innovation through design for behaviour change: full project report. A project funded by the Arts and Humanities Research Council under the 'Design in Innovation' call (2014). Project website: https://www.behavi ourchange.eu. Accessed 22 Feb 2024
14. Ferencz-Kaddari, M., Shifman, A., Koslowsky, M.: Modeling psychologists' ethical intention: application of an expanded theory of planned behavior. Psychol. Rep. **118**(3), 691–709 (2016)
15. Ajzen, I., Nichols, A.J., III., Driver, B.L.: Identifying salient beliefs about leisure activities: frequency of elicitation versus response latency 1. J. Appl. Soc. Psychol. **25**(16), 1391–1410 (1995)
16. Mazloomy-Mahmoodabad, S.S., Navabi, Z.S., Ahmadi, A., Askarishahi, M.: The effect of educational intervention on weight loss in adolescents with overweight and obesity: application of the theory of planned behavior. ARYA Atherosclerosis **13**(4), 176 (2017)
17. Staats, A.W.: Skinner's theory and the emotion — behaviour relationship: incipient change with major implications. Am. Psychol. **43**, 747–748 (1988)
18. Maurice, F.V., Sandra, S.H.: Reinforcement theory: a practical tool. Leadersh. Org. Dev. J. **12**(2), 27 (1991)
19. Scheffers, M., van Duijn, M.A., Bosscher, R.J., Wiersma, D., Schoevers, R.A., van Buss- chbach, J.T.: Psychometric properties of the Dresden body image questionnaire: a multiple-group confirmatory factor analysis across sex and age in a Dutch non-clinical sample. PLoS ONE **12**(7), e0181908 (2017)
20. Cash, T.F.: Body image: past, present, and future. Body Image **1**(1), 1–5 (2004)

21. Röhricht, F., et al.: Consensus paper on the terminological differentiation of various aspect of body experience. Psychotherapie, Psychosomatik. Medizinische Psychologie **55**(3–4), 183–190 (2005)
22. Rosen, J.C.: Improving body image in obesity. In: Thompson, J.K. (ed.) Body Image, Eating Disorders, and Obesity, pp. 425–440. American Psychological Association, Washington, DC (1996)
23. Matz, P.E., Foster, G.D., Faith, M.S., Wadden, T.A.: Correlates of body image dissatisfaction among overweight women seeking weight loss. J. Consult. Clin. Psychol. **70**(4), 1040 (2002)
24. Slade, P.D., Owens, R.G.: A dual process model of perfectionism based on reinforcement theory. Behav. Modif. **22**(3), 372–390 (1998)
25. Cash, T.F., Hicks, K.L.: Being fat versus thinking fat: relationships with body image, eating behaviors, and well-being. Cogn. Ther. Res. **14**, 327–341 (1990)
26. Cash, T.F., Now, P.L., Grant, J.R.: Why do women exercise? Factor analysis and further validation of the reasons for exercise inventory. Percept. Mot. Skills **78**(2), 539–544 (1994)
27. Cash, T.F.: Body-image attitudes among obese enrollees in a commercial weight-loss program. Perceptual Motor skills **77**(3_suppl), 1099–1103 (1993)
28. Grogan, S.: BODY IMAGE Understanding Body Dissatisfation in Man, Woman and Children, 1st edn, p. 10017. Routledge, New York, NY (2017)
29. Palmeira, A.L., et al.: Change in body image and psychological well-being during behavioral obesity treatment: associations with weight loss and maintenance. Body Image **7**(3), 187–193 (2010)

Design of a Framework Based on MCDM and Data Analytics for Improving the Inventory Management of Supplies for Clinical Studies: A Case Study in a Research Center of a High Complexity Clinic

Genett Isabel Jiménez-Delgado[1]([⊠]) [iD], Imran Aslan[2] [iD], Hugo Hernández-Palma[3] [iD], Mario Orozco Bohorquez[4] [iD], Felipe Acosta Ortega[5] [iD], Jonny Plazas-Alvarado[6] [iD], Angélica Jiménez-Coronado[7] [iD], Alberto Roncallo-Pichon[8] [iD], and Roberto Morales-Espinosa[9] [iD]

[1] Department of Industrial Engineering, Institución Universitaria de Barranquilla IUB, Barranquilla, Colombia
gjimenez@unibarranquilla.edu.co
[2] Faculty of Health Sciences, Bingöl University, 12000 Bingöl, Turkey
iaslan@bingol.edu.tr
[3] Faculty of Engineering, Industrial Engineering Program, Corporación Universitaria Iberoamericana IBERO, Bogotá, Colombia
hugo.hernandez@ibero.edu.co
[4] Department of Computer Science and Electronics, Universidad de la Costa CUC, Barranquilla, Colombia
morozco5@cuc.edu.co
[5] Faculty of Economic, Accounting and Administrative Sciences, Business Administration Program, Fundación Universitaria de Popayan, Popayan, Colombia
felipe.acosta@docente.fup.edu.co
[6] School of Basic Sciences, Technology and Engineering – ECBTI, Universidad Nacional Abierta y a Distancia (UNAD), Bogotá, Colombia
jonny.plazas@unad.edu.co
[7] Department of Business Transformation - Business Administration Program, Corporación Unificada Nacional de Educación Superior – CUN, Bogotá, Colombia
angelica_jimenezco@cun.edu.co
[8] Faculty of Economic, Administrative and Accounting Sciences. Accounting Program, Corporación Universitaria Americana, Barranquilla, Colombia
aroncallo@americana.edu.co
[9] International Business Program, Fundación Universitaria CEIPA, Barranquilla, Colombia
roberto_moraleses@virtual.ceipa.edu.co

Abstract. Inventory management in the health sector, specifically in the pharmaceutical service, represents a high percentage of logistics costs, putting pressure on health institutions to optimize inventory management to guarantee the availability of supplies. On the other hand, different regulations worldwide establish the adoption of mechanisms and policies for adequate inventory management, a situation that in low- and middle-income countries is restricted by resource

V. G. Duffy (Ed.): HCII 2024, LNCS 15376, pp. 74–92, 2025.
https://doi.org/10.1007/978-3-031-76809-5_6

limitations and the low implementation of robust techniques and methodologies. Different applications of models for inventory management have been identified in the literature, such as optimization models, Lean tools, and multicriteria decision-making methods. However, integrated approaches to optimize demand management, ordering, and controlling pharmaceutical services supplies are still under development. Therefore, the present study proposes a three-phase hybrid approach based on MCDM techniques and data analytics to improve inventory management of the pharmaceutical service in a health research center. The first stage consisted of characterizing the process to identify aspects for improvement. In the second stage, a multicriteria ABC classification model based on F-AHP and TOPSIS was applied to classify laboratory supplies for three selected clinical studies. Furthermore, the appropriate forecasting method was chosen for each clinical study, and a combined model (P model and FEFO model) was applied to establish the reorder point. Then, strategies, mechanisms, and policies were proposed to improve inventory management and redesign the process flow. As the main results, a multicriteria ABC method was obtained to classify laboratory supplies, taking into account Rotation (GW = 0.512), Criticality (GW = 0.286), and Availability (GW = 0.203). On the other hand, through data analysis and regression models, the exponential smoothing model with $\alpha = 0.10$ was identified as the most convenient forecasting model, as well as the integrated application of the P and FEFO models to calculate the reorder point adapted to the dynamics of the Research Center, and finally, a set of strategies to improve inventory management that underpin the development of clinical studies with an impact on the health of patients.

Keywords: Inventory management · Optimization · Data Analytics · Forecasting · Multicriteria Decision Techniques · Healthcare Logistics · Intuitionistic Fuzzy Analytic Hierarchy Process (F-AHP) · (TOPSIS) · Healthcare · Pharmaceutical Services · Clinical Studies

1   Introduction

Supply management in the health sector is one of the most complex logistics chain processes, considering in addition to criteria such as time and quality and compliance with legal and market requirements. In this regard, Saldivar, cited by Torres Cáceres [1], mentions that pharmaceutical service supply chains face pressure to reduce their inventory levels, considering the demands of their users. In addition, these pharmaceutical services manage a wide variety of products that require appropriate handling based on their storage, use, and helpful life characteristics. No less important is the management of logistics costs, which for the health sector represent around 30% to 45% of the total budget, costs that could be reduced through implementing good practices and adequate supply chain integration [2].

Along the same lines, Arias [3], Uthayakumar, and Priyan [4] highlight that inventory management is an essential point in the strategic management of any organization since it affects the cost structure of any organization, with a significant impact on the health sector, which pursues the constant optimization of its costs given the economic restrictions, especially after the Covid-19 pandemic. In this regard, inventory management in the health sector is one of the most significant challenges for financial management; it already represents between 5 and 10% of the monthly cost in some institutions [5], which must guarantee the availability of the necessary supplies for patient care, in addition to having healthy inventories, that is, not having overstock or shortages.

The above implies efficient management of the supply chain of hospital supplies, which includes inventory management through continuous analysis of processes, technologies, procedures, and human talent, as well as the use of methodologies and techniques that facilitate making effective and data-based decisions. National and international health organizations regulate the management of medical supplies used for clinical studies and hospital medical treatments. As an example, in Colombia, the National Institute for Food and Drug Surveillance – INVIMA [6] establishes that pharmaceutical services must-have criteria, procedures, and resources that allow inventory control to be carried out. This control will be carried out primarily by evaluating inventory rotation and the physical count compared to the stock record and carrying out general inventories, selective tests, or rotating inventories and permanent inventories.

Different initiatives have been developed to improve inventory management in pharmaceutical services, from using technology [7], data analytics, demand forecasts [8], and decision-making models for prioritizing inventories according to their criticality [9], multi-objective mathematical models [4], Lean philosophy [10], and policies for order management and inventory control [11], aiming to guarantee the availability, quality, and safety of medical supplies. Despite efforts to address supply chain improvement and inventory management in pharmaceutical services, the development of innovative and comprehensive solutions is limited, especially in low- middle-income countries, given the restrictions of resources, complexities, and internal dynamics of health systems, which prevents the development of improvement projects and the adoption of good practices with operational, social and economic impact for patients, medical and health personnel, managers, and other actors of the health value chain.

The present research proposes a methodological approach using multicriteria decision-making techniques and data analytics to improve the management of input inventories for clinical studies in a pharmaceutical service to a health institution. The case study of an investigation center of a highly complex clinic in a low- and middle-income country presents problems in managing the supply chain of medications and laboratory kits used in research studies of medicines for oncology patients and children and in testing vaccines for different diseases. The problems include the absence of an inventory management system, the non-use of policies for planning and programming inputs and outputs, the non-application of data analysis methods to forecast the required quantities of supplies inputs, deficiencies in storage methods, management, and control of the quality and availability of supplies. These deficiencies generate losses of laboratory kits, medications, and other medical supplies, whether due to loss, deterioration, or expiration, which in turn translates into delays in the supply of supplies, affecting the development of clinical studies, the decrease in patients, and financial support of the pharmaceutical companies for the different researches, with impacts at a reputational, economic and social level.

To address the challenges above and propose the hybrid model for improvement in inventory management, a mixed approach, non-experimental, cross-sectional design study was developed, collecting relevant information about the process and through expert judgments. In the first phase, the current conditions of the input inventory process were diagnosed through a SIPOC analysis and a survey conducted with the research center staff. In the second phase, the criteria were identified to categorize the critical supplies through a Multicriteria ABC classification F-AHP / TOPSIS applied in three clinical studies. Subsequently, data analytics was used to select the appropriate forecasting model for demand management and supply planning based on the historical data collected for the selected clinical studies. In addition, a mixed inventory replenishment method (P and FEFO models) was used, considering the characteristics of the pharmaceutical service. Finally, in the third phase, strategies and policies were proposed to plan, control, and replace the pharmaceutical service inventory of the research center and redesign the supply orders' process flow.

The proposed methodological Framework constitutes a set of value-added tools for decision-makers in pharmaceutical services in the health sector, contributing to closing gaps in developing supply chain improvement models for medical supplies. The practical implications for research centers and entities in the health sector include improving operational, social, and economic objectives and positively impacting research development that improves patients' quality of life worldwide. The remainder of this paper is organized as follows. Section 2 presents the literature review of inventory management and multicriteria decision methods in pharmaceutical services. In Sect. 3, the proposed methodology is presented. Section 4 covers the results and discussion. Finally, Sect. 5 presents the conclusions and future works.

2 Literature Review

Medicines, the shortage of which can be life-threatening, can account for up to 50% of the cost of consumables, so they need to be effectively stocked and available when they are required. High costs and risks to patient health can result from inadequate management of the flow of medicines. It is, therefore, necessary to have timely access to these items. The order and reorder point, the quantity ordered, and the safety stock can be determined following proper inventory management of medicines [12]. Effective inventory management is required in healthcare institutions due to the rhythm of supply and demand. A professional way to improve the management of resources, processes, and activities is needed due to the various materials and drugs in hospitals and the different inflows and outflows. Effective management systems are required to predict daily drug consumption and uncertainty in healthcare organizations. The main objectives of hospital stock management are to reduce costs by promoting efficient use and having the right amount of each product according to demand. Classes should receive different levels of attention, with the highest-priority classes receiving more attention [13].

The drug categorization plan or drug ranking can be applied to separate essential drugs from trivial ones, which is called drug categorization based on several selected criteria and objectives. ABC, which generally classifies stock items as very important (A), moderately necessary (B), and relatively unimportant (C) based on annual monetary expenditure, and VED, which classifies items as vital, essential, and desirable based on item criticality, are some traditional stock-sorting methods. Fast, Slow, and Non-Moving

(FSN) is another method based on the frequency of consumption without considering other factors such as inventory value, criticality, and cost. Another method is the SDE (Scarce, Difficult, and Easy) method, which focuses only on the availability of inventory items on the market [12, 14]. A single criterion is mainly used in the VED, FSN, SDE, and ABC curve techniques. Because of the complexity of hospital inventory management, a single criterion, such as dollar value, demand, or criticality, may not be sufficient for classifying inventory [13].

Health decisions are complex because of medical, technical, social, ethical, economic, and environmental factors, with multiple competing objectives and different stakeholders requiring more sophisticated techniques for assessment [13]. Unpleasant outcomes, catastrophic consequences, and high costs can result from a wrong decision under uncertainty. Evaluating the performance of the considered alternatives according to these criteria, called Multicriteria Decision Making (MCDM), involves numerous conflicting qualitative and quantitative criteria and requires the intervention of stakeholders such as patients, healthcare workers, doctors, pharmaceutical suppliers, etc. Multicriteria inventory ranking (MCIC) models such as Mathematical Programming, Data Envelopment Analysis, Metaheuristics, Artificial Intelligence, AHP, Fuzzy AHP (FAHP), Technique of Order of Preference (TOPSIS), Simple Multi-Attribute Ranking Technique (SMART), MACBETH, Complex Proportional Rating (COPRAS), Gray Relational Analysis (GRA), PROMETHEE and so on methods have been applied to classify the inventories based on own organizational priorities, values and objectives [15]. MCDM techniques can be used in various areas such as medical devices, disease identification and management, supply chain management, health information systems, quality assessment in health care, risk management, waste management, etc., and many others. These methods can be applied to generate and validate decision rules with multiple strategies, such as monitoring the shelf-life of stocks in terms of their priority. These techniques are superior to single-criteria techniques because they evaluate numerous attributes of the items in stock, including criteria relevant to the decision problem. The availability and efficacy of alternative medicines, unit price, quantity, type of demand, importance, lead time, importance, substitutes, obsolete, and shelf life are some criteria for their classification [12, 13]. Inadequate weight procedures, failure to test model appropriateness, and participants' cognitive difficulty in building models are among MCDM model weaknesses [16].

The healthcare sector requires a multidisciplinary approach to pharmaceuticals, medical devices, waste management, information technology, etc. Healthcare supply chains (HSC) differ from other supply chains due to the high complexity, high-value goods, and weight of human life involved in procuring and distributing products and services from the warehouse to the patient/customer. Due to inventory or waste management, stock shortages, and drug expiration, the Pharmaceutical Supply Chain (PSC) is necessary. Hospitals have complex information and product flows between different departments. The flow of patients, the building of relationships, and authorities must also be included in the HSC. The COVID-19 pandemic has demonstrated the importance of HSC in hospitals as the production and distribution of products and critical services were disrupted. The MCDM modeling framework addressed raw material shortages, short product life, high-quality products and services, patient care, risk prevention/mitigation, and seasonal demand factors affecting HSC. Based on these criteria, MCDM methods such as AHP, Fuzzy AHP, TOPSIS, and VIKOR, etc., which allow the incorporation of uncertainty and subjectivity, were used to make decisions on production, transportation, procurement, blood supply chain, drug supply chain, distribution, after-sales service, and inventory planning [9]. Organizational risk factors include technological, political, human, and environmental disruptions. Natural disasters such as earthquakes, flooding, or manufactured disasters such as war, terrorist attacks, strikes, etc., can affect HSCs, destroying hospitals and clinics, losing power, water, and telecommunications, and damaging transport infrastructure. In these cases, backup suppliers should be prepared [17].

According to Cadena, the Analytical Hierarchy Process (AHP) is "a quantitative method for multicriteria decision-making that allows the generation of priority scales based on expert judgments expressed by pairwise comparisons using a preference scale" [18]. The weighting of classification criteria can be determined using the analytical hierarchy process (AHP) proposed by Saaty [19] for inventory classification by comparing the factors in pairs with a given objective based on expert judgment by using [18], and the fuzzy AHPs (FAHPs) with ambiguity, which include both qualitative and quantitative aspects and include human judgment in the classification process. The subjectivity of decision-makers is a significant drawback of AHP [20]. The advanced form of the AHP, the FAHP, can deal with the potential inaccuracy of human judgment by using natural language in the reasoning and evaluation and eliminating unnecessary criteria [12].

TOPSIS is a reasonably simple MCDA method, and the acronym stands for 'Order Preference Similarity Technique with the Ideal Solution.' As its name suggests, the method is based on searching for an ideal and anti-ideal solution and comparing the distance of each alternative to these solutions" [21]. The TOPSIS method proposed by Hwang and Yoon [22], which states that the best alternative is the one that comes closest to the ideal solution under uncertainty and incomplete information, is used to rank the other options by Euclidean distance from the perfect and anti-ideal solutions. With this method, opportunities for improvement can be realized. The advantages and disadvantages of treatment and individual preferences can be integrated into the method. For example, the best dialysis alternative, diagnosis of diabetes, selection of diabetes treatment, health technology assessment, estimation of usable security hospital management system software from choices, evaluation of the performance of blockchain-based IoT healthcare industry 4. 0 systems, estimating the corresponding criteria weights and usefulness of 20 COVID-19 mobile applications, ranking the hospital site alternatives, a framework of resilient supplier selection, prioritizing multiple chronic disease patients or selecting the most appropriate electronic blood pressure monitor applications, ranking users' feelings and emotions, etc. cases can be carried out with this method to find an optimal decision. Mainly fuzzy AHP or fuzzy TOPSIS hybrid models, which are developed to improve decision-making processes [15, 23, 24]. Failure to consider the relationship between criteria is a drawback of this method [25].

3 Methodology

This research uses a three-phase methodology to improve inventory management, as shown in Fig. 1.

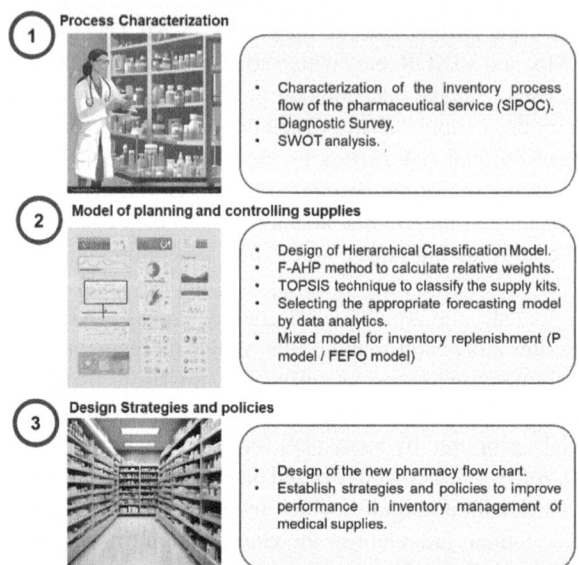

Fig. 1. Proposed Framework Based on MCDM and Data Analytics for Improvement of the Inventory Management of Supplies for Clinical Studies

Phase 1. *Process Characterization.* In this step, the pharmaceutical service's inventory process flow was diagrammed and characterized using the SIPOC diagram [26]. In addition, the current internal and external conditions that affect the inventory process were analyzed through a survey and SWOT analysis.

Phase 2. *Model of planning and controlling supplies.* In this phase, a multicriteria ABC model was used to categorize the essential supplies in three clinical studies. First, the interdisciplinary team of the Research Center identified the criteria for classification. Subsequently, F-AHP was applied to determine the criteria weights under uncertainty in the evaluation process from the definition of fuzzy numbers [27, 28]. TOPSIS was then used to classify the supply kits based on the evaluation criteria through the Closeness Coefficient (CC) [29, 30]. Then, with data analytics, the appropriate forecasting model was selected for input planning based on historical data collected from the three selected clinical studies. Finally, a mixed model was applied for inventory replenishment based on the periodic review model (P model) and the FEFO model, according to the particularities of the pharmaceutical service.

Phase 3. *Strategies and policies for the planning, control, and replenishment of the inventory of the pharmaceutical service.* In this final phase, strategies and policies were proposed to plan, control, and replenish the inventory of kits and supplies for clinical studies to guarantee their availability. Likewise, a new flow of the supply orders process is proposed.

4 Results

4.1 Process Characterization

The first stage characterized the current conditions of the pharmaceutical service inventory process in a clinical research center of a highly complex health entity in a low and middle-income country such as Colombia. To this end, technical visits and interviews were conducted with pharmacy area personnel in the second semester of 2022 to map the current process and determine the project's starting conditions. The interview results showed that the pharmaceutical service does not have an electronic or digital system for inventory management, and they also mentioned that there are no formal protocols for carrying out cyclical counts in the pharmacy warehouse. In addition to the above, it was evident that forecast estimates are not made based on the demand for laboratory kits, nor do they have to reorder point calculations, so it is necessary to improve the inventory management process to guarantee the availability of the supplies required in clinical studies. Subsequently, the current flow of the inventory management process was diagrammed using the SIPOC diagram and flowchart, as seen in Figs. 2 and 3.

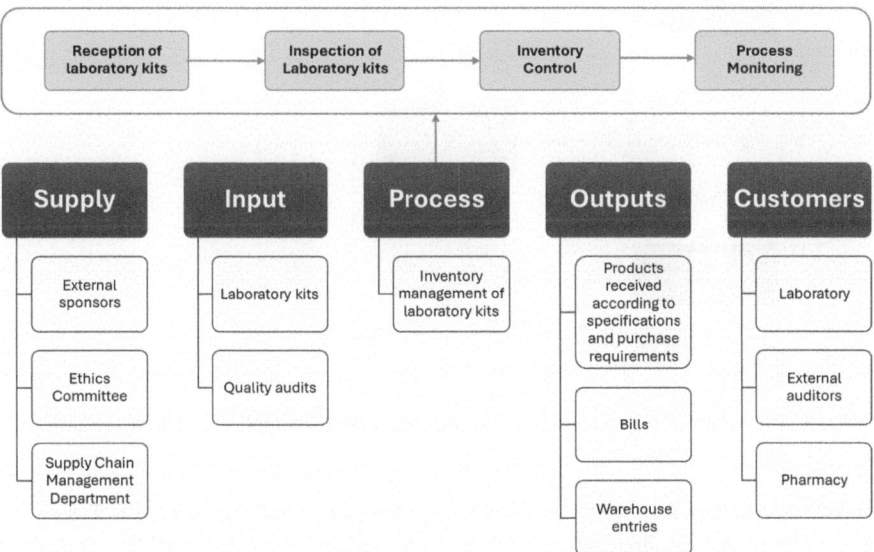

Fig. 2. SIPOC diagram for the inventory management of Supplies for Clinical Studies

Subsequently, a SWOT analysis was carried out (Fig. 4), through which the strengths, weaknesses, opportunities and threats were detected. In this regard, strengths are revealed, such as the variety of supplies for clinical studies, adequate storage spaces, large storage capacity for supplies, and adaptability of the service. Training by pharmaceutical laboratories was identified as an opportunity that would raise the research center's service level. However, the main weaknesses detected are the non-use of digital technologies or applications for inventory management, the lack of personnel training

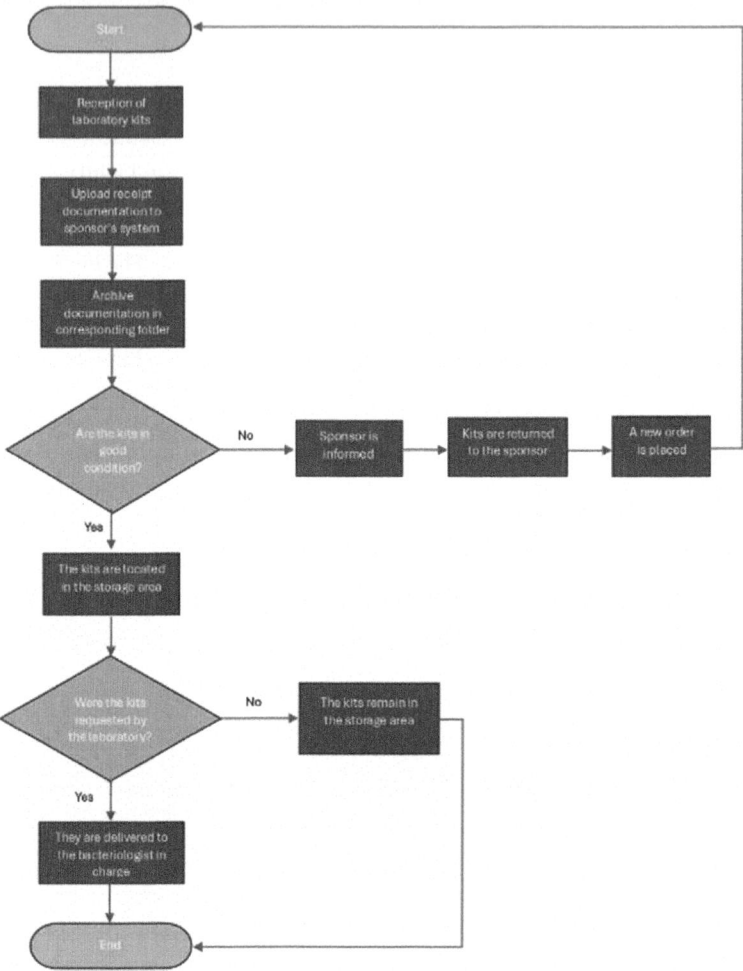

Fig. 3. Flowchart of the inventory management process for Supplies for Clinical Studies

in inventory management, and the absence of policies to control input inventories. In addition to the above, there are threats that the improvement of the process poses to avoid shortages, such as interruptions in the global supply chain due to natural disasters, war conflicts, and pandemics.

5   Model of Planning and Controlling Supplies

For the Second stage, the proposed methodology was piloted in three clinical studies out of 60 managed by the Research Center, as shown in Table 1. For the choice of clinical studies, they were considered the following criteria:

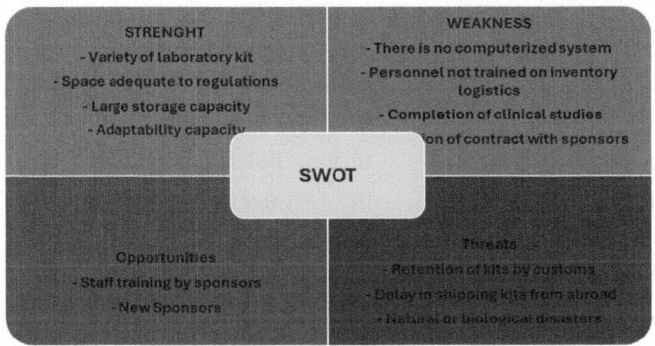

Fig. 4. SWOT of the research center pharmacy

1. **By experience and reputation of the sponsor:** It was considered which studies were with the research center's most important clients, which have national and international recognition. In this sense, the three studies from the three pharmaceutical companies that have developed the most research in the research center were selected to parameterize the inventory of these studies and have a positive response from the external client.
2. **By pathology of the clinical study:** The pathology of the clinical research affects the number of patients for testing and the study time, directly impacting the number of kits to request. In this sense, the pathologies chosen were oncology, pediatrics, and vaccines for the following reasons:
   • The chosen oncological study involved a few patients, so ample storage space for the laboratory kits was not required. In addition, the study time is usually quite long, so orders for laboratory kits will be placed for an extended period.
   • In pediatric studies, there is a high probability that all the patients who started the study will complete it because the study duration is relatively short compared to others. Since it is a young population of patients, it is unlikely that they will suffer events. During the study, adverse events that cause its discontinuation concerning the storage of the kits, such as the requested quantities, will always remain constant.
   • In the study of vaccines, the particularity is the massive recruitment, so the center's directives are interested in managing the storage of laboratory kits adequate for several patients to test the effectiveness of the vaccines.
3. **By impact of the study at a commercial level:** The last criterion for choosing the sample was the effect that the study will have at a commercial level, which must ensure that the study meets the parameters of duration and number of patients for the development of the methodological Framework and the results obtained.

Subsequently, an inventory classification model was designed through the combination of ABC, F-AHP, and TOPSIS techniques, for which a team of five experts was involved, made up of:

• Three professionals in the pharmaceutical service department of the Research Center (Head of Pharmacy, Regent of Pharmacy, Pharmaceutical Chemist).

Table 1. Selected clinical studies

Study	State	Duration time	Phase	Pathology	N° patients	N° visits
A	Active	8 years	III	Oncological	13	53
B	Active	1 year	III	Pediatric	85	5
C	Active, recruitment	2 years	III	Vaccine	1278	14

- Two professionals in Industrial Engineering with knowledge and experience in logistics, inventory management, and multicriteria decision-making techniques.

Then, the team of experts validated the classification criteria shown in Table 2.

Table 2. Criteria description

Criterion (C)	Criterion description
C1. Rotation	This criterion evaluates the quantities of medications or supplies from inventory. [31, 32]
C2. Criticality	This criterion measures the potential of the medication or input in treating and preventing diseases, from minor to critical illnesses. [31, 32]
C3. Availability	This criterion analyzes the quick access of the input or medication in the pharmacy stock. [31, 32]

After applying the Fuzzy AHP methodology, the relative weights of the criteria and consistency ratios were calculated to ensure validity in expert judgments. The results revealed that rotation (GW = 51.2%) was the most crucial criterion for classifying laboratory kits. Table 3 shows the relative weights of the criteria and subcriteria and their consistency indices, less than 0.1, which shows consistent judgments.

Table 3. Global weights and Consistency Index of criteria

Criterion (C)	GW	CR
C1. Rotation	0.512	0.004
C2. Criticality	0.286	
C3. Availability	0.203	

Then, the TOPSIS method was used to classify the supplies (laboratory kits) for the three selected studies. For the application of TOPSIS, evaluation indicators of the supplies were established considering the criteria of Rotation, Criticality, and Availability. Then, the formulation of the TOPSIS method [29] was applied to determine the TOPSIS decision matrices, the normalized matrix R, the weighted and normalized TOPSIS decision matrix V, the separations of the positive ideal solution (PIS) and negative ideal solution (NIS). Finally, a classification index of critical supplies called the ABC Classification Coefficient (CC_{ABCi}) was calculated to rank the laboratory kits according to the CC_{ABCi} preference order (Kit type C: $0 \leq CC_{ABCi} \leq 0.25$ ‖ Kit Type B: $0.25 < CC_{ABCi} \leq 0.75$ ‖ Kit Type A: $0.75 < CC_{ABCi} \leq 1$). For example, Table 4 shows the TOPSIS ABC ranking of the laboratory kits from Study C. This classification allows differentiated control over those kits with greater criticality, availability, and rotation for efficient inventory management.

Table 4 ABC Classification of laboratory kits (Study C) via TOPSIS method

Kit	CC_i	d_i^+	d_i^-	Rank
Kit C	0.756	0.109	1.332	A
Kit D	0.713	0.	1.315	B
Kit E	0.456	0.198	1.166	B
Kit A	0.312	0.313	1.133	B
Kit B	0.244	0.315	1.124	C

Another aspect developed in this Second stage was selecting an appropriate forecast model for demand management and planning supplies and kits. Based on data collected from the previous 24 weeks, three time series forecasting models were applied to determine the most relevant one based on the lowest forecast error. In this sense, the Simple Moving Average (N = 3), Weighted Moving Average, and Exponential Smoothing methods were used with α values of 0.10, 0.20, and 0.30. These methods were used given the ease of use by the research center staff and the short-term data collection. Tables 5, 6, and 7 show each study's application of the predictive models. The best forecasting model for study A is the exponential smoothing model with α = 0.20. The best forecasting model for study B is the exponential smoothing model with α = 0.10. The best forecast model for study C is the exponential smoothing model with α = 0.10.

Table 5. Forecasting methods compared across forecast error measures for Study A

	Simple Moving Average	Weighted Average	Smoothing with α = 0.10	Smoothing with α = 0.20	Smoothing with α = 0.30
MAD	15.25	16.81	16.46	16.59	16.58
MSE	432.14	473.38	346.85	373.37	388.94
MAPE	24.26%	26.00%	27.00%	26.00%	26.00%

Then, a mixed model between probabilistic and deterministic was selected due to the variable demand presented by the sample of the three studies of the center; the model chosen was a combination of the periodic review model or P model and the FEFO model.

Table 6. Forecasting methods compared across forecast error measures for Study B

	Simple Moving Average	Weighted Average	Smoothing with α = 0.10	Smoothing with α = 0.20	Smoothing with α = 0.30
MAD	4.48	4.88	3.86	4.10	4,32
MSE	28.15	33.67	21.50	23.48	25.66
MAPE	14.00%	15.00%	12.00%	13.00%	14.00%

Table 7. Forecasting methods compared across forecast error measures for Study C

	Simple Moving Average	Weighted Average	Smoothing with α = 0.10	Smoothing with α = 0.20	Smoothing with α = 0.30
MAD	84.81	92.75	79.55	84.37	89.06
MSE	12,095.90	13,883.00	10,052.37	10,992.23	12,023.19
MAPE	6%	7%	6%	6%	7%

These models are the ones that are adjusted to the inventory needs in the research center's pharmacy since the periodic review model is used in cases where the inventory level is reviewed in fixed periods in which orders will be placed to sponsors and to in the case of the FEFO model, this method bases its input and output management criteria on the expiration of the products, those that expire first, leave first.

The period selected to carry out the inventory of each study will be two weeks. Given that the research center has more than 60 studies, the pharmacy staff will work on taking inventory every business day of the week. Likewise, the senior management of the pharmacy considered a service fulfillment level in stock of 95%. In this sense, Eq. 1 is used to calculate the order quantity according to model P:

$$q = d(T + L) - I \qquad (1)$$

where:

q = Price Quantity

d(T + L) = Average demand during the vulnerable period

I = Stock available (plus order, if any)

The order quantity for kits was calculated with the 24-week observation period set out above; therefore, the daily consumption was calculated from the demand for each kit concerning the time of 24 weeks or 168 days. Each study's stock safety differed depending on the number of patients. The stock will be half the patients the study has when carrying out the inventory. If the result is a fraction, this will be rounded to the corresponding figure in the Cases of study A, B, and C, respectively, will be 7, 43, and 639, according to the number of patients registered for each study and the delivery time according to what was observed during the execution of this study is from the day of placing the order. The day the laboratory kits arrive is approximately 30 days; therefore, that is the delivery time. Tables 8, 9, and 10 show the order point calculations for each study.

Table 8. Order point calculations for study A kits

Study	Kit required for studies	Kit Quantity Required in the period of 168	Daily consumption	Consumption during the delivery period	Consumption between two replacements	Maximum Stock	Point of order
Study A	KIT A-991	150	0,89	26,79	25,00	58,29	85
	KIT B-991	154	0,92	27,50	25,67	59,67	87
	KIT C-991	111	0,66	19,82	18,50	44,82	65
	KIT D-991	161	0,96	28,75	26,83	62,08	91
	KIT E-991	174	1,04	31,07	29,00	66,57	98
	KIT F-991	93	0,55	16,61	15,50	38,61	55
	KIT G-991	152	0,90	27,14	25,33	58,98	86
	KIT H-991	74	0,44	13,21	12,33	32,05	45
	KIT I-991	133	0,79	23,75	22,17	52,42	76
	KIT J-991	115	0,68	20,54	19,17	46,20	67
	KIT SEROLOGY-991	134	0,80	23,93	22,33	52,76	77
	KIT FRESH TISSUE-991	92	0,55	16,43	15,33	38,26	55
	KIT TYPE BLOCK-991	145	0,86	25,89	24,17	56,56	82
	KIT SLIDES-991	102	0,61	18,21	17,00	41,71	60
	KIT UNS -991	64	0,38	11,43	10,67	28,60	40

Table 9. Order point calculations for study B kits

Study	Kit required for studies	Kit Quantity Required in the period of 168	Daily consumption	Consumption during the delivery period	Consumption between two replacements	Maximum Stock	Point of order
Study B	SCREEN V1	364	2,17	65,00	30,17	137,67	203
	KIT ADHOC DIAGNOSTIC (V2-V4)	43	0,26	7,68	28,26	78,43	86
	KIT W52 (V5)	373	2,22	66,61	30,22	139,33	206

Concerning the applicability of the FEFO method, an inventory matrix is implemented (see Fig. 5) to control Kit entries to verify their expiration dates to locate them so that the kits closest to expiry are on the shelves closest.

Table 10. Order point calculations for study C kits

Study	Kit required for studies	Kit Quantity Required in the period of 168	Daily consumption	Consumption during the delivery period	Consumption between two replacements	Maximum Stock	Point of order
Study C	KIT A	6389	38,030	1140,893	66,030	1845,923	2987
	KIT B	5992	35,667	1070,000	63,667	1772,667	2843
	KIT C	6774	40,321	1209,643	68,321	1916,964	3127
	KIT D	6781	40,363	1210,893	68,363	1918,256	3129
	KIT E	6764	40,262	1207,857	68,262	1915,119	3123

INVENTORY REGISTRATION - ENTRIES AND EXITS								
DATE	PROTOCOL	PRODUCT	FECHA DE VENCIMIENTO	EXPIRATION DATE	QUANTITY	DESCRIPTION	DELIVERY	RECEIVED
5-sep-22	SL-0043	KIT A	Sunday, April 30, 2023	-390	5			
				-45436				
				-45436				
				-45436				
				-45436				
				-45436				
				-45436				
				-45436				
				-45436				
				-45436				
				-45436				
				-45436				
				-45436				
				-45436				
				-45436				
				-45436				

Fig. 5. Inventory Control Matrix

6 Strategies and Policies for the Planning, Control, and Replenishment of the Inventory of the Pharmaceutical Service

Finally, and with the consensus of senior management, the following policies were established for the control and organization of inventory:

1. Apply forecast models for each of the research center's studies. The following statistical models are recommended for forecasting (Simple Moving Average, Weighted Moving Average, and Exponential Smoothing with alpha values of 0.10, 0.20, and 0.30).
2. Arrange the kit request between the pharmacy professional in charge of the inventory and those requesting the kits through emails and meetings.
3. Monitor the input and output of the kits with the matrix proposed in the research.
4. Carry out the request for laboratory kits, considering the quantities established as the order point.
5. Place orders for laboratory kits, considering the periods and quantities established with the inventory model.
6. Dispense the kits considering the FEFO model.

The methods and policies proposed in this study were socialized to the directors and staff of the research center's pharmacy, given that they contain guidelines and techniques for calculating forecasts and recording the delivery and reception of the kits.

The research center staff stated that these strategies are easy to apply, which positively impacted the management and control of the inventories of the selected studies. Furthermore, in Fig. 6, an improved process flow is proposed to manage and control laboratory kit inventories for medical studies.

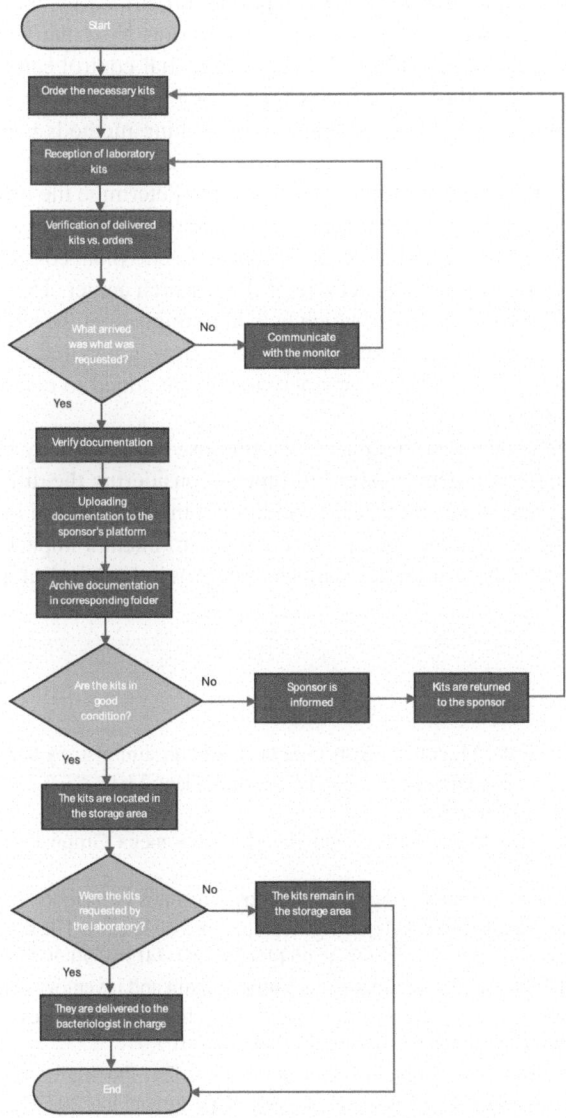

Fig. 6. Proposed flow chart for ordering kits in the research center pharmacy

7 Conclusions and Future Work

This study proposes a hybrid methodological framework based on F-AHP, TOPSIS, and data analytics for the improvement of supply inventory management in the pharmacy service of a health research center. Initially, a diagnosis of the current situation of the pharmaceutical service inventory process was carried out to determine the aspects for improvement through interviews, process flow, SIPOC diagram, and SWOT analysis. In a second phase, a multicriteria ABC model was structured to classify the inventories of laboratory kits, considering criteria such as rotation, criticality, and availability, of which rotation was identified as the most relevant criterion. Next, the TOPSIS technique was applied to classify the inputs with which differential control can be exercised on the inputs. Subsequently, three-time series forecasting methods were used to estimate demand from historical data, with exponential smoothing methods with alpha of 0.10 and 0.20 being the most recommended due to the smallest margin of error. Then, a mixed method based on the P and FEFO models was used to determine the inventory replacement quantities, considering the characteristics of the research center's pharmaceutical service. In phase 3, strategies and policies were proposed to plan, control, and replenish the inventory of the pharmaceutical service of the research center. The results found in phases one and two were socialized, which helped to implement the strategies better. A new proposal was made for the pharmacy's process flow, given that the initial process flow was not working optimally, so new activities were added to control and monitor inventory management.

Future research is intended to replicate the proposed methodology in the remaining research center studies for better control of inputs, considering the different characteristics of the studies and inputs required. In addition, other studies can incorporate other inventory classification criteria, such as cost and environmental impact, among others, and use intuitionistic multicriteria techniques to improve classification under uncertain conditions.

References

1. Torres, N., Calsina. W.: Modelo de gestión de la cadena de suministro y la rentabilidad de los principales laboratorios farmacéuticos del Perú. Ind. Data **23**(1), 53–72 (2020). https://doi.org/10.15381/idata.v23i1.16265
2. Ozores, B.: Logística Hospitalaria (Segunda ed.). Alfaomega Grupo Editor S.A., México (2014)
3. Arias, R.: Control de inventarios de medicamentos e insumos utilizando la metodología multicriterio en la bodega de la unidad quirúrgica en una IPS de la ciudad de Cali. (2015). https://red.uao.edu.co/server/api/core/bitstreams/65446c28-accf-44f3-b690-e07551c16059/content
4. Uthayakumar, R., Priyan, S.: Pharmaceutical supply chain and inventory management strategies: optimization for a pharmaceutical company and a hospital. Oper. Res. Health Care **2**(3), 52–64 (2013). https://doi.org/10.1016/j.orhc.2013.08.001
5. Reddi. Gestión de inventarios en el sector de salud (2024). https://reddicolombia.com/gestion-de-inventarios-en-el-sector-de-salud/#:~:text=El%20manejo%20de%20inventarios%20en%20el%20sector,la%20atenci%C3%B3n%20del%20paciente%2C%20garantizando%20tambi%C3%A9n%20tener. Accessed 23 Mar 2024.

6. Ministry of Social Protection. Resolution 1403 (2007). https://autorregulacion.saludcapital. gov.co/leyes/Resolucion_1403_de_2007.pdf. Accessed 20 Mar 2024

7. Papert, M., Rimpler, P., Pflaum, A.: Enhancing supply chain visibility in a pharmaceutical supply chain: solutions based on automatic identification technology. Int. J. Phys. Distrib. Logist. Manag. **46**(9), 859–884 (2016). https://doi.org/10.1108/IJPDLM-06-2016-0151

8. Zhu, X., Ninh, A., Zhao, H., Liu, Z.: Demand forecasting with supply-chain information and machine learning: evidence in the pharmaceutical industry. Prod. Oper. Manag. **30**(9), 3231–3252 (2021). https://doi.org/10.1111/poms.13426

9. Laganà, I.R., Colapinto, C.: Multiple criteria decision-making in healthcare and pharmaceutical supply chain management: a state-of-the-art review and implications for future research. J. Multicriteria Decis. Anal. **29**(1–2), 122–134 (2022). https://doi.org/10.1002/mcda.1778

10. Argiyantari, B., Simatupang, T., Basri, M. Pharmaceutical supply chain transformation through application of the lean principle: a literature review. J. Ind. Eng. Manag. (JIEM) **13**(3), 475–494 (2020). ISSN 2013-0953. https://doi.org/10.3926/jiem.310

11. Seidman, G., Atun, R.: Do changes to supply chains and procurement processes yield cost savings and improve availability of pharmaceuticals, vaccines, or health products? A systematic review of evidence from low-income and middle-income countries. BMJ Glob. Health **2**, e000243 (2017). https://doi.org/10.1136/bmjgh-2016-000243

12. Nag, K., Helal, M.: Multicriteria inventory classification of diabetes drugs using a comparison of AHP and fuzzy AHP models. In: 2018 IEEE International Conference on Industrial Engineering and Engineering Management (IEEM), pp. 1456–1460. IEEE (2018). https:// doi.org/10.1109/IEEM.2018.8607678.

13. De Assis, A.G., dos Santos, A.F.A., dos Santos, L.A., et al.: Classification of medicines and materials in hospital inventory management: a multicriteria analysis. BMC Med. Inform. Decis. Mak. **22**, 325 (2022). https://doi.org/10.1186/s12911-022-02069-0

14. Hukum, R., Shrouty, V.A.: The study of various tools and techniques of inventory management and experiment with use of ABC analysis. Int. Res. J. Eng. Technol. **6**, 2019 (2019)

15. Chakraborty, S., Raut, R.D., Rofin, T.M., Chakraborty, S.: A comprehensive and systematic review of multicriteria decision-making methods and applications in healthcare. Healthc. Anal. 100232 (2023). https://doi.org/10.1016/j.health.2023.100232

16. Oliveira, M.D., Mataloto, I., Kanavos, P.: Multicriteria decision analysis for health technology assessment: addressing methodological challenges to improve the state of the art. Eur. J. Health Econ. **20**, 891–918 (2019). https://doi.org/10.1007/s10198-019-01052-3

17. Aldrighetti, R., Zennaro, I., Finco, S., et al.: Healthcare supply chain simulation with disruption considerations: a case study from Northern Italy. Glob. J. Flex. . Manag. **20**(Suppl 1), 81–102 (2019). https://doi.org/10.1007/s40171-019-00223-8

18. Cadena, J.: Gestión del Pronóstico Estratégico: una herramienta de planificación en las empresas. CESA-Colegio de Estudios Superiores de Administración, Bogotá (2016)

19. Saaty, T.L.: The Analytical Hierarchy Process: Planning Priority Setting Resource Allocation. Mc Graw Hill, New York (1980)

20. Dowlatshahi, J.R.S.: A rule-based multicriteria approach to inventory classification. Int. J. Prod. Res. **48**(23), 7107–7126 (2010)

21. Papathanasiou, J., Ploskas, N.: Multiple Criteria Decision Aid. Springer Optimization and Its Applications. Springer, Cham (2018). https://doi.org/10.1007/978-3-319-91648-4

22. Hwang, C.L., Yoon, K.: Methods for multiple attribute decision making. In: Hwang, C.L., Yoon, K. (eds.) Multiple Attribute Decision Making: Methods and Applications: A State-of-the-Art Survey, pp. 58–191. Springer, Heidelberg (1981). https://doi.org/10.1007/978-3-642-48318-9_3

23. Aldaghi, T., Muzik, J.: Multicriteria decision-making in diabetes management and decision support: systematic review. JMIR Med. Inform. **12**, e47701 (2024). https://doi.org/10.2196/47701

24. Pehlivan, N.Y., Gürsoy, Z.: Determination of individuals' life satisfaction levels living in Turkey by FMCDM methods. Kybernetes **48**(8), 1871–1893 (2019)
25. Ortíz-Barrios, M., Gutiérrez-Severiche, E., Cómbita-Niño, D., Jiménez-Delgado, G., Ishizaka, A., Barbati, M., Herrera-Fontalvo, Z.: A multicriteria decision-making framework for assessing the performance of gynecobstetrics departments: a case study. Int. Trans. Oper. Res. **30**(1), 328–368 (2023). https://doi.org/10.1111/itor.12946
26. Jimenez, G.: Procedimientos para el mejoramiento de la calidad y la implantación de la Norma ISO 9001 aplicado al proceso de Asesoramiento, no. November, p. 22 (2016)
27. Ortíz-Barrios, M., Neira-Rodado, D., Jiménez-Delgado, G., Hernández-Palma, H.: Using FAHP-VIKOR for operation selection in the flexible job-shop scheduling problem: a case study in textile industry. In: Tan, Y., Shi, Y., Tang, Q. (eds.) ICSI 2018. LNCS, vol. 10942, pp. 189–201. Springer, Cham. https://doi.org/10.1007/978-3-319-93818-9_18
28. Jimenez-Delgado, G., Balmaceda-Castro, N., Hernández-Palma, H., de la Hoz-Franco, E., García-Guiliany, J., Martinez-Ventura, J.: An integrated approach of multiple correspondences Analysis (MCA) and fuzzy AHP method for occupational health and safety performance evaluation in the land cargo transportation. In: Duffy, V. (ed.) HCII 2019. LNCS (LNAI and LNB), vol. 11581, pp. 433–457. Springer, Cham (2019). https://doi.org/10.1007/978-3-030-22216-1_32/COVER.
29. Barrios, M.A.O., De Felice, F., Negrete, K.P., Romero, B.A., Arenas, A.Y., Petrillo, A.: An AHP-topsis integrated model for selecting the most appropriate tomography equipment. Int. J. Inf. Technol. Decis. Mak. **15**, 861–885 (2016). https://doi.org/10.1142/S021962201640006X
30. Jimenez-Delgado, G., et al.: Improving the performance in occupational health and safety management in the electric sector: an integrated methodology using fuzzy multicriteria approach. In: Duffy, V.G. (ed.) HCII 2020. LNCS, vol. 12199, pp. 130–158. Springer, Cham (2020). https://doi.org/10.1007/978-3-030-49907-5_10.
31. Jimenez, V.: Aplicación de metodología multicriterio para la priorización de los procesos objeto de costeo en entidades del sector de la salud. Libre Empresa, 2012, vol. 9, no. 1, pp. 99–123. Universidad del Valle (2029). https://bibliotecadigital.univalle.edu.co/server/api/core/bitstreams/c54224ae-820a-44a5-bb93-a73273963a9b/content
32. Lozada, A., Hernandez, C.: Propuesta de mejora de la gestión de inventarios de Medicamentos y dispositivos médicos tipo a de un hospital Nivel 2 de la ciudad de palmira en el área de farmacia.

AI and Well-Being: Enhancing Health, Happiness and Cultural Understanding

Takashi Kido[✉]

Teikyo University, Advanced Comprehensive Research Organization, 2-21-1 Kaga,
Itabashi-kuTokyo 173-0003, Japan
kido.takashi@gmail.com

Abstract. This study explores Well-being AI's potential to enhance human health, happiness, and cultural understanding through the application of artificial intelligence (AI). It examines the dual impact of digital technology on well-being—its benefits and challenges—including issues like data bias, the need for transparency, and the role of AI in fostering positive human cognition and lifestyle improvements. Moreover, this study addresses AI's societal implications, emphasizing its role in promoting diversity and addressing digital misinformation. We advocate for the ethical and socially responsible development of AI to support individual happiness and broader societal well-being.

Keywords: Well-being AI · machine-learning limitation · personalization technology · self-knowledge technology · happiness science

1 Introduction

At the threshold of the 21st century, the convergence of artificial intelligence (AI) and human existence has sparked profound inquiries into well-being, personal identity, and societal harmony. AI technologies, such as machine learning and natural language processing have left a significant imprint on various facets of our lives, including healthcare, education, entertainment, and communication. While these technologies have the potential to enhance human health and happiness, they also raise critical ethical and social issues that require attention.

For instance, AI-driven personalization tailors content to individual preferences, enriching user experiences; however, it can also create filter bubbles and echo chambers, limiting exposure to diverse viewpoints. Moreover, the use of AI in decision-making processes such as hiring and law enforcement has raised concerns about algorithmic bias and fairness. As we navigate this era of unprecedented digital transformation, the technology of self-knowledge, exemplified by advancements in AI-driven personalization and genetic analysis, has emerged as a vital area of exploration with far-reaching implications for society.

V. G. Duffy (Ed.): HCII 2024, LNCS 15376, pp. 93–102, 2025.
https://doi.org/10.1007/978-3-031-76809-5_7

This study delves into the nuanced dynamics between AI and humans, focusing on how self-knowledge technologies influence individual happiness and contribute to a broader understanding the diversity within society. We consider the potential of these technologies to foster a more inclusive world, in which differences are both tolerated and celebrated. Drawing upon the insights of leading thinkers and the latest research, we embark on a journey to unravel the complex relationship between technological innovation, personal fulfillment, and the collective well-being of humanity.

2 AI and Humans: Well-Being AI

2.1 Well-Being AI

Well-being AI, proposed within the AI community in 2016, aims to enhance human health, happiness, and potential [1–3]. This approach seeks to understand how digital technology impacts human health and sensibilities and aims to create information environments and healthier lifestyles and workplaces that address modern stresses and health issues (e.g., caffeine, fast food, information overload, loneliness, and sleep deprivation). This represents a venture into the frontier between AI, healthcare, and happiness studies, deeply engaging with the effects of AI and the digital information environment on human cognition, sensibility, health, and the essence of true happiness [2].

Figure 1 illustrates the scope of Well-being AI and its applications at the intersection of artificial intelligence and life sciences. This visual representation contextualizes Well-being AI's multifaceted impact on enhancing human health and happiness, highlighting key applications such as mental health monitoring, personalized medicine, and stress management techniques.

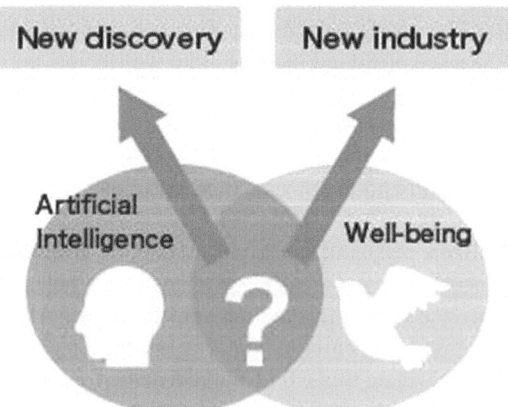

Fig. 1. Interdisciplinary area between Artificial Intelligence and Well-being

2.2 Machine Learning Techniques and Their Limitations

Machine learning allows computer programs to learn from data and extract patterns and rules to predict or classify new data. Deep learning, which is a subset of machine learning, utilizes multilayer neural networks for advanced feature extraction and pattern recognition. For instance, robots can learn to grasp cylinders with high success rates through deep learning, without pre-designed rules. Similarly, research on autonomous driving technology has employed machine learning to detect hazardous situations and automatically stop a vehicle.

Therefore, it is crucial to understand the limitations of machine learning. Recent advancements in statistical machine learning and deep learning, which predict the future based on past data, have led to challenges in forecasting unprecedented events. It is important to recognize that machine learning is not universally applicable. Biases in the training data and adversarial samples, which intentionally mislead AI by inducing subtle perturbations, present significant challenges. The discrepancy between human and computer cognition, where even minor noise can deceive computers, poses problems.

To address these issues, we aimed to explore new research areas, organizing the AAAI International Symposium almost annually at Stanford University for nearly a decade [5–8].

Bias in Machine Learning
Bias in the training data poses critical challenges to fairness and accuracy in machine learning systems. For example, facial recognition systems often exhibit racial bias, whereas hiring algorithms can exhibit gender bias. These biases arise from the data used to train these systems and may not adequately represent diverse populations. Recent research has focused on developing techniques to detect and mitigate bias, such as resampling methods, algorithm fairness constraints, and creation of more diverse training datasets. Additionally, adversarial samples, which are intentionally crafted inputs designed to deceive AI, pose another challenge. These samples exploited minor discrepancies in human and computer cognition, leading to significant errors.

Explainability in AI
Explainability of AI is critical for building trust and ensuring the reliability of AI systems. Many deep learning models operate as "black boxes," making it difficult to understand their decision-making processes. Recent research has focused on developing methods to make these models more transparent and interpretable, thereby helping users to understand and trust AI predictions. Techniques such as Local Interpretable Model-agnostic Explanations (LIME) and Shapley Additive Explanations (SHAP) provide insights into how AI models make decisions.

2.3 The Intersection of AI and Happiness Science Studies

In 2016, we hosted an international symposium to explore the intersection between AI and happiness studies. Following the passing of one of AI's founders, Minsky, his disciples attended his memorial service, revealing his aversion to the word "happiness." Minsky considered happiness not merely a temporary state but a continuous growth process.

We subsequently hosted a symposium titled "How Fair is Fair? Achieving Well-being AI," discussing the importance of fairness and reliability along with the challenges of data bias and evaluating true fairness. The relationship between human happiness and AI remains a key topic for discussion.

Efforts were made to use SoftBank's robots to study the impact of multitasking and human-robot relationships, highlighting the need for new metrics to address machine learning biases.

Explainability has also emerged as a crucial theme, with research progressing to demystify the black-box aspects of deep learning and clarify prediction rationales, aiming to make AI predictions more comprehensible [3].

3   Toward Culturally Situated AI

3.1   Culturally Situated AI

Culturally Situated AI refers to cooperative systems that cooperate with users by adapting to their diverse cultural backgrounds, including diverse languages, beliefs, personalities, motivations, common knowledge, and values. These systems aim to enable software agents and robots to effectively interact with users from different cultural backgrounds.

3.2   Why Culturally Situated Systems Are Needed

At the AAAI-sponsored workshop "Socially Intelligent Agents" held in Boston in 1997, the social capabilities that future software and robots should possess were discussed. For agents to integrate into human society they require not only IQ but also interpersonal (EQ) and social intelligence.

3.3   High Context Culture vs Low Context Culture

To promote intercultural collaboration, it is essential to understand the essence of human-to-human communication. Culture influences every aspect of human personality, communication style, thought processes, values, knowledge, perception, and cognition. The P-F Study, a personality diagnostic method, analyzes how individuals react to different situations depicted in pictures and is used in cultural comparison research. While individual responses vary, interesting results have shown that cultural and linguistic differences affect behavioral patterns.

Understanding the unspoken context is vital for intercultural understanding. Context refers to all physical, social, and temporal environments in which communication occurs (atmosphere, non-verbal meanings, connections with the other person, etc.). In high-context cultures, such as Japan, collectivism and uniformity prevail, and implicit and abstract language expressions and subtle gestures are common ("Silence is golden"). In contrast, in low-context cultures such as the United States, individualism and diversity are developed, and logical, concrete language expressions and bold gestures are prevalent ("Eloquence is golden").

Figure 2 illustrates the differences between high- and low-context cultures.

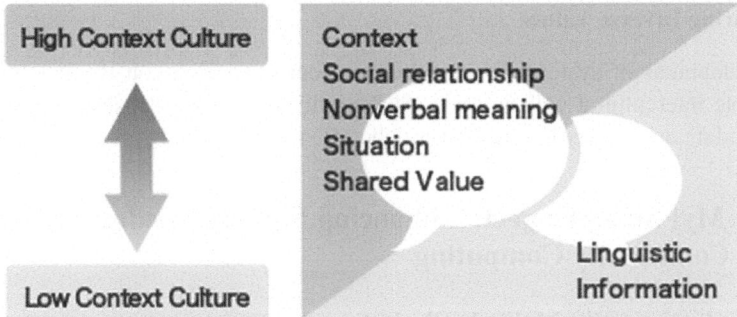

Fig. 2. High Context Culture vs Low Context Culture

From the perspective of information sharing, it is crucial to understand how much context is shared within a community and how to resolve different interpretations when they arise.

3.4 Adaptive Information Retrieval

Information retrieval should be adapted to an individual's interests, search history, location, and shared community knowledge. This process requires the construction of knowledge and concept systems (ontologies) that should be performed collaboratively within the community to ensure consistency and growth.

3.5 Adaptive Interfaces

Designing interfaces that elicit emotional empathy and engagement is essential. Cultural backgrounds influence nonverbal communication, such as facial expressions and gestures. Effective interfaces account for these differences and provide emotional resonance to the users.

3.6 Community Formation

The formation of online communities allows diverse people to collaborate. Social filtering techniques can be used to leverage evaluations of others with similar preferences. In addition, modeling negotiation and consensus-building processes are essential, enabling autonomous agents to negotiate in cyberspace.

3.7 Discussions at International Workshops

In November 1998, the author hosted an international workshop on "Issues on Cross-Cultural Communication: Toward Culturally Situated Agents" in Singapore. The importance of cross-cultural communication and collaboration was also discussed. The workshop shared specific application examples and technological breakthroughs to promote intercultural collaboration.

3.8 Sharing Diverse Values

The development of systems for collaborative content ratings on the internet aims to promote intercultural collaboration. Sharing diverse values and deepening mutual understanding are the key to effective collaboration and knowledge creation.

4   The MyFinder Project: Enhancing Self-Knowledge and Community Computing

4.1   Introduction to the MyFinder Project

The MyFinder Project has two primary goals. The first goal is to identify and maximize innate potential and individual characteristics (individual approach). The second goal is to create a research platform aimed at scientific discoveries through community computing (collective intelligence approach).

4.2   Framework of the MyFinder Project

We believe that constructing a personal genomic information environment will bridge the theoretical and practical domains of artificial intelligence and genetic research. The MyFinder Project is a new research framework that integrates the concept of intelligent agents in AI research with a community-driven genetic research approach for disease-related gene discovery.

Figure 3 illustrates the framework of the MyFinder Project, showing the integration of AI and genetic research to enhance personal and community well-being.

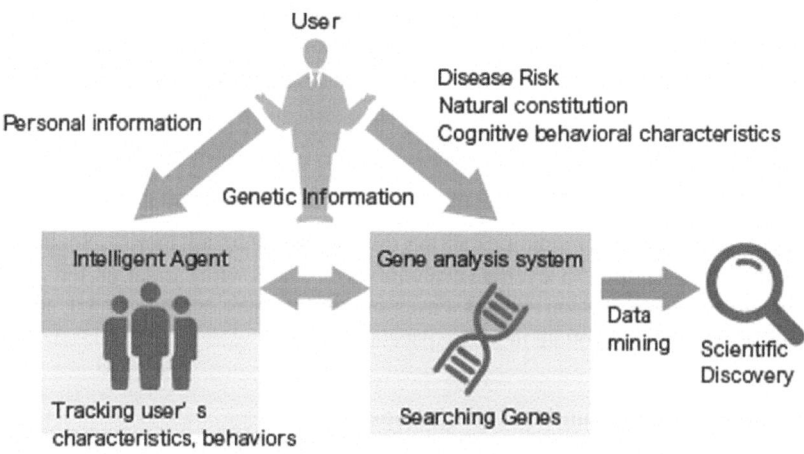

Fig. 3. Framework of MyFinder project

4.3 Individual Approach: Unleashing Innate Potential

One of the goals of the MyFinder Project is to discover and maximize individuals' inherent traits, strengths, and talents. Unlike recent personal genome research, which primarily focuses on personalized medicine, MyFinder emphasizes wellness, mental health, and behavioral science.

This project hypothesizes that physical, chemical, and psychological stresses have significant effects on gene activity, drawing on recent findings in gene expression regulation   and epigenomics. For example, recent studies have reported that laughing can effectively treat diabetes, suggesting that the positive psychological stress from laughing may be involved in the genetic switch that controls gene expression at the cellular level.

By continuously monitoring and analyzing daily physical, chemical, and psychological stress using intelligent agents, we can better understand and manage stress. Intelligent agent technology can effectively learn individual behavioral characteristics and stress states.

4.4 Collective Intelligence Approach: Community Computing for Scientific Discovery

The second goal of the MyFinder Project is to establish a research platform for scientific discovery using community computing. Similar concepts have been explored by initiatives such as 23andMe, which encourages individuals to voluntarily participate in genetic research, potentially leading to groundbreaking discoveries that benefit public health.

In contrast to 23andMe's static surveys for phenotype data collection, MyFinder aims to gather reliable phenotype data using intelligent agents and interactive and intimate interfaces. For example, MyFinder seeks to learn users' personalities by monitoring their daily behavior and providing insights based on psychological and behavioral science theories, such as Enneagram.

This feature helps individuals rediscover their innate potential and unique characteristics, contributing to personal growth and self-awareness.

5 Artificial Intelligence and the Future of Humanity: Considering Self-knowledge Technologies

5.1 Personalization Technology

My particular interest lies in personalization technology, which uses individual information to infer each user's preferences and characteristics and offers tailored information and recommendations. For example, Google's search results vary based on an individual's history, considering location data and past search keywords to present appropriate information. Social media and online shopping also utilize past purchase histories for individual recommendations.

The challenge in Internet advertising is to increase click-through rates, with advertisers developing methods to display ads tailored to individual users.

Recent research has demonstrated the capability to accurately discern political party support based solely on facial features, such as predicting Republican or Democratic support the use of deep learning to analyze over a million facial photos. Advancements in such technologies raises questions regarding their societal impact.

5.2 Fake News, Filter Bubbles, and Echo Chambers

I have a strong interest in the fake news phenomenon, believing that it is crucial to elucidate the process by which false beliefs arise via cognitive biases. This issue is relevant to data science education, as it explores the impact of new information environments on human cognition. The impact of new information environments on human cognition is an essential theme in the evolution of human society.

For example, Google's search engine prioritizes the ability to input appropriate keywords over memorization. How do changes in the information environment affect cognition?

The filter-bubble phenomenon arises from personalization technologies that filter vast amounts of information from the Internet based on user preferences. These technologies potentially narrow an individual's perspective by limiting their exposure to other information. Figure 4 shows a conceptual diagram of the personalization technology and filter bubbles.

The echo chamber phenomenon in social networks, in which users are primarily exposed to opinions that mirror their own, potentially exacerbates societal division. In this diagram, algorithms that learn users' personal information filter vast amounts of information from the Internet and extract content that is likely to be of interest to them. In the filter-bubble phenomenon, these algorithms present highly specialized information based on personal interests. As the personalized algorithm continues to learn from the user's preferences, the loop reinforces the filter, resulting in narrowing of the user's exposure to diverse information. While personalization offers convenience, it may narrow one's perspective by limiting access to diverse information.

Related research, including studies by Facebook researchers, has explored the echo chamber effect, however, the results have not yet been conclusive. Different viewpoints and hypotheses may exist, underscoring the importance of continued research and discussion one these issues.

5.3 Technology of Self-knowledge: Does Knowing Oneself Lead to Happiness?

Whether self-knowledge technologies such as personalization and genetic analysis, lead to happiness varies among individuals. Genetic analysis, used for predicting diseases and selecting medications, is expected to reduce healthcare costs but also raises ethical debates. In non-medical fields, opinions differ regarding the use of this knowledge for educational purposes and for calling for regulation. As we move forward, the ability to envision the future of technological innovation and share diverse values to address problems becomes increasingly important.

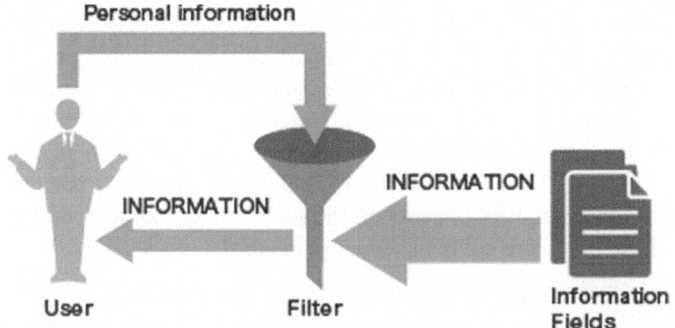

Fig. 4. Concept of Personalization Technology and Filter Bubble

6 Toward a Society that Respects Diversity

Finally, I pose a question regarding diversity. Dr. Temple Grandin, who is on the autism spectrum, has illuminated the differences in perception and thought characteristics of individuals with autism through her encounters with science, conveying the message that these should not be viewed as illnesses but as individualities that society should recognize and utilize to enrich diversity. As research in neuroscience and genetics advances and reveals the scientific nuances of individual differences, we are left to ponder the impact these discoveries will have on society.

The philosophy of respecting diversity involves acknowledging and valuing people's beliefs and perspectives. This idea suggests that innovative concepts may emerge by combining diverse viewpoints and insights to enhance societal cohesion and mutual understanding.

Additionally, there is a viewpoint aimed at reducing the risks of discrimination and prejudice, which often stem from stereotypes and fixed notions. Such attitudes can result in social disadvantages for specific groups or individuals, potentially leading to societal divisions and tension.

Respecting diversity means recognizing differences as opportunities to foster innovation and collaboration, while discrimination and prejudice reduce these differences to grounds for exclusion and inequality. Although these concepts often appear in opposition, in reality, respect for diversity and the presence of discrimination and prejudice can coexist within society, and neither concept is inherently "good" or "bad."

Personally, I believe it's crucial to value differences and move towards a direction that respects diversity ("It's good to be different"), though various viewpoints exist. We hope to continue this discussion in future.

7 Conclusion

As we stand at the crossroads between technological innovation and social evolution, the difference between AI and human well-being underscores the critical narrative of our time. The exploration of self-knowledge technologies reveals a dual-edged sword capable of enhancing individual happiness and amplifying societal diversity, which is fraught with ethical dilemmas and the potential to exacerbate existing disparities. This paper has argued for a balanced approach to AI development that prioritizes ethical considerations, respects individual differences, and actively works towards dismantling the barriers of prejudice and discrimination. The future of AI and humanity, as we have seen, is not predetermined but a canvas we collectively paint. By embracing the richness of diversity and harnessing the power of AI for the greater good, we pave the way for a future that respects and uplifts all members the society. This journey, while challenging, holds the promise of a more equitable and joyful world.

Future Research Directions
Future research should focus on developing AI systems that are not only technically robust but also socially responsible. This includes exploring to mitigate AI bias, enhancing the explainability of AI systems, and ensuring that AI technologies are accessible and beneficial to diverse populations. Interdisciplinary collaboration between technologists, ethicists, and social scientists is crucial in addressing the complex ethical and societal issues surrounding AI.

Acknowledgments. We would like to thank the AAAI Spring 2023 and 2024 program committees for their assistance.

References

1. Kido, T., Takadama, K.: Special issues on Well-being Computing. J. Jpn. Soc. Artif. Intell. **32**(1), 79 80 (2017)
2. Kido, T., Swan, M.: Machine learning and personal genome informatics contribute to happiness science and wellbeing computing. In: The AAAI (The Association for the Advancement of Artificial Intelligence) 2016 Spring Symposia, Wellbeing Computing: AI Meets Health and Happiness Science (2016)
3. Maruyama, H., Kido, T.: Introduction for machine learning engineering. J. Jpn. Soc. Artif. Intell. **33**(2), Special Issue on "AI and Data - Data-Driven Decision Making and Society Innovation Creation" (Ed. By, T. Kido and T. Hayashi), pp. 124–131 (2018)
4. Baldini, I., et al.: AI Magazine **40**(3) (2019). Reports of the AAAI 2019 Spring Symposium Series, FALL 2019, pp. 61–62 (2019)
5. Kido, T., Takadama, K.: AAAI 23 Spring Symposium Report on "Socially Responsible AI for Well-Bing". AI Mag. **44**(2), Summer 2023, pp. 211–212 (2023)
6. Kido, T., Takadama, K.: The challenges for fairness and well-being: how fair is fair? Achieving well-being AI. In: The AAAI 2022 Spring Symposium, How Fair is Fair? Achieving Wellbeing AI, Stanford, CA, 21–23 March 2022, pp. 1–3 (2022)
7. Kido, T., Takadama, K.: The challenges for interpretable AI for well-being -understanding cognitive bias and social embeddedness. In: AAAI 2019 Spring symposia, Interpretable AI for Well-Being: Understanding Cognitive Bias and Social Embeddedness, Stanford, CA, 25–27 March 2019
8. Kido, T., Oono, K., Swan, M.: The challenges for machine learning and subjective computing in well-being AI. In: The AAAI 2017 Spring symposia, Wellbeing AI: From Machine Learning to Subjectivity Oriented Computing, Stanford, CA, 27–29 March 2017, p. 751 (2017)

Analyzing the Interplay of Visual and Auditory Stimuli on Human Physiology and Stress Levels in Virtual Environment

Yik Junn Kuan[1], Mahdiyeh Sadat Moosavi[2]([⊠]), Christophe Guillet[3]([⊠]), Angelina Seow Voon Yee[1]([⊠]), and Frédéric Merienne[2]([⊠])

[1] School of Computing, Asia Pacific University of Technology and Innovation, Kuala Lumpur, Malaysia
{kuan.yikjunn,angelina.yee}@apu.edu.my
[2] Arts et Metiers Institute of Technology, LISPEN, HESAM Université, 71100 Chalon-Sur-Saone, France
{mahdiyehsadat.moosavi,frederic.merienne}@ensam.eu
[3] Universite de Bourgogne, LISPEN, UBFC, 71100 Chalon-Sur-Saone, France
Christophe.Guillet@u-bourgogne.fr

Abstract. This investigation extends prior research on the impact of audio stimuli in Virtual Reality (VR) environments, with an enhanced focus on understanding the relationship between audio stimuli and the level of immersion, as indicated by stress levels. Using the State-Trait Anxiety Inventory (STAI) for psychological assessment and heart rate variability for physiological responses, this study examines the interplay of visual and auditory stimuli across four diverse VR scenarios. These scenarios include combinations of city and forest environments paired alternately with matching and contrasting auditory cues. Correlation analysis was employed to determine how audio stimuli influence the level of immersion, reflected through variations in heart rate and STAI-derived stress indicators. Participants' responses were continuously monitored for real-time physiological effects, while stress assessments were conducted after exposure to each scenario. This methodical approach aims to uncover significant sensory interactions that affect immersion in VR, potentially guiding the design and application of VR technologies across various disciplines.

Keywords: Virtual Reality · Audio Stimuli · Visual Stimuli · Heart Rate · Correlation Analysis

1 Introduction

Virtual Reality (VR) has emerged as a powerful tool for exploring human responses to diverse environments, with applications ranging from entertainment to therapeutic interventions [1]. The importance of VR lies in its ability to revolutionize the way we perceive and interact with digital content. Unlike traditional media formats, VR enables users to fully immerse themselves in virtual environments, providing a sense of presence

© The Author(s), under exclusive license to Springer Nature Switzerland AG 2025
V. G. Duffy (Ed.): HCII 2024, LNCS 15376, pp. 103–117, 2025.
https://doi.org/10.1007/978-3-031-76809-5_8

and embodiment that is unparalleled [22]. This immersion allows users to explore new worlds, learn complex concepts, and engage in realistic simulations that would be otherwise inaccessible in the physical world [2, 3]. In the field of entertainment and gaming, VR offers unprecedented levels of immersion and interactivity, allowing users to step into the shoes of their favorite characters and experience thrilling adventures first-hand. VR has redefined the immersive experience, offering users a new level of realism and engagement that traditional platforms cannot match [7, 8]. Beyond entertainment, VR holds immense potential for applications in healthcare, where it can be used for medical training, rehabilitation, and therapy. VR simulations can recreate realistic medical scenarios, providing healthcare professionals with valuable hands-on training in a safe and controlled environment. Additionally, VR-based therapies have shown promising results in treating various mental health conditions, such as anxiety disorders and phobias, by exposing patients to virtual stimuli in a controlled and therapeutic manner [12]. As VR technology continues to evolve and become more accessible, its potential to shape the future of entertainment, healthcare, education, and beyond is limitless.

In the realm of virtual reality (VR), one of the most compelling aspects experienced by users is the sense of presence—a feeling of being fully immersed and present within the virtual environment [6]. The concept of presence refers to the extent to which users perceive themselves to be physically and mentally present in the virtual world, despite knowing that it is artificially generated. This phenomenon is central to the effectiveness and success of VR experiences, as it directly influences user engagement, enjoyment, and the overall quality of the virtual experience [15]. The importance of sense of presence in VR cannot be overstated. It serves as a fundamental indicator of the level of immersion achieved by VR technology, determining the degree to which users suspend disbelief and perceive the virtual environment as real [5]. When users experience a strong sense of presence in VR, they are more likely to feel emotionally connected to the virtual world, leading to enhanced levels of engagement and immersion [4, 9]. Sense of presence is crucial for various applications of VR, including entertainment, gaming, education, training, therapy, and beyond [16]. In the realm of entertainment and gaming, a strong sense of presence can elevate the gaming experience, allowing players to feel as if they are truly part of the virtual world. This heightened immersion can lead to increased enjoyment, satisfaction, and retention, ultimately making VR games more compelling and memorable. Therefore, the importance of sense of presence in VR lies in its ability to create immersive and impactful experiences that transcend the limitations of traditional media. While VR offering various advantages, one of the primary concern deals with prolonged exposure in virtual environment which leads to motion sickness [17].

Building upon past research [27] examining the influence of audio-visual conflicts on anxiety levels in VR users, this extended study delves into the correlations between various virtual environments and their respective impacts on individuals' heart rates. Understanding these correlations can provide valuable insights into the intricate relationship between immersive virtual experiences and physiological responses.

2 Background

As the study delve into the analysis, the correlations among four different scenarios were examined to identify the potential linear relationship between visual and audio influence towards the subject responses. These correlations aim to provide better insights into the complex interplay between immersive virtual experiences and the human physiology. The hypotheses are grounded in the expectation that scenarios featuring identical stimuli, whether in a stressful city or a calm forest, were expected to exhibit either positive or no correlations with participants' heart rates. The results of correlation analysis underline the importance of audio stimuli in environments. In detail, participants heart rate tends to respond proportionally on calming sound of the forest regardless of visual environment [24]. Meanwhile, in different scenario of similar audio environment of city regardless of visual environment, the heart rate of participants varied with no influence towards the heart rate, suggested that in stressful environment the participants tend to react independently. Lastly, in contradicting environments whereby both visual of the city and forest with the sound of forest and city respectively, the environment tends to be somehow influenced the heart rate of participants due to auditory dominance factor.

This study endeavors to bridge this gap by offering a detailed investigation of visual and audio environments using the heart rates and STAI results. This study provides a more meaningful insights to VR experiences working in different applications including therapeutic interventions, stress management, and the development of personalized virtual experiences. The findings may provide a roadmap and guideline for optimizing the design of VR environments based on the impact on human physiology and psychology, therefore shaping the future of VR applications.

Overall, the motivation behind this study is to advance our understanding of multisensory integration in virtual environments and its impact on user experiences. By investigating the complex interplay between visual and auditory stimuli and their effects on user physiology and emotion, we aim to contribute to the development of more engaging, user-centered, and effective VR applications.

2.1 State-Trait Anxiety Inventory Survey

Many studies use questionnaires to assess the sense of presence experienced by users in virtual environments. These questionnaires typically include items that measure various aspects of presence, such as spatial presence (feeling of being physically present in the virtual environment), involvement (degree of engagement and absorption), and emotional engagement (emotional connection to the virtual experience). Examples of such questionnaires include the Presence Questionnaire (PQ) and the Immersive Experience Questionnaire (IEQ) [18]. Using this method could be not reliable as the results tend to be inconsistent as the responses provided by the participants is subjective, and we should avoid one fit size all methodology for measuring sense of presence. However, we believe that using questionnaires that are relevant to the concept of virtual environment are still could be helpful and provide important information about deep feelings of the participants that they experienced during experiment. For instance, for assessing the level of stress and anxiety of the participants we asked them to fill State-Trait Anxiety Inventory (STAI) [28]. The State-Trait Anxiety Inventory (STAI) is an essential instrument in psychological evaluation, designed to measure anxiety in adults and differentiated into two distinct scales: the State Anxiety Scale and the Trait Anxiety Scale. State Anxiety Scale, assesses transient feelings of anxiety influenced by situational factors, using 20 items to gauge immediate feelings of tension, apprehension, and nervousness. On the other hand, anxiety Scale Measures anxiety as a persistent personal characteristic, with 20 items evaluating general feelings of anxiety and stress experienced on a regular basis. In this experiment we used the State Anxiety Scale.

2.2 Physiological Measure

Researchers also employ physiological measures, such as heart rate variability, skin conductance, and electroencephalography (EEG), to assess the sense of presence [19]. Changes in physiological responses, such as increased heart rate or skin conductance, can indicate heightened arousal and immersion in the virtual environment [14]. EEG studies have shown differences in brain activity patterns between immersive and non-immersive virtual experiences, providing insights into the neural correlates of presence [10].

2.3 Behavioral Observations

Observational studies involve observing users' behaviors and interactions within the virtual environment to assess their sense of presence. Researchers analyze factors such as user movements, gaze patterns, and verbal expressions to infer the level of immersion and engagement experienced by participants [22]. For example, prolonged exploration of the virtual environment, active interaction with virtual objects, and expressions of surprise or enjoyment may indicate a strong sense of presence.

2.4 Neuroimaging Techniques

Advances in neuroimaging techniques, such as functional magnetic resonance imaging (fMRI) and functional near-infrared spectroscopy (fNIRS), have enabled researchers to investigate the neural mechanisms underlying the sense of presence [26]. Neuroimaging studies have identified brain regions associated with presence, such as the prefrontal cortex, parietal cortex, and limbic system, shedding light on the cognitive processes involved in immersive experiences.

2.5 Virtual Reality Technologies

Researchers also utilize advancements in virtual reality technologies, such as head-mounted displays (HMDs), haptic feedback devices, and motion tracking systems, to enhance the sense of presence in virtual environments. By integrating multisensory cues, such as visual, auditory, tactile, and proprioceptive feedback, VR systems can create more realistic and immersive experiences, leading to a stronger sense of presence among users.

3   Contributions

Although there are many studies [1, 8] have been conducted on the visual and audio stimuli in virtual environment, there is limited understanding of how these environments influence user experience and effect of cross-modal sensory integration in virtual reality. Therefore, our study intends to fill in the gap by comparing participants' responses to scenarios set in natural (forest) and urban (city) environments, shedding light on the unique effects of each environment on user experience. The contribution of this paper is as follow:

3.1   New Insight of Multisensory Integration

This study contributes to the understanding of how humans integrate visual and auditory stimuli in virtual environments. By examining the correlation between different combinations of visual and auditory cues and participants' physiological responses, we provide insights into the mechanisms of multisensory integration in immersive experiences.

3.2   Impact Study of Physiological Knowledge Towards Immersive Experiences

The findings of this study have practical implications for the design of virtual reality (VR) environments. By demonstrating the impact of congruent and conflicting visual and auditory stimuli on participants' physiological responses, we offer guidance for VR developers in creating more immersive and engaging experiences.

3.3   New Insight on Factors Affecting Sense of Presence

This research contributes to the broader goal of enhancing user engagement and immersion in virtual environments. By identifying scenarios that elicit synchronized physiological responses and exploring the role of sensory consistency in shaping user experiences, we provide valuable insights into factors that contribute to a sense of presence and immersion in VR.

3.4   Offer Understanding on User Interaction with Immersive Technologies

This study contributes to the field of Human-Computer Interaction (HCI) by examining the complex interplay between sensory stimuli and human physiological responses in virtual environments. By applying principles of psychology and human perception to VR design, we advance our understanding of how users interact with immersive technologies. This research informs the design of future HCI systems and contributes to the development of more user-centered and effective interactive experiences.

4   Methodology

In audio and visual integration, human perceive information through sensory information such as visual and audio. Studies has shown that the information received in virtual environment may affect user responses [9, 13, 21]. Therefore, the requirements considered are based on the experiment that has been conducted in [27].

4.1 Volunteer Participant

A total of 15 participants, consisting of six women and nine men consented to participate in the study. The participants are from diverse background, and all of them did not suffer from any health-related issues.

4.2 Software and Hardware

The simulation of virtual environment involves the development of both city and forest environment using Unity 3D. In terms of hardware or any related devices for simulation, HTC Vive Pro headset and Empatica E4 bracelet to measure physiological data was used.

4.3 Environment Setting

To simulate the subject responses toward the environment, additional elements was considered. In the city environment, loud and disturbing sound was added such as ambulance, car, and dog barking. In terms of visual representation, the case of building on fire, chaotic pedestrian running on the streets and intense raining were used. The brightness setting was set to dim to simulate nighttime brightness. In forest environment, sound of nature such as forest, lake, wind, and animal movements including flying bird were included. As for the visual representation, lake view from a hut, and forest view from another hut were included in the simulation. The brightness setting was set to bright to simulate daytime (Figs. 1 and 2).

Fig. 1. City environment which consists of stressful elements such as dog barking, building on fire, etc.

Fig. 2. Forest environment which consists of relax elements such as nature scenery, sound of wind blowing, etc.

5   Experiments

Before the experiment, physiological data from participants were recorded. Participants were required to experience both environments for fixed duration which passed through certain points. This ensures each participant experienced the visual and audio effect in both environments. Participants were presented with two different scenarios and given three and half minutes to experience a scenario. In between changing of scenario, participants were given two minutes break. The two scenarios are stated as follow.

5.1   Reference Condition

In this scenario, participants were experiencing actual visual element with related to audio environment. For example, the visual of city environment with audio of city environment or the visual of forest environment with audio of forest environment.

5.2   Conflict Condition

In this scenario, participants were experiencing contradiction in between visual and audio elements. For example, the visual of city environment with audio of forest environment or the visual of forest environment with audio of city environment.

6   Results

In this study, two experiments were conducted. The results section provides a detailed analysis of the physiological and psychological data collected from participants during the virtual reality (VR) experiments. This section is divided into two main parts: physiological data, including heart rate (HR) measurements, and psychological data, focusing on anxiety levels as measured by the State-Trait Anxiety Inventory (STAI). The findings highlight how different combinations of visual and auditory stimuli in VR environments affect participants' heart rates and anxiety levels, offering insights into the interplay between sensory inputs and physiological responses. The statistical analyses, including one-way ANOVA and correlation analyses, reveal patterns and relationships that help to understand the impact of sensory congruence and incongruence on the participants' experience.

6.1 Physiological Data

The findings will involve physiological data from participants such as the average heart rate (HR) after experiencing different environments and conditions. In this experiment, the correlation analysis between various conditions were formed to link the possibilities of any relevant hypothesis that were suggested.

The average HR of participants was recorded as shown in Table 1. City reference refers to the visual of city with the sound of city. City conflict refers to the visual of city with the sound of forest. Forest reference refers to the visual of forest with sound of forest and forest conflict refers to the visual of forest with the sound of city.

Table 1. Average heartbeat of participants in various conditions.

Participant	City Reference	City Conflict	Forest Reference	Forest Conflict
1	69.02	64.27	61.04	86.73
2	77.62	70.52	75.00	73.13
3	63.12	76.20	74.81	69.36
4	67.53	65.43	63.91	66.67
5	72.65	57.59	54.62	58.83
6	68.52	68.80	68.10	68.22
7	73.17	75.46	72.18	72.75
8	78.33	77.63	74.67	74.49
9	71.73	65.69	66.31	66.49
10	72.17	77.59	71.62	79.34
11	95.59	71.30	75.18	70.54
12	72.76	75.21	78.34	79.80

In city reference condition, average HR was recorded at 73.52 which is the highest among other conditions. Meanwhile, in forest reference condition recorded the lowest average HR of 69.65 among other conditions. The average HR for city conflict and forest conflict were recorded at 70.47 and 72.20 respectively. The one-way ANOVA test with the p-value greater than 0.05 did not indicate any statistical difference between city and forest environment in different conditions.

Using the existing results, a comprehensive hypothesis can be determined based on correlation between city and forest environment as presented in Table 2. Through the inspection of heartbeat rate, the participants reaction between reference and conflict conditions can be identified using correlation analysis.

Table 2. Correlation analysis between various conditions.

Correlation	City Reference	City Conflict	Forest Reference	Forest Conflict
City Reference	1.00000	0.11481	0.32623	0.00239
City Conflict	0.11481	1.00001	0.88660	0.45463
Forest Reference	0.32623	0.88660	1.00000	0.36381
Forest Conflict	0.00239	0.45463	0.36381	1.00000

Upon finding the average HR in various conditions, it was noticeable in terms of correlation between different set of environments. In this experiment, the correlation ranges from negative one to one, where a correlation closer to one indicates a strong positive correlation, while negative one indicates strong negative correlation. The value close to zero indicates weak correlation.

The correlation between city reference and city conflict is 0.11481 which suggest weak positive correlation. Correlation between city reference and forest reference is 0.326623 indicates moderate positive correlation between the conditions. As for correlation between city reference and forest reference, the value of 0.00239 which very close to zero suggest that there is no correlation between the conditions. Meanwhile, city conflict and forest reference shows there is a very strong positive correlation with the value of 0.88659. The correlation between city conflict and forest conflict shows positive moderate correlation of 0.454633 while the correlation between forest reference and forest conflict also indicates moderate positive correlation of 0.36813.

6.2 State Anxiety Scale

The State-Trait Anxiety Inventory (STAI) was administered to assess the anxiety levels of participants across four different simulated environments (see Table 3). The results reveal variations in state anxiety scores, which appear to be influenced by the auditory environment coupled with the visual settings.

City Reference Environment. The City Reference condition, where participants were exposed to both visual and auditory urban elements, recorded the highest mean anxiety score of 52.92 (SD = 13.89) among the four conditions, with scores ranging from 25 to 71. This suggests a heightened level of anxiety potentially induced by the bustling urban environment.

City with Forest Sound. In contrast, when urban visuals were paired with forest sounds, the mean anxiety score decreased to 44.00 (SD = 13.47), with a range from 20 to 63. This reduction may indicate a soothing effect of natural sounds on anxiety, even when paired with a visually urban setting.

Table 3. Results of State trait Anxiety Inventory for participants in different conditions.

Environment	Mean	Standard Deviation	Range
City Reference	52.92	13.89	25 to 71
City Conflict	44.00	13.4	20 to 63
Forest Reference	34.57	10.68	20 to 57
Forest Conflict	47.08	12.30	24 to 63

Forest Reference Environment. The Forest Reference condition, featuring both forest visuals and sounds, showed the lowest mean anxiety score at 34.57 (SD = 10.68), ranging from 20 to 57. This underscores the potential calming influence of natural environments on participant anxiety levels.

Forest with City Sound. Introducing urban sounds to a forest visual environment resulted in a mean anxiety score of 47.08 (SD = 12.30), with scores ranging from 24 to 63. The increase in anxiety scores compared to the Forest Reference suggests that urban noise may disrupt the tranquil effect typically associated with natural settings.

7   Analysis and Discussion

In this study, the correlation analysis investigated the relationship between various virtual reality (VR) scenarios and participants' heart rates. The assumptions were grounded in the expectation that different combinations of visual and auditory stimuli would elicit distinct physiological responses, as reflected in the correlation coefficients as shown in Table 2. From this analysis, several hypotheses were stated.

7.1   Heightened Sense of Immersion

Scenarios featuring congruent visual and audio stimuli in both city and forest environments (city reference and forest reference) exhibited a moderate positive correlation (correlation: 0.326227). This indicates that participants' heart rates tended to fluctuate together in scenarios where visual and auditory cues aligned. Based on this observation, it can be hypothesized that congruent sensory inputs contribute to a heightened sense of immersion and presence, resulting in synchronized physiological responses across participants [4].

7.2   Auditory Influence in Cognitive Dissonance

In this scenario, when participants experienced congruent visual and audio stimuli in the city environments (city reference and city conflict), it can be observed a weak positive correlation (correlation: 0.114808). This suggests that while the city visuals remained consistent, the conflicting audio may have elicited a mild effect on participants' heart rates. It's plausible to hypothesize that incongruent auditory cues in urban settings could lead to a cognitive dissonance, resulting in a subtle increase in physiological arousal compared to scenarios with congruent stimuli [21, 23]. This supports the assumption that auditory stimuli may exert a greater influence, albeit mild, on heart rates compared to scenarios with congruent stimuli. The presence of conflicting auditory cues in the city environment appears to have a discernible, albeit subtle, effect on participants' heart rates when contrasted with scenarios featuring congruent audio-visual stimuli. Besides, scenarios involving conflicting auditory stimuli in forest environments (forest reference and forest conflict) displayed a moderate positive correlation (correlation: 0.363813). This finding suggests that when participants are immersed in a naturalistic forest setting with incongruent auditory cues, their heart rates exhibit a moderate level of association. This correlation may be attributed to the complex interaction between visual and auditory stimuli in shaping participants' physiological responses. While the soothing visuals of the forest may induce a sense of calmness, the incongruent auditory cues may introduce a degree of cognitive dissonance, leading to a moderate level of physiological arousal.

7.3 Visual Dominance in Stressful Environment

Moving on to scenarios featuring conflicting visual and audio stimuli in forest environments (forest conflict) and congruent visual and audio stimuli in the city environments (city reference), a negligible correlation was observed (correlation: 0.002385). This finding suggests that the weak correlation between the scenario involving congruent city audio but different visual stimuli and the scenario with conflicting city audio and forest visuals indicates that participants' heart rate variations may primarily depend on the visual environment when exposed to stressful auditory cues, such as city sounds. Despite the incongruence between auditory and visual stimuli in the forest conflict scenario, participants' heart rates may not significantly differ from those observed in the city reference scenario. This suggests that in the presence of stressful auditory cues, participants' physiological responses are predominantly influenced by visual stimuli rather than auditory cues.

7.4 Auditory Dominance in Relax Environment

In contrast, scenarios involving congruent visual and auditory stimuli in forest environments (forest reference) with conflicting visual and audio in city (city conflict) displayed a strong positive correlation (correlation: 0.886591). This result underscores the significant impact of congruent sensory cues on participants' physiological responses as supported in [23]. This high positive correlation suggests that participants' heart rates exhibit synchronized fluctuations when exposed to congruent auditory stimuli in both city and forest environments, despite conflicting visual cues. The significant correlation underscores the profound impact of comforting auditory stimuli, such as the calming sound of the forest, on participants' heart rate responses. This finding emphasizes the dominant influence of auditory cues in shaping physiological responses, even in the presence of conflicting visual stimuli. When participants are immersed in a serene forest environment with matching auditory stimuli, their heart rates show a highly synchronized pattern of fluctuation. This alignment between visual and auditory stimuli may evoke a sense of tranquility and presence, leading to a cohesive physiological response characterized by elevated heart rates [24].

7.5 Increase Anxiety in Conflicting Visual and Audio Stimuli

Scenarios featuring conflicting visual and auditory stimuli between city and forest environments (city conflict and forest conflict) exhibited a moderate positive correlation (correlation: 0.454633). This finding suggests that when participants are exposed to cross-modal sensory incongruence, their heart rates demonstrate a discernible association. The moderate correlation observed in these scenarios may be indicative of the interplay between conflicting sensory cues and participants' physiological arousal. The discrepancy between the visual and auditory environments may lead to heightened cognitive processing and emotional arousal, resulting in a more synchronized physiological response [11, 20, 25]. Hence, it shows that conflicting auditory cues may have a noticeable influence on participants' anxiety levels. The significant correlation also suggests that auditory dominance plays a pivotal role in shaping participants' emotional responses in virtual environments, highlighting the importance of considering auditory stimuli in designing immersive experiences.

7.6 Influence of Sensory Congruence on Anxiety Levels

The State-Trait Anxiety Inventory (STAI) results, together with physiological data on heart rates, offer significant insights into how matching audio and visual stimuli impact emotional and physiological states. The study highlights several key findings:

In the City Reference Condition, where both visuals and sounds were urban, the highest anxiety scores were noted. This suggests that urban environments, with their high levels of stimulation, inherently raise anxiety. Heart rates were also highest in this scenario, demonstrating a clear link between the sensory load of urban settings and increased physiological arousal. This condition underscores a direct relationship between elevated heart rates and higher anxiety, confirming that sensory consistency in stimulating environments intensifies both emotional and physical responses. Conversely, the Forest Reference Condition recorded the lowest anxiety and heart rate scores, emphasizing the calming effect of natural environments. This supports the view that serene settings are effective in reducing stress, both psychologically and physically. The marked difference in heart rate and anxiety levels between urban and natural settings illustrates a strong inverse correlation, whereby calming environments significantly lower stress markers. The study also investigated Mixed Sensory Conditions such as city visuals paired with forest sounds and vice versa. The data showed that forest sounds could decrease anxiety even in an urban visual context, suggesting a soothing effect of natural auditory elements. However, urban sounds in a forest setting increased anxiety, highlighting that incongruent auditory stimulus could undermine the calming effect of serene visuals. Heart rates in these scenarios indicated a more complex interplay, where auditory cues significantly influenced emotional regulation, sometimes overriding the effects of visual inputs. Overall, environments with congruent sensory elements (both city and forest) demonstrated a clear relationship between the type of sensory stimulation and changes in heart rate and anxiety—higher in stimulating urban settings and lower in calming natural ones. In contrast, environments with incongruent sensory inputs showed that natural sounds could reduce anxiety in an urban setting, while city noises could increase anxiety in a natural setting, indicating that auditory elements might play a more dominant role in influencing anxiety than visual components.

8 Conclusion

The findings from this study support the hypothesis that conflicting auditory stimuli have a discernible impact on participants' heart rate responses in consistent visual environments. The moderate correlation observed between scenarios with consistent forest visuals and conflicting auditory cues (forest reference) and scenarios with both conflicting forest visuals and auditory stimuli (forest conflict) suggests that auditory stimuli may exert a notable influence on participants' physiological responses, potentially overshadowing the influence of visual cues in conflicting scenarios. These results emphasize the significance of considering auditory elements in virtual environment design, as auditory stimuli can significantly shape participants' physiological and emotional responses, even in the presence of consistent visual cues. Further research in this area is warranted to explore the mechanisms underlying the interaction between auditory and visual stimuli and their impact on participants' experiences in immersive environments. Such insights can inform the development of more effective and immersive virtual reality applications.

Acknowledgments. With profound gratitude, the authors gratefully acknowledge the support received from the France Embassy in Malaysia. We also acknowledge the institutional support provided by Asia Pacific University of Technology and Innovation, Kuala Lumpur, Malaysia, in collaboration with the Arts et Metiers Institute of Technology LISPEN, HESAM Université, Chalon-Sur-Saone, France. Their support and collaboration were instrumental in facilitating this research endeavour.

References

1. Apostolou, K., Liarokapis, F.: A systematic review: the role of multisensory feedback in virtual reality. In: 2nd International Conference on Intelligent Reality (ICIR), pp. 39–42. IEEE (2022)
2. Basharat, A., et al.: Virtual reality as a tool to explore multisensory processing before and after engagement in physical activity. Front. Aging Neurosci. **15**, 1207651 (2023)
3. Canales, R., Jörg, S.: Performance is not everything: audio feedback preferred over visual feedback for grasping task in virtual reality. In: Proceedings of the 13th ACM SIGGRAPH Conference on Motion, Interaction and Games, pp. 1–6 (2020)
4. Chen, H., Dey, A., Billinghurst, M., Linderman, R.W.: Exploring the design space for multisensory heart rate feedback in immersive virtual reality. In: Proceedings of the 29th Australian conference on computer-human interaction, pp. 108–116 (2017)
5. Chen, T., Wu, Y.S., Zhu, K.: Investigating different modalities of directional cues for multitask visual-searching scenario in virtual reality. In: Proceedings of the 24th ACM Symposium on Virtual Reality Software and Technology, pp. 1–5 (2018)

6. Cooper, N., Milella, F., Pinto, C., Cant, I., White, M., Meyer, G.: The effects of substitute multisensory feedback on task performance and the sense of presence in a virtual reality environment. PLoS ONE **13**(2), e0191846 (2018)
7. Grassini, S., Laumann, K., de Martin Topranin, V., Thorp, S.: Evaluating the effect of multisensory stimulations on simulator sickness and sense of presence during HMD-mediated VR experience. Ergonomics **64**(12), 1532–1542 (2021)
8. Halbig, A., Latoschik, M.E.: A systematic review of physiological measurements, factors, methods, and applications in virtual reality. Front. Virtual Reality **2**, 694567 (2021)
9. Hirao, Y., Kawai, T.: Augmented cross-modality: Translating the physiological responses, knowledge, and impression to audio-visual information in virtual reality. Electron. Imaging **31**, 1–8 (2018)
10. Kamińska, D., Smólka, K., Zwoliński, G.: Detection of mental stress through EEG signal in virtual reality environment. Electronics **10**(22), 2840 (2018)
11. Kim, H., et al.: Effect of virtual reality on stress reduction and change of physiological parameters including heart rate variability in people with high stress: an open randomized crossover trial. Front. Psychiatry **12**, 614539 (2021)
12. Kim, J., Luu, W., Palmisano, S.: Multisensory integration and the experience of scene instability, presence and cybersickness in virtual environments. Comput. Hum. Behav. **113**, 106484 (2020)
13. Liu, F., Kang, J.: Relationship between street scale and subjective assessment of audio-visual environment comfort based on 3D virtual reality and dual-channel acoustic tests. Build. Environ. **129**, 35–45 (2018)
14. Marchiori, E., Niforatos, E., Preto, L.: Analysis of users' heart rate data and self-reported perceptions to understand effective virtual reality characteristics. Inf. Technol. Tourism **18**, 133–155 (2018)
15. Melo, M., Gonçalves, G., Monteiro, P., Coelho, H., Vasconcelos-Raposo, J., Bessa, M.: Do multisensory stimuli benefit the virtual reality experience? A systematic review. IEEE Trans. Visual Comput. Graphics **28**(2), 1428–1442 (2020)
16. Oing, T., Prescott, J.: Implementations of virtual reality for anxiety-related disorders: systematic review. JMIR serious games **6**(4), e10965 (2018)
17. Ranasinghe, N., Jain, P., Tolley, D., Karwita Tailan, S., Yen, C.C., Do, E.Y.L.: Exploring the use of olfactory stimuli towards reducing visually induced motion sickness in virtual reality. In: Proceedings of the 2020 ACM Symposium on Spatial User Interaction, pp. 1–9 (2020)
18. Riches, S., Azevedo, L., Bird, L., Pisani, S., Valmaggia, L.: Virtual reality relaxation for the general population: a systematic review. Soc. Psychiatry Psychiatr. Epidemiol. **56**, 1707–1727 (2021)
19. Salgado, D.P., Martins, F.R., Rodrigues, T.B., Keighrey, C., Flynn, R., Naves, E.L.M., Murray, N.: A QoE assessment method based on EDA, heart rate and EEG of a virtual reality assistive technology system. In: Proceedings of the 9th ACM Multimedia Systems Conference, pp. 517–520 (2018)
20. Šalkevicius, J., Damaševičius, R., Maskeliunas, R., Laukienė, I.: Anxiety level recognition for virtual reality therapy system using physiological signals. Electronics **8**(9), 1039 (2019)
21. Sanchez, G.M.E., Van Renterghem, T., Sun, K., De Coensel, B., Botteldooren, D.: Using Virtual Reality for assessing the role of noise in the audio-visual design of an urban public space. Landsc. Urban Plan. **167**, 98–107 (2017)
22. Tabbaa, L., et al.: Vreed: Virtual reality emotion recognition dataset using eye tracking and physiological measures. Proc. ACM Interact. Mobile, Wearable Ubiquit. Technol. **5**(4), 1–20 (2021)
23. Wu, F., Thomas, J., Chinnola, S., Rosenberg, E.S.: Comparison of audio and visual cues to support remote guidance in immersive environments. In: ICAT-EGVE, pp. 121–130 (2020)

24. Wang, X., Shi, Y., Zhang, B., Chiang, Y.: The influence of forest resting environments on stress using virtual reality. Int. J. Environ. Res. Public Health **16**(18), 3263 (2019)
25. Zeng, N., Pope, Z., Lee, J.E., Gao, Z.: Virtual reality exercise for anxiety and depression: a preliminary review of current research in an emerging field. J. Clin. Med. **7**(3), 42 (2018)
26. Shattuck, D.W.: Multiuser virtual reality environment for visualising neuroimaging data. Healthc. Technol. Lett. **5**(5), 183–188 (2018)
27. Moosavi, M.S., et al.: The influence of audio sensory input on the anxiety level of the VR Users. In: International Conference on Future Trends in Smart Communities (ICFTSC), pp. 237–242. IEEE (2022)
28. Spielberger, C.D., Gonzalez-Reigosa, F., Martinez-Urrutia, A., Natalicio, L.F.S., Natalicio, D.S.: The state-trait anxiety inventory. Rev. Interamericana de Psicologia/Interamerican J. Psychol. **5**, 3–4 (1971)

The Design Innovation Space of Intelligent Personal Assistants (IPAs) in Healthy Buildings in the Era of Artificial Intelligence

Yuqi Liu[1]([⊠]), Jiawen Zhang[2], Yibei Zeng[3], Yunlu Liu[4],
and Mohammad Shidujamam[5]

[1] Academy of Arts and Design, Tsinghua University, Beijing, China
liu.yuqi.design@gmail.com
[2] Department of Service Design, School of Design, Royal College of Art, London, UK
[3] Fine Arts College, Shanghai Normal University, Shanghai, China
[4] Faculty of Science, Engineering and Computing, Kingston University, London, UK
[5] Department of Computer Science and Engineering, Independent University, Dhaka, Bangladesh
shidujaman@iub.edu.bd

Abstract. The implementation of Intelligent Personal Assistants (IPA) in healthy buildings cannot just elevate the buildings, intelligence level, but also boost their interactivity and interaction, enhance the quality of life for residents, and establish tailored health management approaches. Given China's status as the world's most populous country and a significant consumer market for emerging smart personal assistant products, this study focuses on the Chinese market. Utilizing a sample of 665 user data, it defines the demand, function, and design domains of IPA products in healthy buildings. Furthermore, it establishes a diversified design innovation space model for IPAs in healthy buildings amidst the artificial intelligence era. Initially, the study quantitatively assesses the impact of demographic variables on the acceptance of IPAs, offering a preliminary clarification and definition of the user profile of Chinese consumers. Additionally, by analyzing user needs and preferences, it explores the specific factors that guide users, purchasing decisions and categorizes these factors into four levels based on their significance. In terms of functional domains, this study has comprehensively gathered and categorized 30 service functions pertinent to Intelligent Personal Assistants (IPA), encompassing both current and anticipated functionalities. Utilizing questionnaire responses and statistical analysis, the study ranked the significance and precedence of these service functions, while employing principal component analysis to categorize user needs for smart speakers into seven distinct dimensions. Additionally, focusing on design domains, this research summarizes the diverse and innovative spatial models for intelligent personal assistants within architectural spaces, drawing insights from the functional domain analysis. This comprehensive study serves as a crucial foundation for the innovative design of IPA products in healthy buildings, while also facilitating the expansion of related enterprises in the Chinese market.

Keywords: Healthy Building · Intelligent Personal Assistant (IPA) · Artificial Intelligence · Design Innovation · User Research · Design Science

V. G. Duffy (Ed.): HCII 2024, LNCS 15376, pp. 118–129, 2025.
https://doi.org/10.1007/978-3-031-76809-5_9

1   Introduction

Human health is influenced by numerous intricate factors, including genetics [1], physical states [2], psychological components [3], lifestyle habits [4–7], and the external environment [8]. Given that individuals spend at least 90% of their lives indoors, with 60% at home and 30% in the workplace [9], architectural design holds significant potential to target and control health-related indicators within buildings [10]. By mitigating harmful factors, promoting beneficial ones, and guiding flexible variables, it can fashion a healthy and cozy indoor environment, furnish comprehensive public service facilities and material terminals, steer towards a healthy and scientific lifestyle, and enhance the physical and mental well-being of building occupants [11, 12]. The health performance of buildings encompasses various aspects such as air quality, water purity, comfort, fitness, humanities, and services. Among the factors influencing comfort are acoustics, lighting, thermal conditions, and ergonomics [13]. In recent years, the exponential advancement of artificial intelligence technology has greatly unleashed the application potential of AI [14] and unlocked boundless opportunities for integrating intelligent personal assistants into buildings [15]. The integration of intelligent personal assistants (IPAs) in buildings not only elevates the intelligence level and regulates various performance indicators more effectively, but also bolsters the interactivity of the built environment, enhancing residents, quality of life and innovating healthcare management techniques [16–18]. China, boasting the world's largest population, launched the "Healthy China 2030" plan in 2016, outlining a roadmap for fostering a healthier nation over the next 15 years [19]. The significance of research on healthy buildings in China is paramount. It serves as a pivotal means to execute the "Healthy China" strategy in the architectural realm, while also significantly contributing to the enhancement of building users, physical and mental well-being, as well as the overall healthy performance of structures. However, what is the design innovation space for intelligent personal assistants in healthy buildings? What factors and human-computer interaction characteristics will affect users, acceptance of related intelligent personal assistants products? [20] By analyzing 665 user data, this study aims to delve into the demand, functionality, and design domains of IPAs in healthy buildings for Chinese users, aiming to spur innovation in related industries. The subsequent sections encompass data collection methods, analysis of user profiles and payment priorities, functional aspects of IPAs in healthy buildings, factor analysis of IPAs design innovation space, and a summation of two-dimensional matrix models.

2   Data Collection and Research Method

This study employed a questionnaire survey format, randomly disseminating questionnaires on the Chinese online platform Wenjuanxing. After approximately a month of data collection, 665 questionnaires were successfully gathered, with a gender distribution of 267 males (40.21%) and 397 females (59.79%). Given that each question was mandatory, the collected data was comprehensive with no missing values. These 665 responses subsequently constituted our analytical sample. For analysis, descriptive statistics were conducted on various demographic and socio-economic factors such as gender, age, residential style, education level, marital status, monthly income, presence of children, and ownership of vehicles. Utilizing IBM SPSS 25.0, T-tests and ANOVA analysis were employed to explore the influence of these variables on the acceptance of smart speaker products. Furthermore, this study categorized the intelligent personal assistant functions within 30 healthy buildings, identified through literature analysis, into seven distinct dimensions using principal component analysis. These dimensions were then prioritized based on their importance. Finally, drawing from the initial data investigation and analysis, a diversified and innovative spatial model for intelligent personal assistants in architectural spaces was proposed.

3   The User Demand Domain of Intelligent Personal Assistants in Healthy Buildings

3.1   User Profile Research

This section conducts a descriptive analysis of the demographic information of the survey respondents, including gender, age, marital status, lifestyle, education level, monthly income, whether they have children, and whether or not they own a family car. ANOVA tests are conducted to determine whether each variable has an impact on the acceptance of intelligent personal assistants in healthy buildings. The resulting user profiles of intelligent personal assistants in healthy buildings are analyzed. The result shows that:

Gender. Gender has a significant impact on the acceptance of intelligent personal assistants in healthy buildings ($T = 0.242$, $p = 0.000 < 0.001$). Among them, the acceptance of men is generally higher than that of women. This is probably because male users prefer high-tech products to women.

Age. The age variable has significant impact on the acceptance of intelligent personal assistants in healthy buildings ($F = 2.786$, $p = 0.017 < 0.05$). Young age group is significantly higher than the old age group, and the younger the user group is, the higher the acceptance they have. This is probably because the younger group are more deeply affected by the Internet, so they are much easier to accept and operate high-tech products.

Marital Status. Marital status has no significant impact on the acceptance of s intelligent personal assistants in healthy buildings ($F = 1.184$, $p = 0.315 > 0.05$).

Way of Living. The way of living has a significant impact on the acceptance of intelligent personal assistants in healthy buildings ($F = 2.250$, $p = 0.029 < 0.05$). The acceptance of users who living with family members is significantly higher than those who living alone, and those who living with parents and children will be more receptive to IPA than those who only live with their spouse. This is presumably because the functions for older parents and children care have been favored by this user group.

Education Level. The education level has a significant impact on the acceptance degree of intelligent personal assistants in healthy buildings ($F = 4.632$, $p = 0.000 < 0.001$), and as the level of education improves, the acceptance degree become higher. This is probably because the horizon will be broadened and the knowledge accumulation will grow as the users receiving higher education level, so that they will have deeper understanding and foresight of smart technology and being more optimistic about how it can improve their life and production efficiency.

Monthly Income. The monthly income variable has no significant impact on the acceptance of intelligent personal assistants in healthy buildings ($F = 0.853$, $p = 0.529 > 0.05$). This is probably because the mainstream IPAs products on the Chinese market are currently cheap with no high purchase threshold. Also, students, as a zero-income group, they have a high level of acceptance of IPAs. An interesting phenomenon is that although the monthly income variable has no significant effect on the level of acceptance, but if you put aside the young group with zero income, the acceptance level of high-income people is still relatively higher than those low-income group. This is probably because in China, higher-income groups are more related and exposed to the internet environment, so they are more sensitive and optimistic to Internet-related intelligence technology and products.

Children. The children variable has no significant effect on the acceptance of intelligent personal assistants in healthy buildings ($F = 0.058$, $p = 0.810 > 0.05$), but the acceptance degree of users who have children are slightly higher than those who not, which indicates that the features and functions of IPAs related to children group will be welcomed by parents but will not constitute a major influence.

Car Driving. The car variable has no significant effect on the acceptance of on the acceptance of intelligent personal assistants in healthy buildings ($F = 1.656$, $p = 0.143 > 0.05$). But the acceptance of users who have car or driving habit stays higher than that those who not, which indicates that some of the in-vehicle functions of smart speaker are favored by car users, but they will not constitute a major influencing factor. The verification summary results of the above hypothesis analysis are shown in Table 1.

Table 1. Anova test on the influence of demographic variables on the acceptance of intelligent personal assistants

Variable	V1	V2	V3	V4	V5	V6	V7	V8
T/F Test	0.242	2.786	1.184	2.250	4.632	0.853	0.058	1.656
p	0.000	0.017	0.315	0.029	0.000	0.529	0.810	0.143
ps	< 0.001	< 0.05	> 0.05	< 0.05	< 0.001	> 0.05	> 0.05	> 0.05
Result	***	**	/	*	***	/	/	/

3.2 The Priorities of User Needs

This section uses descriptive analysis to prioritize the factors that users prioritize when purchasing related smart personal assistant products. Among the surveyed groups, 481 users said that they had the experience of using IPAs, accounting for 72.44% of the total surveyed people, 183 do not have related experience accounting for 28.56%. Among the users who do not have the using experience, 103 announce that they have the plan to purchase an intelligent personal assistant product, accounting for 56.28%, only 19 clearly indicate that they do not intend to buy this product in the future with percentage of 10.38%. 61 users said that they are unsure whether to buy it or not, accounting for 33.33%, that is to say, these users do not have enough recognition about IPAs product or have a wait-and-see attitude towards this industry. All the data being discussed above are shown in Fig. 1. The popularity of IPAs products in Chinese market has grown very fast in recent years.

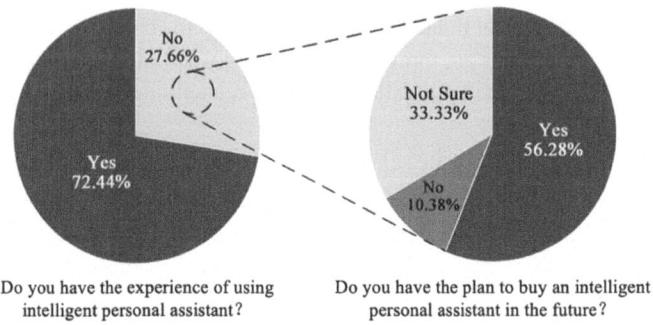

Do you have the experience of using   Do you have the plan to buy an intelligent
intelligent personal assistant?   personal assistant in the future?

Fig. 1. The usage experience and purchase plan of users

For the user group who have the using experience, their IPAs brands distribution is shown in Fig. 2 (a). We can see that Tmall, Baidu and Xiaomi are the mainstream smart speaker product in China while Amazon, Google, and Apple do not account for a large proportion of the Chinese market.

This is mainly because the Chinese Internet environment is completely different with the international. At the same time, Chinese local Internet brands are more family with local customers, needs and expert in local Chinese market. What,s more, it is a very important point that Chinese official language is Chinese so that the international mainstream English speech system is not very attractive to Chinese users. Among the user group who have not bought smart speaker yet, the brands they are mainly interested in are shown in Fig. 2 (b): Tmall Elf, Baidu Xiaodu, and Xiaomi Xiaoai still occupy the top three positions while Huawei SoundX also has strong appeal for users. Among the overseas brands, Chinese users are most interested in the Apple Homepod. This is probably because iphone and ipad from Apple company have accumulated a large number of user groups in China, so that they also showed considerable interest in Apple IPAs product.

When asked what aspects they would pay more attention to when purchasing IPAs products, we got the statistics result shown in Fig. 3. The study found that over 70% of users will consider price factors first; over 60% of users will consider brand, sound quality, and voice recognition; and over 50% will consider product features. These factors can also be said to be the soul of an IPAs product. We can consider them as the first level elements. Over 30% of users will consider appearance design, technical stability, interactive experience, compatibility with products and devices, and ease of operation based on the first level elements; over 29% of users will focus on the content and quality of information, as well as the content quality, supported applications and software, and whether it is portable; over 25% of consumers will consider the length of standby time.

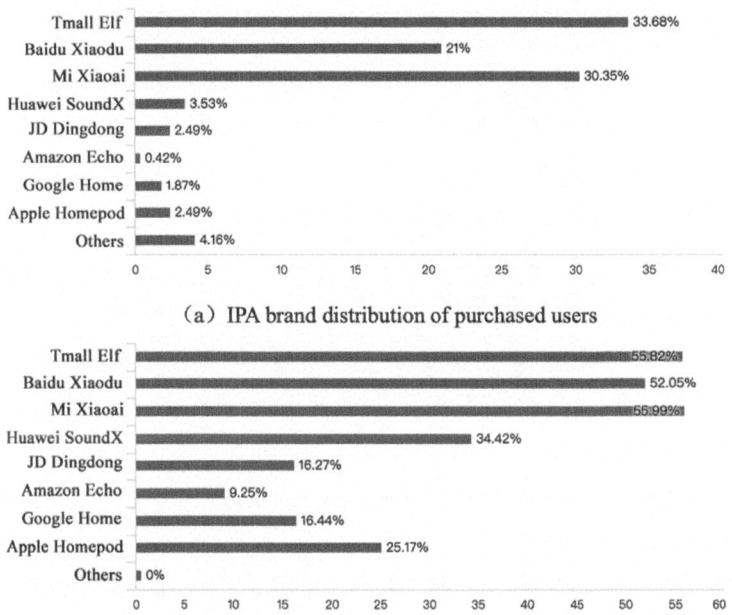

(a) IPA brand distribution of purchased users

(b) IPA brand distribution of users who have not purchased yet but plan to

Fig. 2. Brand distribution

We can classify these as the second level elements; over 10% of users will consider product materials, service platforms, accessories, etc. We can classify them as the third level elements. So basically, we used 50% and 25% as the dividing line and classify all the elements into three levels. Through the above analysis, we can recognize the product elements that consumers mainly look for when purchasing intelligent personal assistant, to provide guidance for our product development and optimization.

Since the users take price as the first considerable element, we also statistic the acceptable prices of Chinese users for IPAs product. As shown in Fig. 4, for most Chinese users, they are more acceptable for an IPAs product whose price is between 200−400RMB, and this type of user group accounts for 43.22%. Secondly, about 30% of users agree that the acceptable price of an IPAs product is between 400−800RMB. So, we can summarize that when the price of an IPA smart speaker is between 200−800RMB, it is more popular acceptable to Chinese users. Moreover, we can notice that there are also low-end user group and high-end user group in IPAs market, which inspires developers to develop products for users with different payment capabilities. From this we can also see the reason why the overseas brands of intelligent personal assistant received bad market performance in China, because when their prices transform from dollar into Chinese Yen, it usually turns out far higher than local Chinese products.

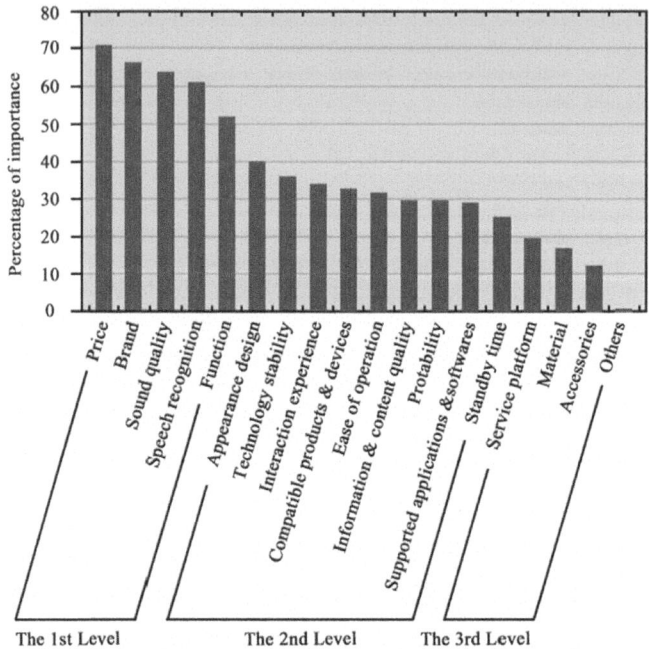

Fig. 3. The consideration factors of IPA while buying

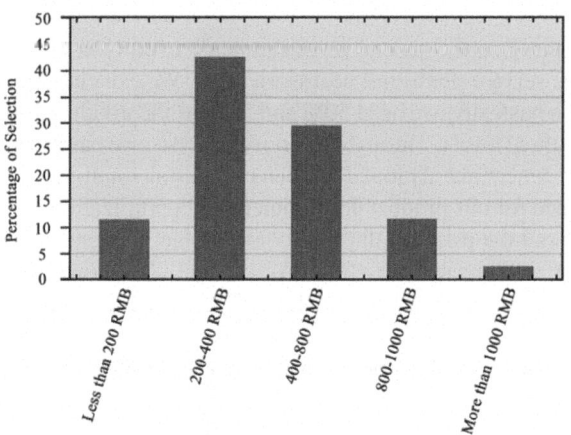

Fig. 4. The appropriate price of an IPA products in China

4   The Product Function Domain of Intelligent Personal Assistants in Healthy Buildings

This section describes descriptive statistical analysis. Through collecting and understanding existing and potential service functions in the market, we have compiled 30 types of user demand for intelligent personal assistant in healthy buildings, as shown in Table 2. We obtained the importance score of each function from 665 users through questionnaire survey. The results are shown in Table 1. We can see that sound-related services remain the core functions of the current IPAs market. And the main motivation for consumers to buy an IPAs product currently is to play music, have weather broadcasting, alarm clock, memo reminder and audio books. The average value of their importance scores is all above 4.00. We even do not rule out the conclusion that the original intention of many users to buy IPAs is to use it as an audio speaker. Secondly, service functions with importance score greater than 3.80 include smart phone, voice message, appliance control, air quality detection, temperature and humidity control, smart doorbell, health management, chat companion, movie and television video, news broadcasting, children and elderly care, early childhood education and family video. From these service functions, we can see that users have gradually formed considerable using habits for IPAs and many Internet giants, strategic layout of using IPAs as the entrance of future smart home has begun to gain fruits, and more and more users are slowly accepting the concept of controlling smart home appliances and products through smart speaker. Service functions with a score more than 3.5 include in-vehicle voice navigation, screen projection, cloud storage, camera snapshot, and in-vehicle entertainment. This shows that users with cars still have expectation for the application of IPAs in in-vehicle environment. Functions like camera snapshot also vary according to the needs of different users in different scenarios. The service features with a score more than 3.0 include online shopping, pet feeder control, online game, and stock market, which shows that the demand of these service functions are not strong and prominent until now, but this does not necessarily mean that those demands will stay weak in the future, because user needs and perceptions of an industry will change over time and their habits will be cultivated as the development and maturity of a certain industry. Taking online shopping as an example, if China's domestic Internet giants, such as Alibaba and Meituan, have developed such online shopping services with good quality and precision, and insert into smart home appliances such as refrigerator in the future, then user habits can be cultivated quickly. To sum up, in terms of the current market environment, the sound services is still the soul and core competition of IPAs products. Taking this as the basis, the market can slowly develop and cultivate other service needs and behaviors mode of users. In the future, the design and development of an IPAs product can unlock many different service scenarios according to different characteristics and needs of users, such as children service scenario, elderly service scenario, pet service scenario, car service scenario, home control service scenario, health management service scenario, social service scenario, entertainment service scenario, etc.

5   The Design Space Domain of Intelligent Personal Assistants in Healthy Buildings

To further elaborate on the design spatial domain of intelligent personal assistants in health buildings, we conducted a principal component analysis on the 30 service functions. The outcomes of this analysis are presented in Table 2, revealing the extraction of seven distinct demand dimensions based on factor loading. Figure 5 depicts the naming of these dimensions along with their corresponding demand factors. These include Factor

Table 2. The importance degree of different service function

Service Function	Importance degree					Ave
	Very Unimportant	Unimportant	General	Important	Very Important	
Play music	1(0.15%)	9(1.36%)	39(5.87%)	292(43.98%)	323(48.64%)	4.40
Alarm clock	11(1.66%)	27(4.07%)	116(17.47%)	233(35.09%)	277(41.72%)	4.11
Weather forecast	8(1.2%)	19(2.86%)	113(17.02%)	291(43.83%)	233(35.09%)	4.09
Reminder	15(2.26%)	26(3.92%)	112(16.87%)	277(41.72%)	234(35.24%)	4.04
Audiobooks	11(1.66%)	29(4.37%)	107(16.11%)	309(46.54%)	208(31.33%)	4.02
Smart phone calling	15(2.26%)	40(6.02%)	112(16.87%)	273(41.11%)	224(33.73%)	3.98
Appliance control	15(2.26%)	32(4.82%)	131(19.73%)	281(42.32%)	205(30.87%)	3.95
Health management	12(1.81%)	34(5.12%)	144(21.69%)	260(39.16%)	214(32.23%)	3.95
Voice message	7(1.05%)	37(5.57%)	147(22.14%)	285(42.92%)	188(28.31%)	3.92
Air quality detection	12(1.81%)	40(6.02%)	140(21.08%)	272(40.96%)	200(30.12%)	3.92
Chat companion	22(3.31%)	49(7.38%)	138(20.78%)	226(34.04%)	229(34.49%)	3.89
Children or elderly care	16(2.41%)	51(7.68%)	144(21.69%)	241(36.3%)	212(31.93%)	3.88
News broadcast	5(0.75%)	34(5.12%)	167(25.15%)	297(44.73%)	161(24.25%)	3.87
Early childhood education	20(3.01%)	40(6.02%)	145(21.84%)	258(38.86%)	201(30.27%)	3.87
Temperature & humidity control	16(2.41%)	31(4.67%)	162(24.4%)	272(40.96%)	183(27.56%)	3.87
Movie&video	8(1.2%)	27(4.07%)	192(28.92%)	261(39.31%)	176(26.51%)	3.86
Smart doorbell	19(2.86%)	29(4.37%)	190(28.61%)	229(34.49%)	197(29.67%)	3.84
In-vehicle smart phone	19(2.86%)	39(5.87%)	155(23.34%)	267(40.21%)	184(27.71%)	3.84
Family video	12(1.81%)	39(5.87%)	182(27.41%)	248(37.35%)	183(27.56%)	3.83
In-vehicle voice navigation	19(2.86%)	52(7.83%)	159(23.95%)	255(38.4%)	179(26.96%)	3.79
Screen projection	19(2.86%)	51(7.68%)	170(25.6%)	274(41.27%)	150(22.59%)	3.73
Cloud storage	23(3.46%)	57(8.58%)	167(25.15%)	252(37.95%)	165(24.85%)	3.72
Camera snapshot	25(3.77%)	61(9.19%)	159(23.95)	253(38.1%)	166(25%)	3.71
Gesture control	27(4.07%)	61(9.19%)	193(29.07%)	249(37.5%)	134(20.18%)	3.61
Gourmet recipes	22(3.31%)	71(10.69%)	210(31.63%)	235(35.39%)	126(18.98%)	3.56
In-vehicle entertainment	17(2.56%)	75(11.3%)	237(35.69%)	224(33.73%)	111(16.72%)	3.51
Online shopping	57(8.58%)	85(12.8%)	230(34.64%)	192(28.92%)	100(15.06%)	3.29
Pet feeder control	47(7.08%)	108(16.27%)	241(36.3%)	184(27.72%)	84(12.65%)	3.23
Online game	45(6.78%)	148(22.29%)	257(38.7%)	132(19.88%)	82(12.35%)	3.09
Stock market	50(7.53%)	135(20.33%)	258(38.86%)	168(25.3%)	53(7.98%)	3.06

1 - Healthy building device control, Factor 2 - Daily reminders, Factor 3 - Entertainment and shopping, Factor 4 - Family members, care and education, Factor 5 - In-vehicle service, Factor 6 - Media linkage, and Factor 7 - Information acquisition. Positioning these seven principal component factors, we consider the internal and external environments of the building, as well as physical and non-physical interactions, as two crucial variables. Within the building,s internal environment, the seven demand factors and their

specifics can be categorized into three main groups: "Social Health," emphasizing family interaction, care, and education; "Psychological Health," focused on entertainment, gaming, and shopping; and "Physical Health," encompassing environmental and building equipment control as well as daily reminders. Moving to the external environment of the buildings, in-vehicle services stand as the primary demand factor. Additionally, there are numerous support systems that enhance product, service, and experience affordability. These are grouped into three categories: software support systems, hardware support systems, and humanware support systems. By delving into these dimensions and support systems, we gain a deeper understanding of how IPAs can comprehensively enhance residents, quality of life in health buildings, addressing both physical, mental, and social well-being.

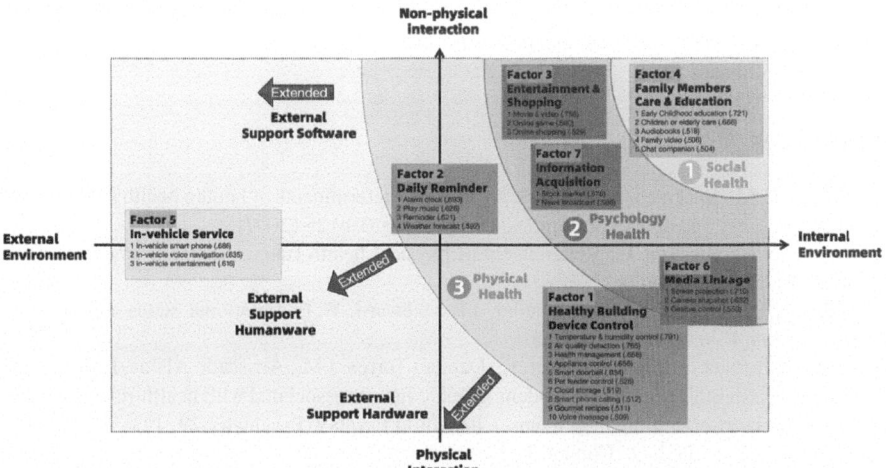

Fig. 5. The design innovation dimension and level of IPA in healthy building

6   Conclusion

This study focuses on the Chinese market, utilizing a robust sample of 665 user data to paint a comprehensive portrait of Chinese consumers. It delves into defining the demand, functional, and design domains of intelligent personal assistants products in healthy buildings within the realm of artificial intelligence. In analyzing the demand domain, we categorize the pivotal factors influencing user purchasing decisions into three level: price, brand, sound quality, speech recognition, and product functionality constitute the first level; appearance design, interactive experience, technical stability, compatibility, ease of use, information/content quality, supported applications/software, portability, and battery life form the second level; and service platform, product materials, and accessories comprise the third level. Within the functional domain, we identify and analyze 30 service functions offered by IPAs. Through statistical analysis, we ascertain the importance and user preferences for each function. To refine the design domain in healthy buildings, we conduct a principal component analysis of these 30 functions, categorizing them into seven distinct dimensions: healthy building device control, daily assistance, entertainment and shopping, family members care and education, in-vehicle services, media linkage, and information acquisition. Notably, in-vehicle services pertain to the external environment, while the remaining six dimensions pertain to the internal environment. The insights gained from this study are invaluable in guiding the utilization of IPAs to enhance residents, quality of life in architectural design, ultimately fostering physical, mental, and social well-being.

Acknowledgments. This study was funded by China Postdoctoral Science Foundation (grant number: 2023M742017).

Disclosure of Interests. The authors have no competing interests to declare that are relevant to the content of this article.

References

1. Martin, G.M., Bergman, A., Barzilai, N.: Genetic determinants of human health span and life span: progress and new opportunities. PLoS Genet. **3**, e125 (2007)
2. Belloc, N.B., Breslow, L.: Relationship of physical health status and health practices. Prev Med (Baltim) **1**, 409–421 (1972)
3. Salovey, P., Rothman, A.J., Detweiler, J.B., Steward, W.T.: Emotional states and physical health. Am. Psychol. **55**, 110 (2000)
4. Jiménez Boraita, R., Gargallo Ibort, E., Dalmau Torres, J.M., Arriscado Alsina, D.: Lifestyle habits, health indicators and sociodemographic factors associated with health-related quality of life and self-esteem in adolescents. Clin. Child Psychol. Psychiatry **29**, 493–512 (2024)
5. Cooper, J., Campbell, Q., Conner, T.: Healthier but not happier? The lifestyle habits of health influencer followers. Cyberpsychology J. Psychosoc. Res. Cybersp. **18**(2) (2024)
6. Brehm, B.J., Summer, S.S., Khoury, J.C., et al.: Health status and lifestyle habits of US medical students: a longitudinal study. Ann. Med. Health Sci. Res. **6**, 341–347 (2016)
7. Rippe, J.M.: Lifestyle medicine: the health promoting power of daily habits and practices. Am. J. Lifestyle Med. **12**, 499–512 (2018)
8. Tomljenović, A.: Effects of internal and external environment on health and well-being: From cell to society. Coll. Antropol. **38**, 367–372 (2014)
9. Bluyssen, P.M.: The Healthy Indoor Environment: How to Assess Occupants, Wellbeing in Buildings. Routledge (2013)
10. Kelly, F.J., Fussell, J.C.: Improving indoor air quality, health and performance within environments where people live, travel, learn and work. Atmos. Environ. **200**, 90–109 (2019)
11. Allen, J.G., Macomber, J.D.: Healthy Buildings. Harvard University Press (2022)
12. Šujanová, P., Rychtáriková, M., Sotto Mayor, T., Hyder, A.: A healthy, energy-efficient and comfortable indoor environment, a review. Energies **12**, 1414 (2019)
13. Wierzbicka, A., Pedersen, E., Persson, R., et al.: Healthy indoor environments: The need for a holistic approach. Int. J. Environ. Res. Public Health **15**, 1874 (2018)
14. Wu, Z., Ji, D., Yu, K., et al.: AI creativity and the human-AI co-creation model. In: Human-Computer Interaction. Theory, Methods and Tools: Thematic Area, HCI 2021, Held as Part of the 23rd HCI International Conference, HCII 2021, Virtual Event, July 24–29, 2021, Proceedings, Part I 23. Springer, pp 171–190 (2021). https://doi.org/10.1007/978-3-030-78462-1_13

15. Mehmood, M.U., Chun, D., Han, H., et al.: A review of the applications of artificial intelligence and big data to buildings for energy-efficiency and a comfortable indoor living environment. Energy Build. **202**, 109383 (2019)
16. Srinivasan, A., Madheswari, A.N.: The role of smart personal assistant for improving personal healthcare. Int. J. Adv. Eng. Manag. Sci. **4**, 268274 (2018)
17. Kubicki, S., Zarli, A., Coujard, C., Guerriero, A.: Health, well-being and comfort in smart buildings innovation: state-of-play and opportunities. In: IOP Conference Series: Earth and Environmental Science, pp. 92019. IOP Publishing (2022)
18. Ermolina, A., Tiberius, V.: Voice-controlled intelligent personal assistants in health care: International Delphi Study. J. Med. Internet Res. **23**, e25312 (2021)
19. Tan, X., Liu, X., Shao, H.: Healthy China 2030: a vision for health care. Value Heal. Reg. issues **12**, 112–114 (2017)
20. Song, X., Liu, M., Gong, L., et al.: A Review of human-computer interface evaluation research based on evaluation process elements. In: International Conference on Human-Computer Interaction, pp 262–289. Springer (2023). https://doi.org/10.1007/978-3-031-35596-7_17

Bi-class Classification System Using Supervised Techniques for Depression Level Detection During and After Covid-19

Fabio Mendoza Palechor[1]([✉]) [iD], Alexis De la Hoz Manotas[2] [iD],
and Dionicio Neira-Rodado[2] [iD]

[1] Corporación Universitaria Minuto de Dios, Bogotá, Colombia
fabio.mendoza.p@uniminuto.edu
[2] Universidad de La Costa, CUC, Barranquilla, Colombia
{adelahoz,dneira1}@cuc.edu.co

Abstract. Depression can be considered a disorder of the state of mind of a person, where some can experience feelings of sadness, anger, and many others. According to Pan American Health Organization (PAHO/WHO), 50 million people in America suffer from depression disorder, and it is the main cause of mental health and disability worldwide. The World Health Organization (WHO) consider that 300 million people live with depression, a 18% increase from 2005 to 2015 [1]. This study analyzes the depression that suffered people through COVID-19 in Barranquilla, Colombia. With this objective, a dataset was built using the Beck's Depression Inventory (BDI) which has been previously used in several studies such as [5–7]. The dataset was collected during pandemic in 2021 between April and may (moment 1), and post-pandemic in 2023 between February and march (moment 2), and both moments (1 and 2) were consolidated, to better identify the levels of depression using classification algorithms such as Decision Tree (DT), Support Vector Machine (SVM), Artificial Neuronal Networks (RNA) and Naïve Bayes (NB), these techniques were used to discover patterns useful to practitioners and patients, and after comparison, the results obtained demonstrated all algorithms were successful to recognize the different levels of depression contained in the dataset nevertheless, the DT method achieved the best result with TPR (98.1%), FPR (1.8%), Precision (98.1%) and Recall (98.1%).

Keywords: Data Mining · Depression · Covid-19 · Decision Tree · Support Vector Machine · Artificial Neuronal Networks · Naïve Bayes

1 Introduction

Depression can be considered a disorder of the state of mind of a person, where some can experience feelings of sadness, anger, and many others. According to Pan American Health Organization (PAHO/WHO), 50 million people in America suffer from depression disorder, and it is the main cause of mental health and disability worldwide. The World Health Organization (WHO) consider that 300 million people live with depression, a 18% increase from 2005 to 2015 [1].

© The Author(s), under exclusive license to Springer Nature Switzerland AG 2025
V. G. Duffy (Ed.): HCII 2024, LNCS 15376, pp. 130–143, 2025.
https://doi.org/10.1007/978-3-031-76809-5_10

WHO defines COVID-19 as the disease produced by the coronavirus known as SARS-COV-2, and propagation can be prevented by conducting confinement of patients, preferably in a medical center where they can receive medical attention and quarantine if necessary, meaning they have to be isolated due exposition to the virus and possibly infection, if there is no special center for it, it can be done in their household [2]. This disease caused a great number of human losses worldwide regardless gender, race, or socio-economic level in population, with 2.623.459 deaths approximately, based on the data by PAHO and WHO in the report N° 71 with date of February 25th of 2022 [3].

Given the huge impact of the pandemic in the population, many authors have studied a correlation between disorders as depression and COVID-19, [4] presents a study of anxiety and depression in COVID-19 survivors and the role of the inflammatory processes and the clinical predictors.

This study analyzes the depression that suffered people through COVID-19 in Barranquilla, Colombia. For this, a dataset was built using the Beck's Depression Inventory (BDI) which has been previously used in several studies such as [5–7]. The data was processed through data mining supervised methods to discover patterns to classify the level of depression. The dataset was collected during pandemic in 2021 between April and may (moment 1), and post-pandemic in 2023 between February and march (moment 2), and both moments (1 and 2) are merged to better identify the levels of depression using classification algorithms such as Decision Tree – **DT**, Support Vector Machine – **SVM**, Artificial Neuronal Networks – **RNA** and Naïve Bayes – **NB**. The study is structured as follows: Sect. 2 previous studies related to study for estimation of depression levels, Sect. 3 presents the materials and methods used, Sect. 4 shows methodology, Sect. 5 presents the results obtained, and Sect. 6, features conclusions and future works.

2 Related Works

Depression is a disorder that affects many people, several factors such psychological or life experiences, can create problems in mental health, so it is relevant to study new tools to help people using intelligent techniques based on big volumes of data. Next, you can find several studies related to the identification of depression.

In [8], authors investigate the method to classify sentiments in the mental health domain. The classical features and sentiment analysis approach is conducted in this preliminary study to detect depression using a sample of data collected from Twitter. By using a combination of the lexical approach and the Naive Bayes model, the highest accuracy is achieved above 69%. The results indicate a combination of lexical and machine learning outperforms several machine learning approaches for classifying depression in individual tweets.

In [9], authors analyze the "depressed" text; by manipulating the data, extracting features, categorizing, and try to understand what are the attributes of "depressed" text, and how they can "predict" whether a text should be marked as depressed or not. Using text analysis and text data mining techniques, the text obtained from the social forums was analyzed and three different machine learning algorithms were used to predict depression. After cross validation overall accuracy of 99.69% was obtained as the best score using the proposed system. This study definitively answers the question regarding using human basic language and communication of personal experiences, for the prediction of depression and can be reached easily.

In [10], authors used data mining and machine-learning methods to crawl 112,537 Sina COVID-19- related microblogs and conduct sentiment and group difference analyses. It was found that: (1) the microblog users' emotions shifted from negative to positive from the second COVID-19 pandemic phase; (2) there were no significant differences in the microblog users' emotions in the different regions; (3) males were more optimistic than females in the early stages of the pandemic; however, females were more optimistic than males in the last three stages; and (4) females posted more microblogs and expressed more sadness and fear while males expressed more anger and disgust. This research captured online information in real-time, with the results providing a reference for future research into public opinion and emotional reactions to crises.

In [11], this study includes 1) Rajyoga practitioners' perceptions of psychological effects, levels of anxiety, stress, and depression are compared to those of the non-practitioners 2) Predictions of mental health disorders such as stress, anxiety and depression using machine learning algorithms using the online survey data collected from Rajyoga meditators and general the population. Decision tree, random forest, Naive Baye, Support vector machine and K nearest neighbor algorithms were used for the prediction as they have been shown to be more accurate for predicting psychological disorders. The support vector machine showed the highest accuracy among all other algorithms (94.9% for depression, 97.8% for Anxiety and 97.4% for stress). The f1 score was also the highest for support vector machine.

In [12], authors developed a model for predicting depression among youth in Thailand, the results showed that most of the respondents had no depressive risk conditions with 1,059 samples (74.95%). However, there are still three risk groups that need to be monitored: mild level with 260 samples (18.40%) moderate level with 78 samples (5.52%), and severe level with 16 samples (1.13%). The observations were taken to develop a prototype model. It was found that the highest accuracy model was the artificial neural networks technique with an accuracy value of 97.88%.

In [13], this study found that students' psychological problems during the COVID-19 epidemic were mainly reflected in four aspects: depression, interpersonal relationship, sleep and eating disorders, and compulsive behavior. Through the discussion of family of origin, self-awareness and motivation attribution, and social pressure, this paper analyzed the causes of psychological problems. In this paper, a data preprocessing system is designed, and three data preprocessing rules are defined: expression data conversion rules, data deduplication rules and invalid data cleaning rules. The characteristics of online community text data are analyzed, and the text feature extraction method is selected according to its characteristics. The results of this study show that the proportion of university students with psychological problems is about 23%, which is slightly higher than the research results during the non-epidemic period. This paper suggests that college students should master methods of self-regulation, improve their levels of physical exercise, improve their physical fitness, and establish and improve their defense mechanisms to alleviate psychological conflicts and pressures.

In [14], COVID-19-related tweets from March 5th, 2020, to January 31st, 2021, were collected through Twitter streaming API using keywords (i.e., "corona," "covid19," and "covid"). By further filtering using keywords (i.e., "depress," "failure," and "hopeless"), they extracted mental health-related tweets from the US. Topic modeling using the Latent Dirichlet Allocation model was conducted to monitor users' discussions surrounding mental health concerns. Deep learning algorithms were performed to infer the demographic composition of Twitter users who had mental health concerns during the pandemic. Results. Authors observed a positive correlation between mental health concerns on Twitter and the COVID-19 pandemic in the US. Topic modeling showed that "stay-at-home," "death poll," and "politics and policy" were the most popular topics in COVID-19 mental health tweets. Among Twitter users who had mental health concerns during the pandemic, Males, White, and 30–49 age group people were more likely to express mental health concerns. In addition, Twitter users from the east and west coast had more mental health concerns.

In [15] authors designed an effective regular expression-based search method and created the largest English Twitter depression data set containing 2575 distinct identified users with depression and their past tweets. To examine the effect of depression on people's Twitter language, they trained three transformer-based depression classification models on the data set, evaluated their performance with progressively increased training sizes, and compared the model's tweet chunk-level and user-level performances. Finally, the study demonstrated the model's capability of monitoring both group-level and population-level depression trends by presenting two of its applications during the COVID-19 pandemic. The fusion model demonstrated an accuracy of 78.9% on a test set containing 446 people, half of which were identified as having depression. Conscientiousness, neuroticism, appearance of first-person pronouns, talking about biological processes such as eat and sleep, talking about power, and exhibiting sadness were shown to be important features in depression classification.

In [16] the effects that COVID-19 had on citizens of Peru have been described. For this, 1699 questionnaires, collected between 2 April and 2 September 2020, were analyzed. Descriptive, bivariate analysis was performed with odds ratio (OR) calculations and a data mining methodology. Sociodemographic variables (from the General Health Questionnaire), health conditions and perception, symptoms, and variables related to contact and preventive measures regarding COVID-19 were analyzed. As compared to other countries, less affectation of mental health and increased use of preventive measures were observed. Psychological distress had a greater incidence in women, young people, people without a partner, and people without university studies. The most significant conditioning variables were self-perceived health status, headache or muscle pain over the past 14 days, level of studies, and age.

In [17] authors proposed a CorExQ9 algorithm that integrates a Correlation Explanation (CorEx) learning algorithm and clinical Patient Health Questionnaire (PHQ) lexicon to detect COVID-19 related stress symptoms at a spatiotemporal scale in the United States. The proposed algorithm overcomes the common limitations of traditional topic detection models and minimizes the ambiguity that is caused by human interventions in social media data mining. The results showed a strong correlation between stress symptoms and the number of increased COVID-19 cases for major U.S. cities such as

Chicago, San Francisco, Seattle, New York, and Miami. The results also show that people's risk perception is sensitive to the release of COVID-19 related public news and media messages.

3 Materials and Methods

3.1 Dataset Description

The dataset was created based on survey using the Beck Depression Inventory [5–7], which can be used to find out if a person suffers from depression. A set of questions were added to the BDI, including several factors related to COVID-19 as shows in Table 1. Data recollection used a website with a survey, and users indicated their current situation, including both physical and mental state. In Table 1, you can see all the questions in the survey. After the survey was ended, all data was preprocessed and get ready to be used by data mining techniques.

The number of entries in the dataset is 1948, and variable VNDepression was calculated using Eq. 1, and the class variable NDepression was set.

$$VNdepression = indicator1 + indicator2 + indicator3 + \ldots indicator21 \qquad (1)$$

The class NDepression is calculated for bi-class problems, referencing the Normal and Anormal values, the Normal label contains the records with depression level between 1 and 16, and the Anormal label contains the values higher than 16.

3.2 Decision Trees

A Decision Tree (DT) [18] is a classification procedure that partitions recursively a dataset in subdivisions, they are composed by a root node and a set of internal nodes, both created through data division, and a set of terminal nodes. Each node has a single parent and two or more descendants. A Decision Tree is commonly used to support decision making processes and set the probability for each possible choice, based on the context of the decision [19]. Decision Trees are implemented through different algorithms including C.4.5 and Random Forest. A J48 classifier [20] is a simple C.4.5 decision tree for classification and produces a binary tree. The decision tree approach is most useful in classification problems.

3.3 Support Vector Machine (SVM)

Support Vector Machines [21] is the most widely used Machine Learning technique, using pattern classification nowadays. Based on statistical learning theory and created by Vapnik in 1995. The objective of this technique is to project nonlinear separable samples onto another higher dimensional space by using different types of kernel functions. SVM has been applied extensively worldwide in different tasks such as handwritten numbers recognition [22], object recognition [23], text classification [24] and human activities recognition [25].

Table 1. Description *of data set attributes*

Attribute	Values
Year	Numeric Value
Age	Numeric Value
Gender	Female Male I rather don't answer
¿Do you suffer from any mental illness or disability?	Yes No
¿Did you contract the COVID-19 virus?	Yes No
¿Did you lose any people around you, from COVID-19?	Yes No
¿Did you lose your employment during COVID-19 confinement?	Yes No
Indicator 1	I don't feel sad I feel sad I feel sad permanently and can't avoid it I feel sad that I can't handle it
Indicator 2	I don't feel especially discouraged about the future I feel discouraged about the future I feel I don't have anything to hope for I feel the future is hopeless and things won't get any better
Indicator 3	I don't feel like a failure I think I have failed more than most people When I look back, I just see failure after failure I feel like a complete failure
Indicator 4	Things in my life satisfy me as before I don't enjoy things in my life as before I don't have any satisfaction from things in my life I'm unsatisfied or bored about everything
Indicator 5	I don't feel especially guilty I feel guilty in several occasions I feel guilty most of the time I feel guilty permanently

(*continued*)

Table 1. (*continued*)

Attribute	Values
Indicator 6	I don't think I have been punished I feel like I'm going to be punished I hope to be punished I feel I'm punished right now
Indicator 7	I'm not disappointed of myself I feel disappointed about me I feel ashamed of me I hate myself
Indicator 8	I don't consider myself worse than anyone else I criticize myself for my weaknesses and mistakes I blame myself constantly for my faults I blame myself for anything bad that happens to me
Indicator 9	I don't have any thoughts about suicide I think about suicide sometimes, but I wouldn't do it I wish to commit suicide I would suicide if I have the chance
Indicator 10	I don't cry more than what I used to do it I cry more often than before I cry permanently I was capable of crying before, now I can't, even if I want to
Indicator 11	I'm not more irritable than usual for me I get angry or irritable easier than before I feel irritated permanently I can't feel irritated by things than bothered me before
Indicator 12	I haven't lost any interest in others I'm less interested in others than before I have lost most interest in others I have lost all interest in others
Indicator 13	I take decisions in my life as usual I avoid taking decisions more than before Taking decisions is more difficult for me now than before It's impossible for me to take any decisions now

(*continued*)

Table 1. (*continued*)

Attribute	Values
Indicator 14	I don't think I have worse aspect than before I'm afraid that I look older or less attractive I think I had permanent changes in my aspect that make me look less attractive now I think I have a horrible aspect
Indicator 15	I work in the same way as before I have to make an extra effort to start working I have to obligate me to start working I can't work in anything at all
Indicator 16	I sleep as good as always I don't sleep as good as before I wake up one or two hours before usual and it's difficult to sleep back again I wake up several hours before usual and I can't sleep again
Indicator 17	I don't feel more tired than usual I get tired easier than before I get tired as soon as I do any chore I'm too tired to do anything
Indicator 18	My appetite has not diminished at all I don't have as good appetite as before I have less appetite now than before I have lost all my appetite
Indicator 19	I have lost little weight or nothing at all I have lost more than 2kg in weight I have lost more than 4kg in weight I have lost more than 7kg in weight
Indicator 20	I'm not worried about my health more than usual I'm worried about physical problems such as pain, discomfort, stomach issues or constipation I'm worried about my physical problems and it's difficult to think on anything else I'm so worried about my physical problems that I'm incapable of thinking about anything else
Indicator 21	I haven't noticed any changes in my interest concerning sex I'm less interested in sex than before I don't have much interest about sex I have lost all interest about sex

(*continued*)

Table 1. (*continued*)

Attribute	Values
VNdepression	Numeric Value
Ndepression	Normal Anormal

Table 2. Summary of findings

Summary of Findings	
Missing Values	3
Atypical Data	0
Variable Removal for higher level of correlation	0

3.4 Multilayer Perceptron (MLP) – Neural Networks

Multi-layer perceptron (MLP) [26] is a feed forward neural network. It consists of three types of layers—input layer, output layer and hidden layer. The input layer receives the input signal to be processed. The required tasks, such as prediction and classification, are performed by the output layer. An arbitrary number of hidden layers that are placed in between the input and output layer are the true computational engine of the MLP. Like any feed forward network, in an MLP, the data flows in forward direction from input to output layer. The neurons in the MLP are trained with a back propagation learning algorithm. MLPs are designed to approximate any continuous function and can solve problems not linearly separable.

3.5 Naïve Bayes (Bayesian Networks)

The Naïve Bayes (NB) method [27] is based on the Bayes theorem with strong independence assumptions between the predicates, a naïve Bayesian model is easy to build, without a complex estimation of the iterative parameters, practical for big datasets. In [28], the study shows this method is based on classic mathematic theory and the model can be implemented for a wide range of activities, since it needs few estimated parameters, and it is insensitive to missing data. Bayesian networks are considered an alternative to classic expert systems oriented to decision making and prediction under uncertainty in probabilistic terms [29].

4   Methodology

The experimental process development begins with the creation of an appropriate dataset, as described in Sect. 3.1, served as the starting point. Subsequently, data cleaning and transformation procedures were carried out, as detailed in Sect. 4.1. This resulted in a baseline dataset that was free of noise, enabling the implementation of data mining algorithms, as detailed in Sect. 4.2. These algorithms were evaluated using a variety of metrics, including TpRate, FpRate, Precision, and Recall. The interpretation of these metrics was the final step, allowing for the comparison of results and the extraction of relevant information from the analysis (Fig. 1).

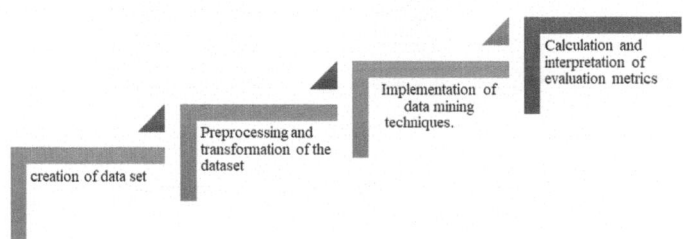

Fig. 1. Methodology used for the development of the experiment.

4.1 Data Cleaning and Preparation

The dataset for this study contains 1948 instances and 31 attributes. First, the data recollected in both moments, 1 (2021) and 2 (2023), was merged to created one single dataset, then the class variable NDepression was analyzed, and it was evident there was a problem with the number of entries, since the normal label contained 1613 instances, and the anormal label contained 335 instances, considering the class variable was certainly imbalanced.

To correct the problem between the depression levels, synthetic data was generated, up to 33% of the data, using Weka and the SMOTE filter [30]. The filter requires: the class to be affected with synthetic data, the number of the nearest neighbors used, the percentage needed to increase the selected class and the random seed for random sampling. Then, all data was revised for identification of atypical or missing data. Finally, the dataset ended with 2953 records. In Fig. 2 you can see the distribution of the data, prior and after the balancing process (Tables 1 and 2).

Instances with missing data are removed from the dataset, in this case, 3 instances were found. To search for atypical data, the numeric variables analyzed were age, year and VNDepression, year represents the moment when the entry is created, so it didn't show any atypical data. The VNDepression attribute is calculated by Eq. 1. Age is a value entered directly by the user and it could possibly have abnormal values in it, but after analysis was done, the process didn't find any atypical data in the age attribute.

The correlation analysis shows the level of relation between variables, taking values of -1 to 1, where -1 indicates a negative relation, zero represents no relation whatsoever and values near to 1, shows a relation between variables, after this analysis was done using the Pearson coefficient, there wasn't any relation shown between variables.

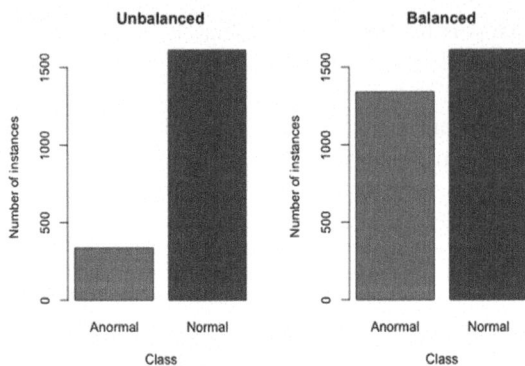

Fig. 2. Distribution of data balanced and unbalanced.

4.2 Activity Classification

After the data preparation stage was completed, a process of training and testing the data was started, using the classification methods: DT, SVM, RNA and NB. All these were compared using the same test scenario, using crossed validation with 10 subsets to guarantee the data was divided randomly, one part for training and one part for test and validation. The validation metrics were precision, coverage, FPR, TPR and F-Measure. In Table 3 you can see the results obtained by DT with the clusters described in Sect. 4.2. These results were considered successful, with a precision rate of 98.9% indicating wrong classification in 8 records only.

Table 3. Results Classifications Methods

Method	TpRate	FpRate	Precision	Recall
DT	98.1%	1.8%	98.1%	98.1%
SVM	96.5%	2.5%	96.5%	96.5%
RNA	97.3%	2.8%	97.3%	97.3%
NB	95.6%	3.8%	95.9%	95.6%

You can also see in Table 3 the comparison between all algorithms, noticing the DT algorithm obtained a precision of 98.1%, Recall 98.1%, TPRate 98.1% and FPRate 1.8%. Nevertheless, the results obtained in the RNA and SMO algorithms with polikernel are promising, with an accuracy like the values achieved by the DT Algorithm and are considered acceptable (Fig. 3).

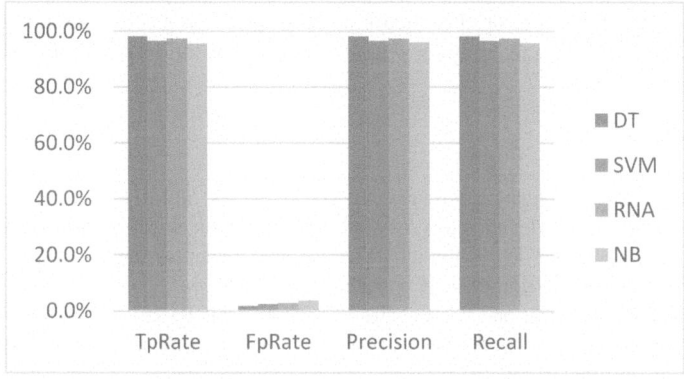

Fig. 3. Classifications Methods Results.

5   Result and Discussion

Depression is a disorder with a huge impact and growth in the population, researchers worldwide are working constantly in the identification of the symptoms to help professionals and people in general. The data intelligence techniques found in Data Mining have a relevant place in the field of the recognition and estimation of depression levels, using data to discover patterns useful to practitioners and patients. In this study, the data mining algorithms DT, SVM, RNA and NB were compared, and the results obtained demonstrated all algorithms were successful to recognize the different levels of depression contained in the dataset. The DT method achieved the best result with TPR (98.1%), FPR (1.8%), Precision (98.1%) and Recall (98.1%). These findings clearly show that it is possible to build a system based on traditional classification methods and data mining methods represent an alternative solution in the estimation of depression levels and they can be used to support decision-making processes.

6   Conclusion and Future Works

Depression can be considered a disorder of the state of mind of a person, where some can experience feelings of sadness, anger, and many others. According to Pan American Health Organization (PAHO/WHO), 50 million people in America suffer from depression disorder, and it is the main cause of mental health and disability worldwide. The World Health Organization (WHO) consider that 300 million people live with depression, a 18% increase from 2005 to 2015 [1], even more 21% of adults are experiencing mental illness of some kind, and 55% of them haven't received any treatment whatsoever [31].

In this research data mining algorithms such as DT, SVM, RNA and NB were compared, and the results obtained demonstrated all algorithms were successfully capable to recognize depression in the dataset. The DT method achieved the best result with TPR (98.1%), FPR (1.8%), Precision (98.1%) and Recall (98.1%). In future works, you could have hybridization with other data grouping techniques, including clustering with

Simple K-Means algorithm, or classification techniques using self-organizing maps, or applying feature selection techniques available in tools as the FEAST toolbox.

References

1. Pan American Health Organization.: Depression: Let's Talk, Says WHO, as Depression Tops List of Causes of Ill Health. https://www3.paho.org/hq/index.php?option=com_content&view=article&id=13102:depression-lets-talk-says-who-as-depression-tops-list-of-causes-of-ill-health&Itemid=1926&lang=es. [Consulted 01,04, 2023]
2. World Health Organization.: Coronavirus Disease (COVID-19) – Answer and Question. https://www.who.int/es/news-room/questions-and-answers/item/coronavirus-disease-covid-19. [Consulted 01,04, 2023]
3. Pan American Health Organization.:COVID-19 – Answer of OPS/OMS - Report 71, 25 of February 2022. https://www.paho.org/es/documentos/covid-19-respuesta-opsoms-reporte-71-25-febrero-2022. [Consulted 01,04, 2023]
4. Mazza, M.G., De Lorenzo, R., Conte, C., Poletti, S., Vai, B., Bollettini, I.: COVID-19 BioB outpatient clinic study group. anxiety and depression in COVID-19 survivors: role of inflammatory and clinical predictors. Brain, behav. Immune. **89**, 594-600 (2020)
5. Cabello Alarcón, H., Benavides Vásquez, A., Jaymez Vásquez, A.: Depresión en pacientes adultos con diabetes. Bol. Soc. Peru. Med. Interna, págs. 3–7 (1996)
6. Flores Ocampo, R., Jiménez Escobar, S.D., Pérez Hernández, S., Ramírez Serrano, P.B., Vega Valero, C.Z.: Depresión y ansiedad en estudiantes universitarios. Rev. electr. psicol. Iztacála **10**(2) (2007)
7. Molina, J.C., Mogrovejo, J.F., Morocho, I., Orellana, A., Delgado, N.: Prevalencia de depresión, diabetes e hipertensión arterial en pacientes geriátricos. Rev. méd. HJCA **5**(2), 145 2013
8. Nazir, N.I., Zainuddin, N., Selamat, A.: Sentiment analysis of depression illness during COVID-19 in social media: a preliminary study. In: 2022 3rd International Conference on Artificial Intelligence and Data Sciences (AiDAS), IPOH, Malaysia, 2022, pp. 238–242 (2022) https://doi.org/10.1109/AiDAS56890.2022.9918805
9. Bagga, N., Vashistha, P., Yadav, P.: Predicting depression from social networking data using machine learning techniques. In: 2021 3rd International Conference on Advances in Computing, Communication Control and Networking (ICAC3N), Greater Noida, India, 2021, pp. 128–132 (2021). https://doi.org/10.1109/ICAC3N53548.2021.9725402
10. Jin, Y., Yan, A., Sun, T., Zheng, P., An, J.: Microblog data analysis of emotional reactions to COVID-19 in China. J. Psychosom. Res. **161**, 110976 (2022). ISSN 0022–3999. https://doi.org/10.1016/j.jpsychores.2022.110976
11. Shobhika, S., Kumar, P., Chandra, S.: Prediction and comparison of psychological health during COVID-19 among Indian population and Rajyoga meditators using machine learning algorithms. Procedia Comput. Sci. **218**, 697–705 (2023). ISSN 1877–0509. https://doi.org/10.1016/j.procs.2023.01.050
12. Wongpanya, S.N., Nasa-ngium, P., Enkvetchakul, P., Nuankaew, P.: A predictive model for depression risk in thai youth during COVID-19. J. Adv. Inf. Technol. **13**(5), 450–455 (2022)
13. Lu, Z.: Analysis model of college students' mental health based on online community topic mining and emotion analysis in novel coronavirus epidemic situation. Front. Public Health **10**, 1000313 (2022). https://doi.org/10.3389/fpubh.2022.1000313
14. Zhang, S., et al.: The COVID-19 pandemic and mental health concerns on Twitter in the United States. Health Data Sci. **2022**, 9758408 (2022). https://doi.org/10.34133/2022/9758408

15. Zhang, Y., Lyu, H., Liu, Y., Zhang, X., Wang, Y., Luo, J.: Monitoring depression trends on Twitter during the COVID-19 pandemic: observational study. JMIR Infodemiology **1** (1), e26769 (2021). https://infodemiology.jmir.org/2021/1/e26769. https://doi.org/10.2196/26769
16. Ruiz-Frutos, C., Palomino-Baldeón, J.C., Ortega-Moreno, M., d.C. Villavicencio-Guardia, M., Dias, A., Bernardes, J.M., Gómez-Salgado, J.: Effects of the COVID-19 pandemic on mental health in peru: psychological distress. Healthcare **9**, 691 (2021). https://doi.org/10.3390/healthcare9060691
17. Li, D., Chaudhary, H., Zhang, Z.: Modeling spatiotemporal pattern of depressive symptoms caused by COVID-19 using social media data mining. Int. J. Environ. Res. Public Health **17**(14), 4988–5023 (2020). https://doi.org/10.3390/ijerph17144988
18. Harous, S., Serhani, M.A., El Menshawy, M., Benharref, A.: Hybrid obesity monitoring model using sensors and community engagement. In: 2017 13th International Wireless Communications and Mobile Computing Conference (IWCMC) (2017)
19. Salehnejad, R., et al.: Leveraging data mining techniques to understand drivers of obesity. In: 2017 IEEE Conference on Computational Intelligence in Bioinformatics and Computational Biology (CIBCB) (2017)
20. Patil, T.R., Sherekar, S.S.: Performance analysis of naive bayes and J48 classification algorithm for data classification. Int. J. Comput. Sci. Appl. **6**(2), 256–261 (2013)
21. Magerman, D.: Statistical decision-tree models for parsing. In: Proceedings of the 33rd annual meeting on Association for Computational Linguistics, vol. 6, pp. 276–283 (1995)
22. Machado, G., Recamonde Mendoza, M., Corbellini, L.G.: What variables are important in predicting bovine viral diarrhea virus? A random forest approach. Vet. Res. **46** (2015)
23. Abirami, S., Chitra, P.: Energy-efficient edge based real-time healthcare support system. In: Advances in Computers, vol. 120, pp. 339–368 (2020)
24. Fath, A.H., Madanifar, F., Abbasi, M.: Implementation of multilayer perceptron (MLP) and radial basis function (RBF) neural networks to predict solution gas-oil ratio of crude oil systems. Petroleum **6**, 80−90 (2020)
25. Kumar Satapathy, S., Dehuri, S., Kumar Jagadev, A., Mishra, S.: «Chapter 1 - Introduction» de EEG Brain Signal Classification for Epileptic Seizure Disorder Detection pp. 1–25 (2019)
26. Landwehr, N., Hall, M., Frank, E.: «Logistic Model Trees» Machine Learning, vol. 59 (2005)
27. Suresh, K., Dillibabu, R.: Designing a machine learning based software risk assessment model using Naïve Bayes algorithm. TAGA J. **14**, 3141–3147 (2018)
28. Naik, D.L., Kiran, R.: Naïve Bayes classifier, multivariate linear regression and experimental testing for classification and characterization of wheat straw based on mechanical properties. Ind. Crops Prod. **112**, 434–448 (2018)
29. Picard, R.W., et al.: Affective learning—a manifesto. BT Technol. J. **22**(4), 253–269 (2004)
30. Chawla, N.V., Bowyer, K.W., Hall, L.O., Kegelmeyer, W.P.: SMOTE: synthetic minority over-sampling technique. J. Artif. Intell. Res. **16**, 321e357 (2002)
31. NextStep Solutions.: The State of Mental Health in America 2023: Adult Prevalence and Access to Care. https://www.nssbehavioralhealth.com/nss-blog-the-state-of-mental-health-in-america-2023-adult-prevalence-and-access-to-care/. [Consulted 01,04, 2023]

Understanding Change Management in Hospital Context with the Integration of Digital Technologies

Beatriz Merino-Barbancho[✉] [iD] and Giuseppe Fico[iD]

Life Supporting Technologies, Universidad Politécnica de Madrid, Madrid, Spain
bmerino@lst.tfo.upm.es

Abstract. Change management is particularly important in the hospital context, as healthcare organizations are constantly evolving and facing new challenges such as changes in regulations, technological advancements, and shifts in patient needs. Effective change management can help hospitals navigate these changes and ensure they continue to provide high-quality patient care. This study emphasizes the importance of effective change management in hospitals, especially when introducing new technologies. Key factors for successful change management include establishing clear Key Performance Indicators (KPIs), having a structured roadmap, ensuring effective communication, and gradually implementing changes. It also stresses aligning technology with hospital goals, considering the well-being of patients and staff, environmental factors, user involvement, and responsiveness.

The present study is part of the activities of the ODIN project, funded by the European Commission (H2020, contract number 101017331), that aims to increase efficiency, productivity, and quality while reducing costs in hospitals by deploying these technologies to empower workers, enhance medical locations, and introduce autonomous and collaborative robots. The project's vision is to revolutionize hospital management with data-driven procedures enabled by Industry 4.0. A multifaceted approach is adopted, which includes a small literature review was conducted to understand change management models and an interactive workshop was held at the Hospital Clínico San Carlos (SERMAS, Madrid, Spain) with 15 participants from different countries to interact and understand the key elements to consider when developing the change management framework. The workshop was divided into two phases: 1) A combination of interactive exercises (3 canvases with key questions) to maintain the interest of the participants and 2) a group discussion. As a result, a comprehensive change management overview on several barriers and challenge is presented. This study presents a framework for overcoming change management by implementing relevant KPIs, offering insights and practical strategies in healthcare settings.

Keywords: change management · key enabler technologies · hospital · management

V. G. Duffy (Ed.): HCII 2024, LNCS 15376, pp. 144–153, 2025.
https://doi.org/10.1007/978-3-031-76809-5_11

1   Introduction

Change management (CM) is particularly key in hospital environments due to the constant evolution and countless challenges healthcare organizations face, such as regulatory changes, technological advances, changing patient needs, or the sudden outbreak of a pandemic such as COVID-19. Furthermore, technological innovation has become an integral aspect of our daily lives, with technologies such as wearable devices and information technology currently helping to transform processes in the healthcare sector. Both patients and professionals are immersed in a digital transformation of hospital processes at both the user and institutional level where they will experience a new era of healthcare with a patient-centered culture [1]. However, this scenario is not easy to manage, and failure rates can be attributed to several factors, including lack of vision and commitment from senior management, insufficient integration with other systems and processes within the organization, and poorly conceived implementation. Promoting change is therefore both demanding and exhausting, requiring managers to challenge established precedents and persist against ingrained habits and norms [2].

Taking this situation into account, the implementation of evidence-based approaches becomes especially difficult. This is because healthcare is complex, and context has a significant impact on the success of implementation and improvement efforts. Thus, there are several methods, tools and approaches that can be implemented in hospital settings to drive success. As an example, Kotter's Change Management Model [3] outlines an eight-step process for implementing change effectively within organizations. These steps include establishing a sense of urgency, forming a powerful coalition, creating a vision for change, communicating the vision, removing obstacles, generating short-term wins, consolidating gains, and anchoring the changes in the corporate culture. Bridges' Change Management Model [4], on the other hand, focuses on the psychological transition individuals undergo during change, consisting of three stages: Ending, Losing, and Letting Go; the Neutral Zone; and the New Beginning. Both models offer valuable frameworks for managing change, but their weaknesses become apparent when dealing with the rapid pace and complexity of digital transformation. So, despite the abundance of literature on new healthcare technologies, few studies exist on the actual change management practices and strategies used during the implementation of digital solutions in hospital processes.

This study focuses on a comprehensive analysis of current change management practices within hospitals, delving into how these practices are implemented and the challenges that healthcare institutions encounter through the case of ODIN project.

2   Materials and Methods

2.1   ODIN Project

The present study is based on the European ODIN project [5] (N° 101017331) that aims to increase efficiency, productivity, and quality while reducing costs in hospitals by deploying these technologies to empower workers, enhance medical locations, and introduce autonomous and collaborative robots. The main objective is to deliver an open digital platform, supporting a suite of services and Key Enabling Resources (KERs) empowered by robotics, Internet of Things (IoT) solutions and specialized AI. These resources will be implemented in three Reference Areas of Hospital Interventions: workers, robots and medical locations and will be tested through seven Clinical User Cases in leading hospitals of six European countries: Spain, France, Germany, Poland Netherlands and Italy.

2.2 Methods

The workshop conducted at Hospital Clínico San Carlos [6] (SERMAS: Madrid Health Service) in Madrid, Spain involved 15 participants whose background comprised engineers, healthcare professionals and hospital managers from different countries (Spain, Netherlands and Italy), with the aim of fostering interaction. The workshop was designed in two phases. **1) Phase One** - Interactive Exercises: The first phase comprised a series of interactive exercises using three different canvases, each with key questions designed to target specific aspects of change management. These exercises were crafted to keep participants engaged and focused on the critical elements of the change management framework. The questions and topics to be discussed have been based on a previous study conducted by Hospodkova et al. [7]. The details are provided in Table 1. **2) Phase Two** - Group Discussion: Following the interactive exercises, the workshop transitioned into a group discussion phase. This phase provided an opportunity for participants to delve deeper into the insights gathered from the previous phase, share their experiences, and discuss potential solutions and strategies. The workshop was led by a facilitator from the Technical University of Madrid partner from ODIN project, who guided the discussions and activities throughout the session.

Table 1. Questions provided to participants in the three canvases

Canvas	Questions/Topics to discuss
1	Identify all the actors involved in change management in your hospital Examine the most common changes in your hospitals
2	What is still missing in change management today
3	Pitfalls to avoid while implementing change management

3 Results

3.1 Canvas 1

Actors Involved in Change Management. As a result of the first dynamics and discussion, at least 9 groups of actors were identified (Table 2) as having an impact on the implementation of change management strategies in the hospital.

Table 2. Actors identified

Actor	Description
Financial departments	Responsible for managing the hospital's finances, including budgeting, accounting, and revenue management
Hospital managers	Responsible for overseeing the day-to-day operations of the hospital and making strategic decisions about its future direction
Data analytics	Responsible for collecting and analyzing data to support decision-making in the hospital
Healthcare professionals	Includes doctors, nurses, and other healthcare providers who work directly with patients involved in implementing new clinical protocols, adapting/adoption to new technology or equipment, and providing input on changes that will affect patient care
Technical team	Includes IT professionals, engineers, and other technical experts who support the hospital's infrastructure and systems
Research departments	Responsible for conducting research to improve patient care and outcomes involved in supporting evidence-based decision-making
Citizens	Members of the community involved in providing input on proposed changes or advocating for changes that will benefit the community as a whole
Patients	The individuals who receive care at the hospital. They are considered to provide feedback on their experiences and suggesting changes that will improve their care
Lawyers (Regulatory staff)	Responsible for ensuring that the hospital is compliant with relevant laws and regulations

The Most Common Changes in Hospitals. Considering the most common changes currently identified in this canvas, the implementation of new technologies driving significant improvements in efficiency and patient outcomes stand out. These changes include the gradual but growing adoption of artificial intelligence (AI), process automation, telemedicine, new software and implementation of electronic health records (EHR). The digitisation of hospital processes streamlines administrative tasks, freeing healthcare professionals to focus more on patient care. Telemedicine broadens access to care, allowing patients to receive remote consultations and follow-ups, improving convenience and continuity of care. The adoption of new IT systems, particularly the EHR, centralises patient information, facilitating better coordination between healthcare professionals and improving the quality of care. However, there is still some resistance to change from users, professionals and organisations. In addition to technological changes, hospitals are also introducing changes in their procurement processes, including modifications in the way they acquire and manage supplies and equipment, as well as alterations in their relationships with vendors or suppliers, which often entails an extra burden. In addition, legal and regulatory changes significantly affect the operation of hospitals, in particular those related to strict healthcare policies or regulations that need to be adopted into their practices quickly. Finally, the humanisation of care remains a critical aspect of hospital operations. While integrating advanced technologies, it is essential to maintain patient-centred care. Balancing technological advances with the need to humanise care ensures that patients receive value-based care. Figure 1 shows the most repeated words among the participants answers.

Fig. 1. Most common changes in hospital contexts extracted from the discussion

3.2 Canvas 2

What is Still Missing in Change Management Today. In the context of hospital change management, several critical aspects remain underdeveloped or inadequately addressed, as highlighted in Canvas 2 (see Table 3 for a summary). These aspects include proactive needs detection, an innovative mindset, technical trust, KPI measurement, feedback loops on KPIs, resource allocation, transparency, knowledge evidence, planning for change, SMART objectives, long-term vision, attitude, effective communication, leadership, and process optimization. Effective change management requires the ability to anticipate future needs and challenges before they become pressing issues, so this involves continuous monitoring of internal and external environments to identify trends, potential disruptions, and opportunities for improvement. By **proactively detecting needs**, hospitals are prepared and implement changes in a timely and efficient manner, minimizing reactive responses that often lead to suboptimal outcomes. Besides that, cultivating an **innovative mindset** within the hospital workforce is essential for fostering creativity and openness to new ideas. This encourages staff to think beyond traditional methods and explore novel solutions to complex problems. Also, building **technical trust** involves ensuring that staff (healthcare professionals and managers) have confidence in new technologies and systems so they can transmit this trust into daily care. This trust can be achieved through training and education, and clear communication about the benefits and limitations of the technologies (explainability). Nowadays we are still missing the **establishment and measurement of Key Performance Indicators (KPIs)** that are fundamental for assessing the progress and impact of change initiatives. KPIs provide quantifiable metrics that help hospitals track performance, identify areas for improvement, and ensure that objectives are being met. To improve the outcomes, **feedback loops** on KPIs should be implemented to involve regularly reviewing and analyzing performance data to make informed decisions. The **proper allocation of resources**, including financing, personnel and technology, is also lacking today. Resource limitations significantly hinder progress, making it essential for hospital leadership to secure and manage resources effectively to support change efforts. Maintaining transparency is a no-brainer either and fosters trust and collaboration between stakeholders. **Clear communication** about the goals, processes, and outcomes of change initiatives helps manage expectations and mitigate resistance. Likewise, using **evidence-based knowledge** is essential for making informed decisions in change management. This involves leveraging scientific research, best practices, and data analysis to guide the development and implementation of change strategies. A gap is found in a **well-defined plan** that provides a roadmap to achieve change objectives and ensures coordinated efforts across the hospital organization. This can be done by setting SMART (Specific, Measurable, Achievable, Relevant, Time-bound) objectives as they provide a structured framework for evaluating progress and success, ensuring that change initiatives are realistic and aligned with the organization's priorities. Also, today there is a clear lack of a long-term vision that is essential to sustain change and achieve lasting improvements as it articulates the future state of the hospital and guides strategic planning and decision making. Fostering a growth and resilience mindset helps staff accept change as an opportunity for development and improvement rather than a threat. Finally, **optimizing processes and workflows**, eliminating redundancies, and leveraging technology to improve process performance is key to providing high-quality care. Table 3 provides a summary of the results from Canvas II (Table 4).

Table 3. Results from Canvas II

Proactive needs detection	Innovative mindset
Technical trust	Digital hospital
KPI measurement	Feedback loops on KPIs
Resources	Transparency
Knowledge evidence	Plan for a change
SMART objectives	Long-term vision
Attitude	Effective communication
Leadership	Processes

Table 4. Results from Canvas III

Not define KPIs to evaluate results	Forget about environmental factors
Not have a roadmap	Not involving users
Bad communication between teams	Not acting upon feedback
Too many changes too quickly	
Technology push	
Avoiding some stages of the process	
Lack of humanity	
Lack of coordination	

3.3 Canvas 3

Pitfalls to Avoid While Implementing Change Management. In this canvas, participants dynamically analyzed the current efforts to implement changes in the hospital context. One critical pitfall to avoid, as highlighted in Canvas 2, is the failure to define Key Performance Indicators (KPIs) to evaluate the outcomes of the change. Without clear KPIs, measuring the success of the change becomes challenging, and hospitals may struggle to determine if the change positively impacts patient care and outcomes. Another identified pitfall is the absence of a roadmap or plan for the change. Without a clear plan, hospitals may face difficulties in implementing the change effectively, leading to confusion and frustration among staff and patients.

Effective communication is crucial in change management; poor communication between teams can be a significant pitfall. Communication must be clear and transparent to ensure alignment around the hospital's goals and objectives. Hospitals should also avoid implementing too many changes too quickly, as rapid changes can overwhelm staff and patients, hindering effective implementation and causing confusion and frustration.

Participants highlighted that another pitfall is the push for technology adoption without alignment with the hospital's needs. Ignoring certain stages of the change management process is also detrimental; each stage is essential for achieving successful outcomes, and hospitals should complete each stage thoroughly. Lack of humanity in change management is a major concern; hospitals must ensure that changes prioritize the well-being of patients and staff. Finally, not involving users in the change management process and failing to act upon feedback are also significant pitfalls to avoid.

Through this dynamic analysis, it became clear that ODIN must consider these aspects to drive significant change, effectively integrate technologies, and improve patient care and outcomes.

3.4 Group Discussion

After completing the execution of phase 1, the group discussion took place on the aspects that caught the most attention among the participants of those mentioned above. In this sense, the lack of KPIs was notoriously a hot topic. After several iterations, a consensus was reached on several KPIs that must be taken into account in change management. Figure 2 provides a detailed view of the different KPIs, illustrating their importance through specific examples. For example, the "Feedback Response Time" measures how quickly feedback is addressed, ensuring that responses are timely and effective. By tracking patient satisfaction, hospitals can gauge the impact of changes on patient/professional experiences, helping to ensure that improvements are positively received by patients/professionals. Additionally, the "Trustworthiness" KPI measures patients' trust in the healthcare system, which is essential for maintaining a strong patient-healthcare professional relationship. KPIs approaching "Training Completion Rate" monitor the effectiveness of training programs for healthcare staff, ensuring that all members are adequately prepared to implement and sustain changes while adopting the new technologies. Monitoring "Acceptance" (TAM-003) helps to understand the adoption and inclusion of new technologies. As a result, they could potentially provide a structured way to monitor, evaluate, and refine hospital processes continuously.

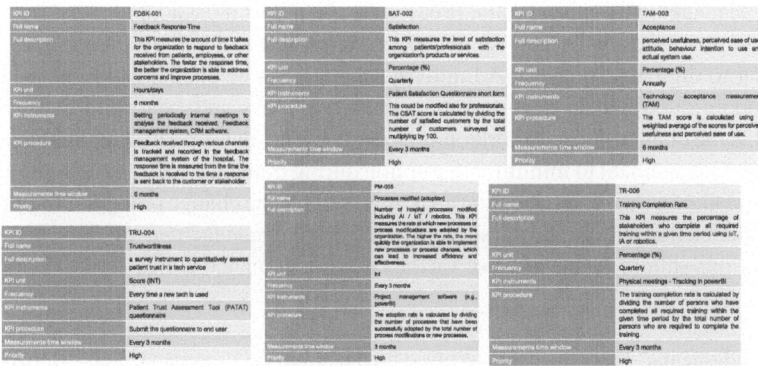

Fig. 2. KPIs designed based on the group discussion

Finally, ODIN's proposed change management framework (Fig. 3) illustrates a comprehensive approach to digital transformation in healthcare. It emphasizes the integration of four key players: patients, healthcare workers, technology and organizational structures. The key factors for the success of this transformation are comprised of ensuring buy-in for change, building trust in new technologies, and providing comprehensive training programs for healthcare staff. The framework is guided by a digital transformation strategy that aligns these actors and factors considering continuous monitoring over time involving the use of Key Performance Indicators (KPIs) to measure progress and the collection of feedback.

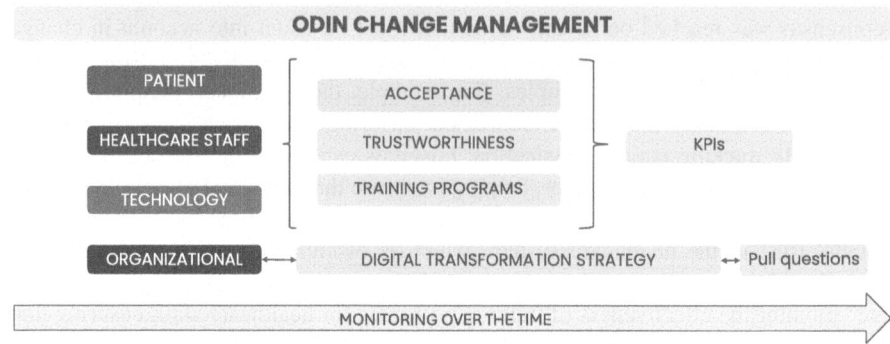

Fig. 3. ODIN change management approach

4 Conclusion

Change management is an essential process that hospitals must adopt to ensure the successful implementation of new strategies, systems and technologies, especially when they plan to digitize a process. Admittedly, change can be challenging and, without a well-thought-out approach, can lead to resistance, delays and even failure. This study highlights the challenges and shortcomings encountered in hospitals and the importance of change management to minimize disruption during transitions. Communication, feedback, acceptance, trust and education are key aspects of the change process. Furthermore, it is concluded that to evaluate the success of the change management process, healthcare organizations should define and use various key performance indicators (KPIs) for this purpose.

Acknowledgments. This project has received funding from the European Union's Horizon 2020 research and innovation programme under grant agreement N° 101017331. We would like to thank all the participants, especially Dra. Maria Luaces, Dr. Julio Mayol, Jorge Nieto, and Laura Llorente, for hosting the workshop at Hospital Clínico San Carlos.

References

1. Stoumpos, A.I., Kitsios, F., Talias, M.A.: Digital transformation in healthcare: technology acceptance and its applications. Int. J. Environ. Res. Public Health **20**(4), 3407 (2023). https://doi.org/10.3390/ijerph20043407
2. Al-Abri, R.: Managing change in healthcare. Oman Med. J. **22**(3), 9–10 (2007)
3. Kotter, J.P.: Leading Change, With a New Preface by the Author, 1R edn. Harvard Business Review Press, Boston, Mass (2012)
4. 'Transitions: Making Sense of Life's Changes, Revised 25th Anniversary Edition - William Bridges - Google Libros'. Accessed 23 May 2024. https://books.google.es/books/about/Transitions.html?id=U8dHzQEACAAJ&redir_esc=y

5. 'Odin Smart Hospitals | Odin Smart Hospital'. Accessed 23 May 2024. https://odin-smarthosp itals.eu/
6. 'Hospital Clínico San Carlos', Hospital Clínico San Carlos. Accessed 23 May 2024. https:// www.comunidad.madrid/hospital/clinicosancarlos/
7. Hospodková, P., Berežná, J., Barták, M., Rogalewicz, V., Severová, L., Svoboda, R.: Change management and digital innovations in hospitals of five european countries. Healthcare **9**(11), 1508 (2021). https://doi.org/10.3390/healthcare9111508

Design of Dashboards for CRM Associated with Health and Wellbeing Tourism

Célia M. Q. Ramos[1,3(✉)] ⓘ, Rashed Isam Ashqar[3,2] ⓘ, and Alexandre Contreiras[1] ⓘ

[1] ESGHT, University of Algarve, 8005-139 Faro, Portugal
cmramos@ualg.pt
[2] Al Zaytona University of Science and Technology (ZUST), Salfit, Palestine
[3] CinTurs, University of Algarve, 8005-139 Faro, Portugal
riashqar@ualg.pt

Abstract. Design of dashboards is strategic for the Customer Relationship Management (CRM) associated with Health and Wellness Tourism, considering all the knowledge acquired about Health and Wellness Tourism, the Machine Learning algorithms identified, and the characteristics to be considered in the development of the reports. It is intended to identify the components to be used in the development of the dashboards, which allow for control of the information associated with this business and to detect deviations in operation, taking into account concepts associated with User Experience/Consumer Experience and the Customer Journey of this type of customers in order to identify opportunities to innovate and grow economically, through the creation of intelligence about this business. In this paper, the presentation of examples of dashboards developed in Power BI, it was possible to show that customer capital indicators can be included, under different dimensions that characterize it. However, the lack of real data to apply in the formulas of the new indicators is one of the limitations of this paper.

Keywords: CRM · Data Storytelling · User Experience (UX) · Data mining · Health and Wellness Tourism · Hospitality

1 Introduction

The implementation of a social consumer relationship management (Social CRM), or CRM 2.0, must integrate the possibility of developing customer-centered co-creation processes [1] to involve the customer. This leads to the co-creation of personalized experiences in the area of health and well-being. With interaction in different communication channels and the proliferation of customer contact points, offering personalized services continuously and throughout the entire customer journey [2].

The CRM system can be enriched with gamification mechanisms [2]; it must allow communication between all interested parties (customers, hotels, event companies, that is, the entire market ecosystem and the company ecosystem). With a view to monitoring and evaluating the hotel's performance, taking into account financial results and contextual factors (such as personality, customer profiles, and needs, privacy, ethical and legal issues, cultural and social values, and other market factors) that can influence relationships of the tourist's health and well-being satisfaction. This implies the acquisition and enjoyment of services and products linked to health-related and private information of the customer, for their loyalty and loyalty. It is necessary to guarantee the security and privacy of their data while the hotel establishes a trusting and secure relationship with personal data protection mechanisms.

The need to understand relationships between customers and the hotel's financial performance is one of the most critical factors for the success and competitiveness of this industry [3], which takes on a more demanding dimension when it comes to a hotel. That offers services in health and well-being tourism, which deals with different aspects related to the health and well-being of its customers, where it is necessary to include biometrics and health information. The metrics associated with the concepts of Customer Lifetime Value (CLV) [4] are no longer sufficient. It is necessary to include new metrics, as well as the concepts of hotel intellectual capital indicators. Metrics that evaluate the customer in the context of social media, combined not with the most straightforward statistics, but with business intelligence tools, data mining and machine learning techniques, and concepts of customer analytics, customer experience metrics, customer interaction metrics, customer satisfaction metrics, online reach metrics and online financial metrics, customer engagement affective, behavioral, and cognitive metrics [2].

According to Sigala [2], the implementation of a Social CRM must include (1) relational information processes referring to companies' tools and capabilities to monitor, capture, analyze valuable customers and market insights, infrastructure and integration of information systems; (2) internal (with employees) and external (with customers and customer communities) information communication capabilities; and (3) ability to manage various engagement management issues, including managing customer communities, employees, customer engagement, user permission, and ethics/privacy.

Taking into account the dynamics that exist in the relationship between the customer and the company, or between the guest and the hotel, the importance of developing social CRM or even more innovative ones. It is extremely important to create dashboards that allow analyzing all associated metrics to the User experience, where the concepts of Data Storytelling must be combined with metrics that analytically evaluate consumer behavior (customer analytics).

2 Knowledge Management and Competitive Intelligence

2.1 User Experience (UX)

The definition of User Experience (UX) considers simplicity and elegance and goes far beyond a set of items on a checklist or giving customers what they say they want, in the words of Norman and Nielson [5]. The quality of the user experience is defined by a set of several services that come together in a single space: engineering, marketing, graphics, and interface design, which is sometimes confused with User Interface and Usability.

UX is part of the concepts associated with HCI (Human Computer Interaction) combined with interaction design [6], where "it ranges from traditional usability to beauty, hedonic, affective or experiential aspects of the use of technology" [6, p. 91], as shown in Fig. 1.

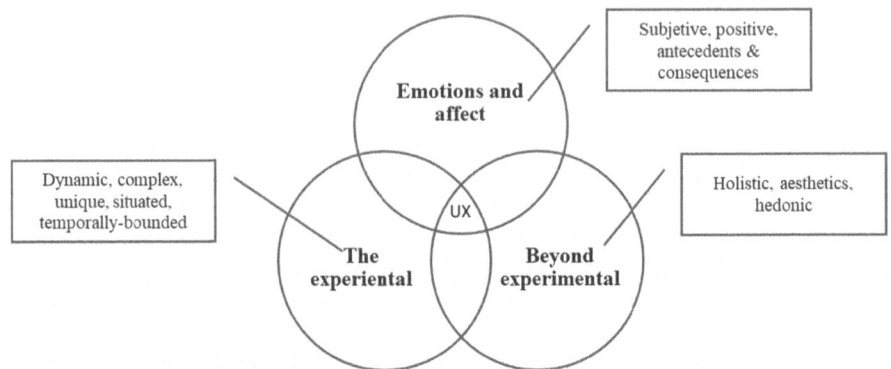

Fig. 1. UX Components. Source: Hassenzahl and Tractinsky [6, p. 95].

Emotions. In human decision-making, the aspects considered are emotions and affection, so in interaction with technology, they are also considered. In this sense, UX must consider positive emotions such as joy, fun, and pride so that the interaction with the user results in an emotionally positive interaction that provides subjective well-being [6, 7].

Experiential Perspective. The experiential component has an impact on the user's well-being, as it assumes that the way the experience and the experience itself can influence the consumer; although they are related, they are not the same.

UX focuses on positive aspects of the relationship between humans and technology, it depends on the user's condition, the context in which they are inserted, and the design characteristics. So, it should privilege exceptional experiences in terms of quality rather than just preventing usability problems, the latter being associated with the efficiency and ease of use of a device or interface, on the part of the user/consumer.

2.2   UX Design

User Experience Design (UED) is defined by the International Organization for Standardization (ISO) [8] as the perceptions and responses that human beings perceive because of the use or anticipation of the use of a product, system, or service. This definition can be divided into two parts: the user's perception and response, which is not controlled by how the design is conceived, and the use of the product, system, or service, which can be managed by designers through the features developed to elicit a behavioral reaction on how it should be used. The designer should consider aspects that can answer questions about how the product or system will be used, such as: why it is used, how it will be used, and what components will be used. In addition, concepts of visual design, psychology, and interaction with the product or system should be considered from a user-centered perspective.

User-centered design involves understanding who the consumers are through interviews, focus groups, and surveys, to identify the "persona" and "customer journey maps" and understand the needs of users to develop appropriate "user stories". After the development of a prototype, usability tests, A/B tests, heuristic estimates, inclusion tests, and accessibility limitations should be carried out [9].

In user-centered design, the development of the User Interface (UI) should be considered, combining the following components: content, functionality, information architecture (inverted pyramid), interaction, and visual aspects (buttons, colors, icons).

2.3 User Interface (UI)

The User Interface is the point of interaction and communication between the human being and the computing device, while the UX is about the experience that the human being has when interacting with the User Interface, developed with the components mentioned above.

UI has seen its relevance increase in terms of new partnerships, such as in the development of dashboards to support the decision-making process of companies associated with Business Intelligence tools, where data visualization plays an extremely relevant role, such as in the analysis of relationships associated with consumer behaviour or as components of CRM systems. Developing a data-driven dashboard can be challenging due to the complexity of the datasets, poor UI design, and insufficient storytelling [10].

Suprata [10] considered that it must be understood which data will be used, which metrics to include in the appropriate context, and how to transmit numerical information. This contributes to the involvement of the decision-maker, and understanding which decision to make is a challenge. Understand who will use the dashboard and choose which data and metrics to view in the right context. Knowing how to convey information, generate engagement, and persuade the public are essential in today's business practices. Therefore, it is necessary to define appropriate dashboards for the decision-making process, which contribute to promoting knowledge about consumers and the business and include concepts that allow the creation of a narrative associated with data (data storytelling).

2.4 Data Storytelling

Data storytelling is a way of using information to create a narrative. According to Zanan and Aziz [11], "Data storytelling" is becoming a process of the effectiveness of visualization tools, as it has the potential to increase the effectiveness of communication [12].

The development of effective dashboards, which support decision-making and include the essentials of data storytelling to communicate with decision-makers, is an aspect that should also be considered in the analysis of the consumer and their consumer experience since companies have to analyze data that increases 24 h a day, 7 days a week.

Data storytelling is an approach that combines data analysis, visualization, and narrative techniques to communicate complex information and insights in a compelling way (Segel & Heer, 2010). It recognizes the innate human tendency to understand and remember information through stories, making data more accessible and engaging [13].

Also, data storytelling involves transforming raw data into meaningful narratives that captivate audiences, increase understanding, and drive action [14]. Key concepts in data storytelling include data analysis, visualization, narrative structure, and audience focus. Data analysis involves optimizing insights, patterns, and correlations of datasets using statistical methods and analytical techniques [15]. Visualization techniques, such as charts, graphs, and infographics, are employed to represent data visually and facilitate understanding [16]. The narrative structure provides a framework for organizing the story, incorporating an introduction, a clear, proven supporting objective, and a conclusion [15]. Finally, an audience-centric approach adapts the narrative to the target audience's level of data literacy, domain knowledge, and preferences [17].

Evolution of Data Storytelling. The evolution of data storytelling can be traced back in time to the theory of information visualization, which aimed to make complex data more accessible through visual representations [18]. Over time, the focus shifted from static visualizations to interactive, narrative-driven approaches [13]. Additionally, advances in data analytics and big data processing have contributed to the splendor of data storytelling. The abundance of data generated across multiple domains requires effective communication of insights and knowledge findings [19]. Data storytelling has emerged as a response to this need, offering a structured and engaging approach to conveying data-driven insights to diverse audiences.

Practical Applications. Data storytelling finds practical applications in various domains. In business, it helps organizations present key performance indicators, market trends, and customer insights to support decision-making and strategic planning [18]. In marketing, data storytelling is used to convey brand-associated narratives, consumer behavior insights, and campaign performance indicators [20]. Journalists use data storytelling to communicate investigative reports, election results, and social issues, increasing transparency and public engagement [21].

To effectively utilize data storytelling, several steps are typically followed. This includes identifying the purpose of the story, selecting relevant data sources, conducting exploratory data analysis, gaining insights, and structuring a coherent narrative. Additionally, choosing appropriate graphics and visualizations is crucial for conveying information accurately and engagingly [17]. As analyzed in Fig. 2, graphs should be aligned with the nature of the data and the message to be communicated, considering factors such as data types, relationships, and reliance on specific patterns [22–25].

Nowadays, business intelligence tools such as Power BI and/or Tableau provide easy-to-use interactive interfaces for creating visually appealing data stories. These tools offer a range of customizable visualizations and data storytelling features that make it easy to create engaging narratives and interactive dashboards. The versatility and effectiveness of data storytelling make these tools valuable in various industries, allowing for effective communication of insights, influencing decision-making, and generating positive results.

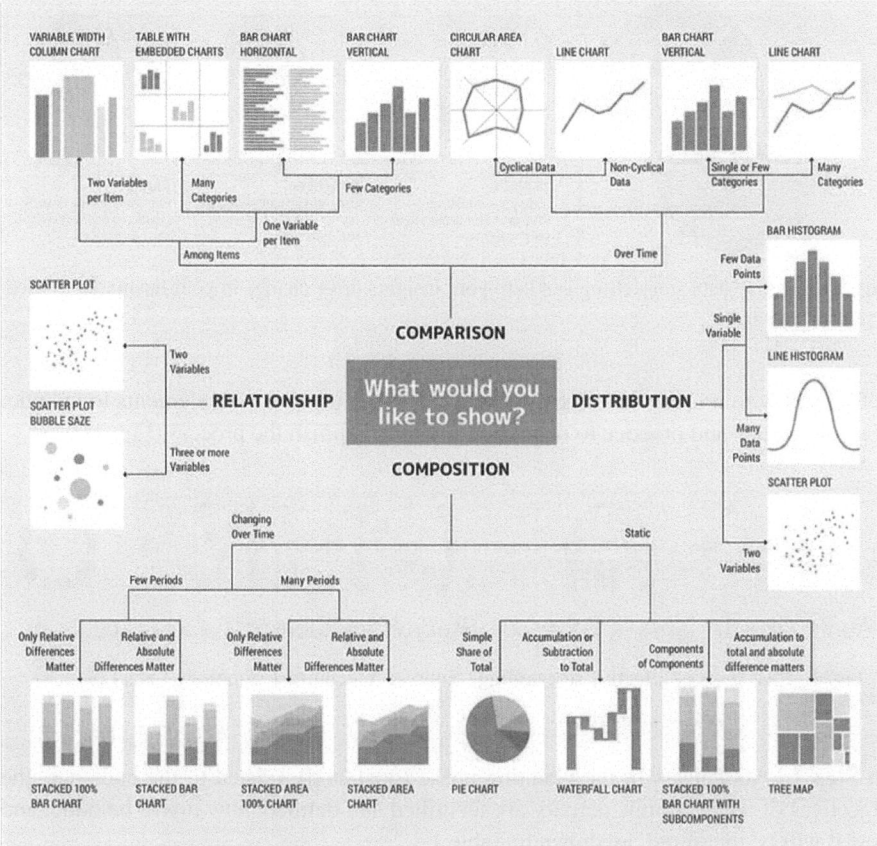

Fig. 2. Which visual element to use? Source: Abela [23].

2.5 Data Storytelling and Dashboards

Data storytelling is an approach that combines data, visual, and narrative aspects [26], which allows for an explanation, involvement, and clarify aspects of the business and consumer behavior, which allows involving the user in terms of credibility, emotional, logical, and rational, as shown in Fig. 3.

In an organization, dashboards can be of three types: operational, tactical, and strategic. The main role of the operational one is the monitoring of operations, the tactical one is the analysis of the measures that represent progress, and the strategic one is the management regarding the execution and definition of strategies [10, 27].

In order to design an effective dashboard that allows the definition of a business measurement model, the following steps should be considered [10, 26]: (1) Planning to define the audience, in terms of knowledge, objectives, and needs; (2) Define the insights, through the collection and relationship of the data; (3) Create context, whether on mobile devices or in person to choose the best view; (4) Adapt to the audience, by

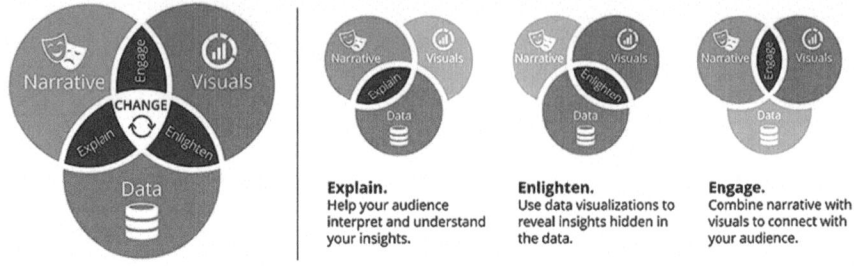

Explain.
Help your audience interpret and understand your insights.

Enlighten.
Use data visualizations to reveal insights hidden in the data.

Engage.
Combine narrative with visuals to connect with your audience.

Fig. 3. Effective data storytelling can help your insights drive change in your business. Source: Dykes [17, p. 32].

defining how to present the insights (Freytag's Pyramid) and what elements to include; (5) Consolidate and practice to receive feedback and finish the process (Fig. 4).

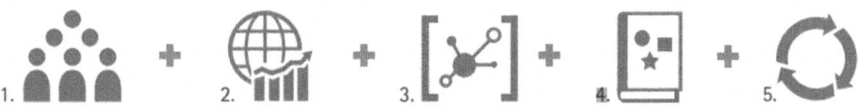

Audience + Insights + Context + Storytelling Elements + Practice

Fig. 4. Five steps of effective storytelling. Source: Accenture Technology Labs [28, p. 4].

In Step 1. Audience - In the planning phase (goal step), related to the audience, the objectives of the economic activity are identified and defined, how it will be done, and how it will be measured, as shown in Table 1.

Table 1. Stage of planning a business model and questions that must be answered by the board.

What's the objective?	How will it be done? (customer journey)	How will it be measured? (customer journey)
Increase customers	By email marketing	KPI to be defined according to the objective
Sell a new product	By social media	
Testing a new concept	By social media	
Measure the degree of satisfaction	By email and mobile	
Launch a new product	Across all channels	

Source: Adapted from Zeferino [26, p. 238]

In Step 2. Insights - Data & Tool step: Phase define the data sources and tools to use in data analysis Table 2, to obtain the insights.

Table 2. Insights step to define data sources and technology tools.

What data?	What technology?	What integration?
Internal and external (metrics, KPI, etc.)	Analytics tools, email, social media, mobile, etc.	How will they be integrated? By API?

Source: Adapted from Zeferino [26, p. 240]

Table 3. Phase of auscultation of results.

What evidence?	What actions?
Low level of subscriptions	Consider 2nd wave of emails
Low level of product purchase	Consider promotional action
High level of product purchase	Spread the degree of endorsement
Low search level	Rephrase keywords
Low CTR (Click through rate)	Rephrase content (engagement)

Source: Adapted from Zeferino [26, p. 241]

In Step 3. Context – Listening step: This phase in which the dynamics and results are evaluated to see if adjustments are needed, as shown in Table 3.

In Step 4. Elements of Storytelling – Analysis and knowledge production phase (Intelligence step): This phase in which knowledge is generated and the decision-maker can evaluate the operation of the business and the plan, as shown in Table 4.

Table 4. Analysis and knowledge production phase (Intelligence step).

What information?	What knowledge?	What insights?
Sales exceeded the target (KPI)	The product had an excellent acceptance (feedback)	This product is unique in this market segment with this positioning (perceived attributes)
Subscription volume (form) exceeds objectives (KPI)	Subscriptions were received from geographic regions that were not segmented (source)	The level of interest is far above the initial expectations (sales potential)

Source: Adapted from Zeferino [26, p. 242]

In addition to the one shown in Fig. 2, it is important to identify how the visual elements of each graph should be used. Table 5 presents suggestions, in terms of types and what is proposed for use.

To communicate information through a narrative, it must be elaborated as the structure of a story, for example, according to Freytag's Pyramid, presented in Fig. 5.

Table 5. Charts and chart components as visuals to consider in a dashboard.

Chart Type	Proposed for use?
Plain text	Can be used to display a number
Tables	Used to present and communicate different units of measurement
Pie charts	Represent a distribution or the relative share of each segment (slice) over the total, which represents 100%. Used to contribute to the revenue of each product
Line graphs	To show trends over a period of time. It should be used with models that are intended to emphasize a sequence or trend over time
Column or Bar chart	Ideal for comparing items over a period of time for a given set of values, such as categories
Stacked columns or stacked bars	Allows you to compare several variables at the same time, each category in a color and each portion of each variable
Radar Graphs	Allows the comparison of several values in a radial format
Area charts	Can be thought of as a subset of line charts, where the area below the line is colored. It can be useful when comparing data series
Composite charts, rows, and columns	To compare two variables that are expressed at different scales two Y-axes can be used

Source: Adapted from Suprata [10, p. 5]

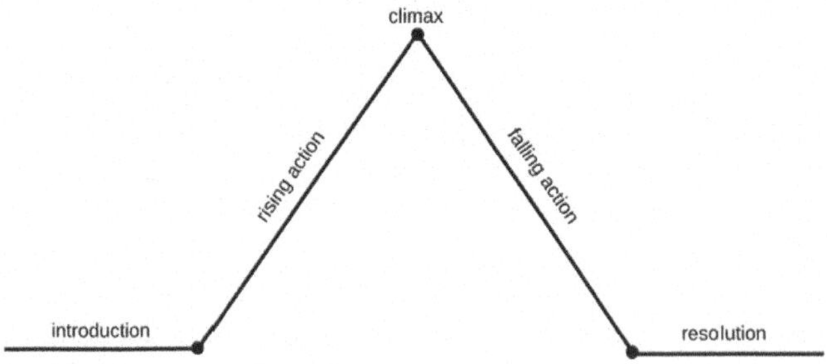

Fig. 5. Freytag's Pyramid. Source: Adapted from Suprata [10, p. 6].

Figure 5 represents Freytag's Pyramid and the moments: (1) Introduction or exposition, to identify the data sources; (2) Rising action on what can be found in the data? (3) Climax to present key insights, (4) Falling action where details, contexts, interpretation, and explanations are presented; (5) Resolution or catastrophe to analyze the key insights and their importance.

In Step 5. Practice - Actionable step (Intelligence step): This phase in which the knowledge generated in the previous steps should be used, and new strategies should be defined, as shown in Table 6.

Table 6. Business optimization phase through the developed dashboards.

What insights?	What decisions?	What actions?
This product is unique in this market segment with this positioning (perceived attributes)	Review sales objectives and consider increasing goals for the year	Design a new short-term campaign introducing a new product feature
This product was not configured correctly for this segment (causes for failure)	Review the communication strategy and understand which digital media can support this decision	New Proof of Concept

Source: Adapted from Zeferino [26, p. 243]

Currently, companies are looking for methods that allow them to obtain information about their business. However, a methodology that combines the presentation of data with visual elements, communicated in visual support such as dashboards, is needed to increase the speed of knowledge acquisition. As well as to enhance the emergence of insights and innovation easily and intuitively in data visualization.

3 Methodology for Elaboration of Dashboard with Indicators Associated with the Hotel Customer Experience

3.1 Research Context

The experience is associated with economic offers and differentiated services provided to the customer, where the focus is no longer centered on the product and shifts to the customer. In addition, management has shifted from physical asset-centric to experience-based assets, which causes a disruptive effect that forces the integration of innovations [29].

In the area of hospitality, innovations must be customer-centric, considering the concepts of "customer centricity, empowerment, and engagement" [30, p. 19]. As the main factors of the new type of customer service, innovation occurs mainly to improve the quality of service and the customer experience [29].

Customer-centric innovations can be considered as functional or experiential innovation [29]. The functional ones are related to the needs associated with the guest's stay. Moreover, experiential ones are related to the resources, the location of a hotel, and the skills and competencies of the employees providing the services.

Preparing a strong customer experience is a new goal for the hotel manager [38], it must be implemented through CRM with a focus on metrics that allow the evaluation of the value of the guest, such as CLV [31], together with other metrics (or performance indicators, as shown in Fig. 6.

The innovation associated with hotel services can be accomplished through new ways of delivering a benefit, new service concepts, or business models through continuous operational improvement, technology, investment in employee performance, or the management of the guest customer experience [29]. This challenge can be overcome with the use of CRM if the objective is to increase competitiveness, face competition, create differentiation, and evaluate the value of each customer [2]. Also, the creation of new performance indicators and innovation in the indicators such as intellectual capital of an organization in general, and in particular of a hotel.

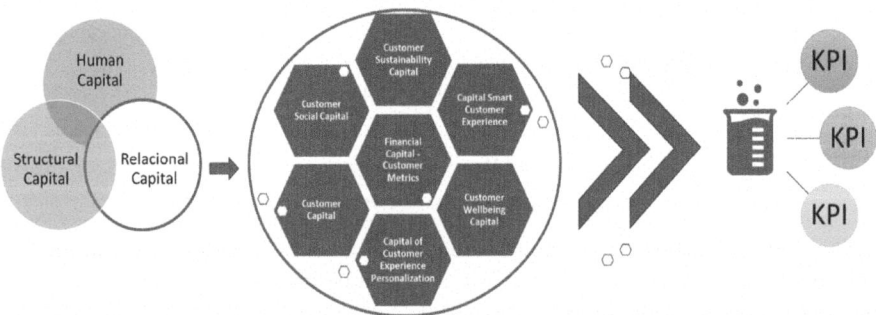

Fig. 6. Conceptual model of the relationship between the Guest's capital and Performance Indicators. Source: Author's elaboration.

Methodology for Defining New KPIs. For the definition of new performance indicators associated with the hotel, health and wellness tourism, and the guest experience, the following methodology was considered:

1. Literature review on intellectual capital indicators and all metrics associated with different areas of society that are related to the client–guest.
2. Identification of indicators associated with each dimension.
3. Conceptual development of the relationship between guest capital and Performance Indicators.
4. Definition of the methodology for data collection.
5. Transforming data so analytics can be performed.
6. Apply Text Mining Algorithm (for Online Comments).
7. Prepare the variables to consider in the model.
8. Define and estimate the regression model.
9. Evaluate results.
10. Create Dashboards with KPIs.

3.2 New Indicators of Capital Associated with the Client

New indicators were presented in the form of formulas, which express the relationship between the variables that measure the client's capital in various dimensions:

First, Health & Wellness Customer Capital (HWCC) is presented in Eq. 1.

$$HWCC = \beta_1 + \beta_2 * CC + \beta_3 * CFC + \beta_4 * SC + \beta_5 * SEC$$
$$+ \beta_6 * SUC + \beta_7 * WBC + \beta_8 * CEPC \tag{1}$$

where CC – Customer Capital, CFC – Customer Financial Capital, SC – Social Capital, SEC – Smart Experience Capital, SUC - Sustainability Capital, WBC – Well-Being Capital and CEPC – Customer Experience Personalization Capital.

Second, the Key Performance Indicator (KPI) of the HWCC Client, whose Eq. 2 expresses the calculation to be performed.

$$KPI_i = \frac{\sum_{i=1}^{n}(\alpha_i * X_i)}{\sum_{i=1}^{n}\alpha_i} \tag{2}$$

Third, the Health and Well-Being Customer Index (HWBCI) defines the positioning of a client when compared to others in terms of their capital in the different dimensions, which is expressed in Eq. 3.

$$HWBCI_i = \frac{\sum_{i=1}^{n}(KPI_i)}{n} \tag{3}$$

3.3 Methodology to Develop a Dashboard, a Business Measurement Model for the Health and Wellness Tourism Client

As mentioned above, the methodology to develop an effective dashboard, taking into account the concepts of data storytelling, which allows the definition of a business measurement model for the Health and Wellness Tourism client, is defined by five steps:

1. Planning to define the audience, in terms of knowledge, objectives and needs.
2. Define insights, through the collection and relationship of data.
3. Create the context, whether on mobile devices or in person to choose the best view and what elements.
4. Adapt to the audience, by defining how to present insights (Freytag's Pyramid).
5. Consolidate and practice to receive feedback and finish the process.

4 Results

In this section, the focus is on the elaboration of dashboards that allow the analysis of the consumer experience of health and wellness tourism, and, at the same time, it is possible to calculate metrics that define the relationship capital associated with the customer, in the various dimensions associated with it.

4.1 Planning to Define the Audience and Objectives

One of the main aspects to consider at this stage is to define the objectives, that is, who the dashboard is for, what its functions, its knowledge. And what indicators you need for your decision-making.

In terms of objectives, as presented in Table 1, applied to the hotel industry and relevant to the strategic decision-maker, the following can be considered: increasing the number of customers, measuring the degree of satisfaction, or launching a new product.

4.2 Define Insights by Collecting and Linking Data

After defining the objective(s), the next step is to collect the data. The guest data considered in this study belong to the Hotel Booking Demand Dataset [32] although it does not refer to health and wellness tourism guests, it is one of the most complete datasets found by the authors with characteristics of hotel customers. This dataset is made up of booking information for an urban hotel and a resort hotel. In total, there are 119,390 reservations scheduled to arrive between July 1, 2015, and August 31, 2017.

The identification of the variables, the type of data, and the statistical description are presented in Table 7, which totals twenty-eight variables, not all of which will be used in the present study.

Create the Technology Context for Better Data Visualization. At this stage, it is important to identify where the dashboard will be visualized and which technology should be used for it; in the present study, Microsoft Power BI and its reports visualized on PCs were considered.

Tailor to the Audience or How to Present the Insights. The concepts of data storytelling, from its visual elements, and other characteristics that were not considered in this study, such as colors, and fonts, among other graphics, are highlighted in this stage, in which the dashboards are prepared according to the metrics and indicators considered.

One of the limitations of the present study is the lack of a panoply of dimensions associated with the customer, including the data necessary to calculate the new indicators, as well as other older ones associated with customer analytics such as Recency, Frequency, Monetary value (RFM), and Customer Lifetime.

However, it was possible to use the database, use the concepts of data storytelling, and develop dashboards that allow the analysis of the business model, such as Fig. 7, 8, 9, and 10.

In Fig. 7, the concepts of Data Storytelling were applied to analyze reservations made by countries and channels, which allows the analysis of revenue, number of meals and number of adults per reservation.

In Fig. 8 it is possible to analyze the reservations for the three countries, with the most reservations, with the aim of understanding the behavior of their guests.

Figure 9 shows a dashboard where it is possible to verify that visual elements are combined with visualizations of artificial intelligence algorithms, as is the case of the main influencers.

In Fig. 10, it is possible to visualize the result of unsupervised Machine Learning algorithms that assigned a cluster to each guest; of the four that were obtained, the application of an artificial intelligence visualization (main influencers) also appears. This dashboard aims to show the characteristics of each cluster, the daily average per cluster *(adr)*, if they ask for parking or if they have other special requests, the type of meal chosen, as well as the characteristics in terms of the household that positions them in cluster 2, as an example, which can be chosen another from the combo box.

Table 7. Variables contained in the data are to be considered in the present study.

ID	Variable	Data type	Description
1	*is_canceled (dependent variable, DV)*	Categorical	2 categories: canceled and not canceled
2	*hotel*	Categorical	2 categories: resort hotel and city hotel
3	*lead_time*	Numerical	Number of lead days
4	*arrival_date_year*	Variable related to time	Arrival year: 2015–2017
5	*arrival_date_month*	Variable related to time	Arrival month: 1–12
6	*arrival_date_week_number*	Variable related to time	Arrival week: 1–53
7	*arrival_date_day_of_month*	Variable related to time	Arrival day in month: 1–31
8	*stays_in_weekend_nights*	Numerical	Number of weekend nights
9	*stays_in_week_nights*	Numerical	Number of week nights
10	*adults*	Numerical	Number of adults
11	*children*	Numerical	Number of children
12	*babies*	Numerical	Number of babies
13	*meal*	Categorical	4 categories: type of booked meal
14	*country*	Categorical	Customer source country
15	*market_segment*	Categorical	8 categories: market segment designation
16	*distribution_channel*	Categorical	5 categories: booking distribution channel
17	*is_repeated_guest*	Categorical	2 categories: whether is a repeat consumer
18	*previous_cancellations*	Numerical	Number of previous cancellations
19	*previous_bookings_not_canceled*	Numerical	Number of previous bookings not canceled
20	*reserved_room_type*	Categorical	9 categories: reserved room type
21	*booking_changes*	Numerical	Number of booking changes

(*continued*)

Table 7. (*continued*)

ID	Variable	Data type	Description
22	*deposit_type*	Categorical	3 categories: deposit type
23	*agent*	Categorical	Travel agency ID
24	*days_in_waiting_list*	Numerical	Number of days in the waiting list
25	*customer_type*	Categorical	4 categories: type of booking
26	*adr*	Numerical	Number of average daily rate
27	*required_car_parking_spaces*	Numerical	Number of parking spaces
28	*total_of_special_requests*	Numerical	Number of special requests

Source: Adapted from António et al. [32]

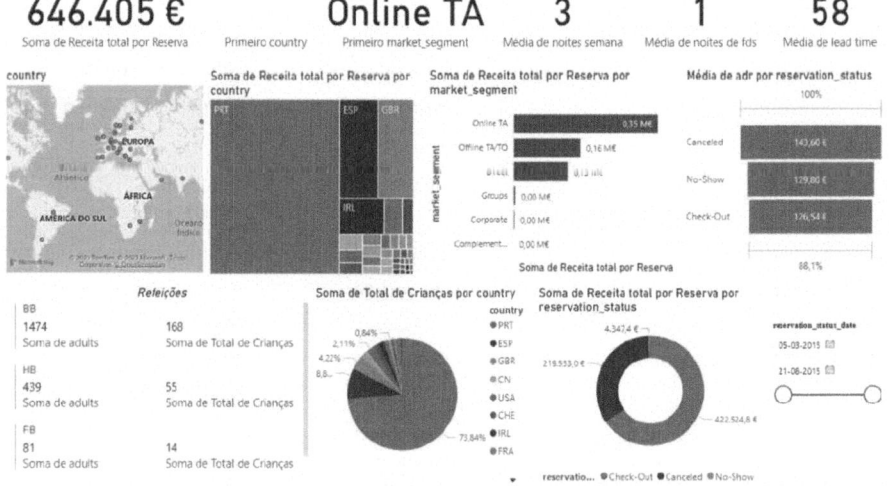

Fig. 7. Dashboard for global business measurement associated with all guests.

4.3 Consolidate and Practice to Receive Feedback and Finish the Process

At this stage, the business objectives and the business strategy should be reviewed, so that it is possible to either continue to have good results or to control deviations so as not to have failure and losses in the business.

The area of Digital Marketing Analytics is increasingly a need for decision-makers and marketers, it should be considered by companies in general, and specifically by those in tourism, to monitor, analyze, and manage their resources, especially those related to

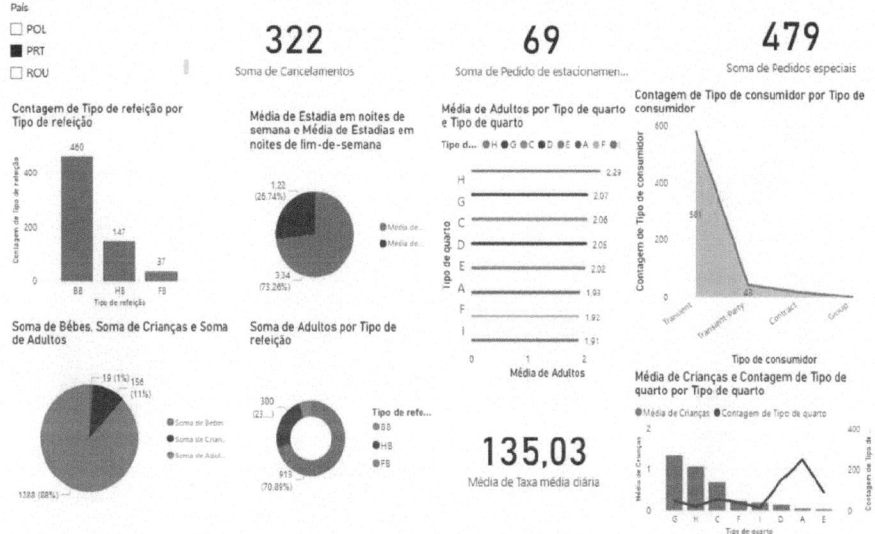

Fig. 8. Dashboard for measuring global business associated with all national guests.

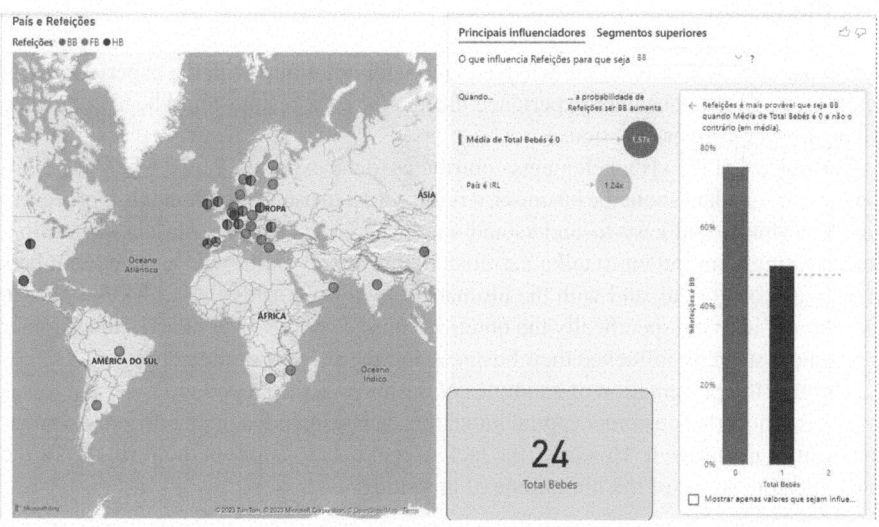

Fig. 9. Dashboard for measuring the global business associated with BB (Bed & Breakfast) meals.

their customers [33–35]. Gamification mechanisms should be considered to enhance their engagement [36], among other strategies, and the various Machine Learning algorithms [37] should be explored to detect and receive insights into the potential and capabilities of the company itself, i.e. the hotel [38, 39].

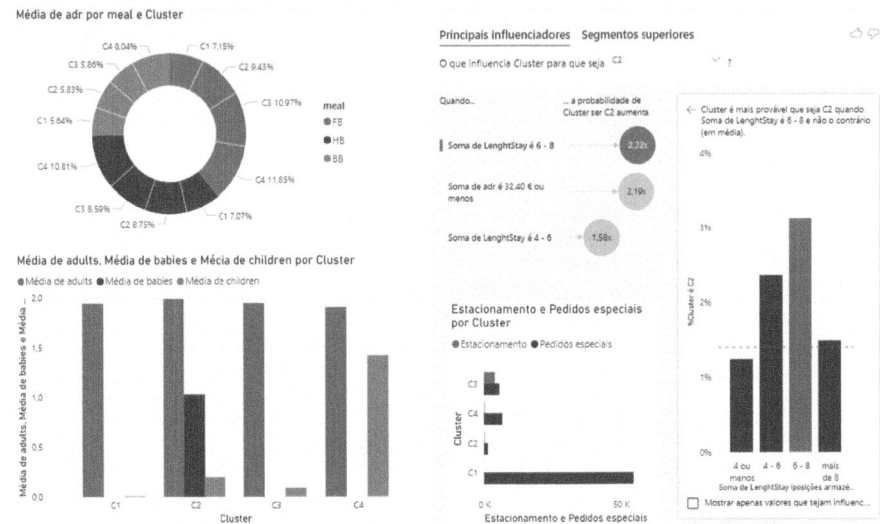

Fig. 10. Dashboard for global business measurement associated with a cluster or guest segment.

5 Conclusion

User experience is an area of knowledge that relates emotions, with the experience with technology and the consumer experience itself, where the result should be to contribute to a positive consumer experience.

The quality of the visual elements contributes to the experience, and when the intention is to present data about the business, it is important to use visual elements that present them in a simple and easy-to-understand way, where the concepts of data storytelling are increasingly important to tell a narrative that is mostly built by values and numbers mixed with categorical, and with the ultimate goal of supporting the decision-maker in any sector of activity, specifically the hotelier whose customer experience and customer engagement strongly influence their business and the success of the hotel.

Through the presentation of examples of dashboards developed in Power BI, it was possible to show that customer capital indicators can be included, under different dimensions that characterize it. However, the lack of real data to apply in the formulas of the new indicators is one of the limitations of this study.

Acknowledgments. This paper is financed by National Funds provided by FCT- Foundation for Science and Technology through project UIDB/04020/2020 and project Guest-IC I&DT nr. 047399 financed by CRESC ALGARVE2020, PORTUGAL2020 and FEDER.

References

1. Trainor, K.J., Andzulis, J.M., Rapp, A., Agnihotri, R.: Social media technology usage and customer relationship performance: a capabilities-based examination of social CRM. J. Bus. Res. **67**(6), 1201–1208 (2014)
2. Sigala, M.: Implementing social customer relationship management: a process framework and implications in tourism and hospitality. Int. J. Contemp. Hosp. Manag. **30**(7), 2698–2726 (2018)
3. Gupta, S., Zeithaml, V.: Customer metrics and their impact on financial performance. Mark. Sci. **25**(6), 718–739 (2006)
4. Venkatesan, R., Kumar, V.: A customer lifetime value framework for customer selection and resource allocation strategy. J. Mark. **68**(4), 106–125 (2004)
5. Norman, D., Nielson, J.: The Definition of User Experience (UX). Nielson Norman Group. https://www.nngroup.com/articles/definition-user-experience/. Accessed 12 Dec 2023
6. Hassenzahl, M., Tractinsky, N.: User experience - a research agenda. Behav. Inf. Technol. **25**(2), 91–97 (2006)
7. Suh, E., Diener, E., Fujita, F.: Events and subjective well-being: only recent events matter. J. Pers. Soc. Psychol. **70**(5), 1091 (1996)
8. DIS, I.: 9241-210: 2010. Ergonomics of human system interaction-Part 210: Human-centred design for interactive systems. International Standardization Organization (ISO). Switzerland (2009)
9. Fonseca, M., Campos, P., Gonçalves, D.: Introdução ao Design de Interfaces. FCA editora, Lisboa (2012)
10. Suprata, F.: Data storytelling with dashboard: accelerating understanding through data visualization in financial technology company case study. J. Metris **20**(01), 1–10 (2019)
11. Zanan, M., Aziz, M.: A review on the visual design styles in data storytelling based on user preferences and personality differences. In: 2022 IEEE 7th International Conference on Information Technology and Digital Applications (ICITDA), pp. 1–7. IEEE (2022)
12. Echeverria, V., et al.: Driving data storytelling from learning design. In: Proceedings of the 8th International Conference on Learning Analytics and Knowledge, pp. 131–140 (2018)
13. Kosara, R., Mackinlay, J.: Storytelling: the next step for visualization. Computer **46**(5), 44–50 (2013)
14. Ryan, L.: Visual Data Storytelling with Tableau: Story Points, Telling Compelling Data Narratives. Addison-Wesley Professional, Boston (2018)
15. Zhang, Y., Reynolds, M., Lugmayr, A., Damjanov, K., Hassan, G.M.: A visual data storytelling framework. Informatics **9**(4), 73 (2022)
16. Fry, B.: Visualizing Data: Exploring and Explaining Data with the Processing Environment. O'Reilly Media, Newton (2008)
17. Dykes, B.: Effective Data Storytelling: How to Drive Change with Data, Narrative and Visuals. Wiley, New York (2019)
18. Segel, E., Heer, J.: Narrative visualization: telling stories with data. IEEE Trans. Vis. Comput. Graph. **16**(6), 1139–1148 (2010)
19. Gillis, A., Laskowski, N.: Data Storytelling (2022). Retrieved from TechTarget website: https://www.techtarget.com/searchcio/definition/data-storytelling. Accessed 30 Sept 2023
20. Maritz, V.: Strategic use of data visualisation and storytelling in marketing research firms. University of Johannesburg (South Africa) (2013)
21. D'Ignazio, C., Klein, L.: Data Feminism. MIT Press, Cambridge (2020)
22. Hardin, M., Hom, D., Perez, R., Williams, L.: Which chart or graph is right for you? Tell impactful stories with data (2012). https://www.tableau.com/learn/whitepapers/which-chart-or-graph-is-right-for-you. Accessed 15 Oct 2023

23. Abela, A.: Data sets and chart types. https://www.lizadamsblog.com/post/data-sets-and-chart-types. Accessed 08 Feb 2024
24. O'sullivan, D., Abela, A.: Marketing performance measurement ability and firm performance. J. Mark. **71**(2), 79–93 (2007)
25. Clark, B., Abela, A., Ambler, T.: An information processing model of marketing performance measurement. J. Mark. Theory Pract. **14**(3), 191–208 (2006)
26. Zeferino, A.: Digital Marketing Analytics. Sabedoria Alternativa Edições, Lisboa (2016)
27. Eckerson, W.: Performance Dashboards: Measuring, Monitoring, and Managing Your Business. Wiley, New York (2010)
28. Accenture Technology Labs: Accelerating Understanding Through Data Visualization - the power of storytelling. Silicon Valley: Accenture. https://www.accenture.com/t20150523t02 1054__w__/us-en/_acnmedia/accenture/conversion-assets/dotcom/documents/global/pdf/digital_2/accenture-accellerating-understanding-through-data-visualization.pdf. Accessed 15 Oct 2023
29. Bharwani, S., Mathews, D.: Customer service innovations in the Indian hospitality industry. Worldwide Hospital. Tour. Themes **8**(4), 416–431 (2016)
30. Lemon, K.N.: Verhoef: understanding customer experience throughout the customer journey. J. Mark. **80**(6), 69–96 (2016)
31. Gupta, S., Lehmann, D.R., Stuart, J.: Valuing customers. J. Mark. Res. **41**(1), 7–18 (2004)
32. Antonio, N., de Almeida, A., Nunes, L.: Hotel booking demand datasets. Data Brief **22**, 41–49 (2019)
33. Liu, X., Burns, A.: Designing a marketing analytics course for the digital age. Mark. Educ. Rev. **28**(1), 28–40 (2018)
34. Wedel, M., Kannan, P.: Marketing analytics for data-rich environments. J. Mark. **80**(6), 97–121 (2016)
35. Xu, Z., Frankwick, G., Ramirez, E.: Effects of big data analytics and traditional marketing analytics on new product success: a knowledge fusion perspective. J. Bus. Res. **69**(5), 1562–1566 (2016)
36. Kaur, J., Lavuri, R., Parida, R., Singh, S.: Exploring the impact of gamification elements in brand apps on the purchase intention of consumers. J. Glob. Inf. Manag. (JGIM) **31**(1), 1–30 (2023)
37. Grigsby, M.: Marketing Analytics: A Practical Guide to Improving Consumer Insights Using Data Techniques. Kogan Page Publishers, London (2022)
38. Cao, G., Tian, N., Blankson, C.: Big data, marketing analytics, and firm marketing capabilities. J. Comput. Inf. Syst. **62**(3), 442–451 (2022)
39. Dykes, B.: Data storytelling: what it is and how it can be used to effectively communicate analysis results. Appl. Mark. Anal. **1**(4), 299–313 (2015)

MatrikalinDiabetes: User-Centered Design of a mHealth App for Gestational Diabetes Mellitus Management and Education Among Bangladeshi Women

Mohammad Arshad Hossain Ratul[1,2], Tunisha Yanoor Bristy[1,2], Noorjahan Sayeed[1,2], Ashraful Islam[1,2(✉)], and Beenish Moalla Chaudhry[3]

[1] Center for Computational and Data Sciences,Independent University Bangladesh,Dhaka, Bangladesh
{1930319,1930639,1811026,ashraful}@iub.edu.bd
[2] Department of Computer Science and Engineering,Independent University Bangladesh,Dhaka, Bangladesh
[3] School of Computing and Informatics,University of Louisiana at Lafayette,Louisiana, USA
beenish.chaudhry@louisiana.edu

Abstract. This study employs the User-Centered Design (UCD) methodology to develop a mobile health (mHealth) application (app) specifically tailored for Bangladeshi women with Gestational Diabetes Mellitus (GDM). GDM affects approximately 10% of pregnant women globally and around 35% within Bangladesh, as reported by the World Health Organization (WHO). Despite its high prevalence, there is a significant lack of awareness and education about GDM in Bangladesh, compounded by language barriers that make existing digital solutions less accessible. The *MatrikalinDiabetes* mHealth app aims to overcome these barriers by providing comprehensive management and educational resources for GDM in the Bangla language, addressing both pre-pregnancy and post-pregnancy needs. To ensure the app meets the actual needs of potential users, personas were created based on a literature review, and a survey was conducted. This process informed the development of both a low-fidelity, paper-based prototype and a high-fidelity digital prototype. Key features of the *MatrikalinDiabetes* app include tracking of food and water intake, physical activity monitoring, reminders, GDM education, chat forums for community support, blood glucose level (BGL) monitoring, an SOS button for emergency contacts, and quizzes for user engagement. Preliminary feedback indicated that 53.8% of participants favored the integrated features and expressed willingness to use and recommend the app. The survey of the high-fidelity prototype yielded positive responses, with 57.9% of participants strongly

---

M. A. H. Ratul, T. Yanoor Bristy, N. Sayeed—Authors contributed equally.

V. G. Duffy (Ed.): HCII 2024, LNCS 15376, pp. 173–188, 2025.
https://doi.org/10.1007/978-3-031-76809-5_13

agreeing and 42.1% agreeing that the features were beneficial. The user-friendly design of the high-fidelity prototype ensures intuitive interaction, aiding in health management, enhancing GDM understanding, and promoting a healthier lifestyle among pregnant women in Bangladesh.

Keywords: Gestational Diabetes Mellitus · mHealth · User-Centered Design · World Health Organization · Pregnancy · Antenatal · Postnatal · Women Health · Language Barriers

1   Introduction

Gestational Diabetes Mellitus (GDM) is a form of diabetes that manifests during the second or third trimester of pregnancy [6]. It poses significant health risks to both mothers and their offspring. In mothers, GDM increases the likelihood of developing Type 2 Diabetes (T2D), cardiovascular diseases, postpartum hemorrhage, cesarean delivery, preeclampsia, and dystocia of labor [15]. For the baby, GDM can lead to fetal overgrowth, known as macrosomia, neonatal hypoglycemia, and respiratory complications. Additionally, offspring of women with GDM are approximately seven times more likely to develop T2D and childhood obesity [14,15]. Early detection and appropriate treatment of GDM can significantly mitigate these risks [18].

In Bangladesh, barriers such as lack of knowledge, language, and cultural factors impede access to quality healthcare. Research shows that around 35% of Bangladeshi pregnant women are affected by GDM [13], a figure that is steadily rising [12]. Alarmingly, only about 31% of pregnant women in Bangladesh attend at least four prenatal care appointments, which is less than half the global average of 65% [12]. Awareness of GDM and its management remains low among the population in Bangladesh [8].

Mobile health (mHealth) applications (apps) offer a promising solution to manage health issues and provide an innovative approach to healthcare [17]. These smartphone apps can effectively support medical treatments and promote healthy lifestyles, including regular exercise, balanced diets, and weight management [10]. Through social support networks, mHealth apps not only provide valuable health information but also foster community engagement [10]. By equipping users with the necessary tools and resources, these apps empower them to make informed health decisions and continuously monitor their health [6].

The growing concern surrounding GDM has spurred global research efforts. In developing the *MatrikalinDiabetes* app using a User-Centered Design (UCD) approach, we examined several studies to enhance our understanding. Ekezie et al. [6] evaluated a mobile app, identifying user challenges while emphasizing its potential to promote behavior change, self-monitoring, awareness of healthy lifestyles, and reduced T2D risk. Park et al. [15] developed the *Breastfeeding for Gestational Diabetes Mellitus App*, which encourages breastfeeding and provides educational videos about GDM and breastfeeding. Potzel et al. [16] created the

Triangle app, which monitors health habits, aids in analyzing cardiometabolic problems, and supports mothers with GDM in adopting healthier lifestyles. Garnweidner-Holme et al. [7] introduced the *Pregnant+* app for managing GDM through lifestyle guidance and blood glucose monitoring, with Borgen et al. [1] evaluating its impact on maternal and newborn outcomes. Garfield et al. [20] conducted a feasibility study of the *Mother App*, which facilitates self-monitoring and provides multimedia resources. While Daley et al. [3] explored the use of artificial intelligence (AI) in mHealth apps for GDM management, Eberle et al. [5] performed a systematic review highlighting the potential of mHealth apps in improving glycemic control and patient compliance. Despite these advances, no prior research or app specifically tailored to Bangladeshi women and their needs was identified.

The primary objectives of this research are: (i) to design and develop a mHealth app in the Bangla language using the UCD methodology; (ii) to assist Bangladeshi women in managing GDM utilizing smartphones; and (iii) to educate women about GDM and its implications. Our research followed a series of steps guided by the UCD methodology, as illustrated in Fig. 1. We began by reviewing scientific papers, creating personas based on this review, and conducting surveys to gather user feedback on desired features. A low-fidelity prototype was initially sketched by hand. After collecting feedback on this prototype, we developed a high-fidelity version using the Figma tool. The high-fidelity prototype was evaluated through a survey, revealing that most participants found the design appealing, navigated it easily, and successfully interacted with all features. Overall, participants rated the prototype highly, with an average rating of 4.578 out of 5.

2   Prototype Development

In the early stage of prototype development, we focused on eliciting design requirements by reviewing relevant literature and identifying key features available in our prior work [2]. To gain a deeper understanding of the interactive needs of women with GDM, we created two personas based on insights from the reviewed papers. These personas helped us visualize the real challenges faced by women with GDM during pregnancy, allowing us to identify additional essential features [2]. We conducted brainstorming sessions to further expand the feature set, aiming to enhance the management and educational aspects of the app for women with GDM. To ensure that the app addresses real-life preferences, we conducted a survey among women with GDM. This survey enabled us to prioritize features that the target users would find most beneficial in a mHealth app [2]. The various methods used to gather and shortlist feature ideas are summarized in Table 1.

2.1   User Personas and Interaction Scenarios

User personas are conceptual representations crafted to embody the experiences and challenges of the target population [9]. These personas are instrumental

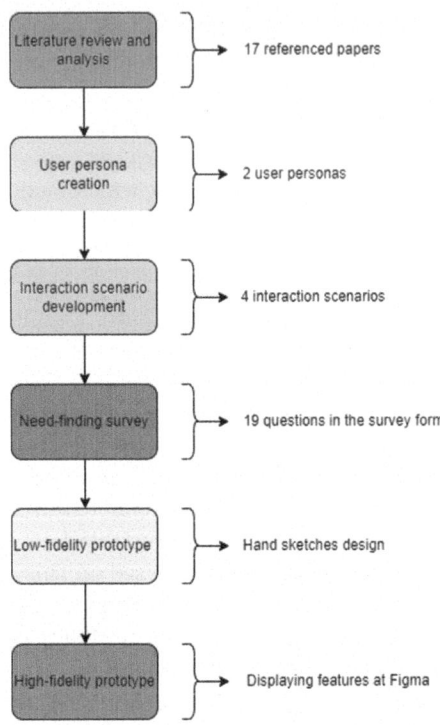

Fig. 1. The sequential phases of the entire design process, starting with requirement analysis and ending with prototype creation.

in providing insights into the real-life circumstances of the users, enabling the development of app features that address their specific needs and preferences [4]. Interaction scenarios, on the other hand, are narrative constructs that illustrate how these personas navigate and utilize the features of the mHealth app. These scenarios are developed to depict the practical application of the app by the personas, highlighting their interaction with various functionalities and how these features aid in managing gestational diabetes [2].

Persona 1. Faiza is a 30-year-old woman who works as a sales team leader, adhering to a demanding 9 am to 5 pm schedule. Recently, Faiza discovered she is pregnant and is currently in her second month of gestation. Balancing her professional responsibilities with personal health has proven challenging. Due to her hectic work environment, Faiza often struggles to remember essential daily tasks such as taking her prescribed medications, scheduling and attending medical appointments, and monitoring her water intake. Given that she spends a significant portion of her day away from home, her meals often consist of quick, convenient options rather than nutritionally balanced choices. This is a

Table 1. Feature ideas collected from literature review, brainstorming, and survey and the features in MatrikalinDiabetes app.

Features	Literature Review	Brainstormed	Survey	MatrikalinDiabetes
Breastfeeding	✓			✓
Food Intake	✓		✓	✓
Water Intake		✓		✓
Blood Glucose Level Monitoring	✓	✓	✓	✓
Physical Activity	✓	✓		✓
SOS		✓	✓	✓
Sleep Tracking		✓		✓
Personalized Recommendations		✓		✓
Quiz		✓		✓
Chat Forum	✓	✓		✓
GDM Education		✓	✓	✓
Reminders	✓	✓		✓

particular concern now that she is pregnant, as maintaining a healthy diet is crucial for her and her developing baby.

Persona 2. Lamia is a 20-year-old housewife who is currently five months pregnant and has been diagnosed with GDM. This is her first pregnancy, and she is deeply concerned about managing GDM. To alleviate her worries, Lamia frequently browses the Internet to gather information about pregnancy and GDM-related issues. However, due to stress, she sometimes overeats. Her family, prioritizing her and her baby's well-being, restricts her from engaging in household activities, urging her to rest. This enforced rest leads to boredom, prompting Lamia to seek out others with similar experiences for support and to learn more about GDM.

In response to the needs highlighted by personas and feedback from our surveys, we have developed a Reminder feature. This allows users to set reminders for doctor's appointments or medication schedules, ensuring tasks are completed on time. For users like Faiza, who struggles with maintaining regular meal times, this feature provides timely alerts to help manage her schedule effectively. Additionally, Faiza's difficulty in tracking her calorie intake prompted us to design the Food Intake feature. This allows users to log their daily food consumption, helping them monitor their eating habits and receive tailored dietary suggestions.

Considering Lamia's specific concerns about GDM, we have introduced the GDM Education feature. This feature provides users with comprehensive information on GDM, delivery methods, and dietary guidelines through a series of informative videos. To address Lamia's limited physical activity due to enforced rest, we have also included a Physical Activity feature. This enables users to log activities such as walking and sleeping, helping them track their physical activity levels and receive appropriate suggestions to maintain a healthy lifestyle [4].

3   Low-Fidelity Prototype Development

Utilizing insights gained from user persona interactions and need-finding survey results, the features for the *MatrikalinDiabetes* app were finalized, as detailed in Table 1, and a low-fidelity prototype was subsequently developed [2]. Notably, to the best of our knowledge, there is no existing mHealth app in Bangla that offers comprehensive features similar to our proposed *MatrikalinDiabetes* app. Considering the target audience's unfamiliarity with such technology, the design was intentionally kept simple to enhance usability. Through multiple iterations of sketching, the prototype gradually took shape, offering a clear visual representation of the envisioned app. The finalized low-fidelity prototype was then subjected to evaluation via a survey to gather further user feedback [2].

4   High-Fidelity Prototype Development

Prior to developing the high-fidelity prototype, the low-fidelity prototype was evaluated with the participation of 13 women, who had a mean age of 29.5 years [2]. The analysis revealed that 53.8% of the participants appreciated all the features of the low-fidelity prototype, with the "GDM Education" and "Food Intake" features being the most favored. Additionally, 53.8% of the participants expressed interest in using such an app in the future, and an equal percentage indicated their willingness to recommend the app to others. The participants also requested a clickable prototype to better visualize and interact with the app's functionalities [2]. Based on these satisfactory results and feedback, the high-fidelity prototype was developed.

Using the design tool Figma (https://www.figma.com/), the high-fidelity prototype was created entirely in Bangla to ensure ease of use for the target audience, who may not be accustomed to navigating such apps. The design was kept straightforward and user-friendly, with a light blue theme chosen to minimize eye strain and create a calming environment. Two sample transformations from the low-fidelity to the high-fidelity prototype are depicted in Fig. 2.

The high-fidelity prototype is now clickable, offering users an enhanced, interactive experience of the app design. This allows for a live demonstration, enabling users to provide real-time feedback. The inclusion of detailed images and interactive scenarios in the high-fidelity prototype aims to address potential issues and further improve the overall user experience.

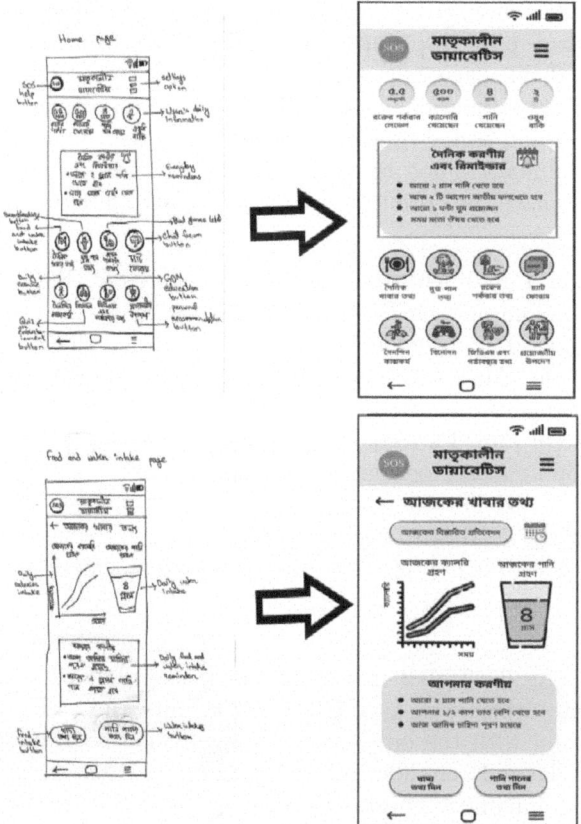

Fig. 2. Transformation from hand-sketched low-fidelity prototype to polished high-fidelity prototype using Figma (Homepage and Food Intake features).

4.1 Prototype

Homepage. As depicted in Fig. 3a, the top left of the screen features an SOS button, providing a one-tap solution to send emergency alerts to the user's trusted contact. This button is consistently available on every page of the app. User data for blood glucose level (BGL), calorie intake, water intake, and medicine reminders are displayed in four distinct circles. The central box presents daily reminders and suggestions tailored for the user. The bottom section of the homepage contains eight buttons: 'Food Intake', 'Blood Glucose Level Monitoring', 'Chat Forum', 'GDM Education', 'Quiz', 'Physical Activity', 'Breastfeeding Information', and 'Personalized Recommendation'. Each button directs the user to the corresponding feature's page. The design of the homepage is intentionally intuitive, ensuring that users can navigate and utilize the buttons easily without confusion.

Food Intake. As illustrated in Fig. 3b, selecting the "Food Intake" option redirects the user to a page displaying their daily calorie count and water intake. At the bottom of this page, two buttons are available: Food Intake Information and Water Intake Information, each leading to their respective pages. Users can input their food and water consumption on these dedicated pages. Based on these inputs, the main "Food Intake" page will provide tailored recommendations. Users also have the option to delete their inputs if necessary.

Blood Glucose Level Monitoring. As illustrated in Fig. 3c, this feature enables users to monitor their BGL. The page includes a calendar to help users track their BGL readings over time. Users can input their BGL readings directly below the calendar. After entering their data, users can click on the "Results" button to determine if their BGL exceeds a specified threshold. Based on these results, the system provides recommendations for stabilizing BGL. The feature also includes pop-up alerts for high, low, and optimal BGL levels. At the bottom of the page, three text buttons address common user queries: "Why is it important to know BGL?", "How to measure BGL?", and "What is a Glucometer?". Each button leads to a pop-up that provides comprehensive answers to these questions.

Chat Forum. As illustrated in Fig. 3d, this feature allows users to connect and interact with others who have GDM. Users can write and share blog posts within this forum, with the option to post anonymously to maintain privacy. They can also like and comment on each other's posts, fostering a supportive and interactive community. This feature enables users to share their experiences, seek advice, and provide support to one another regarding their GDM journey. By facilitating social interaction and engagement, the Chat Forum helps users overcome the stigma associated with GDM.

GDM Education. As illustrated in Fig. 3e, this feature is designed to educate users about GDM, pregnancy, childbirth, food & nutrition, BGL, and exercise. The feature includes video resources to help users gain a comprehensive understanding of these topics. The videos will be clearly articulated, providing relevant information in high resolution for an effective learning experience. This feature aims to address the primary concerns of users, such as managing GDM, understanding the childbirth process, and selecting a suitable diet.

Quiz. As illustrated in Fig. 3f, this feature allows users to engage in educational quizzes during their free time. Designed with a game-like interface, this feature aims to attract users and encourage their active participation. Users will be provided with brief notes related to GDM, which they need to study to answer short quiz questions. Upon selecting "Participate in the quiz," users will be redirected to the quiz page. Correct and incorrect answers will trigger different alert pages: correct answers will reward users with trophies, while incorrect answers will result in the loss of trophies. This feature transforms leisure time into a productive and educational experience.

Reminder. As illustrated in Fig. 3g, this feature provides users with reminders for doctor's appointments, food intake, water intake, and medication. Users can also create custom reminders tailored to their specific needs. Upon selecting the "Reminder" option, users are redirected to a page displaying all their set reminders in an organized box. At the bottom of the page, a button labeled "Set Reminder" allows users to add new reminders. Options include reminders for doctor's appointments, medication, walking, sleep, and hospital visits. By clicking each reminder button, users can customize and set reminders according to their preferences.

Breastfeeding Information. As illustrated in Fig. 3h, many mothers are unaware of the critical importance of breastfeeding and its positive impact on managing GDM. This page is designed to help users track their breast-feeding schedules effectively. The interface features two buttons at the top: "Improving Breastfeeding Method" and "Breastfeeding Schedule," along with two charts displaying their baby's growth and breastfeeding information. Click-ing on "Improving Breastfeeding Method" redirects users to two video popups. One video demonstrates techniques to increase milk flow, while the other pro-vides information on foods that can aid in milk production. By selecting "Breast-feeding Schedule," users are taken to a page where they can input and track their breastfeeding routine. Users have the flexibility to update or delete their input as needed, ensuring the information remains accurate and relevant.

Physical Activity. As illustrated in Fig. 3i, this page enables users to track their daily walking, sleeping, and exercise activities. Users can input the duration of these activities, and after saving the inputs, a pop-up will provide tailored recommendations. The "Weekly Mean" button calculates the average weekly progress, offering insights based on this data. The app also visualizes progress through graphs and charts, encouraging users to make informed choices about their physical health. This feature serves as an active wellness coach, guiding users toward better physical health management.

Personalized Recommendations. As illustrated in Fig. 3j, this feature pro-vides users with visual charts displaying their daily, weekly, and monthly progress. Initially, users receive tailored advice regarding their health and dietary habits. Subsequently, various graphs and charts illustrate their progress over time, based on the data they have input into the app. This page primarily serves as a visual tool, enabling users to identify and address any deficiencies by closely monitoring their progress.

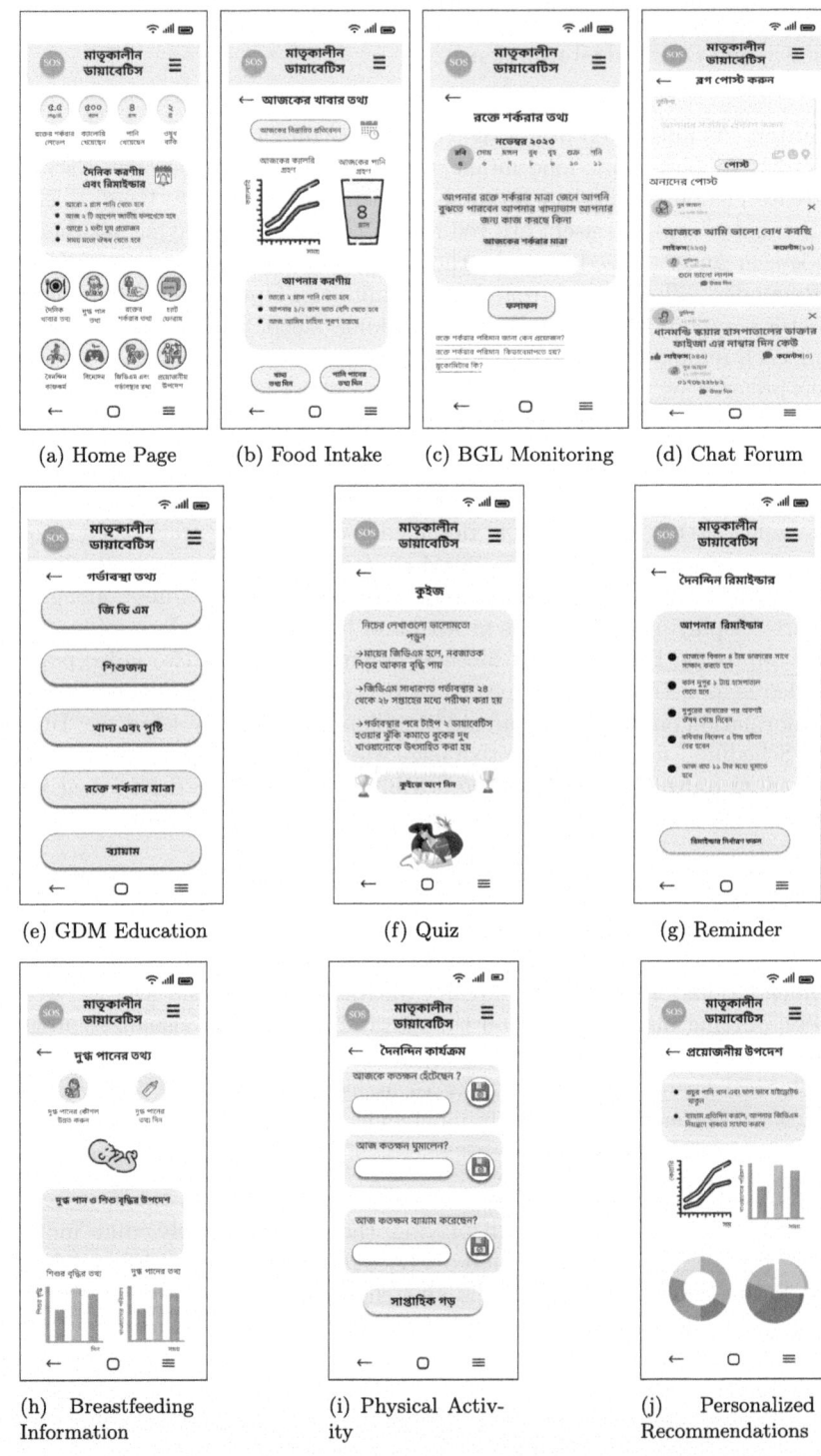

(a) Home Page   (b) Food Intake   (c) BGL Monitoring   (d) Chat Forum

(e) GDM Education   (f) Quiz   (g) Reminder

(h) Breastfeeding
Information

(i) Physical Activity

(j) Personalized
Recommendations

Fig. 3. High-fidelity Prototype of MatrikalinDiabetes

5   Usability Evaluation

The purpose of this study was to assess the acceptance and perceived usefulness of the *MatrikalinDiabetes* app among users, as well as their willingness to utilize it. Specifically, the study investigated several theories: the perceived value of the prototype in helping women with GDM maintain their health, the acceptance of the prototype to evaluate user comfort with its features and quality, and the willingness of users to engage with the app and deepen their understanding of GDM.

5.1   Study Design

At the beginning of the survey (quantitative in nature), participants were provided with an outline of the study, followed by the informed consent process. This study was exempt from the institutional review board of Independent University Bangladesh and the participation was fully anonymized. Participants were then asked to submit basic demographic information including age range, number of pregnancies, and prior experience with mHealth apps. They also provided information about their current pregnancy status and any family history of diabetes. Following this, participants interacted with the high-fidelity prototype, experiencing each described interaction independently. Each interaction scenario lasted for 2–4 minutes. Participants assessed the quality and helpfulness of *Matrikalin-Diabetes* in each scenario and rated the prototype's features and functionality on a Likert scale after completing their overall interaction. Additionally, participants indicated their willingness to use the *MatrikalinDiabetes* app on a Likert scale and expressed whether they were willing to accept the app as a tool to help pregnant women manage GDM and improve their health conditions.

5.2   Participants

The survey, along with feedback on the high-fidelity prototype, was collected online through Google Forms shared via mailing lists. Specific criteria were established for user testing, requiring all participants to be married women with at least a high school education, capable of using smartphones, Bangladeshi nationals, and currently residing in Bangladesh. To maintain privacy, no personal information such as name, contact number, or email address was collected, and participation was entirely voluntary. The recruitment process yielded 19 responses from individuals aged 18 to 46 years, with a mean age of 32.68 years and a standard deviation of 5.22. The age distribution included 2 responses from individuals aged 18 to 22 years, 6 responses from those aged 23 to 27 years, 3 responses from individuals aged 28 to 32 years, 2 responses from those aged 33 to 37 years, 2 responses from individuals aged 38 to 42 years, and 4 responses from those aged 43 to 47 years.

5.3   Measures and Data Analysis

A variety of methods were employed to collect survey responses, including 5-point Likert scales, multiple-choice questions, and checkboxes. Data collection was facilitated through Google Forms, and the resulting data was stored in Google Sheets, which provided various functionalities for quantitative analysis. Descriptive analysis involved calculating means, standard deviations, percentages, and frequencies, which were visualized using pie charts and bar charts generated in Google Sheets. A total of 19 participants completed the survey, providing valuable feedback for the study.

5.4   Findings

In the usability evaluation survey for the high-fidelity prototype, feedback was collected using a Likert scale ranging from "Very Bad" to "Very Good," as shown in Table 2. The "Food Intake" feature received highly positive ratings, with 57.9% of participants rating it as "Very Good." The Chat Forum was well-received, with 15.8% rating it as "Good" and 57.9% as "Very Good." The Reminder feature garnered positive feedback, with 42.1% rating it as "Good" and another 42.1% as "Very Good." The Quiz feature received a "Good" rating from 42.1% of participants. Although the Physical Activity feature received fewer "Very Good" ratings compared to other features, it still achieved a 52.6% "Good" rating. Both the GDM Education and Blood Glucose Level Monitoring features received exceptionally positive ratings, with 84.2% and 73.7% of participants, respectively, rating them as "Very Good." The SOS Button also received positive feedback, with 63.2% of ratings being "Very Good." The Breastfeeding Information and Personalized Recommendations features had more ratings of "Good" (47.4% and 36.8%, respectively) compared to "Very Good" (21.1% each), indicating potential areas for improvement in user satisfaction.

A significant 63.2% and 57.9% of participants suggested improvements for the Personalized Recommendation and Breastfeeding Information features, respectively. Additionally, 84.2% of participants expressed a desire for a new feature that would allow direct contact with doctors. Moreover, 57.9% of participants wanted a feature that enables hospitals to directly track the patient's health. A majority, 73.7% of participants, reported that all the buttons were functioning perfectly, and 47.4% found the app's theme appealing and comfortable. 10 out of 19 participants reported no difficulty navigating through the prototype. The GDM Education feature achieved the highest average rating of 4.84, as shown in Fig. 4. Overall, 63.2% of participants considered the features in the high-fidelity prototype to be very useful, demonstrating a willingness to use the app.

Table 2. Features rated by participants for the high-fidelity prototype and average rating on a scale of 5 for each feature.

Features	Very Bad	Bad	Neutral	Good	Very Good	Average rating on a scale of 5
	1	2	3	4	5	
Food Intake	0.00%	5.30%	5.30%	31.60%	58%	4.42
Chat Forum	0.00%	0.00%	26.30%	15.80%	57.90%	4.32
Reminder	5.30%	5.30%	5.30%	42.10%	42.10%	4.11
Quiz	0.00%	0.00%	21.10%	42.10%	36.80%	4.16
Physical Activity	0.00%	0.00%	31.60%	52.60%	15.80%	3.84
GDM Education	0.00%	0.00%	0.00%	15.80%	84.20%	4.84
Blood Glucose Level Monitoring	0.00%	0.00%	0.00%	26.30%	73.70%	4.74
Breastfeeding Information	5.30%	5.30%	21.10%	47.40%	21.10%	4.74
SOS Button	0%	10.50%	10.50%	15.80%	63.20%	4.32
Personalised Recommendation	0%	5.30%	36.80%	36.80%	21.10%	3.74

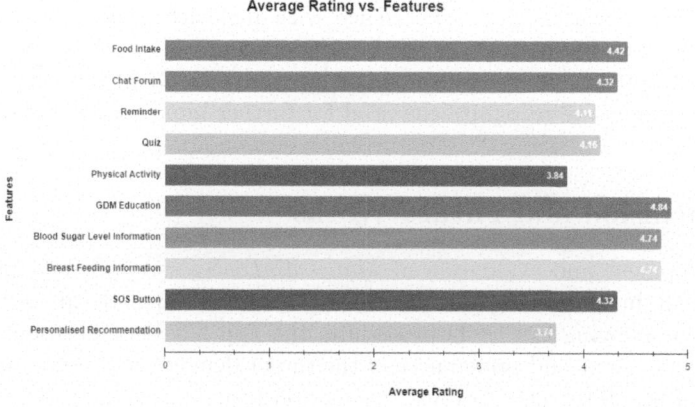

Fig. 4. Average rating given by the participants to the features

6   Discussion

In this research, we reviewed 17 studies to identify and accumulate features for *MatrikalinDiabetes* using the UCD methodology. The app includes several features similar to those in *Pregnant+* such as monitoring blood glucose levels (BGL), providing suggestions, and tracking physical activities and food preferences [6]. Additionally, *MatrikalinDiabetes* incorporates features found in "Health-e Mums," including setting reminders for doctor appointments and a social community page where users can connect and share their experiences [11]. Unique features in *MatrikalinDiabetes* include the SOS button, breastfeeding information, and a quiz for user engagement.

From our survey, 60% of interviewees reported a family history of diabetes, 10% mentioned heart problems, and 40% indicated high blood pressure as identified by their doctors during the low-fidelity prototype survey. Users who had never used a mHealth app before exhibited more curiosity and engagement than those who had previous experience. While there is potential for further improvement and additional features, the existing features in *MatrikalinDiabetes* are beneficial for pregnant women with GDM.

A limitation of our design is its exclusive use of Bangla, which may discourage non-Bangla speakers from using the app. The initial survey feedback was gathered from a limited participant pool, and future surveys should include participants from across Bangladesh to obtain a broader range of perspectives and experiences. One major challenge is addressing the cultural variations in dietary habits across different regions of Bangladesh, which makes delivering universally applicable nutritional recommendations difficult. Accurate and consistent user input regarding food intake, water intake, and physical activity is crucial for the app to effectively assist in managing GDM.

Our current objective is to determine the usefulness of these features before developing a fully functional app. The study indicates that participants, particularly those with no prior experience with mHealth apps, have a positive attitude toward the features in the high-fidelity prototype. We are confident that *MatrikalinDiabetes* will aid pregnant women with GDM in managing their condition, even as we recognize the need for further improvements and cultural adaptations.

7   Conclusion and Future Works

The development and evaluation of *MatrikalinDiabetes* represent a significant advancement in addressing the healthcare needs of Bangladeshi women with GDM. By employing the UCD procedure, the app has been customized to fit the cultural context and preferences of the target demographic, ensuring its relevance and usability. The thorough evaluation process demonstrated the app's effectiveness in improving GDM management and educational outcomes among users. *MatrikalinDiabetes* holds promise for enhancing healthcare access, promoting healthier pregnancy outcomes, and contributing to efforts to reduce maternal and neonatal morbidity and mortality rates in Bangladesh. This study synthesized ideas from previous research papers, survey questions, brainstorming user personas, and interactive scenarios. A high-fidelity prototype was created using Figma, and its acceptance was evaluated through user feedback. The study revealed that while some features were highly favored by participants, others required improvement.

In future work, we plan to include educational videos about GDM with subtitles to accommodate users with hearing impairments. Additionally, we aim to integrate more features to evaluate multimodal functions. To enhance user-friendliness, we will introduce multiple regional languages. When evaluating the fully functional app, we will employ usability measurement scales such as the System Usability Score (SUS) [21] and the Mobile Application Rating Scale (MARS) [19]. These scales will provide comprehensive quantitative and qualitative feedback on the app's design, focusing on effectiveness, efficiency, and user satisfaction.

We also plan to incorporate perspectives and features for other types of users, such as doctors or hospitals, allowing them to access patients' health data while maintaining privacy and permissions. Additionally, family members, such as husbands, can use the app to monitor their wives' health and gain knowledge about GDM, enabling them to provide better care. By offering the app in Bangla, we ensure that Bangladeshi women can use it more comfortably, thereby spreading information and awareness about GDM and aiding in its management through activity tracking and guided support. Optimistically, this mHealth app will significantly improve the lifestyles and health management of pregnant women with GDM.

References

1. Borgen, I., et al.: Effect of the pregnant+ smartphone application in women with gestational diabetes mellitus: a randomised controlled trial in Norway. BMJ Open **9**(11), e030884 (2019)
2. Yanoor Bristy, T., Ratul, M.A.H., Sayeed, N., Badrul, T., Islam, A.: Preliminary design validation of a mHealth tool for gestational diabetes mellitus management and education in Bangladeshi women. In: 2024 Advances in Science and Engineering Technology (ASET) International Multi-Conferences. IEEE (2024)
3. Daley, B.J., et al.: mHealth apps for gestational diabetes mellitus that provide clinical decision support or artificial intelligence: a scoping review. Diabet. Med. **39**(1), e14735 (2022)
4. Dam, R.F., Siang, T.Y.: Personas - a simple introduction (2024). https://www.interaction-design.org/literature/article/personas-why-and-how-you-should-use-them#:~:text=Personas%20are%20fictional%20characters%2C%20which,%2C%20%20experiences%2C%20behaviors%20and%20goals
5. Eberle, C., Loehnert, M., Stichling, S.: Effectivness of specific mobile health applications (mHealth-apps) in gestational diabtetes mellitus: a systematic review. BMC Pregnancy Childbirth **21**(1), 1–7 (2021)
6. Ekezie, W., Dallosso, H., Saravanan, P., Khunti, K., Hadjiconstantinou, M.: Experiences of using a digital type 2 diabetes prevention application designed to support women with previous gestational diabetes. BMC Health Serv. Res. **21**, 1–10 (2021)
7. Garnweidner-Holme, L.M., Borgen, I., Garitano, I., Noll, J., Lukasse, M.: Designing and developing a mobile smartphone application for women with gestational diabetes mellitus followed-up at diabetes outpatient clinics in Norway. In: Healthcare, vol. 3, pp. 310–323. MDPI (2015)
8. Halim, A., Abdullah, A.S.M., Rahman, F., Biswas, A.: Exploring the perceptions, practices and challenges of gestational diabetes detection and management among health care providers in a district of Bangladesh. F1000Research **9**, 189 (2020)
9. Islam, A., Chaudhry, B.M.: Identifying user personas for engagement with a COVID-19 health service delivery relational agent. In: Proceedings of the 9th International Conference on Human-Agent Interaction, pp. 364–366 (2021)
10. Jakob, R., et al.: Factors influencing adherence to mHealth apps for prevention or management of noncommunicable diseases: systematic review. J. Med. Internet Res. **24**(5), e35371 (2022)
11. Kalhori, S.R.N., Hemmat, M., Noori, T., Heydarian, S., Katigari, M.R.: Quality evaluation of English mobile applications for gestational diabetes: app review using mobile application rating scale (Mars). Curr. Diabet. Rev. **17**(2), 161–168 (2021)

12. Kim, Y., Lee, J.L., Jang, I.S., Park, S.: Knowledge and health beliefs of gestational diabetes mellitus associated with breastfeeding intention among pregnant women in Bangladesh. Asian Nurs. Res. **14**(3), 144–149 (2020)
13. Mazumder, T., Akter, E., Rahman, S.M., Islam, M.T., Talukder, M.R.: Prevalence and risk factors of gestational diabetes mellitus in Bangladesh: findings from demographic health survey 2017–2018. Int. J. Environ. Res. Public Health **19**(5), 2583 (2022)
14. O'Reilly, S.L., Laws, R.: Health-e mums: evaluating a smartphone app design for diabetes prevention in women with previous gestational diabetes. Nutr. Diet. **76**(5), 507–514 (2019)
15. Park, S., Kwak, E., Lee, J.: Breastfeeding mobile application for mothers with gestational diabetes mellitus: designed by mothers and experts. BMC Public Health **22**(1), 1510 (2022)
16. Potzel, A.L., et al.: A novel smartphone app to change risk behaviors of women after gestational diabetes: a randomized controlled trial. PLoS ONE **17**(4), e0267258 (2022)
17. Pustozerov, E., Popova, P., Tkachuk, A., Bolotko, Y., Yuldashev, Z., Grineva, E., et al.: Development and evaluation of a mobile personalized blood glucose prediction system for patients with gestational diabetes mellitus. JMIR mhealth uhealth **6**(1), e9236 (2018)
18. Shen, J., et al.: An innovative artificial intelligence-based app for the diagnosis of gestational diabetes mellitus (GDM-AI): development study. J. Med. Internet Res. **22**(9), e21573 (2020)
19. Terhorst, Y., et al.: Validation of the mobile application rating scale (Mars). PLoS ONE **15**(11), e0241480 (2020)
20. Varnfield, M., et al.: Mother, an mHealth system to support women with gestational diabetes mellitus: feasibility and acceptability study. Diabet. Technol. Ther. **23**(5), 358–366 (2021)
21. Vlachogianni, P., Tselios, N.: Perceived usability evaluation of educational technology using the system usability scale (SUS): a systematic review. J. Res. Technol. Educ. **54**(3), 392–409 (2022)

A Preliminary Exploration of the Effectiveness of Portable Simulated Pet Systems Based on UI/UX Design in Alleviating Mental Stress Among Caregivers

Jiang Wu[1,4] ⓘ, Yihang Dai[2(✉)], Peize Wu[3,4], Jing Li[4], Tianze Wang[4], and Jingbo Ge[4,5]

[1] The University of Tokyo, 7-3-1 Hongo, Tokyo 113-8656, Japan
[2] Tama Art University, 2-1723 Yarimizu, Tokyo 192-0394, Japan
daiyihang6@gmail.com
[3] Tokyo University of Technology, 1404-1 Katakuramachi, Tokyo 192-0982, Japan
[4] Ichikawa Academy, 4-6-6 Takadanobaba, Tokyo 169-0075, Japan
[5] Waseda University, 2-7 Hibikino, Kitakyushu 808-0135, Japan

Abstract. This study preliminarily explores the effectiveness of a UI/UX design-based portable simulated pet system (KEDAMA application) in alleviating mental stress among caregivers. As countries like Japan enter a super-aged society, caregivers are increasingly burdened physically and mentally, especially due to lumbar pain and psychological stress from transferring elderly individuals. The KEDAMA application aims to offer caregivers a tool for stress relief by providing a customizable virtual pet experience. The system framework includes creation, voice, personal, and more pages, supporting personalized customization of pet appearances and sounds. Preliminary evaluations indicate that interaction with KEDAMA significantly improves caregivers' performance across six dimensions: emotional, linguistic, visual, behavioral, social interaction, and excitement levels, thereby reducing their mental stress. The study also finds that long-term interaction with KEDAMA positively impacts caregivers' emotional dimensions without affecting the overall user experience. Thus, KEDAMA has the potential to serve as a long-term use device, offering continuous improvements in mental health for both caregivers and general users.

Keywords: UI/UX design · mental health · portable simulated pet systems · welfare equipment

1 Introduction

In Asia, Japan, as one of the earliest countries to enter an aging society, has now advanced into a super-aged society, with an aging rate of 29.0% [1]. As the aging society continues to evolve, the number of elderly individuals in care facilities is expected to keep increasing. Caregivers working in elder welfare facilities face a high incidence of lower back pain, with 80% of caregivers reporting experiencing lower back pain during their work [2, 3]. Addressing lower back pain issues is crucial for improving the working environment of caregivers. It is particularly noted that caregivers engage in physically demanding tasks such as assisting the elderly from sitting to standing positions, often adopting bending and twisting postures. This not only makes it difficult for them to get sufficient rest but also adds to their psychological burden [4]. According to a report by the Ministry of Health, Labour and Welfare (MHLW) of Japan, 70% of the causes of lower back pain among caregivers are attributed to the physical strain involved in assisting the elderly with transfers (e.g., from wheelchair to bed, from wheelchair to toilet, etc.) [5].

In response to the lumbar pain challenges faced by caregivers during the transfer of elderly, extensive efforts have been made to review literature on transfer assistance and develop transfer assistance systems [6–9]. Building on our preliminary work, this study has developed a transfer assistance device specifically designed for elderly with limited upper body mobility to aid in their movement. This device not only meets the needs of on-site facilities but also significantly reduces the lumbar load on caregivers during transfer tasks. It is specifically designed for the seamless transfer of elderly from their rooms to the bathroom, supporting them in independently managing their excretion within the bathroom [10].

Moreover, the study thoroughly considered the physical contact between caregivers and the elderly, aiming to lessen the psychological burden on elderly and enhance their acceptance of the transfer assistance device. Given the potential interference of conditions such as Parkinson's disease and cognitive impairments with the system's effective use, caregivers maintain physical contact with the elderly during the transfer assistive movements. This approach not only helps stabilize the elderly physically but also alleviates their anxiety, thereby facilitating the optimal synergistic effect of the human-machine collaborative transfer system [11].

However, in the aforementioned research, our primary focus was on the quantitative assessment of lumbar load among caregivers, with a relatively limited exploration into the psychological state of caregivers when using the human-machine collaborative transfer system. This indicates that while addressing the issue of caregivers' lower back pain, research into their psychological burdens [12–16] is equally indispensable. Particularly during the 2020–2023 COVID-19 global pandemic, the direct fatalities aside, the adverse impacts on the mental health of many individuals [17] cannot be overlooked. In response to these challenges, a series of recently developed digital mental health tools [18] and welfare devices [19, 20] have played a positive role in emotional regulation, skill enhancement, and education, offering new strategies for addressing mental health challenges. Thus, exploring suitable design approaches for improving the mental health of caregivers has become an important focus of our research.

Therefore, recognizing the significance of alleviating the psychological stress experienced by caregivers due to their work responsibilities, this study proposes a user interface/user experience (UI/UX) based design methodology for developing a customizable portable simulated pet system (mobile application). This system is intended to mitigate the psychological stress of caregivers and to preliminarily assess its potential effects.

2 System Framework Based on UI/UX Design Methodology

Building upon previous research, it becomes clear that the portable simulated pet application, KEDAMA, features a core framework divided into four main sections: create, voice, personal and more pages (Fig. 1) [21, 22]. Specifically, it includes functionalities such as basic personal information, software updates, generation of personal QR codes, and personalized designs based on each user's pet rearing experiences. Additionally, the selection and recording of personalized pet sounds have been considered in the design.

The innovative aspects of KEDAMA's design are twofold. Firstly, it offers customization based on individual preferences, personalizing the design according to each user's pet preferences, thus breaking away from the traditional stereotypes associated with virtual pets. The design process emphasizes not only the appearance of pets but also a personalized and customized approach, suggesting attention to virtual pet characteristics from various aspects such as fur length, color, and texture. Secondly, the selection and customization of pet sounds are tailored according to users' experiences with pets, types of pets, breeds, and individual characteristics.

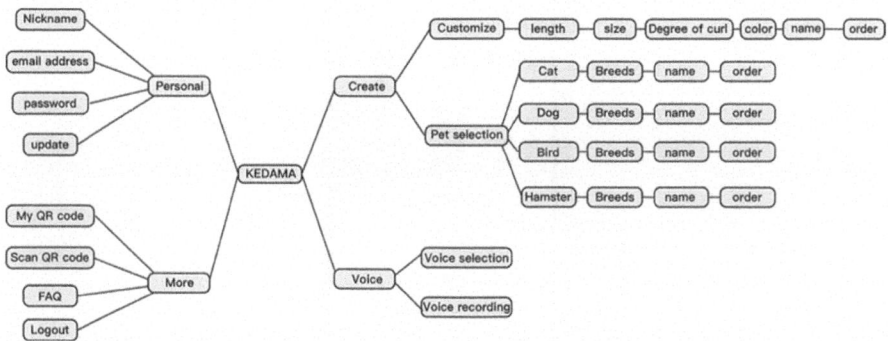

Fig. 1. The core framework of the portable simulated pet application KEDAMA [21].

2.1 Initial Page Design

Throughout the design process of the entire application, we consistently employed rounded rectangles, also referred to as circular design elements. This design approach aims to provide users with a sense of comfort, aligning with the original intent of the design. As demonstrated in the login interface shown in Fig. 2, the top of the interface features an illustration depicting a traveler carrying a ball of wool. Below the illustration are input fields where users are required to enter their email address and password. For new users, a "New User" button is available at the lower left corner for registration purposes; for those who have forgotten their password, a "Forgot Password" button is also provided. Moreover, the application offers the option to log in using Facebook or Google accounts, facilitating convenient account access for users.

For newly registered users who initially possess no information within the app, the first step is to create a hairball. By tapping on the plus icon, users can add a hairball, with two avenues for creation: selecting the type and breed of the pet, or opting for a personalized customization. For those without prior pet-owning experience or who have not made specific decisions regarding their preferences, selecting a pet type or breed directly is available. For users with unique customization ideas, personalizing a hairball is an option. The specifics of what can be customized will be elaborated on in subsequent sections.

On the home page, users can view the hairballs they have created, along with their basic information. The upper left corner of the screen displays the user's avatar, name, and number. The upper right corner contains additional buttons, which upon clicking, offer access to functions such as password modification, customer service, and logout.

If users wish to create another hairball after having created one, they can slide to the hairball and then click on the plus icon to create it. At the bottom of the screen, the option to modify the hairball's voice through recording or importing is available.

Fig. 2. Pages for new user registration, login, and forgotten password.

2.2 Customization Page Design

In the design of the customization page, Fig. 3 illustrates a method for personalized customization based on characteristics of hairballs such as length, size, and curliness. This customization process is divided into three steps, designed to allow users to make detailed selections based on the specific appearance of their pets.

The first step focuses on the selection of the hairball's length, where users can choose from "long," "medium," and "short," depending on the actual appearance of their pet.

The second step involves the customization of the hairball's size. Again, users select the most suitable option from "large," "medium," and "small," based on their pet's size.

The third step is to determine the degree of curliness of the hairball. Users can choose from "straight," "medium," and "curly," according to the natural state of their pet's fur, thereby more accurately replicating the natural charm of their pet.

Fig. 3. Pages for personalizing hairball characteristics such as length, size, and curliness.

As shown in Fig. 4, the fourth step involves selecting the texture of the hairball to better match the appearance of one's pet. The options available include solid color, polka dots, and stripes. For those who choose polka dots or stripes, there is also the option to select two colors, adding an extra layer of customization.

The fifth step is to confirm the appearance of the hairball and to assign a name to it. The sixth step is to place the order and make the payment. On the following payment page, it is necessary to fill in various information, including the recipient's name, postal code, and phone number. After completing these details and clicking on the shopping cart button, payment can be made. The product will be shipped to the home within a few business days.

2.3 Pet Selection Page Design

As mentioned in Sect. 2.1, another method for creating hairballs involves selecting the type of pet (see Fig. 5).

The initial step requires users to choose the general category of their pet. Subsequently, in the second step, the selection of the pet's breed takes place, after which the system automatically generates a hairball that closely matches the selected breed's characteristics, including fur color, length, and curliness. Although this list encompasses a wide range of common pet breeds and types, if the user's pet breed is not included, they may return to the homepage to select the option for custom hairball creation. Following the selection of the pet's type and breed, the subsequent steps resemble the customization process of hairballs, with the third step focusing on confirming the appearance of the hairball and naming it, and the fourth step moving towards order placement and payment.

Fig. 4. Pages for personalizing hairball characteristics such as texture, appearance, and payment.

Fig. 5. Pages for pet selection page design

Whether users opt to select based on the characteristics of their pets directly or prefer to customize hairballs according to their own tastes, our designed application offers a pathway to customization grounded in individual preferences. This method allows for the creation of hairballs that align precisely with the user's personal tastes, as opposed to being limited to the options available in the commercial market. This approach to customization is capable of significantly enhancing the emotional bond between users and their hairballs, as well as mitigating psychological stress in future use, thereby enhancing the emotional well-being of the user. By providing a creative platform for users, we encourage personalized expression and believe that such deep customization can forge a closer connection on an emotional level between users and their pets.

3 Preliminary Evaluation of the Effectiveness of KEDAMA Stroking in Alleviating Psychological Stress Among Caregivers

Hairballs designed by using the KEDAMA application, based on prototypes of animals such as Persian cats, Teddy dogs, Samoyed dogs, Shiba Inus, and hamsters, as depicted in Fig. 6.

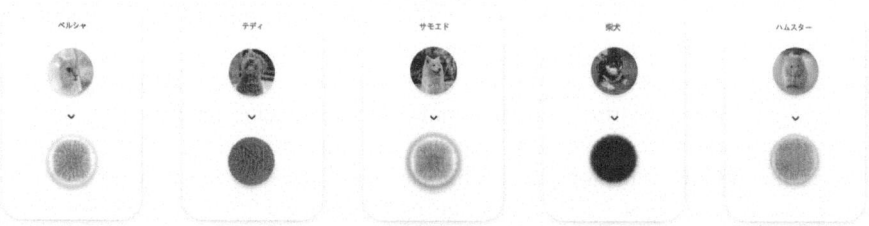

Fig. 6. Appearance of hairballs.

VC-IOE Checklist(KEDAMA)

Date:_____   Name:_____   Video time:_____

感情的な反応
(Emotional)   -2   -1   0   1   2

言葉による反応
(Verbal)   -2   -1   0   1   2

視覚による反応
(Visual)   -2   -1   0   1   2

行動に見られる反応
(Behavioural)   -2   -1   0   1   2

他者やグループとして反応
(Collective)   -2   -1   0   1   2

興奮、動揺
(Agitation)   -2   -1   0   1   2

Name of rater:_____

Fig. 7. VC-IOE checklist for touching KEDAMA.

3.1 Experimental Settings for Touching KEDAMA

We recruited 5 subjects with a caregiver background (average age 33, standard deviation 6) who lived with KEDAMA for three weeks. Based on the subjects' available times each week, specifically, a selected time once per week, we arranged for 10-min interaction sessions with KEDAMA, which were recorded on video. By analyzing the subjects' responses captured in the videos, we conducted observational evaluations and assessed the effect of using KEDAMA by calculating the average of these responses, comparing the outcomes before and after the three-week period.

Jones in 2015 developed a novel approach utilizing a Video Coding Protocol-Incorporating Observed Emotion (VC-IOE) to explore the behavioral responses of dementia patients [23]. This methodology facilitates the quantitative analysis of the extent to which machinery impacts various human aspects through scoring patients' reactions. The creation of the VC-IOE metric aims to provide a more intuitive means of measuring impact, to meet research objectives. It is specifically designed for the study of interactions between virtual pet robots and dementia patients under varying environmental conditions, with a significant emphasis on comparing changes before and after participation. VC-IOE encompasses six dimensions of the experiencer: emotional, linguistic, visual, behavioral, social interaction, and excitement levels. Experiences across each dimension should be independently evaluated and aggregated to derive an overall outcome.

In our study, the evaluation criteria used a 5-point scale (-2 for significant deterioration, -1 for slight deterioration, 0 for no change, $+1$ for improvement, $+2$ for significant improvement) to rate entries in the observed video recordings list (Fig. 7), numerically representing the degree of impact. The scoring method is: emotion score times 2, verbal score times 2, visual score times 2, behavioural score times 1, collective score times 2, and agitation score times 1. This method increases the weight of emotion, verbal, visual, behavioural, as well as collective and agitation values.

3.2 Results and Discussion

Based on the VC-IOE assessment checklist, we conducted scoring on the subjects' performances observed in video recordings over a three-week period, selecting one evaluation session each week. The scores obtained by the subjects across six dimensions—emotion, verbal, visual, behavioural, collective, and agitation—are presented in Fig. 9. Comparative analysis clearly shows that the scores in all six evaluation dimensions were significantly higher in the third week compared to the first week, indicating marked improvement in the subjects' performance in various aspects by the third week.

To substantiate the statistical significance of these observations, we calculated p-values for the performances across the six dimensions. Specifically, the p-value for the emotion dimension was 0.001082298, for the verbal dimension it was 0.0000153406517978879, for the visual dimension it was 0.024824458, for the behavioral dimension it was 0.004308785, for the collective dimension it was 0.003032055, and for the agitation dimension it was 0.00008082875159678889. These p-value results further confirm our initial observations that, over a three-week period using the VC-IOE assessment methodology, there were statistically significant improvements in subjects' performances across key dimensions such as emotion, verbal, visual, behavioural, collective, and agitation levels (Fig. 8).

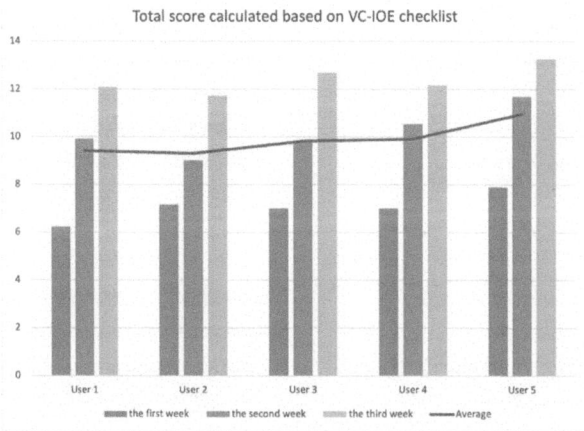

Fig. 8. Total score calculated based on VC-IOE checklist.

Further comparative analysis shows that scores across all six evaluation dimensions were significantly higher in the third week compared to the first week, indicating marked improvement in the subjects' performance in various aspects by the third week. To further substantiate these observations' statistical significance, we calculated p-values for the performances across the six dimensions. The p-value for the emotion dimension was 0.001082298, for the verbal dimension it was 0.00001534065179788879, for the visual dimension it was 0.024824458, for the behavioural dimension it was 0.004308785, for the collective dimension it was 0.003032055, and for the agitation dimension it was 0.00008082875159678789. These p-value results further confirm our initial observations that, over a three-week period using the VC-IOE assessment methodology, there were statistically significant improvements in subjects' performances across key dimensions such as emotion, verbal, visual, behavioural, collective, and agitation levels.

After a detailed statistical analysis of the data, it was particularly noted that there were significant positive responses in the dimensions of verbal and agitation when interacting with KEDAMA. This observation underscores the unique benefits of the KEDAMA experience in enhancing verbal abilities and increasing user agitation levels. Further comprehensive analysis of the summary data revealed a clear upward trend in individual user response effects over the three-week experience period, indicating a sustained positive impact of KEDAMA on users. Specifically, the average efficacy rating of KEDAMA significantly increased from 7.05 before the experience to 12.38 after three weeks of engagement. This outcome not only confirms the significant positive impact of the portable virtual pet KEDAMA on individuals but also reflects that the user experience with KEDAMA over three weeks did not lead to aversion; instead, it resulted in positive progress and improvements across various aspects (Fig. 9).

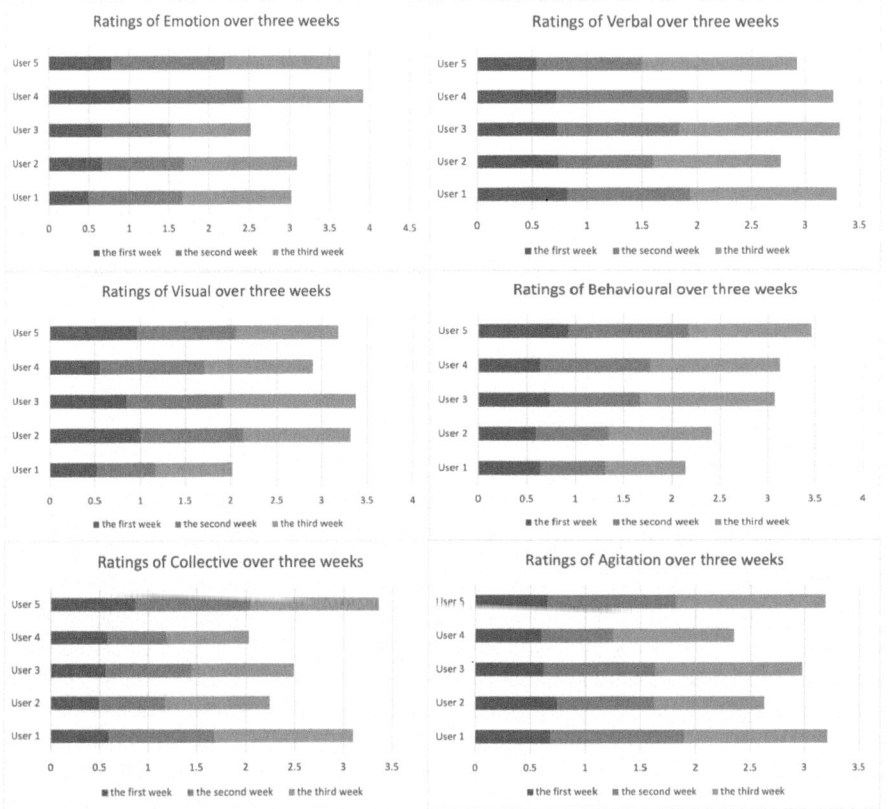

Fig. 9. Over the course of three weeks, the scores of subjects across six dimensions (emotion, verbal, visual, behavioural, collective, and agitation) based on the VC-IOE checklist.

4   Conclusion

This study aimed to thoroughly investigate whether users with caregiving backgrounds are inclined towards long-term engagement with KEDAMA as an interactive device. Through comprehensive survey and analysis across various dimensions, it was found that 55.2% of participants rated KEDAMA's performance as good, while 42% pointed out areas for improvement, with virtually no participants rating it poorly, and no experiencers expressing outright negative feedback. These test outcomes provide substantial evidence of KEDAMA's potential as a device suitable for long-term use, demonstrating its capability to sustain positive effects.

The findings suggest that the longer users interact with KEDAMA, the more pronounced its positive impact on emotional dimensions becomes. Additionally, the study revealed that long-term usage of KEDAMA does not adversely affect the overall user experience. On the contrary, users reported a sense of emotional stability and enhanced well-being with prolonged use. This indicates that KEDAMA can potentially serve as a reliable companion, akin to traditional pets, without the drawbacks associated with live animals, such as the need for physical care and the possibility of allergies.

Furthermore, the integration of KEDAMA into daily routines could lead to continuous improvements in mental health for caregivers and general users alike. This is particularly beneficial in contexts where traditional pets may not be feasible, such as in small apartments or for individuals with mobility issues. The data collected from the study underscores KEDAMA's role not only as an interactive device but also as a significant contributor to emotional and mental well-being. Given these positive research findings, we propose that KEDAMA can be effectively integrated into people's daily lives over the long term, serving as a potential alternative to traditional pets and facilitating sustained mental health improvements.

However, to alleviate the psychological stress of caregivers and conduct an initial exploration of the effects, only five participants with caregiving backgrounds were recruited. While the small sample size provided valuable initial insights, it limits the generalizability of the findings. In future research, we plan to recruit a larger and more diverse group of participants, ensuring a balanced gender ratio and an even distribution of age groups. This will enable a more comprehensive analysis and understanding of KEDAMA's long-term impact on a broader population. Despite these limitations, the current study successfully highlights the promising potential of KEDAMA, paving the way for further exploration and validation in subsequent studies. Thus, while acknowledging the limitations, this research lays a solid foundation for future work and underscores the significant implications of integrating KEDAMA into daily caregiving routines.

Acknowledgments. This research was supported by JSPS KAKENHI Grant Number JP20J10461.The authors would like to thank the JSPS Program for Leading Graduate School (Graduate Program in Gerontology, Global Leadership Initiative for an Age Friendly Society, The University of Tokyo) for providing financial support to Jiang Wu. Special thanks to Dr. Mio Nakamura for her help and comments on the evaluation of this system.

Disclosure of Interests.   The authors have no competing interests to declare that are relevant to the content of this article.

References

1. Reiwa 1st Edition White Paper on Aging Society (Whole Version). https://www8.cao.go.jp/kourei/whitepaper/w-2023/zenbun/05pdf_index.html. Accessed 20 Mar 2024
2. Mehrdad, R., et al.: Prevalence of low back pain in health care workers and comparison with other occupational categories in Iran: a systematic review. Iran. J. Med. Sci. **41**(6), 467 (2016)
3. Rasmussen, C.D.N., et al.: Prevention of low back pain and its consequences among nurses' aides in elderly care: a stepped-wedge multi-faceted cluster-randomized controlled trial. BMC Publ. Health **13**(1), 1–13 (2013)

4. Kurumatani, N., et al.: Work related movement disorders of nurses – basic of prevention and countermeasures (special collection of human care services and ergonomics). J. Labor Sci. **59**(12), 709–713 (2004)

5. Study group report on revision and spread of low back pain prevention measures guidelines in the workplace. Ministry of Health, Labor and Welfare (2013). https://www.mhlw.go.jp/stf/shingi/2r98520000034qqlatt/2r98520000034qs-0.pdf. Accessed 22 Feb 2021

6. Sivakanthan, S., Blaauw, E., Greenhalgh, M., Koontz, A.M., Vegter, R., Cooper, R.A.: Person transfer assist systems: a literature review. Disabil. Rehabil. Assist. Technol. **16**, 270–279 (2021)

7. Blaauw, E.R., et al.: Assessment of muscle activation of caregivers performing dependent transfers with a novel robotic-assisted transfer device compared with the Hoyer advance. Am. J. Phys. Med. Rehabil. **100**, 885–894 (2021)

8. Krishnan, R.H., Pugazhenthi, S.: Design and development of a robotic self-transfer device for wheelchair users. J. Enabling Technol. **11**, 59–72 (2017)

9. Ulrey, B.L., Fathallah, F.A.: Subject-specific, whole-body models of the stooped posture with a personal weight transfer device. J. Electromyogr. Kinesiol. **23**, 206–215 (2013)

10. Wu, J., Shino, M.: Hip lift transfer assistive system for reducing burden on caregiver's waist. Sensors **21**, 7548 (2021)

11. Wu, J., Shino, M.: Proposal for a human–machine collaborative transfer system considering caregivers' lower back pain and cognitive factors in the elderly during transfer movements. Actuators, 96 (2024)

12. Kurumatani, N., Morita, N.: Work related movement disorders of nurses—basic of prevention and countermeasures (special collection of human care services and ergonomics). J. Labor Sci. **59**, 709–713 (2004)

13. Ebrahim, O.S., Al-Attar, G.S., Gabra, R.H., Osman, D.M.: Stigma and burden of mental illness and their correlates among family caregivers of mentally ill patients. J. Egypt. Publ. Health Assoc. **95**, 31 (2020)

14. Shetty, J., Shetty, A., Mundkur, S.C., Tantri, K.D., Prachi, P.: Economic burden on caregivers or parents with down syndrome children—a systematic review protocol. Syst. Rev. **12**, 3 (2023)

15. Zwar, L., König, H.H., Hajek, A.: Gender differences in mental health, quality of life, and caregiver burden among informal caregivers during the second wave of the COVID-19 pandemic in Germany: a representative, population-based study. Gerontology **69**, 149–162 (2023)

16. Kayaalp, A., Page, K.J., Rospenda, K.M.: Caregiver burden, work-family conflict, family-work conflict, and mental health of caregivers: a mediational longitudinal study. Work Stress. **35**, 217–240 (2021)

17. Panchal, N., et al.: The implications of COVID-19 for mental health and substance use. Kais. Fam. Found. **21**, 1–16 (2020)

18. Petrovic, M., Gaggioli, A.: Digital mental health tools for caregivers of older adults—a scoping review. Front. Publ. Health **8**, 128 (2020)

19. Kedama, Welfare Equipment Contest 2021. https://www.resja.or.jp/contest/data/2021/202121.jpg. Accessed 20 Mar 2024

20. Wu, J., et al.: UI/UX design of portable simulation pet 'KEDAMA' hairball for relieving pressure. In: Stephanidis, C., Antona, M., Ntoa, S.. (eds.) HCII 2021. CCIS, vol. 1499, pp. 215–223. Springer, Cham (2021). https://doi.org/10.1007/978-3-030-90179-0_28

21. Wu, J., et al.: UI/UX design methodology of portable customizable simulated pet system considering human mental health. In: 2022 IEEE 4th Global Conference on Life Sciences and Technologies (LifeTech), pp. 41–45. IEEE (2022)

22. Wu, J., et al.: Feasibility study of portable simulated pet 'KEDAMA' for relieving depression. In: Gao, Q., Zhou, J. (eds.) HCII 2022. LNCS, vol. 13331, pp. 290–304. Springer, Cham (2022). https://doi.org/10.1007/978-3-031-05654-3_20
23. Jones, C., Sung, B., Moyle, W.: Assessing engagement in people with dementia: a new approach to assessment using video analysis. Arch. Psychiatr. Nurs. **29**(6), 377–382 (2015)

Exploring the Potential of Design Thinking in Healthcare Through the Integration of VR for Educational Purposes

Lizhu Zhang, Swetha Anand, and Cecilia Xi Wang[✉]

University of Minnesota, Minneapolis, MN 55455, USA
{zhan8909,ceciw}@umn.edu

Abstract. *Background:* The healthcare education landscape has become increasingly complex, presenting a growing need for innovative problem-solving. One approach that has gained traction in recent years is design thinking, which prioritizes a patient-centric approach to solving complex medical challenges. As a result, design thinking has been integrated into the medical field to tackle these intricate issues.

Objective: In order to gain a deeper understanding, we conducted a thorough literature review to analyze the outcomes of design thinking when applied to the use of virtual reality technology in medical training decision-making. The focus of our paper is to provide insights into the following research inquiries:

RQ1: How has design thinking been incorporated in pre-training in Healthcare education?

RQ2: How has technology such as virtual reality been used in educating medical students and practitioners?

Methodology: An extensive search was conducted using virtual reality in healthcare training scientific research data between 2015 and 2024. The extensive search was done using databases including EBSCOhost, Springer, Pub Med, and Science Direct. The searches retrieved n = 10 original articles that were quality-checked and included for the review based on the search criteria.

Conclusion: According to existing literature, Design Thinking in conjunction with VR technologies will be an effective means of pre-training medical students and practitioners. Although many healthcare studies incorporate Design Thinking without explicit recognition, there is still a lack of understanding and implementation of this approach in the healthcare industry to tackle the multifaceted challenges within the field.

Keywords: Health and DUXU · Design Thinking Healthcare · Healthcare design thinking · medical simulation · Clinical training · Simulation training · Healthcare VR · VR · education · UX · literature review

© The Author(s), under exclusive license to Springer Nature Switzerland AG 2025
V. G. Duffy (Ed.): HCII 2024, LNCS 15376, pp. 202–211, 2025.
https://doi.org/10.1007/978-3-031-76809-5_15

1 Introduction

1.1 Challenges in Healthcare

Healthcare has become increasingly challenging, with the demand for patient-centric care taking precedence. This has added to the stress experienced by practitioners and medical students. Not only are medical students and practitioners required to acquire vast amounts of information, but they are also expected to develop their clinical skills [1]. Educational materials in medical education and other health-related professional training involve the study of extensive material and the acquisition of various new skills [2]. Students are expected to retain voluminous information in order to obtain clinical skills [14]. In response to the challenges and stress faced by students and medical schools, there is a growing trend of incorporating technology to achieve learning objectives within a limited time frame. Methods such as active learning, flipped classrooms, and the integration of technologies like augmented reality are being adopted to enhance learning within curricula, offering educators a variety of options [1].

Additionally, educators have made efforts to incorporate new technologies into the curriculum in order to enhance engagement and comprehension. Institutions are now promoting the use of technologies like VR, AR, and serious games to make learning more interactive and accessible for students [2]. These technology-based tools are designed to avoid overwhelming students with information and to personalize skill development based on individual student needs.

In this paper, we will focus on the challenges that medical students and healthcare professionals encounter during their simulation training prior to their clinical rotations. Traditionally, medical students and surgical residents have primarily learned through observing and discussing cases among experienced colleagues [3, 4]. However, this approach often provides limited exposure to decision-making and the practice of motor skills necessary for rotational training, leading to lower confidence and increased stress when starting rotations. Due to inadequate training methods, four out of every ten novice surgeons lack confidence in performing major procedures [15]. To address these challenges, educators can incorporate interactive technologies such as augmented reality (AR), virtual reality (VR) [3], and serious games to better prepare students and practitioners for the demands of surgical training. Additionally, the need for design thinking with different stakeholders to build the technology-based curriculum is of great need.

1.2 How Design Thinking Plays a Role in Healthcare

The importance of clinicians possessing strong medical knowledge and clinical skills, as well as effective problem-solving abilities, cannot be overstated [16]. In the face of these challenges, innovative problem-solving is crucial, and can be accomplished through the application of design thinking and the integration of technology into medical education.

Design thinking is a methodical and structured approach to solving intricate problems in collaboration with users and other stakeholders, resulting in the development of innovative patient care. It fosters creative problem-solving by leveraging various data sources to produce groundbreaking solutions [6, 7]. At its core, the key principle is that creating high-quality products and services necessitates a profound understanding of user needs and collaborative prototyping with users, including patients. Design thinking is a systematic approach to innovation and problem-solving, commonly taught in leading business schools and widely utilized in the technology industry. Its fundamental premise is that the development of exceptional products and services requires a genuine comprehension of user needs and close collaboration with users to create prototypes [6].

Design thinking has been increasingly utilized in the medical field to tackle the complexities of patient care. This involves integrating design thinking into the development of healthcare products and services, as well as incorporating it into medical education to equip healthcare professionals with skills and knowledge beyond basic and clinical sciences [8]. For instance, American medical schools have introduced an elective program in innovation and entrepreneurship (I&E) for undergraduate students, providing them with opportunities to participate in workshops, studio-based classes, and hackathons to devise solutions for real-world problems [6].

Consequently, this approach not only fosters the development of innovative medical practitioners but also cultivates essential skills such as critical thinking, teamwork, and interdisciplinary collaboration, ultimately leading to improved patient care.

2   Use of VR in Healthcare

The integration of interactive VR, AR, serious games, and other technologies as tools by medical educators into simulation training curricula has shown promising results. In a study by Ribaupierre et al., 98% of 200 medical students expressed support for incorporating technology into medical curricula for better integration, and 95% of the students were in favor of including new media technology in surgical training for academic and skill acquisition benefits. The study emphasized the importance of medical educators as facilitators to enhance the simulation training sessions [2]. This indicates a growing acceptance of technology, particularly VR, in the medical field among both students and practitioners. Additionally, we delved deeper into understanding how VR is utilized in healthcare and in pre-training or clinical training to address the second research question.

2.1   Understanding VR

VR technology has seen increasing use due to its promising potential. It has been adopted in various fields, such as entertainment, education, firefighting, and medicine [9, 10]. The interactive nature of VR engages users and provides an immersive experience. In healthcare education, VR helps bridge the gap between theory and practice by creating a realistic environment for students and practitioners to enhance their clinical skills. The immersive environment, more specifically a 3D simulated environment [9], helps to concentrate on the task, and the aspect of virtual wards with interactive patients helps in effective training in the dynamic environment. Scenario-based virtual environments also facilitate the practice of surgical tasks and improve motor and other skills based on the person. Additionally, Dynamic case scenarios with interactive and sensory feedback help students learn effectively and enhance their surgical and clinical skills [3, 9].

2.2 Simulation and Clinical Training Using VR

Efforts to find effective complements to traditional training methods have led surgeons to explore the use of simulation, serious games, and virtual reality to train novice surgeons, similar to the way pilots use flight simulators [17]. The following is a brief overview of advancements in surgical training methods. The primary purpose of simulation is to provide a safe environment for practitioners, students, and surgeons to practice [4]. In many cases, specialty-based training involves a case scenario with role-playing, requiring students to prepare based on their assigned roles. Additionally, student practice sessions are sometimes recorded, and feedback is given afterward. These physical sessions necessitate significant use of imagination by the students [2]. Moreover, limited accessibility and availability of simulation labs can restrict knowledge and skill transfer for students. To tackle this challenge, simulation training is increasingly incorporating technology-based solutions such as VR and serious games [2, 4]. The limited out-of-hours access and reduced availability for trainees during the initial three years of surgical training underscore a critical requirement for the advancement of future surgical simulators. However, the substantial production costs and investment associated with the development of realistic surgical simulations impede their widespread adoption on a global scale [4].

Furthermore, VR, AR, and serious game simulators are not only adaptable to different platforms but the simulation environment can also be tailored to the specific needs of practitioners. It is customizable to the needs of students, and it can help in the development of students of diverse skill sets [12]. It's worth noting that in certain healthcare fields, such as nursing, VR and serious games are utilized to train professionals in decision-making under pressure, providing a safe and realistic simulated environment for skill acquisition [13].

Based on the literature, it is evident that numerous studies have demonstrated the effectiveness of integrating gamification through serious games as a complementary approach to VR. This not only facilitates realistic simulation but also provides opportunities for practice and feedback [3] that help students continue practicing to obtain the required knowledge. Additionally, it allows the analysis of direct consequences of conduct without cost to the patient's life [3].

One example of how VR is used in simulation [5] is second life which is a web-based tool used for the simulation training [11, 12]. Although initially intended for medical education training, Second Life is also utilized by non-medical students to learn about the medicine by immersing into the environment [5]. Since its launch in 2003, the tool has seen new medical and health projects [11] introduced, incorporating case-based and multiplayer simulation features [5]. Medical educators are currently assessing its adaptability for their needs [11].

Another example of VR simulation is CliniSpace, which is specifically designed for simulating emergency medicine [5, 12] and is currently utilized by Stanford University. While its graphical interface may not be top-notch, it effectively covers the necessary information for medical students. Because of the custom case ability and the enhanced usability addressing the needs of students, it has been also used by other universities for training medical students and practitioners [5].

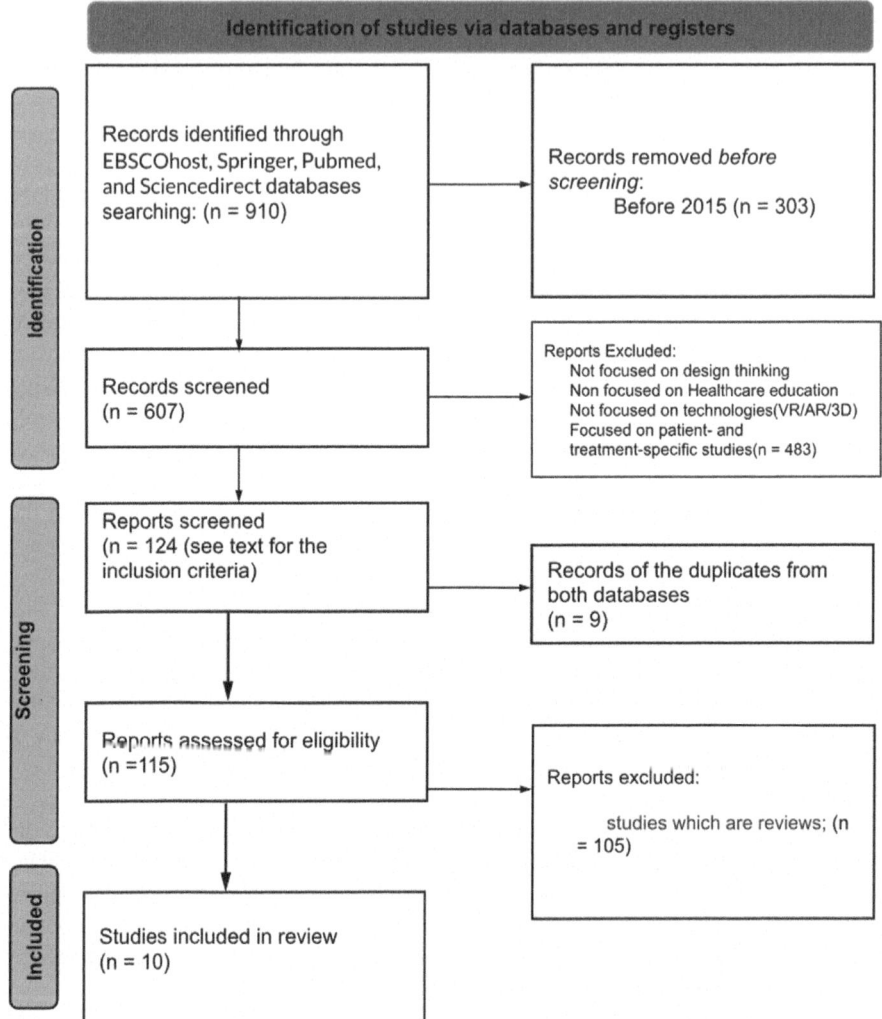

Fig. 1. A figure showing the data collection and filtering process is depicted based on the search criteria of VR.

3 Methodology

In order to understand the use of technology that is the use of Virtual Reality (VR) in the simulation training or clinical training of healthcare we conducted a search criterion mentioned below was the process carried out to understand the growth of VR in the medical field.

3.1 Eligibility Criteria

The search was limited to peer-reviewed papers published between January 2014 and March 2024.

3.2 Search Strategy

Use the following search terms and their different combinations: "healthcare education" AND "using serious games" AND "virtual reality or VR or augmented reality" AND "user experience design," with the Boolean operators (AND, OR). MeSH terminology was also used in the review. In addition, a manual search of the references of the included articles was performed. No restrictions were used in the search. In addition, a manual search was conducted on the references of the included articles. We used these keywords searched in EBSCOhost, Springer, Pubmed, and ScienceDirect databases, these four paper search platforms.

The inclusion criteria for this review were as follows: (1) qualitative or quantitative studies involving healthcare professionals or nursing/medical students from different disciplines; (2) design thinking to realize healthcare education studies; and (3) studies in which the authors defined the technology as 3D or AR or VR.

The exclusion criteria were as follows: (1) studies not dedicated to medical training; (3) studies not focusing on technologies such as VR; (3) review studies; and (4) patient- and treatment-specific studies. Non-scientific and anecdotal papers were excluded. Figure 1 shows a detailed description of how the process was followed.

Virtual reality is a computer-generated simulation environment that allows users to immerse themselves in and interact with it. Based on the results, we were able to analyze that VR is increasingly used in the healthcare and pre-training or clinical training sectors, filling the gap between theory and practice to help medical students and professionals learn complex surgical procedures and improve their skills and confidence in creating realistic simulated environments.

3.3 Search Outcomes

A total of 910 studies were collected, comprising 13 from EBSCOhost, 557 from Springer, 334 from ScienceDirect, and 3 from PubMed. 303 studies dating before 2015 were excluded. Two independent researchers evaluated the remaining 607 articles. At first, we reviewed the titles and abstracts of the papers and selected 124 that were relevant. We excluded 483 studies that did not focus on design thinking, health education, or scientific and technological purposes, as well as content that focused on patients and treatment modalities. Subsequently, 9 duplicate studies and 105 review papers were excluded. Following individual reviews and researcher discussions, the selection and exclusion criteria were confirmed, leading to the final selection of studies for review. A total of 10 studies were included in the analysis. The process of data collection and filtering is depicted in Fig. 1 (Table 1).

Table 1. Table shows the VR and other technologies usage from the 10 articles.

Healthcare	Year	Technology	Description
Surgical simulators	2014	VR, serious games	The VR simulator along with serious game elements are used for surgical training including neonatal care, cardiovascular drugs, and abnormal blood clot formation etc.
Surgical simulators	2017	VR, serious games	An immersive VR operating room experience for oral and maxillofacial surgery trainees using simulation, serious gaming, and VR. Trainees to virtually participate in surgical procedures and interact with the patient's anatomy. Into VR Surgery is useful visualization aid for surgical trainees and a practice-based learning tool for senior surgeons
VR case study	2018	VR, serious games	Immersive VR improves simulation outcomes, such as increasing learning gain and knowledge retention and improving clinical outcomes for rehabilitation
Virtual medical environment	2023	VR	Technologies are used to build virtual medical environment for primary care for diabetic foot, providing users with a range of trusted experiences
Simulations in Nursing Education	2021	VR	Demonstration of the application of epistemic network analysis (ENA), a quantitative ethnography (QE) technique, to model how one nursing educator facilitated clinical judgment, and nurtured quality and safety education for nurses' competencies through the use of the Simulation Learning System with Virtual Reality (SLS with VR)

(*continued*)

Table 1. (*continued*)

Healthcare	Year	Technology	Description
Medical Education	2020	VR	VR tool for patients' treatment and help for educating the patients
Virtual Reality Simulations	2019	VR, serious games	A virtual reality serious game for Recreational therapy as a study case of iPlus, a methodology for the design of SGs. iPlus allows educational, based on a participative, user-centered approach
VR Case Study	2018	VR, serious games	A development case for making a new training tool using multi-user virtual reality (VR) and serious game methods for anaphylactic shock critical care auxiliary medical cases. VR training outcome depends on high presence effects and is limited by usability issues
Virtual medical environment	2018	VR	Current applications of virtual environments in training and assessment, including limitations and challenges of implementing virtual environments in medical education programs

4 Result

The use of virtual reality (VR) has been dominant in recent years, particularly in clinical training and skill acquisition. Our literature review revealed a growing trend in designing simulation and clinical training using VR and other technologies. Most studies covered the need of virtual reality in education and how the existing VR tools are not used by all medical universities because of the lack of common agreement. Furthermore, there is a need for more research on the impact of technology on students' clinical training. Analyzing the papers helped us to address the research question of "How has technology such as virtual reality been used in educating medical students and practitioners?" and helped us to understand that there is a need for the technology and also the aspect of what would be the implementation of the adoptions of such technology into clinical training, which in the long term will help in patient care.

In terms of design thinking, a lot of recent literature shows that design thinking has been adopted into medical and healthcare in recent years. The demand for innovative solutions and the development of problem-solving skills among medical students and professionals has led medical universities across the United States to incorporate design thinking into their curricula. However, it is worth noting that design thinking has not yet been integrated into clinical simulation training programs. In the literature review, none of the articles has design thinking adopted into the process. This is concerning because of the need to involve other stakeholders, including the patients and students, in providing and building useful and better-performing clinical simulation training. Therefore, this review has sought to address the research question, "How has design thinking been incorporated into pre-training in healthcare education?".

5   Conclusion

According to existing literature, VR technologies have been shown to be an effective method for pre-training (clinical training) medical students and practitioners. While many healthcare studies implicitly incorporate Design Thinking, there is still a lack of understanding and implementation of this approach in the healthcare industry to address the complex challenges within the field. Therefore, the incorporation of design thinking not only aids in developing innovative healthcare solutions, but also in understanding the implementation of technology and its limitations when applied in the healthcare industry. Most studies indicate that the use of VR and other technologies can have negative effects such as dizziness and cybersickness. This suggests that further studies are needed after the implementation of technologies like AR, VR, and others in simulation training.

References

1. Moro, C., Phelps, C., Redmond, P., Stromberga, Z.: HoloLens and mobile augmented reality in medical and health science education: a randomised controlled trial. British J. Educ. Technol. **52** (2020). https://doi.org/10.1111/bjet.13049
2. de Ribaupierre, S., Kapralos, B., Haji, F., Stroulia, E., Dubrowski, A., Eagleson, R.: Healthcare training enhancement through virtual reality and serious games. Virt. Augment. Real. Seri. Games Healthcare **1**, 9–27 (2014). https://doi.org/10.1007/978-3-642-54816-1_2
3. Riva, G., Dores, W., Damasio, A., Cacione, D.G., Jorge, J., Zorzal, E.: Virtual Reality applied to medical education and training on Diabetic Foot (2023). https://doi.org/10.1109/vrw58643.2023.00043
4. Pulijala, Y., Ma, M., Ayoub, A.: VR surgery: interactive virtual reality application for training oral and maxillofacial surgeons using oculus rift and leap motion. Serious Games Edutain. Appl. 187–202 (2017). https://doi.org/10.1007/978-3-319-51645-5_8
5. Kleinert, R., Wahba, R., Chang, D.-H., Plum, P., Hölscher, A.H., Stippel, D.L.: 3D immersive patient simulators and their impact on learning success: a thematic review. J. Med. Internet Res. **17**, e91 (2015). https://doi.org/10.2196/jmir.3492
6. Trowbridge, M., Chen, D., Gregor, A.: Teaching design thinking to medical students. Med. Educ. **52**, 1199–1200 (2018). https://doi.org/10.1111/medu.13699
7. Marcus, D., Simone, A., Block, L.: Design thinking in medical ethics education. J. Med. Ethics. medethics-2019–105989 (2020). https://doi.org/10.1136/medethics-2019-105989
8. van de Grift, T.C., Kroeze, R.: Design thinking as a tool for interdisciplinary education in health care. Acad. Med. **91**, 1234–1238 (2016). https://doi.org/10.1097/acm.000000000000 1195

9. Baniasadi, T., Ayyoubzadeh, S.M., Mohammadzadeh, N.: Challenges and practical considerations in applying virtual reality in medical education and treatment. Oman Med. J. **35**, e125–e125 (2020). https://doi.org/10.5001/omj.2020.43

10. Menin, A., Torchelsen, R., Nedel, L.: An analysis of VR technology used in immersive simulations with a serious game perspective. IEEE Comput. Graph. Appl. **38**, 57–73 (2018). https://doi.org/10.1109/mcg.2018.021951633

11. Alselaiti, N.: Enhancing student engagement and learning outcomes through education technologies in medical education. World J. Adv. Res. Rev. **19**, 1356–1367 (2023). https://doi.org/10.30574/wjarr.2023.19.3.1922

12. McGrath, J.L., et al.: Using virtual reality simulation environments to assess competence for emergency medicine learners. Acad. Emerg. Med. **25**, 186–195 (2017). https://doi.org/10.1111/acem.13308

13. Calik, A., Kapucu, S.: The effect of serious games for nursing students in clinical decision-making process: a pilot randomized controlled trial. Games Health J. **11**, 30–37 (2022). https://doi.org/10.1089/g4h.2021.0180

14. D'Antoni, A.V., Mtui, E.P., Loukas, M., Tubbs, R.S., Zipp, G.P., Dunlosky, J.: An evidence-based approach to learning clinical anatomy: a guide for medical students, educators, and administrators. Clinical Anatomy. New York, N.Y. (2019). https://doi.org/10.1002/ca.23298

15. Geoffrion, R., Lee, T., Singer, J.: Validating a self-confidence scale for surgical trainees. J. Obstet. Gynaecol. Canada: JOGC = Journal d'obstetrique et gynecologie du Canada: JOGC. **35**, 355–361 (2013). https://doi.org/10.1016/S1701-2163(15)30964-6.Geoffrion

16. Sezer, B., Sezer, T.A., Teker, G.T., Elcin, M.: Developing a virtual patient: design, usability, and learning effect in communication skills training. BMC Med. Educ. **23** (2023). https://doi.org/10.1186/s12909-023-04860-7

17. Jackson, C., Gibbin, K.: 'Per ardua…' Training tomorrow's surgeons using inter alia lessons from aviation. J. Royal Soc. Med. **99**, 554–558 (2006). https://doi.org/10.1177/014107680609901112

Ergonomics and Digital Human Modelling

Relationship Between Work Performance and Exercise Load with Virtual Reality Active Workstation: Application to Type 2 Diabetes Prevention

Eisuke Aoki[1], Jun Motomura[2], and Takehiko Yamaguchi[3]([✉])

[1] Suwa University of Science Graduate School of Engineering and Management, Chino City Toyohira 5000-1, Japan

[2] Department of Health Informatics, Faculty of Human Health Sciences, MEIO University, Nago, Japan
j.motomura@meio-u.ac.jp

[3] Suwa University of Science, Chino City Toyohira 5000-1, Japan
tk-ymgch@rs.sus.ac.jp

Abstract. Type 2 diabetes is a chronic, persistent disease of high blood sugar due to insufficient insulin sensitivity, and it is often accompanied by the three major complications of retinopathy, nephropathy, and neuropathy. Type 2 diabetes is mainly caused by a combination of lifestyle habits that include overeating and lack of exercise. In Japan, the number of people suspected of having type 2 diabetes is approximately 18.7 million people, or one in six adults. Exercise therapy is a method of treating diabetes by having the patient perform an appropriate exercise for an appropriate amount of time. In the case of type 2 diabetes, the goal is to maintain a heart rate of 100 or higher for at least 20 min, at least three times a week, for a total of at least 150 min. Currently, active workstations are being studied as one way to enable exercise therapy. An active workstation is a desk environment that allows patients to work while performing aerobic exercise, and it enables them to change their posture and improve muscle activation while working. Previous studies have not been able to balance physical activity and work when active workstations were used. We believe that one of the reasons for this is the inability to switch attention. Therefore, in the present study, we investigate changes in office work and performance by forcing the switching of attention using a VR (virtual reality) system to balance exercise and work, and we report on the relationship between the two. This experiment was conducted after typing speed was measurements without an aerobic bike. Results showed that typing speed was significantly faster when the VR active workstation was used, and typing speed increased after attention switching.

Keywords: Diabetes · Active workstations · Exercise therapy · Virtual reality

V. G. Duffy (Ed.): HCII 2024, LNCS 15376, pp. 215–232, 2025.
https://doi.org/10.1007/978-3-031-76809-5_16

1   Introduction

1.1   Diabetes

Diabetes mellitus is a disease in which blood sugar levels are chronically high due to a lack of insulin action. There are two types of diabetes: type 1 diabetes and type 2 diabetes. Type 2 diabetes has become a major problem. Type 2 diabetes is called insulin-independent diabetes and is caused by a combination of genetic factors and by lifestyle habits, such as overeating and lack of exercise. In Japan, the number of people suspected of having type 2 diabetes is about 18.7 million people, or one in six adults [1].

1.2   Exercise Therapy

Exercise therapy is the use of exercise to treat or prevent disorders and diseases; it has been proven effective in the treatment and prevention of type 2 diabetes.

For patients with type 2 diabetes, the amount and duration of exercise therapy generally considered to be the most effective is exercise at least three times per week for a total of at least 150 min. Exercise that is of moderate intensity (heart rate of 100 bpm to 120 bpm, or within 100 bpm for those over 50 years old), full-body aerobic exercise, and an exercise duration of at least 20 min are recommended [2].

However, it was also found that about half of people with type 2 diabetes are unable to engage in exercise therapy, mostly because they "don't have the time" [3].

1.3   Active Workstation

An active workstation is a desk environment that allows for changes in posture and improved muscle activation during work. Podrekar, Nastja et al. conducted a meta-analysis of performance on an active workstation and found that it significantly decreased typing speed and increased the number of typing errors. Furthermore, they found that there was no decrease in performance at low workloads and a decrease in performance at high workloads. Marusic et al. also examined the feasibility of regular four-hour standing sessions and more dynamic standing sessions for elderly type 2 diabetics while they were performing routine desktop activities. The results showed that longer standing sessions could be performed without serious side effects [4–6].

However, previous studies that used active workstations have not been able to combine physical activity and work.

1.4   Goal Habituation Model

The goal habituation model is based on the idea that people's attention is divided in parallel, and that their attentional resources are allocated to the object they perceive as important at any given time. Switching between objects that are perceived as important is called attentional switching. I consider that the failure of previous research to achieve this attentional switching was the cause of the inability to balance exercise and work. Therefore, I assumed that the situation could be improved by forcing the switching of attention.

1.5 Virtual Reality (VR)

VR is intended to engineer and implement an experience that is equivalent to an experience in the real world and consists of three major elements: three-dimensional spatiality, real-time interactivity, and self-projection [7].

In VR, interactions in the real world change the VR space. Therefore, we believe that changing the environment can force the switching of attention.

1.6 Purpose

The purpose of this study is to propose a new active workstation that eliminates the trade-off between the exercise goals and work performance. Furthermore, this study investigates the extent to which the trade-off is eliminated by forced attention switching.

We also examine the effectiveness of this system as a preventive system for type 2 diabetes.

2 Methods

2.1 Development System

The framework of the developed system is shown in Fig. 1.

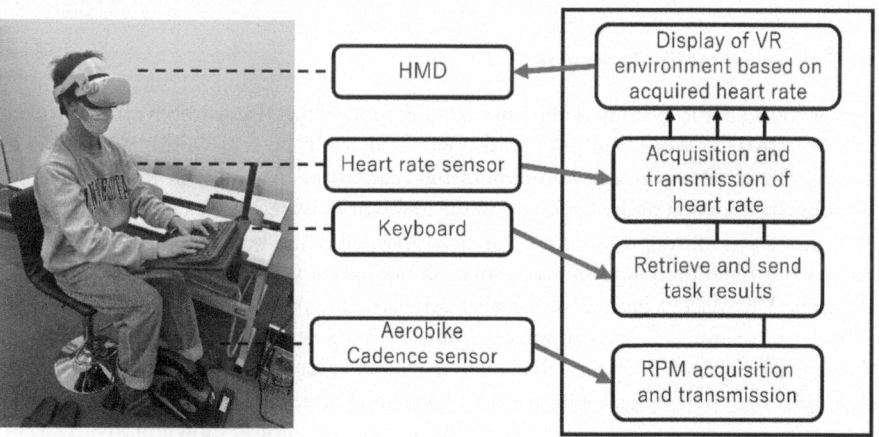

Fig. 1. Framework of the developed system.

2.2 Research Policy

In order to conduct this study, it was necessary to determine the experimental task, how the keyboard would be displayed in VR, and how the environment would be changed.

2.3 Experimental Tasks

The task to be performed by the participants was determined to be a typing task, considering the tasks that could be performed in a VR space. In the typing task, the participants were asked to type sentences that were displayed on a screen.

The numbers of correct and incorrect answers were obtained to determine speed and accuracy as indicators of typing performance.

Because typing performance varies greatly from person to person, we decided to investigate changes in performance by comparing performance in a baseline experiment in which participants were asked to type while pedaling an aerobic bike.

During the task, 259 English-language questions were presented in random order. Examples of questions are shown in Table 1.

Table 1. Examples of questions

The only impossible journey is the one you never begin.
Life is really simple, but we insist on making it complicated.
All you need in this life is ignorance and confidence, and then success is sure.
Being honest may not get you many friends but it will always get you the right ones.

2.4 Experimental Environment

In order to use a VR system, a head mounted display (HMD) must be worn. However, when the HMD is worn, the user is disconnected from the real world, which makes it impossible to obtain information about the real world. As a result, the user cannot determine the location of the keyboard in the real world, which makes it difficult to type. Therefore, a pass-through function was used to display the keyboard. A pass-through function is a function that allows information in the real world to be viewed through a hole in the VR space. Figure 2 shows a screen using the pass-through function.

Next, we examine the environment within the VR system and how the environment changes when the exercise load falls below the target value, i.e., when the heart rate falls below 100. The environment within the VR system includes only a single monitor in the space in front of the subject's eyes. The screen of the monitor is shown in Fig. 3.

When the exercise load was below the target value, the transparency of the monitor would change and would become completely transparent within 3 s from the time point when the exercise load fell below the target.

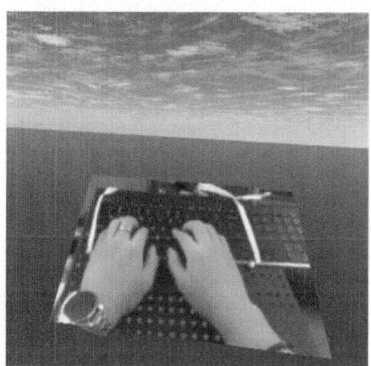

Fig. 2. Screen with pass-through function.

Fig. 3. Monitor in VR space.

2.5   Questionnaire

In this experiment, a questionnaire was administered to investigate changes in performance as well as perceptions of the aerobics and typing. The questionnaire was administered before and after the typing task was performed. A pre-task questionnaire was used to obtain information about the subjects and their physical condition. A post-task questionnaire investigated video sickness and task-related content.

Video Sickness was investigated using R. S. Kennedy's Simulator Sickness Questionnaire (SSQ) questionnaire [8].

The post-task questionnaire was prepared differently for the baseline than for the main experiment. The post-baseline questionnaire investigated only typing, and the post-test questionnaire investigated aerobic riding in addition to the post-baseline questionnaire. The content of the baseline questionnaire is shown below. In the actual questionnaire, the questions were given in a random order, and the responses were recorded on a 5-point scale (1: Not at all; 5: Very much).

Table 2. Baseline questionnaire administered after the experiment.

Q1	Found it was easy to type
Q2	Typing speed felt fast
Q3	Typing speed felt slow
Q4	Typing speed felt as expected
Q5	My typing speed was consistently the same
Q6	Felt I made a lot of typing errors
Q7	Fewer typing errors
Q8	My typing errors were as expected
Q9	My typing errors were consistently the same
Q10	Fatigue from typing was high
Q11	Fatigue from typing was low
Q12	Fatigue for typing was as expected
Q13	Fatigue for typing was consistently the same

Table 3. Questionnaire administered only after the experiment.

Q14	Aero bike felt heavy
Q15	Aero bike felt light
Q16	The weight of the aero bike was as expected
Q17	The aero bike felt consistently the same weight
Q18	I felt the aero bike was fast
Q19	I felt the aero bike was slow
Q20	The aero bike felt as fast as expected
Q21	The speed of the aero bike felt consistently the same
Q22	Felt fatigued from pedaling the aero bike
Q23	Felt less fatigued from rowing the aero bike
Q24	Felt as fatigued as expected on the aero bike
Q25	Felt consistently the same fatigue from rowing the aero bike
Q26	Typing errors made the aero bike feel heavier
Q27	Typing errors made the aero bike feel lighter
Q28	Typing errors made the aero bike feel consistently heavier regardless of typing error
Q29	Faster typing made the aero bike feel heavier
Q30	Faster typing made the aero bike feel lighter

(continued)

Table 3. (*continued*)

Q31	The weight of the aero bike felt consistent regardless of typing speed
Q32	Typing errors seemed to increase when the aero bike felt lighter
Q33	When the aero bike felt lighter, typing errors seemed to decrease
Q34	Typing errors seemed to be consistent regardless of how light the aero bike felt
Q35	I felt my typing speed increase when the aero bike felt lighter
Q36	I felt my typing speed slow down when the aero bike felt lighter
Q37	Typing speed felt consistent regardless of how light the bike felt
Q38	Felt more focused on typing
Q39	Felt more focused on pedaling the bike
Q40	Felt that typing interfered with concentration on the aero bike
Q41	Felt that rowing the aero bike interfered with concentration on typing

2.6 Experimental Instrumentation

In this study, a MetaQuest2 from Meta was used as the HMD that provided the VR space. A heart rate sensor was used to measure heart rate, and a cadence sensor was used to measure rotation speed; both were made by Magene. A small aero bike manufactured by ALINCO was used. The keyboard for the typing task was a Logitech MX Keys mini, which could be positioned using a laptop arm as shown in Fig. 1.

2.7 Experimental Procedures

Subjects were first asked to take baseline experiment. The room in which the experiment was conducted was set to a room temperature of 23 °C and the windows were opened for ventilation. When the subjects entered the room, they were asked to fill out the pre-questionnaire. After the subjects completed the questionnaire, we explained the tasks that were to be performed during the experiment and asked the subjects to adjust the positions of the keyboard and the aerobic bike in the experimental environment to the position that was comfortable for them. After they had adjusted the keyboard and the aerobic bike, the participants were asked to wear the heart rate sensor. After they had attached heart rate sensor, the participants put on the HMD and executed the program. When the task execution screen appeared, the participants were asked to start the task on their own initiative. The baseline task measurement lasted 23 min. The first 3 min were intended for familiarization with the VR space and typing and for adjusting the volume. After the task was completed, the subjects completed the SSQ questionnaire and the post-questionnaire in Table 2 to complete the baseline measurement. Next, the experiment was conducted in the same classroom at least one day later.

In this experiment, we explained the task to be performed, told the subjects that the monitor was linked to the heart rate and that the monitor would not be visible unless the heart rate was above a certain value, and instructed them to start pedaling the aero bike before they began the task so that their heart rate would increase and the monitor would be visible. The participants were then asked to adjust the position of the keyboard and aero bike as they did during the baseline measurement, and to wear the heart rate sensor and the HMD. When the task execution screen was reached, the participants were asked to increase their heart rate by pedaling the aero bike until the monitor on the screen where the task was to be performed was displayed, and then they were allowed approximately 1 min to stabilize before the task was begun. The task lasted 21 min. The first minute was considered intended for familiarization with the VR space and for adjusting the volume. After the task was completed, the participants completed the SSQ questionnaire and the post-test questionnaires in Tables 2 and 3 to complete the entire experiment.

3   Results and Discussion

3.1   Task Results

The typing data for the 12 subjects collected during the baseline and main experiment are shown in Tables 4 and 5 below.

Table 4. Baseline results

Subject No.	Correct Answers	Incorrect Answers	Correct Answer rate (%)
1	1989	434	82.09
2	4259	246	94.54
3	1102	682	61.77
4	2949	549	84.31
5	3290	656	83.38
6	772	295	72.35
7	1587	943	62.73
8	1749	864	66.93
9	1240	500	71.26
10	4532	300	93.79
11	1935	643	75.06
12	2468	259	90.5

Next, a t-test was carried out on the results to check for normality. The analyzed results are shown in Tables 6 and 7 and in Fig. 4 (Table 8).

The analysis showed that only the number of correct answers was significantly different, and typing speed increased with the use of the aerobic bike.

Next, we investigate the effect of attention switching. During this experiment, there were five subjects whose heart rate fell below the target value a total of 10 times. We then examined the data from these five subjects to determine if there was a difference in the state of their heart rate for 1 min before it fell below the target value and 1 min after

Table 5. Experiment results

Subject No.	Correct Answers	Incorrect Answers	Correct Answer rate (%)
1	2352	561	80.74
2	4581	264	94.55
3	1476	763	65.92
4	3288	560	85.45
5	3758	735	83.64
6	1060	334	76.04
7	1675	1136	59.59
8	1841	767	70.59
9	1229	337	78.48
10	4641	351	92.97
11	1795	872	67.3
12	2861	291	90.77

Table 6. Normality of typing results

Test of Normality (Shapiro-Wilk)

			W	p
Correct_0	-	Correct_1	0.913	0.235
Miss_0	-	Miss_1	0.957	0.739
CorrectPercent_0	-	CorrectPercent_1	0.961	0.792

Note. Significant results suggest a deviation from normality.

Table 7. Results of t-test for typing data

Paired Samples T-Test

Measure 1		Measure 2	t	df	p	Cohen's d	SE Cohen's d	95% CI for Cohen's d	
								Lower	Upper
Correct_0	-	Correct_1	-4.097	11	0.002	-1.183	0.055	-1.915	-0.420
Miss_0	-	Miss_1	-1.592	11	0.140	-0.460	0.119	-1.047	0.146
CorrectPercent_0	-	CorrectPercent_1	-0.545	11	0.596	-0.157	0.098	-0.723	0.416

Note. Student's t-test.

it exceeded the target value, i.e., before and after the switching, as shown in Fig. 16. The results are presented in Tables 9 and 10 (Fig. 5).

The obtained data were checked for normality and the corresponding t-tests were performed. The confirmation results are represented in Tables 10 and 11 and Fig. 6.

Table 8. Typing speed results before heart rate drop

No.	Correct Answer	Incorrect Answer	Correct Answer Rate(%)
1	166	28	85.57
2	46	15	75.41
3	36	22	62.07
4	82	49	62.6
5	100	69	59.17
6	55	76	41.98
7	41	52	44.09
8	94	43	68.61
9	88	53	62.41
10	78	41	65.55

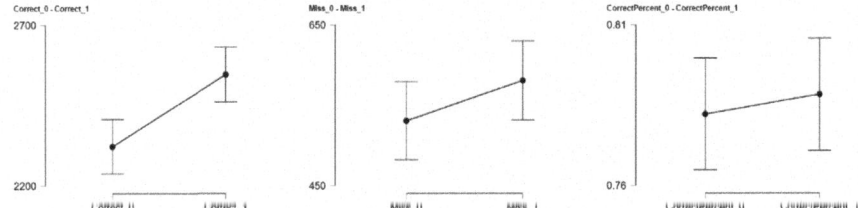

Fig. 4. Statistical chart of the number of correct typing answers and percentage of correct answers

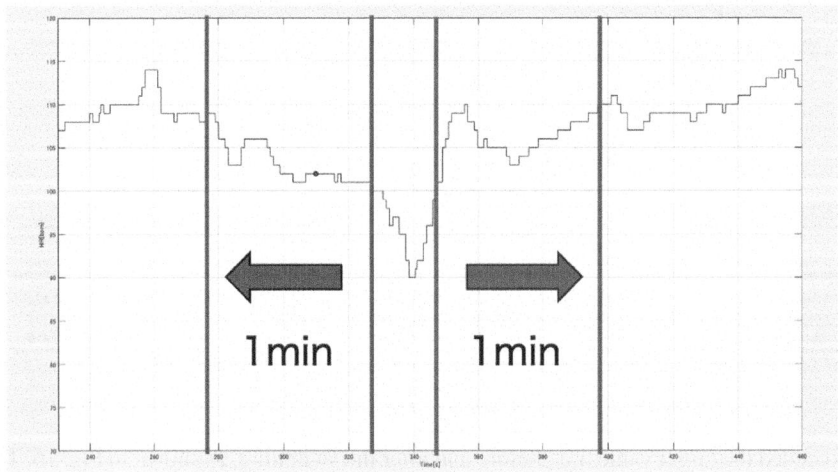

Fig. 5. Heart rate 1 min state

Table 9. Typing speed results after heart rate increase

No.	Correct Answer	Incorrect Answer	Correct Answer Rate(%)
1	189	23	89.15
2	43	13	76.79
3	54	19	73.97
4	84	56	60
5	106	67	61.27
6	89	60	59.73
7	84	39	68.29
8	82	52	61.19
9	97	46	67.83
10	107	41	72.3

Table 10. Normality of typing results before and after heart rate change

Assumption Checks ▼

Test of Normality (Shapiro-Wilk) ▼

			W	p
Correct_0	-	Correct_1	0.981	0.969
Miss_0	-	Miss_1	0.959	0.773
Percent_0	-	Percent_1	0.961	0.796

Note. Significant results suggest a deviation from normality.

Table 11. Results of t-test for typing data before and after heart rate change

Paired Samples T-Test

Measure 1		Measure 2	t	df	p	Cohen's d	SE Cohen's d	95% CI for Cohen's d	
								Lower	Upper
Correct_0	-	Correct_1	-2.694	9	0.025	-0.852	0.166	-1.566	-0.104
Miss_0	-	Miss_1	1.302	9	0.225	0.412	0.134	-0.246	1.049
Percent_0	-	Percent_1	-2.115	9	0.064	-0.669	0.276	-1.345	0.036

Note. Student's t-test.

The t-test results showed a significant increase in typing speed and a significant trend in the percentage of correct answers. This indicates that attention switching affects typing.

3.2 Analysis and Discussion of the Questionnaire

The scored SSQ questionnaire results for each experiment are shown in Tables 12 and 13.

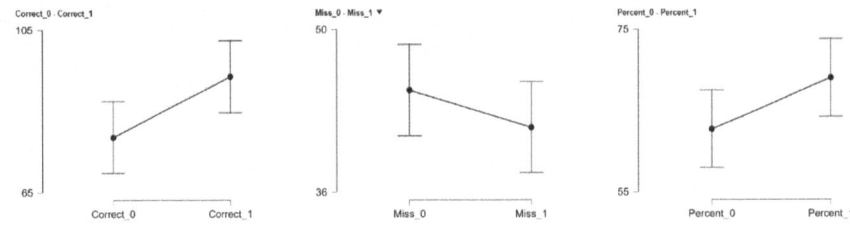

Fig. 6. Statistical chart of typing results before and after heart rate change

Table 12. Questionnaire results at baseline experiment

Subject No.	Nausea	Oculomotor	Disorientation	Total Score
1	19.08	30.32	13.92	14.96
2	9.54	30.32	13.92	14.96
3	38.16	75.8	69.6	52.36
4	28.62	37.9	13.92	22.44
5	9.54	30.32	55.68	26.18
6	19.08	15.16	13.92	14.96
7	19.08	37.9	27.84	26.18
8	19.08	22.74	0	14.96
9	76.32	128.86	153.12	89.76
10	19.08	37.9	27.84	26.18
11	9.54	45.48	69.6	26.18
12	9.54	30.32	27.84	18.7

Next, we performed normality checks on the SSQ scores. The results are shown in Table 14.

According to these results, normality was not found for disorientation but was confirmed for all other variables. Therefore, we conducted t-tests for items other than disorientation. The results are shown in Table 15 and Fig. 7.

The results of the analysis showed that only nausea was significantly different, and aerobics were more likely to cause nausea and other symptoms. This is thought to be due to an increase in sweating and a decrease in concentration in response to rowing the aero bike, which might have influenced the calculated results. In addition, the degree of intoxication was also considered to be affected by fatigue from rowing the aero bike, which might have affected the calculated results.

Next, we analyze the post-questionnaire. The results of the questionnaires conducted both at baseline and in the experiment will be subject to normality checks and t-tests. The four items subjected to normality checks were ease of doing, typing speed, errors, and fatigue. The results are shown in Tables 16, 17, and 18.

Table 13. Questionnaire results at the time of this experiment

Subject No.	Nausea	Oculomotor	Disorientation	Total Score
1	28.62	15.16	13.92	14.96
2	19.08	7.58	0	11.22
3	57.24	68.22	69.6	56.1
4	0	7.58	0	3.74
5	57.24	30.32	41.76	44.88
6	76.32	53.06	41.76	48.62
7	38.16	30.32	13.92	29.92
8	28.62	30.32	27.84	29.92
9	66.78	53.06	55.68	48.62
10	47.7	53.06	69.6	44.88
11	57.24	98.54	83.52	63.58
12	9.54	15.16	13.92	11.22

Table 14. Confirmation of score normality

Test of Normality (Shapiro-Wilk) ▼

			W	p
Nausea_0	-	Nausea_1	0.963	0.824
Oculomotor_0	-	Oculomotor_1	0.957	0.745
Disorientation_0	-	Disorientation_1	0.821	0.016
TotalSeverity_0	-	TotalSeverity_1	0.965	0.853

Note. Significant results suggest a deviation from normality.

Table 15. SSQ score of t-test results

Paired Samples T-Test

Measure 1		Measure 2	t	df	p	Cohen's d	SE Cohen's d
Nausea_0	-	Nausea_1	-2.421	11	0.034	-0.699	0.373
Oculomotor_0	-	Oculomotor_1	0.530	11	0.606	0.153	0.328
TotalSeverity_0	-	TotalSeverity_1	-0.787	11	0.448	-0.227	0.307

Note. Student's t-test.

According to the above results, normality was observed only for typing speed. Therefore, a t-test was performed for speed. The results are shown in Table 19 and Fig. 8.

These results indicate that there is no significant difference in the awareness of typing speed. Therefore, we can say that there is no significant difference in the awareness of

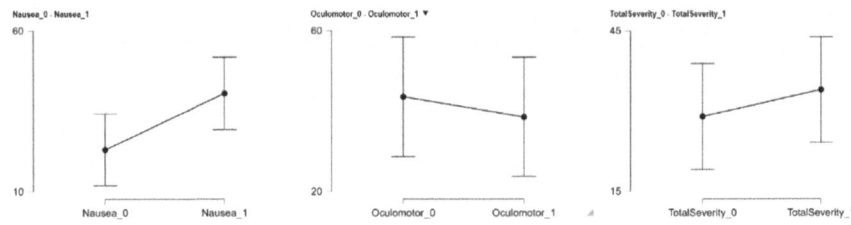

Fig. 7. Statistical chart of SSQ scores

Table 16. Questionnaire about typing after baseline experiment

Subject No.	Ease	Speed	Error	Fatigue
1	2	3	9	7
2	4	11	9	8
3	1	6	14	12
4	3	8	10	9
5	2	10	10	12
6	1	2	13	8
7	1	4	11	9
8	1	3	13	10
9	1	2	11	10
10	2	9	13	9
11	2	3	10	10
12	3	5	12	10

typing with and without an aero bike. However, because this questionnaire is unique, it may not be reliable.

Table 20 below shows the results of the aero bike questionnaire.

In the questionnaire on aerobics, most respondents felt that the aerobics were heavy. However, no uniformity was found regarding speed and fatigue.

Table 17. Questionnaire about typing after experiment

Subject No.	Ease	Speed	Mistake	Fatigue
1	2	7	10	9
2	4	12	7	6
3	2	10	12	12
4	3	7	9	7
5	2	5	10	9
6	1	2	11	8
7	1	9	13	9
8	2	4	11	6
9	2	7	9	7
10	2	2	12	6
11	1	3	11	7
12	3	6	11	7

Table 18. Confirmation of normality for typing

Test of Normality (Shapiro-Wilk) ▼

			W	p
confort	-	confort_6	0.753	0.003
speed	-	speed_7	0.900	0.157
miss	-	miss_8	0.831	0.022
tired	-	tired_9	0.861	0.050

Note. Significant results suggest a deviation from normality.

Table 19. Results for t-test on typing speed data

Paired Samples T-Test ▼

Measure 1		Measure 2	t	df	p	Cohen's d	SE Cohen's d	95% CI for Cohen's d	
								Lower	Upper
speed	-	speed_7	-0.616	11	0.551	-0.178	0.341	-0.744	0.397

Note. Student's t-test.

3.3 Task Considerations

The results of the task in this study showed a significant increase in typing speed. The results also showed a significant increase in typing speed before and after switching as well.

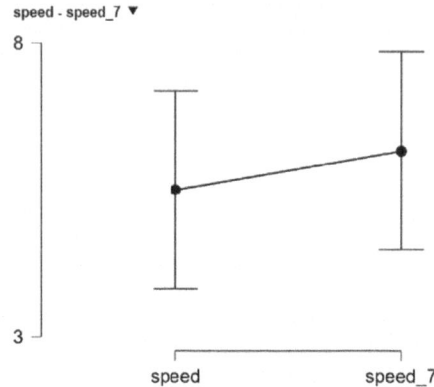

speed - speed_7 ▼

Fig. 8. Statistical chart of typing speed

Table 20. Results of the aero bike questionnaire

Subject No.	Weight	Speed	Fatigue
1	10	10	9
2	6	5	8
3	11	7	13
4	11	9	6
5	7	8	6
6	9	8	8
7	9	9	11
8	9	8	9
9	7	9	8
10	9	5	7
11	10	5	12
12	11	7	11

A previous study on the effects of switching examined the relationship between sustained attention and performance. The results showed that switching attention causes a recovery of attention and performance [9].

Therefore, it is conceivable that in the present experiment, performance may also have been restored by switching, as shown in Fig. 9.

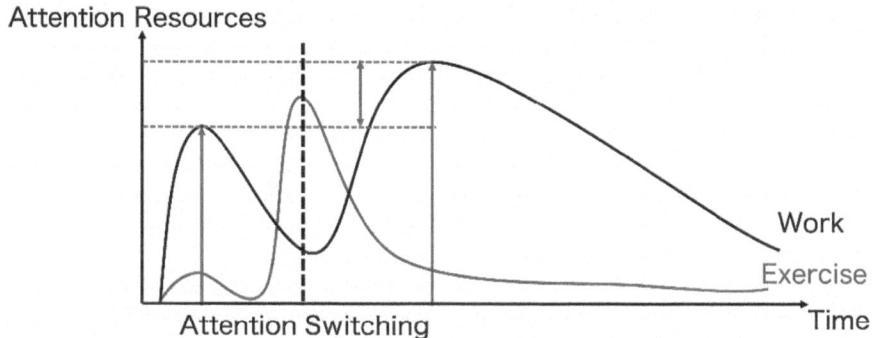

Fig. 9. Anticipated recovery chart with attention switching

4 Conclusion and Outlook

4.1 Conclusion

The VR active workstation was found to significantly increase typing speed compared with typing speed with no aerobics. Similarly, when they were subjected to switching, subjects also significantly increased their typing speed and produced a significant trend in the percentage of correct answers. However, there was no significant difference in the subjects' own perceptions of typing.

Based on these results, we can say that VR active workstations are expected to further improve performance as a preventive measure against diabetes. However, because the present experiment did not eliminate the effects of habituation to the problem and learning, it is possible.

4.2 Outlook

Although this experiment included two recommendation items of exercise therapy, namely that the heart rate must be above 100 and that the exercise must be at least 20 min per session, we have not been able to investigate the item of exercise at least three times per week. Therefore, we believe it is necessary to conduct a long-term study to determine if there is any impact on performance and physical activity.

The task in this experiment was a typing task, but typing is not the only activity that is performed in actual office work. For example, there are also mouse operations and combined mouse operations. Therefore, we believe it is necessary to investigate performance when such tasks are being carried out.

References

1. Ministry of Health, Labour and Welfare. https://www.e-healthnet.mhlw.go.jp/information/dictionary/metabolic/ym-048.html
2. Ministry of Health, Labour and Welfare. https://www.e-healthnet.mhlw.go.jp/information/exercise/s-05-005.html

3. Arakawa, S., et al.: Current status of diet and exercise therapy in diabetes care: Results of a nationwide survey of diabetic patients. Diabetes **58**(4), 265–278 (2015)
4. Podrekar, N., Kozinc, Ž, Šarabon, N.: The effects of cycle and treadmill desks on work performance and cognitive function in sedentary workers: a review and meta-analysis. Work **65**(3), 537–545 (2020)
5. Cho, J., Freivalds, A., Rovniak, L., Sung, K., Hatzell, J.: Using a desk-compatible recumbent bike in an office workstation. In: Proceedings of the Human Factors and Ergonomics Society Annual Meeting, vol. 58(1), pp. 1662–1666. SAGE Publications, Sage CA, Los Angeles, CA (2014)
6. Marusic, U., Müller, M.L., Alexander, N.B., Bohnen, N.I.: Feasibility and behavioral effects of prolonged static and dynamic standing as compared to sitting in older adults with type 2 diabetes mellitus. BMC Geriatr. **20**(1), 1–8 (2020)
7. Tachi, A.: Virtual reality and transversal core science and technology. Measure. Control **42**(3), 196 (2003). https://www.jstage.jst.go.jp/article/sicejl1962/42/3/42_3_193/_pdf
8. Kennedy, R.S., Lane, N.E., Berbaum, K.S., Lilienthal, M.G.: Simulator sickness questionnaire: an enhanced method for quantifying simulator sickness. Int. J. Aviat. Psychol. **3**(3), 203–220 (1993)
9. Ariga, A., Lleras, A.: Brief and rare mental "breaks" keep you focused: deactivation and reactivation of task goals preempt vigilance decrements. Cognition **118**(3), 439–443 (2011)

Domain-Tailored Generative AI for Personalized Assistant

Nina Jiang, Sogand Hasanzadeh, and Vincent G. Duffy(✉)

Industrial Engineering, Purdue University, Grissom Hall, West Lafayette,
IN 47906, USA
{jiang841,sogandm,duffy}@purdue.edu

Abstract. Development of the generative artificial intelligence has
made notable progress over recent years. Especially with the exponential prevalence of the large language models and foundation models.
Although there is extensive research on the improvements of the algorithms, users often need to provide complex prompts if they want to
filter the credible responses in specific domains. To improve the interaction and learning experience between users and the generative artificial intelligence system, this paper presents the literature that aims
to identify research gaps and introduce the development of a Domain-
Tailored Generative AI system. This domain-tailored generative AI system is designed to provide in-depth domain-tailored response for the
users and to improve the effectiveness and positive impact for the users.

Keywords: Generative AI · Domain-tailored assistant · Large
Language Model · Personalized Learning · Synthetic Datasets

1 Introduction

The exponential expansion of artificial intelligence (AI) in recent years is leveraging the development of various technologies to a higher level and reshaping
various domains, including healthcare, education, finance, and professional practices for people. Generative AI, which is one of the most transformative advances
in recent years, has received significant attention in the field of education [1].
Researchers explore its impacts on education, including engineering education,
non-STEM fields, medical education, graduate education, and K12 education
[2–5]. These researches investigated the development and potential of generative
AI to personalize learning experiences and innovative approaches to pedagogy
[5,6].

However, the majority of current large language models (LLMs) are trained
in generalized databases, which poses a challenge to provide domain-specific

N. Jiang and S. Hasanzadeh—Contributing authors.

knowledge to users [7,8]. Furthermore, these models can hallucinate when generating information, leading to inaccurate or misleading responses. Therefore, there is an increasing demand for customized AI systems. Such a system could provide for domain-specific assistant to improve users' learning experience and outcomes.

In this paper, we present the literature to identify current research gaps in the field of generative AI in education. The methodology and framework for developing generative AI based on the customized domain is introduced to provide personalized learning experience to the users. Our system aims to improve user engagement through customized content generation, improve user experience, system usability, and learning effectiveness, particularly for students with low performance [9,10].

2   Literature Review

Generative Artificial Intelligence (Gen AI) is the machine learning model that can generate unseen output data that are similar to trained data samples [11,12]. Those models are not only limited to text-to-text generation, but also have capacity on text-to-image, such as DALL-E [13], MidJourney [14] and Stable Diffusion [15]. In addition, there are also models capable of generating other types of media, such as text-to-video [16–18], text-to-audio [19,20], and even text-to-3D models [21–24].

As illustrated in Fig. 1, the evolution of research on generative AI has experienced exponential growth in publications since 2022.

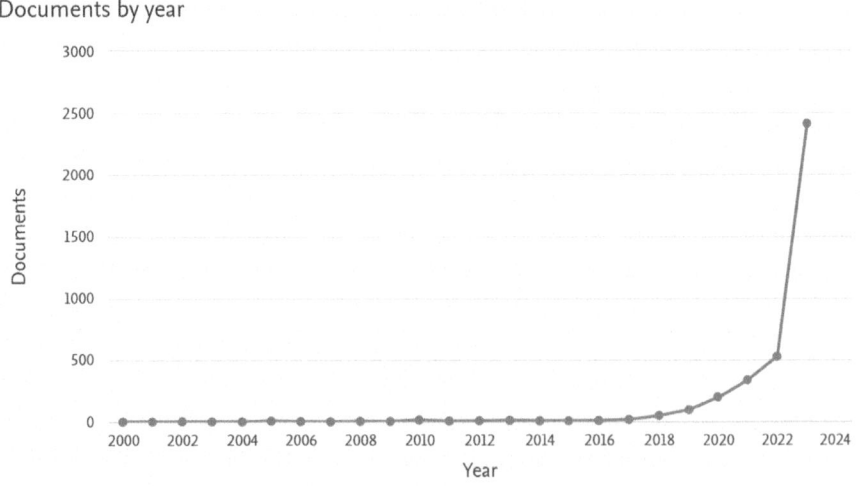

Fig. 1. Trend analysis of Generative AI from Scopus.

Comparison of research publications among three interrelated domains: Generative AI, Generative AI & learning, and Generative AI & assist is illustrated in

Fig. 2. The data is exported from the Web of Science within the time range from 2010 to 2024. Between 2010 and approximately 2018, the increase in generative AI research publications maintains only a relatively minimal level and remains flat. However, from 2019, there is a significant increase in generative AI. More recently, 2022 has experienced the dramatic increase in these fields. Furthermore, the sharp increase observed in the trend reflects that there has been a significant increase in generative AI and its application in learning and assistance. Educational institutions and companies have begun to adopt generative AI to provide personalized learning experiences to students, automate administrative tasks, and intelligent tutoring systems. This widespread application of generative AI has accelerated its research and implementation, driving rapid growth in these areas.

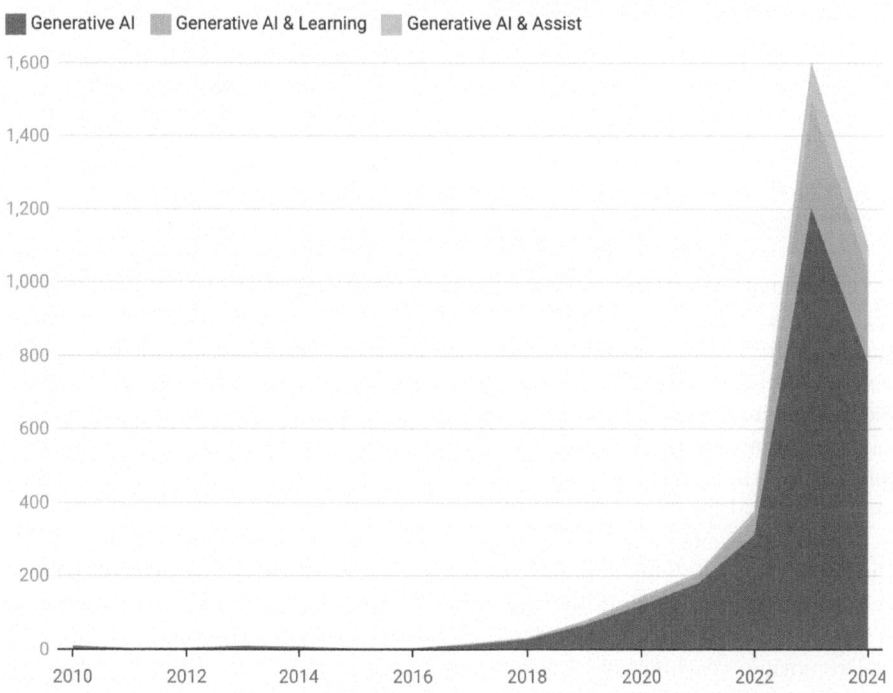

Fig. 2. Trend analysis of Generative AI from Web of Science.

Rapid expansion implies that this field is a cutting-edge and emerging research topic, aligned with the rise of generative AI and other advanced LLM outside of traditional education. The trends indicate the growing emphasis on AI technologies in education and the appearing acknowledgment of the application of generative models in this field.

In the tree map chart of Fig. 3, it presents the research categories on generative AI and education. It reflects the wide application and the nature of inter-disciplinary collaborations of the development of generative AI in education.

Fig. 3. Tree map chart of "Generative AI & Education" research papers.

Generative AI are able to provide a more personalized and personalized learning experience for students 24/7, including personalized feedback, recommendations, tailored responses, and detailed explanations based on specific queries for diverse disciplines [20,25]. Fatima rigorously selected 22 studies on AI-assisted medical training [26]. This review reveals that AI-assisted training is applied in various domains in the field of medical education, including training laboratories, followed by the surgery domain, orthopedics, ophthalmology, surgery medicine, and behavioral health.

Table 1 presents more leading papers and their citation counts imported from Publish or Perish. This summarizes influential research in the field of generative AI in education. Notably, the paper "Education in the Era of Generative Artificial Intelligence (AI): Understanding the Potential Benefits of ChatGPT in Promoting Teaching and Learning" by D Baidoo-Anu and LO Ansah, with 1114 citations, stands out as the most referenced work, underscoring its significant impact on the academic community. In this paper, the authors systematically review and explore the interactivity of ChatGPT, its benefits, possible drawbacks, and potentials. The reviewed articles range from November 2022 to March 2023. Baidoo-Anu et al. suggest that educators could adapt to technological evolution and incorporate these powerful tools into their practices to improve their teaching and students' learning experience. They also emphasize the need to build professional generative AI to help teachers harness the power of AI effectively [27].

As notated, all of the papers listed were published in 2023 and 2024, indicating the recent surge for the researchers' attention to generative AI's application in education. This also indicates the rapidly expansion of the generative AI and its application in education, as also illustrated in the Figs. 1 and 2.

Although AI has shown promising potential impacts on education, it often does not provide significant additional benefits to a wide range of students, not only due to cost concerns, as the development and maintenance of AI systems can be expensive [5]. Furthermore, researchers have noted that most AI techniques are developed for general scenarios and do not meet the specific requirements of educational domains, including educational fields, learning activities, and instruction objectives [7,28,29]. However, they also face multiple challenges, including bias, hallucinations, lack of contextual awareness, limited or outdated knowledge, and privacy [30].

Hallucination is one of the most challenging issues in generative AI, which means that the content generated by LLMs is factually incorrect or nonsensical, sometimes disconnected from the source content provided [31,32]. The responses generated seem plausible, but actually unfactual [33]. As presented in Figs. 4, 5, and 6, these are some instances of inaccuracy of incorrect responses generated by ChatGPT [34]. It will fabricate non-exit item like makeup reference. Or it fails to generate the required content. Most of all, Its not able to provide in-depth response in many subjects. Those shortcomings limit the power of gen ai as a learning assistant.

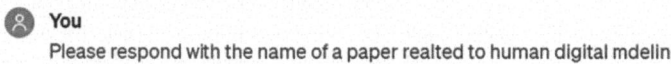

👤 **You**
Please respond with the name of a paper realted to human digital mdeling

💠 **ChatGPT**
One paper related to human digital modeling is "A Survey of Human Modeling and Simulation Technologies in Product Design" by Shaochun Li, Wenxiu Peng, and Chengtao Wang.

Fig. 4. Fabricate non-exit reference.

👤 **You**
Please response with a single sentence in which the 3rd word is \"dog\"

💠 **ChatGPT**
The dog barks loudly at night.

Fig. 5. Fail to generate the required content.

Table 1. Leading Papers

Cites	Authors	Title	Year
1114	D Baidoo-Anu, LO Ansah	Education in the era of generative artificial intelligence (AI): Understanding the potential benefits of ChatGPT in promoting teaching and learning	2023
503	J Qadir	Engineering education in the era of ChatGPT: Promise and pitfalls of generative AI for education	2023
437	WM Lim, A Gunasekara, JL Pallant, JI Pallant	Generative AI and the future of education: Ragnarök or reformation? A paradoxical perspective from management educators	2023
418	G Cooper	Examining science education in ChatGPT: An exploratory study of generative artificial intelligence	2023
194	CKY Chan, W Hu	Students' voices on generative AI: Perceptions, benefits, and challenges in higher education	2023
171	A Bozkurt, X Junhong, S Lambert	Speculative futures on ChatGPT and generative artificial intelligence (AI): A collective reflection from the educational landscape	2023
153	Y Wu	Integrating generative AI in education: how ChatGPT brings challenges for future learning and teaching	2023
139	J Su, W Yang	Unlocking the power of ChatGPT: A framework for applying generative AI in education	2023
127	A Bozkurt	Generative artificial intelligence (AI) powered conversational educational agents: The inevitable paradigm shift	2023
109	Z Bahroun, C Anane, V Ahmed, A Zacca	Transforming education: A comprehensive review of generative artificial intelligence in educational settings through bibliometric and content analysis	2023
97	R Michel-Villarreal, E Vilalta-Perdomo	Challenges and opportunities of generative AI for higher education as explained by ChatGPT	2023
96	FM Megahed, YJ Chen, JA Ferris, S Knoth	How generative AI models such as ChatGPT can be (mis) used in SPC practice, education, and research? An exploratory study	2024
76	EA Alasadi, CR Baiz	Generative AI in education and research: Opportunities, concerns, and solutions	2023
75	TKF Chiu	The impact of Generative AI (GenAI) on practices, policies and research direction in education: A case of ChatGPT and Midjourney	2023
66	W Holmes, F Miao	Guidance for generative AI in education and research	2023
66	Y Dai, A Liu, CP Lim	Reconceptualizing ChatGPT and generative AI as a student-driven innovation in higher education	2023
60	H Yu, Y Guo	Generative artificial intelligence empowers educational reform: current status, issues, and prospects	2023
51	A Bozkurt, RC Sharma	Reimagining the role of generative AI in distance education and online learning	2023
50	R Kaplan-Rakowski, K Grotewold	Generative AI and teachers' perspectives on its implementation in education	2023

Those examples reveal the imperfections of ChatGPT's answer for specific and expert domains. Also implies the limitation of the ChatGPT model, including incomplete or outdated knowledge, especially for domain-specific data [8, 30].

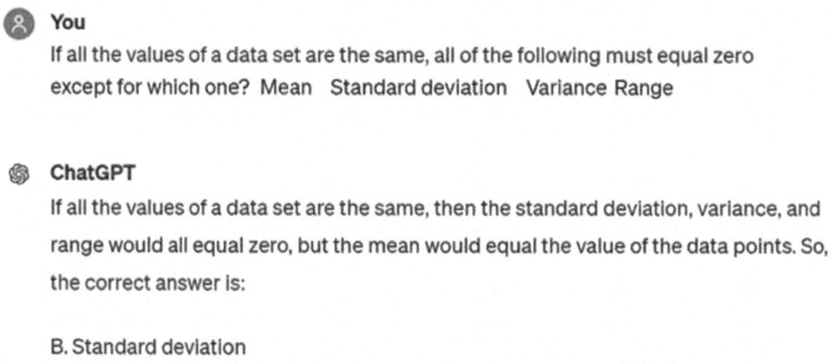

(8) **You**

If all the values of a data set are the same, all of the following must equal zero
except for which one? Mean   Standard deviation   Variance   Range

(®) **ChatGPT**

If all the values of a data set are the same, then the standard deviation, variance, and
range would all equal zero, but the mean would equal the value of the data points. So,
the correct answer is:

B. Standard deviation

Fig. 6. Unable to provide correct responses in statistic.

This is partially caused by the models' training processes, which involve
learning patterns from vast datasets without the ability to verify the truthfulness
or relevance of the generated content in real-time. Despite the extensive nature
of the training datasets, particularly for some commercially available models,
the hallucination phenomenon is still inevitable. For example, the ChatGPT-
4 training dataset is 570 gigabytes, and Google Bard is trained on a dataset
comprising 1.56 trillion words [35–37].

Detecting and mitigating hallucinations in LLMs is difficult because it is
mainly caused by the lack of ground truth in the responses generated. AI systems,
especially generative models, generate responses based on patterns learned from
vast datasets [33,38]. Unlike humans, they do not have connection with the
real world to access the ground truth or objective reality, making it hard to
distinguish between accurate information and hallucinations.

Personalized learning is a main focus in the field of Generative AI in education. As shown in Fig. 7, the personalized learning has emerged as a significant
and rapidly growing area of research, closely connected with other key AI technologies such as machine learning and neural networks. This trend highlights
the increasing emphasis on developing adaptive learning systems that can tailor
educational experiences to individual learners' needs and preferences, leveraging
the capabilities of Generative AI to enhance personalization and effectiveness in
educational environments [29].

The majority of current large language models (LLMs) are trained in generalized databases, which poses a challenge to provide domain-specific knowledge
to users [7,8]. Although AI has shown promising potential impacts on education, it often does not provide significant additional benefits to a wide range of
students, not only due to cost concerns, as the development and maintenance
of AI systems can be expensive [5]. Furthermore, researchers have noted that
most AI techniques are developed for general scenarios and do not meet the specific requirements of educational domains, including educational fields, learning
activities, and instruction objectives [7,28,29].

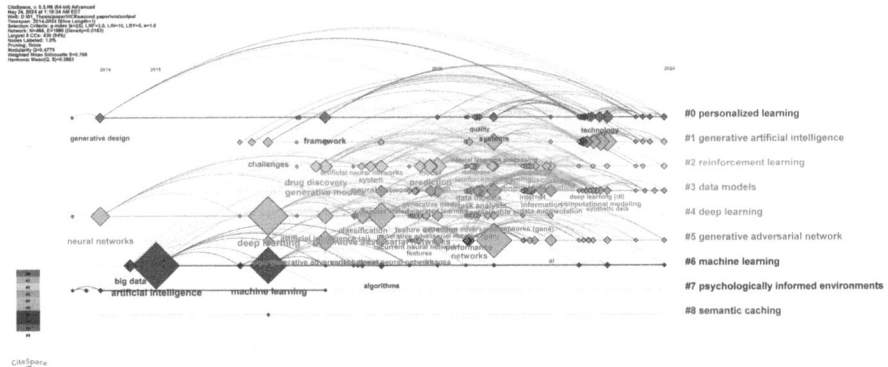

Fig. 7. Timeline view of the keywords clustering in CiteSpace

Therefore, there is an increasing demand for customized, assisted generative AI systems. Injecting domain-tailored knowledge to LLM could counter the hallucination of it. Such a system could provide for domain-specific assistant to improve users' learning experience and outcomes. For example, ClinicalGPT [39], which is a GPT model that is fine-tuned on extensive professional medical data, leverages the capabilities of GPT for medical language understanding and generation, specifically focusing on improving healthcare applications. It utilizes a dataset of medical literature and information to train its models, in order to improve the accuracy and utility of AI in medical contexts. The project seeks to address the critical need for advanced AI tools in healthcare care, with the aim of improving diagnosis, treatment planning, and patient care through the advancements in natural language processing.

Therefore, there is a pressing need for the development of more flexible and domain-tailored generative AI to satisfy the specific and diverse needs of various learning domains.

3   Methods

In order to develop the domain-tailored generative AI, we need to provide the domain-specific dataset to the models. There are some domain-specific datasets, including the MedQA datasets in the medical domain [40]. In the legal domain, the JEC-QA datasets, collected from the National Judicial Examination of China [41]. Furthermore, in the finance domain, the FINQA data set [42] includes 8k pairs of questions and answers from 2.8k financial reports to study numerical reasoning with structured and unstructured evidence.

However, these data sets only cover a small portion of subjects and not enough to meet the needs of the rest of the users. Not only because the limited resource of domain specific dataset, but also because of the rapidly evolving nature of various fields, the increasing complexity of user queries, and the extensive effort to construct such dataset [43].

Therefore, in order to better personalize the generative AI to adapt different goals to the users, the needs to create ones own domain-tailored generative AI is raised.

3.1   Dataset

In order to ensure the quality of the data set, we primarily identify the framework used to synthesize domain-tailored quality data sets for the target domains. Then collect the authenticated files within the target domains. After collecting the text and PDF files, we need to preprocess the files before feeding the text into the selected framework.

To choose the optimal framework, we reviewed multiple comprehensive evaluation models for LLMs and adopted the ranking methods in [44] due to the objective of generating data sets of question-answer pairs. We perform crowd-sourced battles on Chatbot Arena on the MT-bench dataset. As illustrated in Fig. 8, the GPT-4-turbo is the best model among all. Therefore, we use GPT-4-turbo as a base model to synthesize the questions and answers for all input source files.

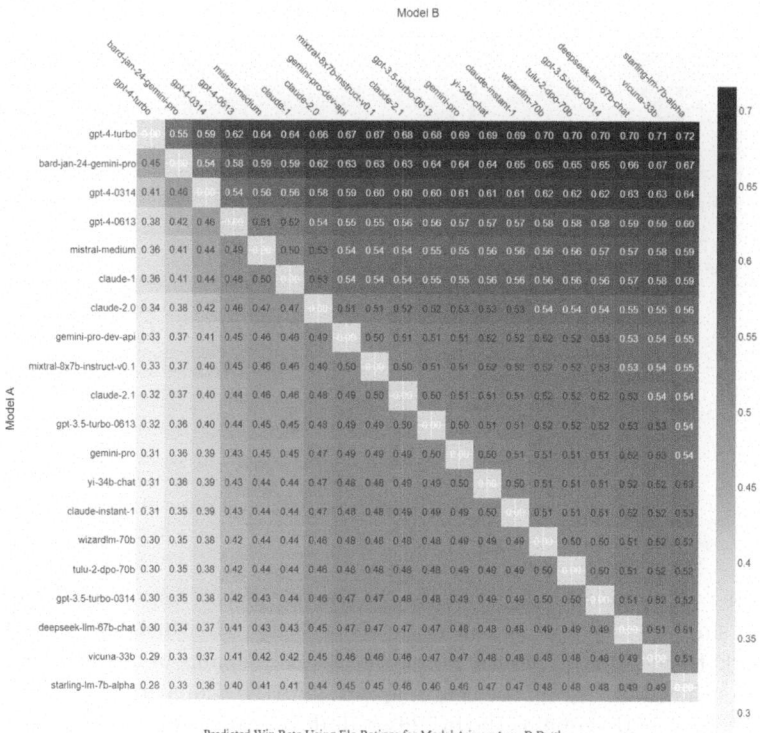

Fig. 8. Average win rate against all other model.

After incorporating the input documents into the predefined structure, there is a subsequent step of constructing the synthetic dataset. The synthetic data set undergoes preparation to align with the format of the required file format to fine-tune on the GPT model. The demonstration of fine-tuned results will be discussed in the following section.

Figure 9 presents the question distribution of the synthetic dataset and illustrates the diversity of question prompts. The innermost level shows segments corresponding to the first word of the question prompts. Each segment's size represents the or proportion of prompts that begin with that word. Moving outwards, the next level details the second word in the question prompts, and each segment is connected to the first word in the inner level, showing common pairings of the first and second words in the question prompts.

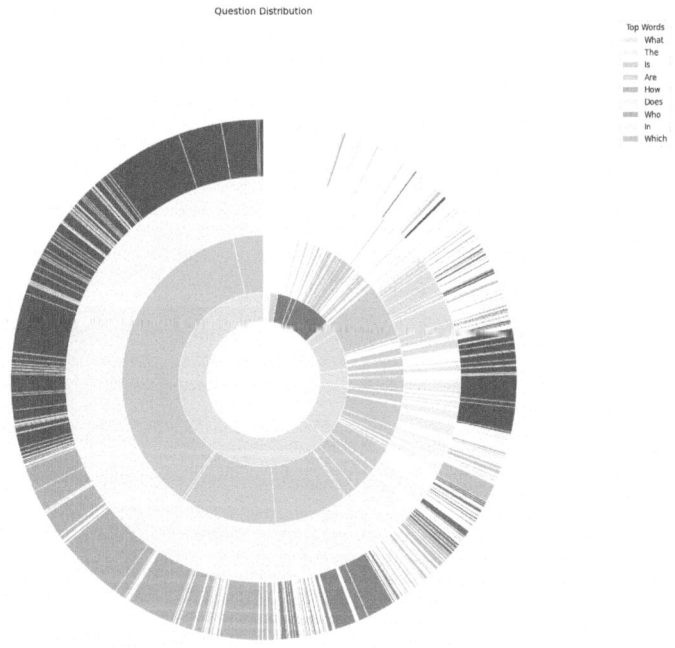

Fig. 9. Question distribution of synthetic dataset.

In order to quantitatively evaluate the quality of the response, the pairwise response similarity of the response matrix is adopted, which is an analytical framework to measure semantic similarity between pairs of textual responses [45, 46]. As shown in Fig. 10, the heat map presents the similarity of each response to the others. The diagonal is the brightest uniform color and serves as a baseline that indicates the maximum similarity value.

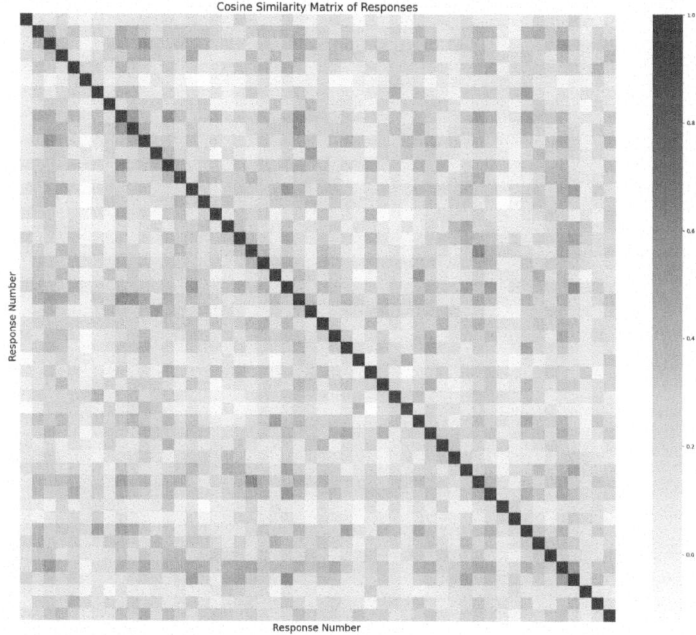

Fig. 10. Pairwise answer similarity of responses.

3.2   Domain-Tailored GPT

Therefore, we developed a pipeline to bridge this gap by infusing the domain specific knowledge to generative models. We built a domain-tailored GPT that could provide in-depth domain specific knowledge to the user and interact with participants via chatting. To enhance usability, we deployed the model online, enabling instant interaction between the system and users. As shown in the Fig. 11, the model is deployed online and tested by the users.

4   Experiment Design

This study aims to evaluate the effectiveness of various AI-assisted learning methods of three independent variables: eBook, Domain-tailored GPT, GPT and their impact on student performance across different difficulty levels of quizzes. Participants were randomly assigned to one of those learning assistant conditions and learning topics: basic statics, introduction to machine learning, and human factors. This research recruited volunteered participants from Purdue University. We introduced the detailed experiment design to all participants at the beginning. Participants will read the consent form and ask the researcher any questions they may have regarding the study. The participants will start the experiment once they have reviewed the consent form.

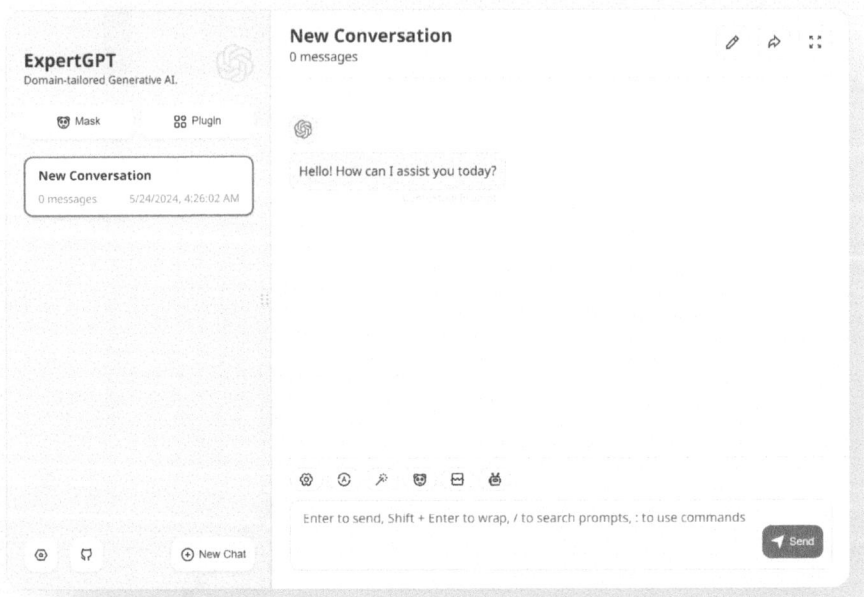

Fig. 11. Interface of Domain-Tailored GPT.

The pretest questionnaires are designed to evaluate the participant's comprehension of the learning subjects, which will serve as the baseline for the learning outcome comparison for all three learning materials. After this, the participants will start learning one of the materials with the first random assigned method. Participants will take two quizzes corresponding to learning materials when they finish learning with the system: one easy quiz and one hard quiz. The order of two quizzes is randomly assigned. They can collaborate with the assigned learning method during the open book quiz.

Once the quizzes are completed, participants will be asked to evaluate the system they used in the post-test questionnaire, which also includes the mental workload questionnaire (NASA-TLX) [47], usability evaluation [48], and trust towards the system [49]. After finishing the interaction and evaluation with the first assigned system, participants will collaborate with the second and third randomly assigned systems with the same procedure as described above.

5   Results

The domain-tailored GPT is trained on three domains: basic statics, introduction to machine learning, and human factors. Figure 12 presents the comparison of ChatGPT and Domain-Specific GPT objective quiz scores in these three domains. On average, the Domain-tailored GPT outperforms ChatGPT by 43.3% across various domains. This suggests that domain-specific tailoring of generative AI models significantly enhances their performance, providing more accurate and relevant responses compared to the general-purpose model like ChatGPT. Improvement in various fields underscores the value of specialized models in achieving superior results in targeted applications.

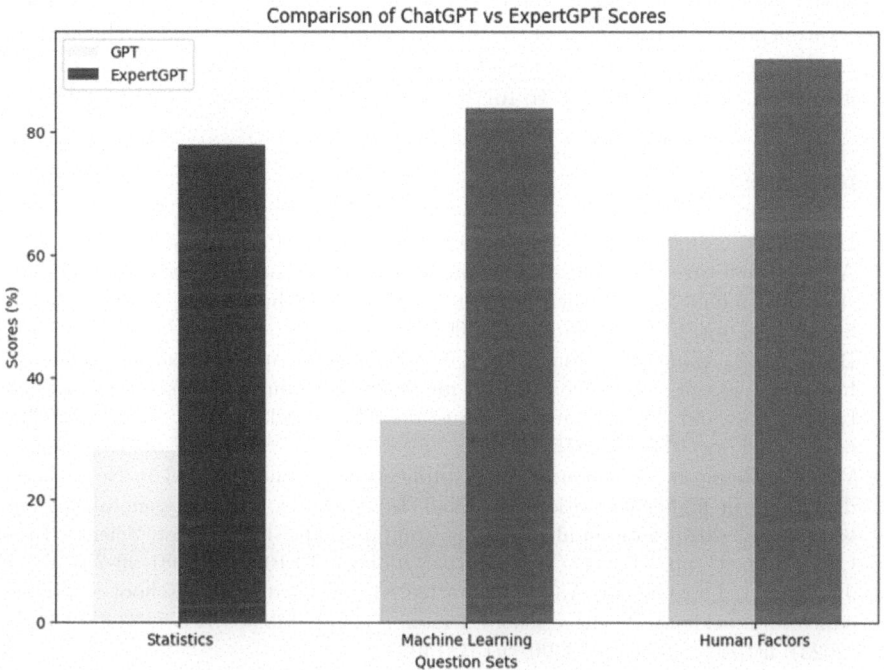

Fig. 12. Comparison of GPT vs Domain-tailored GPT scores.

During the debrief with the participants, most participants who have backgrounds in the assigned learning materials tend to provide more favorable feedback on our Domain-tailored GPT. This can be explained by the fact that those with prior knowledge are better equipped to assess the quality of the system's responses compared to uninformed individuals.

6   Conclusion and Future Works

This paper includes the review of generative AI, and its application in learning and assistance. After reviewing current research and challenges in these fields, we introduce an approach to construct a generative AI system that could provide customized content in specific domains to provide better computer-human interaction and address the current research gaps in hallucination and adaptability, which could potentially improve user experience, usability, and learning outcome. By creating the domain-specific dataset from valid sources and training the LLM on the dataset, we deployed the domain-specific GPT online and conducted experiments to investigate the impact of this system.

As part of future work, we intend to explore the long-term effects of the system by conducting interaction experiments with users, employing both state-of-the-art generative AI systems and the domain-tailored generative AI system. The system could be further improved by introducing the retrieval in the system to improve the user trust of the system. The user interface will also be improved according to the user feedback to further improve the usability of the system.

References

1. Lim, W.M., Gunasekara, A., Pallant, J.L., Pallant, J.I., Pechenkina, E.: Generative AI and the future of education: Ragnarök or reformation? A paradoxical perspective from management educators. Int. J. Manage. Educ. **21**(2), 100790 (2023). https://doi.org/10.1016/j.ijme.2023.100790
2. Bahroun, Z., Anane, C., Ahmed, V., Zacca, A.: Transforming education: a comprehensive review of generative artificial intelligence in educational settings through bibliometric and content analysis. Sustainability (Switzerland) **15**(17) (2023). https://doi.org/10.3390/su151712983
3. Wu, T., Zhang, S.: Applications and implication of generative AI in Non-STEM disciplines in higher education. In: Zhao, F., Miao, D. (eds) AI-generated Content. AIGC 2023. Communications in Computer and Information Science 1946 CCIS(August), pp. 341–349 (2024). https://doi.org/10.1007/978-981-99-7587-7_29
4. Jauhiainen, J.S., Guerra, A.G.: Generative AI and ChatGPT in school children's education: evidence from a school lesson. Sustainability (Switzerland) **15**(18) (2023). https://doi.org/10.3390/su151814025
5. George, A.S.: The potential of generative AI to reform graduate education. Partners Universal International Research Journal (PUIRJ). The Potential of Generative AI to Reform Graduate Education (December) (2023). https://doi.org/10.5281/zenodo.10421475
6. Smolansky, A., Zeivots, S., Cram, A., Huber, E., Raduescu, C., Kizilcec, R.F.: Educator and student perspectives on the impact of generative AI on assessments in higher education. dl.acm.org, pp. 378–382 (2023). https://doi.org/10.1145/3573051.3596191
7. Zhai, X., et al.: A review of artificial intelligence (AI) in education from 2010 to 2020. Complexity **2021** (2021). https://doi.org/10.1155/2021/8812542
8. Saka, A., et al.: GPT models in construction industry: opportunities, limitations, and a use case validation. Dev. Built Environ. **17**, 100300 (2024). https://doi.org/10.1016/J.DIBE.2023.100300arXiv:2305.18997
9. Sayed, W.S., et al.: AI-based adaptive personalized content presentation and exercises navigation for an effective and engaging E-learning platform. Multimedia Tools Appl. **82**(3), 3303–3333 (2023). https://doi.org/10.1007/S11042-022-13076-8/TABLES/7
10. Tiwari, R.: The integration of AI and machine learning in education and its potential to personalize and improve student learning experiences. Int. J. Sci. Res. Eng. Manage. **07**(02) (2023). https://doi.org/10.55041/IJSREM17645

11. Liu, J., et al.: A bibliometric analysis of generative AI in education: current status and development. Asia Pacific J. Educ. **44**(1), 156–175 (2024) https://doi.org/10.1080/02188791.2024.2305170

12. Ali, S., Ravi, P., Williams, R., DiPaola, D., Breazeal, C.: constructing dreams using generative AI. In: Proceedings of the AAAI Conference on Artificial Intelligence, vol. 38, issue (21), pp. 23268–23275 (2024). https://doi.org/10.1609/AAAI.V38I21.30374, arXiv:2305.12013

13. Marcus, G., Davis, E., Aaronson, S.: A very preliminary analysis of DALL-E 2 (2022). arXiv:2204.13807

14. Hanna, D.M.: The use of artificial intelligence art generator "Midjourney" in artistic and advertising creativity. J. Design Sci. Appl. Arts **4**(2), 42–58 (2023). https://doi.org/10.21608/JDSAA.2023.169144.1231

15. Borji, A., Ai, Q., Francisco, S.: Generated Faces in the Wild: quantitative comparison of stable diffusion, midjourney and DALL-E 2 (2022). arXiv:2210.00586

16. Singer, U., et al.: Make-A-Video: text-to-video generation without text-video data (2022). arXiv:2209.14792

17. Hong, W., Ding, M., Zheng, W., Liu, X., Tang, J.: CogVideo: large-scale pretraining for text-to-video generation via transformers (2022). arXiv:2205.15868

18. Li, Y., Min, M.R., Shen, D., Carlson, D., Carin, L.: Video generation from text. In: Proceedings of the AAAI Conference on Artificial Intelligence, vol. 32, issue (1), pp. 7065–7072 (2018). https://doi.org/10.1609/AAAI.V32I1.12233arXiv:1710.00421

19. Yuan, Y., Liu, H., Liu, X., Huang, Q., Plumbley, M.D., Wang, W.: Retrieval-augmented text-to-audio generation, 581–585 (2024). https://doi.org/10.1109/ICASSP48485.2024.10447898arXiv:2309.08051

20. Huang, A.Y.Q., Lu, O.H.T., Yang, S.J.H.: Effects of artificial Intelligence-Enabled personalized recommendations on learners' learning engagement, motivation, and outcomes in a flipped classroom. Comput. Educ. **194** (2023). https://doi.org/10.1016/J.COMPEDU.2022.104684

21. Chen, Y., et al.: IT3D: improved Text-to-3D generation with explicit view synthesis. In: Proceedings of the AAAI Conference on Artificial Intelligence, vol. 38, issue (2), pp. 1237–1244 (2024). https://doi.org/10.1609/AAAI.V38I2.27886, arXiv:2308.11473

22. Raj, A., et al.: DreamBooth3D: subject-driven Text-to-3D generation (2023). https://dreambooth3d.github.io

23. Lin, Z.: Why and how to embrace AI such as ChatGPT in your academic life. Royal Soc. Open Sci. **10**(8) (2023). https://doi.org/10.1098/rsos.230658

24. He, X., et al.: GVGEN: Text-to-3D generation with volumetric representation (2024). arXiv:2403.12957

25. Su, J., Yang, W.: Unlocking the Power of ChatGPT: a framework for applying generative AI in education. ECNU Rev. Educ. **6**(3), 355–366 (2023). https://doi.org/10.1177/20965311231168423

26. Nagi, F., et al.: Applications of artificial intelligence (AI) in medical education: a scoping review. Stud. Health Technol. Inform. **305**, 648–651 (2023). https://doi.org/10.3233/SHTI230581

27. Baidoo-Anu, D., Owusu Ansah, L.: Education in the era of generative artificial intelligence (AI): understanding the potential benefits of ChatGPT in promoting teaching and learning. J. AI **7**(1), 52–62 (2023). https://doi.org/10.61969/jai.1337500

28. Preiksaitis, C., Rose, C.: Opportunities, challenges, and future directions of generative artificial intelligence in medical education: scoping review. JMIR Med. Educ. **9**(1), 48785 (2023). https://doi.org/10.2196/48785

29. Yu, H., Guo, Y.: Generative artificial intelligence empowers educational reform: current status, issues, and prospects. Front. Educ. **8**, 1183162 (2023). https://doi.org/10.3389/FEDUC.2023.1183162/BIBTEX

30. Ray, P.P.: ChatGPT: a comprehensive review on background, applications, key challenges, bias, ethics, limitations and future scope. Internet of Things Cyber-Phys. Syst. **3**, 121–154 (2023). https://doi.org/10.1016/J.IOTCPS.2023.04.003

31. Rawte, V., Sheth, A., Das, A.: A survey of hallucination in "Large" foundation models. arXiv:2309.05922v1

32. Huang, L., et al.: A survey on hallucination in large language models: principles, taxonomy, challenges, and open questions. arXiv:2311.05232v1

33. Towhidul Islam Tonmoy, S., et al.: A comprehensive survey of hallucination mitigation techniques in large language models. arXiv:2401.01313v3

34. Xu, Z., Jain, S., Kankanhalli, M.: Hallucination is Inevitable: an innate limitation of large language models (2024). arXiv:2401.11817

35. Ahmad, N., Murugesan, S., Kshetri, N.: Generative Artificial Intelligence and the Education Sector. Computer **56**(6), 72–76 (2023). https://doi.org/10.1109/MC.2023.3263576

36. Bin Shiha, R., Atwell, E., Abbas, N.: Detecting Bias in university news articles: a comparative study using BERT, GPT-3.5 and Google bard annotations. In: Bramer, M., Stahl, F. (eds) Artificial Intelligence XL. SGAI 2023. Lecture Notes in Computer Science, vol. 14381, pp. 487–492 (2023). https://doi.org/10.1007/978-3-031-47994-6_42

37. Thirunavukarasu, A.J., Ting, D.S.J., Elangovan, K., Gutierrez, L., Tan, T.F., Ting, D.S.W.: Large language models in medicine. Nat. Med. 2023 **29**(8), 1930–1940 (2023). https://doi.org/10.1038/s41591-023-02448-8

38. Galitsky, B.A.: Truth-O-Meter: collaborating with LLM in fighting its hallucinations (2023). https://doi.org/10.20944/PREPRINTS202307.1723.V1

39. Wang, G., Yang, G., Du, Z., Fan, L., Li, X.: ClinicalGPT: large language models finetuned with diverse medical data and comprehensive evaluation (2023). arXiv:2306.09968

40. Jin, D., Pan, E., Oufattole, N., Weng, W.H., Fang, H., Szolovits, P.: What disease does this patient have? A large-scale open domain question answering dataset from medical exams. Appl. Sci. (Switzerland) **11**(14) (2020). https://doi.org/10.3390/app11146421arXiv:2009.13081

41. Zhong, H., Xiao, C., Tu, C., Zhang, T., Liu, Z., Sun, M.: JEC-QA: a legal-domain question answering dataset. In: AAAI 2020 - 34th AAAI Conference on Artificial Intelligence, pp. 9701–9708 (2019). https://doi.org/10.1609/aaai.v34i05.6519, arXiv:1911.12011

42. Chen, Z., et al.: FinQA: a dataset of numerical reasoning over financial data. In: EMNLP 2021 - 2021 Conference on Empirical Methods in Natural Language Processing, Proceedings, pp. 3697–3711 (2021). https://doi.org/10.18653/v1/2021.emnlp-main.300, arXiv:2109.00122

43. Ruiz-Rojas, L.I., Acosta-Vargas, P., De-Moreta-Llovet, J., Gonzalez-Rodriguez, M.: Empowering education with generative artificial intelligence tools: approach with an instructional design matrix. Sustainability 2023 **15**(15), 11524 (2023). https://doi.org/10.3390/SU151511524

44. Zheng, L., et al.: Judging LLM-as-a-Judge with MT-bench and chatbot arena (NeurIPS), pp. 1–29 (2023). arXiv:2306.05685

45. Hussain, Z., Nurminen, J.K., Mikkonen, T., Kowiel, M.: Command similarity measurement using NLP. OpenAccess Ser. Inform. **94**, 13–1130 (2021). https://doi.org/10.4230/OASICS.SLATE.2021.13/-/STATS

46. Singh, R., Singh, S.: Text similarity measures in news articles by vector space model using NLP. J. Institut. Eng. (India): Ser. B **102**(2), 329–338 (2021). https://doi.org/10.1007/S40031-020-00501-5/TABLES/12

47. Rubio, S., Díaz, E., Martín, J., Puente, J.M.: Evaluation of subjective mental workload: a comparison of SWAT, NASA-TLX, and workload profile methods. Appl. Psychol. **53**(1), 61–86 (2004). https://doi.org/10.1111/J.1464-0597.2004.00161.X

48. Bangor, A., Kortum, P.T., Miller, J.T.: An empirical evaluation of the system usability scale. Int. J. Hum.-Comput. Interact. **24**(6), 574–594 (2008). https://doi.org/10.1080/10447310802205776

49. Shamszare, H., Choudhury, A.: The impact of performance expectancy, workload, risk, and satisfaction on trust in ChatGPT: cross-sectional survey analysis. JMIR Hum. Fact. **11**(1), e55399 (2024)

Lower Limb Musculoskeletal Stiffness Analysis of Crouch Gait During Swing Phase Modelled as a Cable-Driven Serial Chain System

Sanjeevi Nakka[(✉)] [iD]

Ecole Centrale School of Engineering, Mahindra University, Hyderabad, India
sanjeevi.nakka@mahindrauniversity.edu.in

Abstract. Walking is a primary therapeutic goal since it significantly improves physical health and general well-being, especially in children with motor disabilities. Nevertheless, the majority of children with cerebral palsy (CP), the most common mobility disability in childhood, lose the ability to walk. Early research on robotic gait trainers has produced encouraging results. However, the scope of these clinic-based solutions is restricted to brief programmes that are too short to sustain enhanced function in a lifetime handicap like cerebral palsy. CNS makes continuous adjustments through the musculoskeletal system to generate suitable joint stability by modulating the multi-joint stiffness through subtle adjustments in limb posture and muscle contraction level. Understanding lower limb musculoskeletal stiffness variations in CP-affected individuals can be used to design a more efficient design and control for the robotic device.

This work uses a cable-driven serial chain model for the lower limb musculoskeletal system during the swing phase of walking to compare the lower limb multi-joint stiffness variations in healthy and CP individuals. The number of cables and routing are adapted from the available lower limb musculoskeletal structure. A multi-joint stiffness matrix, hip and knee joint, is formulated for the serial chain system considering different numbers of muscles. Inferences on the joint stiffness variations observed at hip and knee joints of the CP individuals when compared with healthy musculoskeletal systems were presented.

Keywords: Musculoskeletal stiffness · Cerebral Palsy · Cable-Driven System

1 Introduction

Crouch gait is thought to be one of the most common pathological patterns associated with Cerebral Palsy (CP) affected individuals [1]. It is characterized by excessive flexion of the hip, knee, and ankle during the gait cycle [2]. This walking pattern is inefficient [3,4] and if left untreated can lead to joint pain [5], formation of boney deformities [6], and loss of independent gait [7,8].

© The Author(s), under exclusive license to Springer Nature Switzerland AG 2025
V. G. Duffy (Ed.): HCII 2024, LNCS 15376, pp. 250–261, 2025.
https://doi.org/10.1007/978-3-031-76809-5_18

To improve the functional walking of individuals with crouch gait, different gait rehabilitation paradigms have been proposed in the literature to provide repetitive practice sessions to train the affected leg [9]. To this extent, robotic devices have become popular in the gait rehabilitation community for their advantages in providing controlled repetitive motion, better quantification of motor recovery, and reduced labor need. It is observed that, treadmill-based body weight support locomotor training [10] and robot-assisted gait trainers [11] are more efficient than traditional approaches and have shown some effectiveness in children and adults with CP. However, in controlled trials, improvements were not superior to therapies of equal intensity, indicating that these new treatments should not replace overground training [12]. Further, treadmill-based approaches are constrained to clinical or research facilities, which limits treatment frequency and duration; thus, retention of improvements is unlikely after training ends [12].

Treatments for crouch gait that are both more sustainable and efficacious are obviously needed. For this population, powered exoskeletons offer an unutilized resource. The main goal of robotic devices for gait rehabilitation has been to help adults who have suffered a spinal cord injury or stroke restore function that has been lost owing to paralysis [13,14]. To accomplish the desired joint trajectories, these systems often use impedance-based controllers, a control that allows users to determine how much robotic guiding is essential, and an assist-when-needed approach [15]. But they are implemented above ground. Since the main objective of these technologies is to learn a different walking pattern rather than to restore lost walking capability, translating them to children with gait disorders is a challenging task. Moreover, the neurological deficiencies that underlie the gait pathology associated with cerebral palsy (CP), such as spasticity, poor selective motor control, and muscle weakness, make the effect of motorized assistance difficult to predict in this population.

Essentially, to implement impedance bases controllers or robot design, the choice of usage of proper stiffness and damping values in the control architecture, and the nature of imposed dynamics, during the operation plays a significant role in the outcome of rehab paradigm [15,16]. In particular, as human musculoskeletal system, with the help of central nervous system (CNS) adjusts muscle contraction level to modulate a joint stiffness or multi-joint stiffness to provide joint stability for a movement task. The changes in the human gait pattern during a robotic gait rehabilitation reflect modulation of lower limb stiffness due to the applied external forces on the leg segments. Thus, a model of lower limb musculoskeletal stiffness variations during walking can be used to design a better human-robot interaction paradigm.

One way to estimate a single joint stiffness, a dynamic relationship between joint angle and the torque acting about it, is to apply external perturbation at the joint and measure the joint reaction, for example, ankle stiffness estimates in [15]. Serial chain models have been proposed for arm movements in a plane [17], where end-point perturbations are applied and joint responses are measured, to estimate the multi-joint stiffness behavior. Similar modeling can be used to estimate the lower limb multi-joint stiffness but the end-point perturbations are difficult to apply during walking.

In this work, we explore the variations in lower limb multi-joint stiffness between healthy and CP patients using a cable-driven serial chain model of the lower limb musculoskeletal system during the swing phase of walking. The primary joint actuators in the human body are the muscles, whose lengths and contraction velocities determine how much force they can produce [18]. The literature has examined the characteristics of muscles and their patterns of activation during walking in great detail [19]. An elastic cable that obeys the unilateral tension property and actuation dynamics of the muscle is used to simulate a muscle in this context. The rigid linkages are thought to be the bones.

Subsequently, in this work, a two-link serial chain system is used for the sagittal plane motion of a leg in the swing phase. The number of cables and their routing are adapted from the available structure [20]. Opensim, an open-source musculoskeletal simulation software, is used to analyze muscle forces. Later, the Multi-joint stiffness matrix is formulated for the serial chain system considering dominant muscles during gait. Further, the multi-joint stiffness behaviour of a healthy human lower limbs with that of a couch gait individual during the swing phase of walking.

2   Method

2.1   Lower Limb Musculoskeletal Structure

Human lower extremity comprises of pelvis, thigh, shank and foot segments which are connected by hip, knee and ankle joints connected in series. These segments are composed mainly of muscles and bones. Subsequently, the lower extremity can be thought of as a serial chain system with pelvis as base, thigh, shank and foot as links, and muscles as actuators as shown in Fig. 1. Muscles have unilateral force application property similar to cables, where it can only pull and cannot push. In this work, a two degree of freedom (DOF) leg model is considered to model the sagittal plane motion of hip and knee joints during swing phase of walking. Femur, the main bone of thigh, and tibia, the main bone of shank, are modelled as rigid links and are connected in series. Further, muscles responsible for hip and knee joint sagittal plane motion are considered.

Swing phase of human walking begins with hip and knee joint flexion followed by knee extension. Iliacus (ILI), Psoas (PS) and Rectus Femoris (RF) are the hip flexor muscles which are in the anterior part of the lower limb. Biceps Femoris - Long Head (BFLH) and Biceps Femoris- Short Head (BFSH) muscles, belong to hamstring muscle group are knee flexor muscles. Rectus Femoris (RF) and Vastus Intermedius (VI) muscles, belong to quadriceps femoris muscle group, are knee extensor muscles and act to move the foot forward. Adductor Magnus and Gluteus Medius form the antagonistic pair during the swing phase of walking. Gluteus Medius muscle is made up of three independent units, GM1, GM2 and GM3, out of which GM1 and GM3 are considered as shown in Fig. 1. Overall, Muscle investigated in present work include GM1, GM3, ILI, PS, RF, VI, BFLH and BFSH. The choice of these muscles are inspired from the stiffness analysis results presented in the work [20].

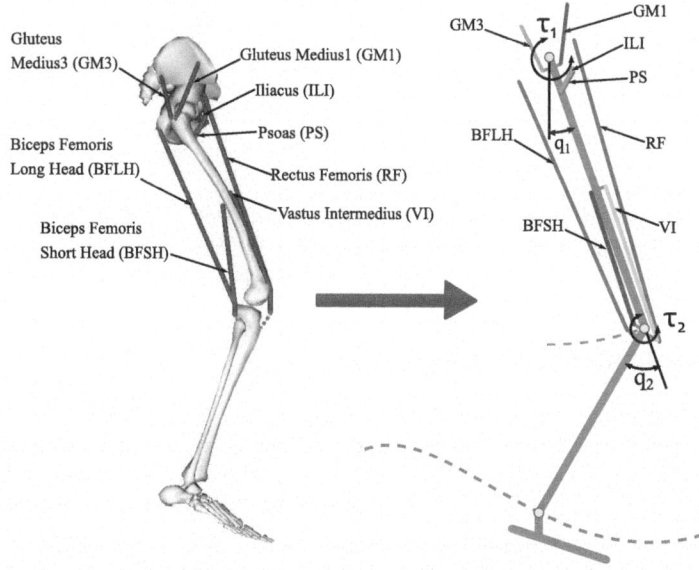

Fig. 1. Sagittal plane modeling of the lower limb musculoskeletal system as a cable-driven serial chain system. Muscles responsible for hip and knee joint motion during the swing phase are modeled as cables.

2.2   Muscle Dynamics

In this work, muscles in the musculoskeletal system are modelled as cables. Notably, a cable functions as the perfect force generator in a cable-driven system, enabling the generation of positive tension values within a specified range and irrespective of manipulator postures. In a musculoskeletal system, however, muscle force is determined by the length of the muscle and the speed of contraction.

The state-dependency of a muscle as an actuator is expressed using the Hill-type muscle model [21] to model the muscle as a cable. Muscle comprises of two elements, an active element capable of generating force, F_a, and a passive element that always produces force, F_p. At any given time t, magnitude of active force F_a, and passive force F_p, depend on state parameters like muscle activation level $a(t)$, muscle instantaneous length $l(t)$, muscle contraction velocity $v(t)$ and muscle properties like optimum muscle fiber length l_o, and maximum isometric muscle force F_o. For the static equilibrium, force dependency on velocity can be ignored. Further, $\eta(t) = l(t)/lo$ and $\hat{F} = F(t)/Fo$ represent normalized muscle fiber length and normalized muscle fiber force respectively, then normalized muscle force is given by,

$$\hat{F} = \hat{F}_a.a(t) + \hat{F}_p \tag{1}$$

$$\hat{F}_a) = \begin{cases} 1 - \left(\frac{\eta(t)-1}{0.5}\right)^2, & 0.5 \leq \eta(t) \leq 1.5 \\ 0, & \text{otherwise.} \end{cases} \tag{2}$$

$$\hat{F}_p = \eta(t)^3.e^{8\eta(t)-12.9} \tag{3}$$

$$F(t) = \hat{F}.F_o \tag{4}$$

It is to be noted that, the normalized active force, $\hat{F}_a$ and the normalized passive force $\hat{F}_a$ relationships are taken from [18, 22]. Subsequently, in the current work, the total muscle force value is used as the tension value in a cable.

2.3   Lower Limb Cable Driven Model

In the sagittal plane leg model shown in Fig. 1, the hip and knee joint motion is given by generalized coordinate q_1 and q_2. Torque values at the hip and knee joints are represented as generalized torque τ_1 and τ_2. An open-source 3D computer model of the human musculoskeletal system, Gait2354, as part of OpenSim library (a biomechanics simulation software [23, 24]) is used for the left leg swing phase joint angle data. Further, details of the muscle activation level, muscle length, and muscle attachment positions are also available from the model.

As a cable can only apply a pulling force, an n-DOF cable-driven system needs at least n+1 actuators for force closure [25]. Thus, to completely actuate a 2 DOF serial chain leg model, a minimum of 3 muscles are required. However, in this work, bases on the results reported in the literature [20], a total of 8 muscles were chosen. Accordingly, the dynamic model of the cable-driven serial chain system is expressed using the Lagrange's approach as follows.

$$\frac{d}{dt}\left(\frac{\partial L}{\partial \dot{q}_i}\right) - \frac{\partial L}{\partial q_i} = \tau_i, \quad i = 1, 2, .., n \tag{5}$$

where L defines the Lagrangian and q_i represent generalized joint variable. Further, τ_i represents the joint torque values. During the swing phase, there are no external torque but only torque generated by the leg muscles. Thus, $\tau_i = \tau_i^c$, where τ_i^c represents torque generated by cable forces. Using Lagrange's method τ_i^c can be expressed as,

$$\tau_i^c = \sum_{j=1}^{m}\left(T_j l_j.\frac{\partial r_j}{\partial q_i}\right) \tag{6}$$

$$\tau_i^c = \begin{bmatrix} l_i.\frac{\partial r_1}{\partial q_i} & l_2.\frac{\partial r_2}{\partial q_i} & \cdots & l_m.\frac{\partial r_m}{\partial q_i} \end{bmatrix} \begin{bmatrix} T_1 \\ T_2 \\ \vdots \\ T_m \end{bmatrix} \tag{7}$$

$$\begin{bmatrix} \tau_1^c \\ \tau_2^c \\ \vdots \\ \tau_n^c \end{bmatrix} = \begin{bmatrix} l_1 \cdot \frac{\partial r_1}{\partial q_1} & \cdots & l_m \cdot \frac{\partial r_m}{\partial q_1} \\ \vdots & \ddots & \vdots \\ l_1 \cdot \frac{\partial r_1}{\partial q_{dof}} & \cdots & l_m \cdot \frac{\partial r_m}{\partial q_{dof}} \end{bmatrix} \begin{bmatrix} T_1 \\ \vdots \\ T_m \end{bmatrix} \tag{8}$$

$$\tau = \mathbf{A}t \tag{9}$$

Here, m represents total number of cables and n represents DOFs of the system, such that $m \geq n + 1$. The matrix $\mathbf{A} \in \mathbb{R}^{n \times m}$ in Eq. 9 is referred as structure matrix. For the considered 2 DOFs system, $n = 2$ and m is 8 as 8 muscles are considered for the analysis.

2.4   Stiffness Formulation

Small changes in hip and knee joint torques result in small changes in corresponding joint angles and they can be related by,

$$\begin{bmatrix} d\tau_1 \\ d\tau_2 \end{bmatrix} = \begin{bmatrix} K_{HH} & K_{HK} \\ K_{KH} & K_{KK} \end{bmatrix} \begin{bmatrix} dq_1 \\ dq_2 \end{bmatrix} \tag{10}$$

$$d\tau = \mathbf{K}dq \tag{11}$$

Here, $\mathbf{K}$ denotes the relation between joint torques and joint angles and is referred as the multi-joint stiffness of the leg. Elements K_{HH} and K_{HK} represent stiffness produced at hip joint and elements K_{KH} and K_{KK} represent stiffness produced at knee joint. Notably, the diagonal elements of $\mathbf{K}$ represent the effect of joint angle on corresponding joint torque and the off-diagonal elements represent the coupling effect. From Eq. 9, it can be written as [26],

$$d\tau = (dA)T + A(dT) \tag{12}$$

From Eqs. 11 and 12,

$$\mathbf{K}dq = (dA)T + A(dT) \tag{13}$$

dT in Eq. 13 represents the changes in cable tension values, which can be related to the changes in cable lengths.

$$dT = k_c dl \tag{14}$$

where k_c is the cable stiffness matrix. It is a diagonal matrix with values computed by differentiating the total muscle force (Eq. 4) with respect to instantaneous muscle lengths. Here, dl is the change in cable lengths, which can be related to the change in joint angles as,

$$dl = -A^T(dq) \tag{15}$$

By substituting Eqs. 14 and 15 in Eq. 13,

$$\mathbf{K}dq = (dA)t - A k_c A^T dq$$

Dividing both sides with dq results in,

$$\mathbf{K} = \left[\frac{dA}{dq_1}t \quad \frac{dA}{dq_2}t \quad \cdots \quad \frac{dA}{dq_n}t \right] - Ak_cA^T \tag{16}$$

$$\text{where, } dA = \sum_{i=1}^{n} \frac{\partial A}{\partial q_i} dq_i$$

$$\mathbf{K} = \mathbf{K}_d + \mathbf{K}_c \tag{17}$$

$$\text{where, } \mathbf{K}_d = \left[\frac{dA}{dq_1}t \quad \frac{dA}{dq_2}t \quad \cdots \quad \frac{dA}{dq_n}t \right]$$

$$\text{and } \mathbf{K}_c = -Ak_cA^T$$

Stiffness ellipse is constructed across the swing phase in order to analyse the overall behaviour of multi-joint leg stiffness, $\mathbf{K}$. The eigen values of $\mathbf{K}$, λ_1 and λ_2 ($\lambda_1 > \lambda_2$) respectively, provide the major and minor axis radius. The respective eigen vectors of $\mathbf{K}$ correspond to the main and minor axes of the ellipse. The major axis denotes the dominant stiffness direction, whereas the minor axis denotes the least stiffness. Further, the condition number, CN, is defined as the absolute ratio of the maximum eigen value of $\mathbf{K}$ to the minimum eigen value of $\mathbf{K}$.

$$\text{CN} = \frac{\lambda_{max}}{\lambda_{min}} \tag{18}$$

A large value of CN, i.e., ratio of the eigen values, implies an anisotropic multi-joint stiffness matrix close to singularity.

3   Results

Multi-joint stiffness analysis of a lower limb during the swing phase of walking is presented for different cases of dominant muscles. Multi-joint stiffness matrix, $\mathbf{K}$, is computed, and the obtained data for both healthy and Cerebral Palsy (CP) individuals is used to plot stiffness ellipse during the swing phase. Figure 2 present the stiffness ellipse at specific point of the swing phase, i.e., 0, 30, 70, 80 and 100%. It is to be noted that ellipses in Fig. 2 have been reduced by factor of 10 due to their large sizes. A significant changes were observed in size and orientation of ellipse across the swing phase gait trajectory. Further, significant differences in size and orientation of ellipse is observed between healthy and CP individuals. This indicates the effect of muscle activation and force values on the perceived value of the leg joint stiffness. Also, the variation of condition number of the multi-joint stiffness matrix, CN, along the swing phase is presented in Fig. 3.

Figure 2 presents the stiffness ellipse comparison for healthy and CP individuals across the swing phase of the gait cycle. Notably, eight dominant lower-limb muscle muscles were used to model the swing phase multi-joint stiffness. The combined effect of these muscles resulted in a skewed stiffness behaviour at the beginning of the swing phase, as the stiffness ellipse is skewed with a minor axis

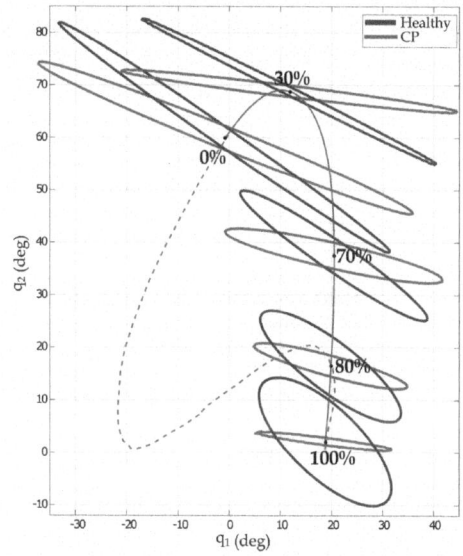

Fig. 2. Stiffness ellipse is plotted at 0, 30, 70, 80 and 100% of the swing phase for both healthy and CP data. Stiffness ellipse has been scaled down by a factor of 10.

nearly aligned with the gait trajectory. However, the stiffness behaviour changes along the swing phase trajectory as the skewness reduces at 70% to 100% of the swing phase. This is also reflected in CN values; refer Fig. 3. It is observed that the stiffness behaviour of CP is skewed throughout the swing phase, unlike the healthy. Further, the major axis of the stiffness ellipse is nearly parallel to the hip joint axis, i.e., q_1 axis. As the ellipse's major axis implies dominant stiffness, it can be inferred that the hip joint is stiffer for CP individuals.

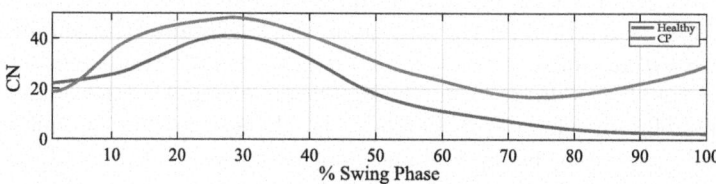

Fig. 3. Condition number of stiffness matrix, **K**, during the swing phase of walking.

Figure 3 presents the comparison of the variation of Condition Number, CN, of **K** between healthy and CP individuals across the swing phase of the gait cycle. CN increases in the initial swing phase for both healthy and CP, implying anisotropic stiffness behaviour. Further, a decrease in the CN is observed for the healthy as the swing phase progressed, whereas it increased for CP. It implies that for healthy individuals, the musculoskeletal system modulates stiffness to be near isotropic at the end of the swing phase, probably to prepare both joints for the impact of a heel strike. Contrastingly, for CP individuals, the CN value is larger, implying anisotropic behaviour. Now, by observing the stiffness ellipse orientation in Fig. 4, the major axis of the ellipse at 80% and 100% is along the Hip-axis, implying a stiffer hip joint. It infers that, while developing a rehab paradigm for CP individuals, the focus should be on making the exoskeleton impose high stiffness at the hip during the late swing phase.

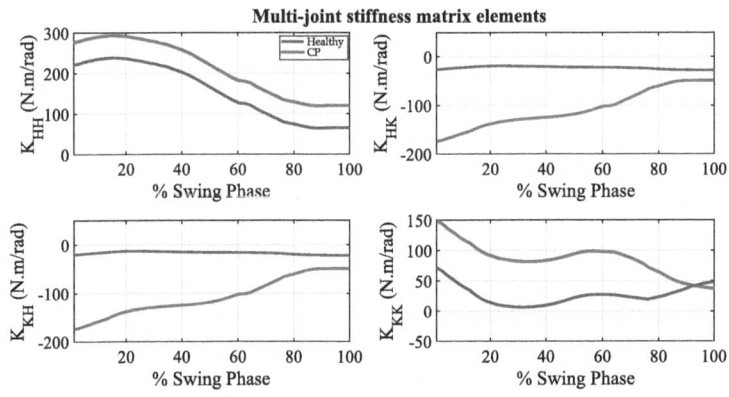

Fig. 4. Multi-joint Stiffness matrix elements variation over the swing phase. Magnitude of elements of K are increased for CP data compared to healthy.

The individual elements of the multi-joint stiffness matrix, **K**, are presented in Fig. 4 during the swing phase for both healthy and CP data. It is observed that the K_{HH} has large values for CP compared to Healthy throughout the swing phase, implying stiffer hip joints for CP individuals. This would imply muscle contraction to produce large hip joint stiffness to facilitate the distal joint motion. The behaviour is observed for the knee joint, K_{KK}. Notably, the coupling terms K_{HK} and K_{KH} magnitudes decrease are lower for healthy compared to CP. The changes in coupling stiffness result in significant changes in the orientation of the stiffness ellipse; refer Fig. 2. Further, the changes in the coupling stiffness pattern and increase in the hip and knee joint stiffness in CP individuals can be seen as a response by the human musculoskeletal system to increase the stability of the deviant gait.

Lower limb multi-joint stiffness values computed from the healthy subject joint data show significant differences with CP subjects over the swing phase. This observation suggests a continuous adjustment by the muscles to generate a desired joint motion. In this work, a set of eight muscles was chosen based on the muscle force values. Notably, consideration of more muscles in the present lower-limb model can bring more information to comprehend changes in the presented stiffness variation. However, the presented model of multi-joint stiffness as a cable-driven serial chain system can still be helpful in understanding the lower limb musculoskeletal system. The presented results can be useful for developing a better human-robot interaction paradigm using exoskeletons for CP individuals. In particular, it helps in tuning the control parameters of the system and understanding the requirement of the level of imposed stiffness. As external forces are applied during the gait rehabilitation paradigm to assist the foot trajectory, such understanding of lower-limb multi-joint stiffness can be used to adjust the applied force values to develop better gait training paradigms.

4   Conclusion

This work presents the comparison of the multi-joint stiffness behaviour of a healthy human lower limb with that of a couch gait individual during the swing phase of walking. The lower limb musculoskeletal system is modelled as a two-link cable-driven serial chain system, where bones and muscles are represented as rigid links and elastic cables, respectively. The multi-joint stiffness matrix is formulated considering eight dominant swing phase muscles. The analysis shows a significant variation in the perceived values of the multi-joint stiffness, both in terms of magnitude and orientation, between both groups. It is observed that for CP individuals, the hip joint is much stiffer compared to healthy. Also, significant coupling stiffness across the hip and knee joints exists for CP individuals. This implies that lower limb muscles are contracted to generate suitable coupling stiffness between joints to control proximal and distal joint motion. This understanding will provide a means to design effective musculoskeletal rehab paradigms and tune control parameters of rehab devices for the crouch gait individuals. In future, the analysis will be extended to comprehend the stiffness behaviour during the stance phase of gait.

References

1. O'Sullivan, R., Marron, A., Brady, K.: Crouch gait or flexed-knee gait in cerebral palsy: is there a difference? A systematic review. Gait Posture **82**, 153–160 (2020)
2. Wren, T.A.L., Rethlefsen, S., Kay, R.M.: Prevalence of specific gait abnormalities in children with cerebral palsy: influence of cerebral palsy subtype, age, and previous surgery. J. Pediatric Orthopaedics **25**(1), 79–83 (2005)
3. Rose, J., Gamble, J.G., Medeiros, J., Burgos, A., Haskell, W.L.: Energy cost of walking in normal children and in those with cerebral palsy: comparison of heart rate and oxygen uptake. J. Pediatric Orthopaedics **9**(3), 276–279 (1989). https://doi.org/10.1097/01241398-198905000-00004
4. Waters, R.L., Mulroy, S.: The energy expenditure of normal and pathologic gait. Gait Posture **9**(3), 207–231 (1999)
5. Jahnsen, R., Villien, L., Aamodt, G., Stanghelle, J., Holm, I.: Musculoskeletal pain in adults with cerebral palsy compared with the general population. J. Rehabil. Med. **36**(2), 78–84 (2004). https://doi.org/10.1080/16501970310018305
6. Graham, H.K., Selber, P.: Musculoskeletal aspects of cerebral palsy. J. Bone Joint Surgery. British vol. **85-B**(2), 157–166 (2003). https://doi.org/10.1302/0301-620X.85B2.14066

7. Johnson, D.C., Damiano, D.L., Abel, M.F.: The evolution of gait in childhood and adolescent cerebral palsy. J. Pediatric Orthopaedics **17**(3), 392–396 (1997)
8. Opheim, A., Jahnsen, R., Olsson, E., Stanghelle, J.K., Walking function, pain, and fatigue in adults with cerebral palsy: a 7-year follow-up study. Dev. Med. Child Neurol. **51**, 381–388 (2009)
9. Lerner, Z.F., Damiano, D.L., Park, H.-S., Gravunder, A.J., Bulea, T.C.: A robotic exoskeleton for treatment of crouch gait in children with cerebral palsy: design and initial application. IEEE Trans. Neural Syst. Rehabil. Eng. **25**(6), 650–659 (2017). https://doi.org/10.1109/TNSRE.2016.2595501
10. Dodd, K.J., Foley, S.: Partial body-weight-supported treadmill training can improve walking in children with cerebral palsy: a clinical controlled trial. Dev. Med. Child Neurol. **49**(2), 101–105 (2007)
11. Borggraefe, I., et al.: Improved gait parameters after robotic-assisted locomotor treadmill therapy in a 6-year-old child with cerebral palsy. Movement Disorders **23**(2), 280–283 (2008)
12. Dobkin, B.H., Duncan, P.W.: Should body weight-supported treadmill training and robotic-assistive steppers for locomotor training trot back to the starting gate? Neurorehabil. Neural Repair **26**, 308–317 (2012)
13. Farris, R.J., Quintero, H.A., Murray, S.A., Ha, K.H., Hartigan, C., Goldfarb, M.: A preliminary assessment of legged mobility provided by a lower limb exoskeleton for persons with paraplegia. IEEE Trans. Neural Syst. Rehabil. Eng. **22**(3), 482–490 (2014). https://doi.org/10.1109/TNSRE.2013.2268320
14. Bortole, M., et al.: The H2 robotic exoskeleton for gait rehabilitation after stroke: early findings from a clinical study. J. NeuroEngineering Rehabil. **12**(1) (2015). https://doi.org/10.1186/s12984-015-0048-y
15. Sanjeevi, N.S.S., Singh, Y., Vashista, V.: Recent advances in lower-extremity exoskeletons in promoting performance restoration. Curr. Opinion Biomed. Eng **20**, 100338 (2021)
16. Nakka, S., Vashista, V.: External dynamics dependent human gait adaptation using a cable-driven exoskeleton. IEEE Robot. Autom. Lett. (2023)
17. Singh, R., Sanjeevi, N.S.S., Vashista, V.: Upper limb musculoskeletal stiffness analysis during planar motions as a cable-driven serial chain manipulator. In: Proceedings of the 2023 6th International Conference on Advances in Robotics (2023)
18. Martin, C.F., Schovanec, L.: The control and mechanics of human movement systems. New Trends, Interfaces, and Interplay. Birkhäuser Basel, Dynamical Systems, Control, Coding, Computer Vision (1999)
19. Zajac, F.E.: Muscle and tendon: properties, models, scaling, and application to biomechanics and motor control. Crit. Rev. Biomed. Eng. **17**(4), 359–411 (1989)
20. Panchal, N., Sanjeevi, N.S.S., Vashista, V.: Lower limb musculoskeletal stiffness analysis during swing phase as a cable-driven serial chain system. In: 2018 7th IEEE International Conference on Biomedical Robotics and Biomechatronics (Biorob). IEEE (2018)
21. McMahon, T.A.: Muscles, reflexes, and locomotion, vol. 10. Princeton University Press (1984)
22. Vilimek, M.: Musculotendon forces derived by different muscle models. Acta Bioeng. Biomech. **9**(2), 41 (2007)
23. Delp, S.L., Loan, J.P., Hoy, M.G., Zajac, F.E., Topp, E.L., Rosen, J.M.: An interactive graphics-based model of the lower extremity to study orthopaedic surgical procedures. IEEE Trans. Biomed. Eng. **37**(8), 757–767 (1990). https://doi.org/10.1109/10.102791

24. Delp, S.L., et al.: OpenSim: open-source software to create and analyze dynamic simulations of movement. IEEE Trans. Biomed. Eng. **54**(11), 1940–1950 (2007). https://doi.org/10.1109/TBME.2007.901024
25. Ming, A.: Study on multiple degree-of-freedom positioning mechanism using wires (part 1). Int. J. Japan Soc. Precis. Eng. **28**, 131–138 (1994)
26. Sanjeevi, N.S.S., Vashista, V.: On the stiffness analysis of a cable driven leg exoskeleton. In: 2017 International Conference on Rehabilitation Robotics (ICORR). IEEE (2017)

Digital Human Modeling and Digital Twin: A Literature Review and Case Study

Satyaswaroop Nanda[1]([⊠]), Martin Pohlmann[1], Sameeran Kanade[1], and Vincent G. Duffy[1,2]

[1] School of Industrial Engineering, Purdue University, 315 N. Grant St, West Lafayette, IN 47907, USA
{nanda11,kanade,duffy}@purdue.edu, mpohlmann@humaneticsgroup.com
[2] Agricultural and Biological Engineering, Purdue University, 225 S. University Street, West Lafayette, IN 47907, USA

Abstract. This paper focuses on Digital Human Modeling [DHM], the ergonomic analysis of heavy truck drivers using 3D software, and Digital Twin, an emerging technology. A systematic literature review was conducted to understand DHM and Digital Twin and its current application. To demonstrate the application of DHM, a 3D software - RAMSIS was used to perform an ergonomic analysis of a heavy truck driver. DHM is a technique used for creating a virtual environment of a product to simulate human interaction with it. In contrast, Digital Twin is a virtual representation of a real device across its lifecycle that can be understood, learned, and reasoned with real-time data from the field. A brief analysis of the current development of these technologies, their application, and their limitations is documented in the literature review. To show a significant application of DHM an advanced ergonomics analysis for comfort, reachability, visibility obstruction, and potential reflection during nighttime is carried out for a heavy truck driver using the RAMSIS software. To optimize the driver's position and reduce the discomfort level on the body parts, several adjustments in the virtual environment were carried out and the results were documented.

Keywords: Digital Human Modeling · Digital Twin · RAMSIS · Ergonomic Analysis · Bibliographic Analysis

1 Introduction

Digital Human Modeling [DHM] is a computer-based simulation of human beings for various purposes such as ergonomics, product Design, and safety analysis. This virtual environment evaluation process is useful in creating user-centered products by incorporating human factor principles at an early design stage and results in reducing overall design time and cost and improving the quality. It is like the advanced quality planning process done in the manufacturing industry before the start of any manufacturing which helps reduce the quality defects, and cost which results in improving productivity. Digital human modeling software is a computer-aided design tool for the construction of 2D and 3D human models from anthropometric data of targeted users/populations for ergonomic analysis of virtual human fit to virtual workstation components [1]. A few popular DHM softwares, which are commercially available include JACK, SAMMIE, RAMSIS, DELMIA, SANTOS, etc. RAMSIS is an ergonomic analysis software with embedded tools to create human-representative manikins and place them into the human-machine CAD model to quantitatively assess comfort and other ergonomic interactions [2]. Digital Twin serves as a virtual counterpart mirroring real-world entities, processes, and systems in real time. While it can depict digital entities independently, its primary function lies in bridging the gap between the physical and digital realms. This innovation holds significant importance in meeting the diverse needs of Industry 4.0. It gives a digital image of a factory's operations, a communications network's activities, or the movement of items through a logistics system [3]. In this study, a literature review was carried out on DHM and the emerging Digital Twin and Human Digital Twin [HDT] field. Additionally, a step-by-step ergonomic analysis for a heavy truck driver was carried out to demonstrate the application of DHM software, RAMSIS. Using this 3D software a 5th percentile female manikin was created from the anthropometric database and positioned in a truck environment. Subsequently, the resulting postures were evaluated concerning ergonomic criteria such as discomfort, reachability, visibility and reflection during nighttime.

2   Literature Review

2.1   Data Collection and Trend Analysis

Efficient utilization of computational modeling and simulation tools at the beginning of the design process has been progressively regarded as a standard for modern product development. The growing integration of computer, sensor, and visualization technologies has given rise to digital human modeling (DHM) as an advanced design support approach. DHM enables the representation and simulation of human entities within computer-aided design (CAD) or virtual environments (VE). On the other hand, Digital Twin represents a software-based emulation of a tangible object or entity. It provides a digital depiction of a physical entity, such as an automobile engine, a building, a solar farm, or even an entire urban area. Digital Twin (DT) technology is now widely used in personal and professional settings, driving the growth of Human-Centered Digital Twin (HDT) applications, especially in fields like medicine and sports. Human-Centered Digital Twin (HDT) is not yet widely used in industries because the focus is more on improving production quality and efficiency rather than considering human needs.

The analysis utilized the Google Ngram research tool to track the percentage usage of three Ngrams: 'Digital Human Modeling', 'Digital Twin', and 'Human

Digital Twin' in English-written Google Books from 1980 to 2019. Figure 1 illustrates the trends for these technologies during this period. It indicates that Digital Human Modeling (DHM) was more prevalent between 1995 and 2013, while Digital Twin (DT) was in its early stages. However, from 2014 onwards, there was a significant surge in the usage of DT technology. Additionally, the chart reveals no discernible trend for Human Digital Twin technology up to 2019, suggesting that this emerging technology is still in its infancy. Our paper primarily focuses on Digital Human Modeling (DHM) and the emerging technology of Digital Twin (DT).

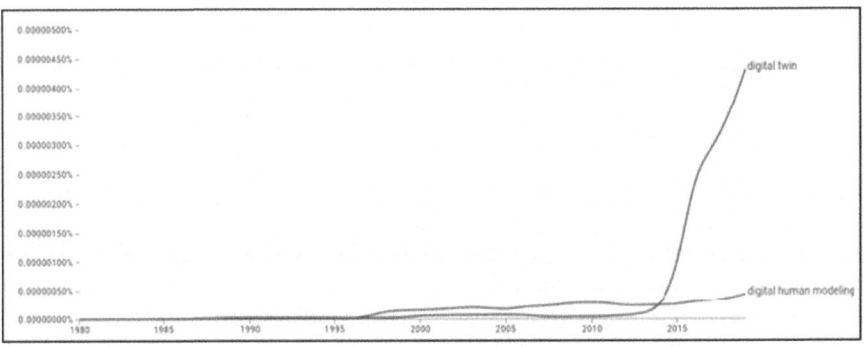

Fig. 1. Trend chart from Google Ngram for 'Digital Human Modeling', 'Digital Twin' AND 'Human Digital Twin' [4].

To understand more about the research articles being published in the areas of 'Digital Human Modeling' and emerging areas like 'Digital Twin', data was collected on the published articles using Scopus and Web of Science. VOSviewer is a software application utilized to build and present bibliometric networks, allowing the visualization of connections between various elements such as journals, researchers, or individual Publications [5]. Figure 2 shows a rising trend in the number of articles being published in the areas of DHM and DT. The Scopus database with the keyword search was used to collect this relevant information for further analysis. There were a total of 12806 articles published on DHM till the year 2023 with the first research article being published in the year 1961. Alternatively, on DT there were a total of 21475 documents published till 2023. The number of research articles on DT experienced a notable rise from 2019 to 2023, increasing from 1,019 to 7,428, respectively. This shows the growing importance of DT as an emerging field. To elaborate further on this, an analysis was done on countries that are leading in these areas of research topics. From Fig. 3, it is evident that China followed by the USA and Germany have published 50% of the research articles on DT. Similarly in the field of DHM, the USA has published a higher number of articles followed by China and the UK.

Digital Human Modeling [DHM]   **Digital Twin [DT]**

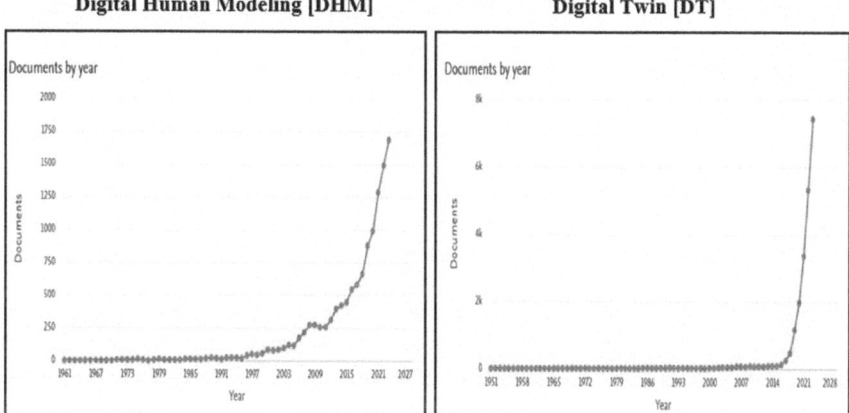

Fig. 2. Trend chart of articles published in Scopus Database on DHM and Digital Twin [6].

[DHM]   **[DT]**

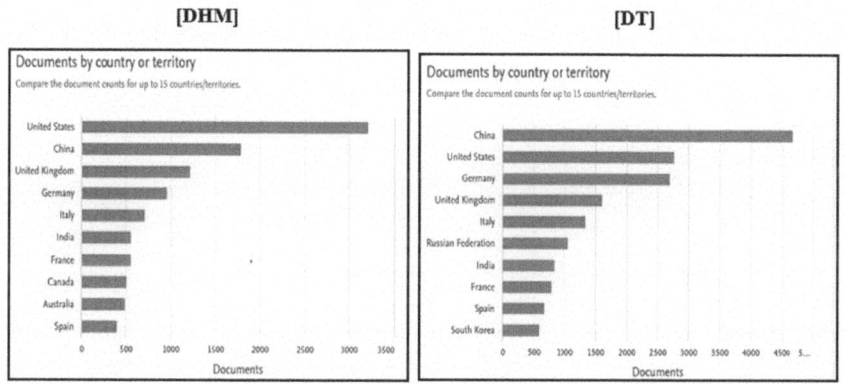

Fig. 3. Pareto Chart demonstrating the number of research articles by countries [6].

2.2 VOSviewer Analysis

A further deep dive was done on the research articles on DHM/DT related to manufacturing using VOSviewer software. A keyword search strategy in the 'Title and Abstract field' was utilized to understand the research articles' relevance to manufacturing. Figure 4 shows the Content analysis results on some of the keywords associated with DHM related to manufacturing. For this analysis, data exported from Scopus was used and the 'Minimum number of Occurrence of a term' was set to 3 and a total of 19 keywords were extracted. The results show some of the applications of DHM in intelligent manufacturing, and simulation.

Fig. 4. Keyword analysis using VOSviewer on the relevance of DHM in manufacturing [7].

For DT, the top 5,000 recently published research articles were selected for a similar analysis. Figure 5 shows the Content analysis results on some of the keywords associated with DHM related to manufacturing. Here the 'Minimum number of Occurrence of a term' was set to 1 and a total of 240 keywords were extracted. The results show some of the applications of DT in manufacturing like 'Tool wear' in terms of wear and condition, 'Tool life' prediction, etc. Table 1 lists some of the keywords found in the top 5,000 latest research articles. From this, it is evident that application in manufacturing is an Emerging Technology.

Fig. 5. Keyword analysis using VOSviewer on the relevance of DT in Manufacturing [7].

Table 1. Keywords related to the relevance of DT in manufacturing from VOSviewer analysis [7].

Term	Occurrences	Relevance
automated machining	1	1.37
cutter wear	1	1.37
cutter wear condition	1	1.37
individual tool wear prediction	1	1.37
intelligent manufacturing process	1	1.37
milling cutting wear status	1	1.37
milling tool wear online monitoring	1	1.37
milling tool wear state	1	1.37
milling wear experiment	1	1.37

2.3   Co-citation Analysis

"Citation analysis is used to examine the degree of connectivity between pairs of papers" [8]. Co-citation analysis is used to find articles that have been cited together in another article. This provides information regarding the degree of connectivity between articles [9]. Citespace software was used for this analysis. Pairs of papers that have been cited together form clusters [8]. For this analysis, DHM data relevant to manufacturing was exported from Web of Science and imported into the Citespace software. Figure 6 shows the co-citation analysis for DHM. The number of research articles that could be imported was 500 since the Citespace software is a free downloaded version. The years from 2020 to 2024 were analyzed and the top 3 reference papers were displayed in the citation burst. This figure depicts research papers where each node represents a paper, and the node's size reflects how often that paper has been cited. Hence, larger nodes indicate papers with higher citation frequencies.

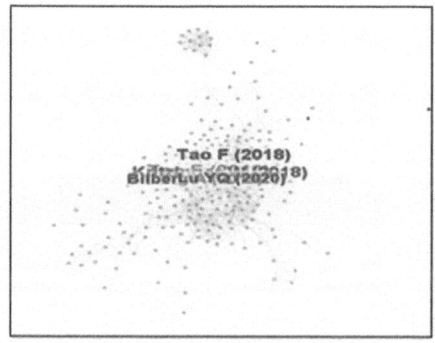

Top 3 References with the Strongest Citation Bursts

References	Year	Strength	Begin	End	2020 - 2024
Ding K, 2019, INT J PROD RES, V57, P6315, DOI 10.1080/00207543.2019.1566661, DOI	2019	2.62	2020	2021	
Tao F, 2017, IEEE ACCESS, V5, P20418, DOI 10.1109/ACCESS.2017.2756069, DOI	2017	2.12	2020	2021	
Alam KM, 2017, IEEE ACCESS, V5, P2050, DOI 10.1109/ACCESS.2017.2657006, DOI	2017	1.84	2020	2021	

Fig. 6. Co-citation and Citation burst analysis using Citespace on the relevance of DHM in manufacturing [10,11].

A similar analysis was also carried out on the relevance of DT in manufacturing and here the citespace software did not show any citation burst. Similar to the previous analysis, 500 research articles were exported from the Web of Science. Figure 7 shows the co-citation analysis of the DT related to manufacturing.

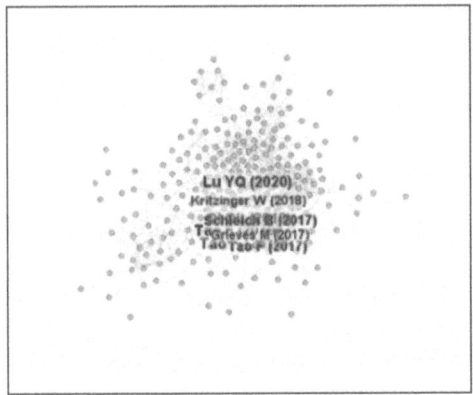

Fig. 7. Co-citation analysis using Citespace on the relevance of DT in manufacturing [10,11]

2.4 Application of DHM and DT in Manufacturing

To understand the application of this technology in manufacturing further, a deep dive was done using the data from the above analysis with a relevant keyword search as'manufacturing'. Figure 8 shows the number of articles published on DHM and DT in the last 10 years related to the manufacturing domain. The bar chart shows a rising trend with a significant increase in DT technology from the year 2019 to 2024. This concludes the wide application of DT as an emerging technology in the manufacturing domain that is being discovered.

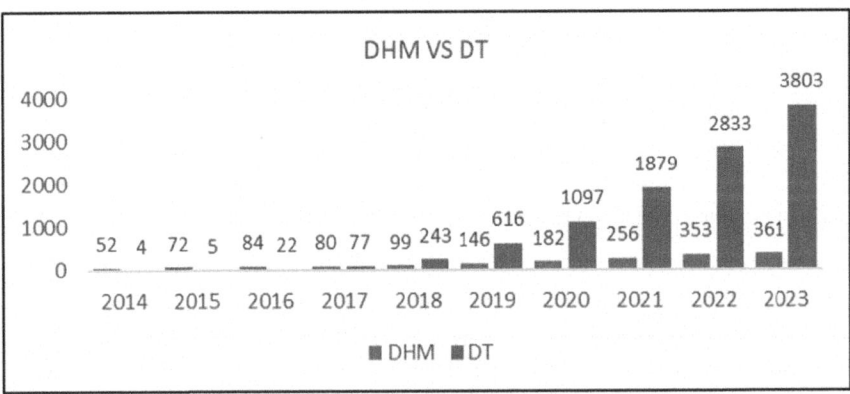

Fig. 8. A comparison of articles published in DHM and DT in manufacturing domain [6].

3   Discussion

3.1   Digital Human Modeling [DHM]

Digital Human Modeling (DHM) has surfaced as a design methodology, portraying human size, and proportions, as well as specific musculoskeletal and cognitive traits. It enables the modeling and simulation of humans within a computer-aided design (CAD) or virtual environments (VE). Designers can utilize it to generate manikins representing particular population percentiles using anthropometric libraries and explore various design alternatives through what-if scenarios. This process aids in mitigating the expenses and time involved in reworking and retrofitting physical prototypes. Figure 9 shows the integration of the DHM into the design process. The direct feedback loop between the CAD modeling, CAE, and DHM provides the potential to detect safety and reliability concerns early in the design process [12]. It also creates opportunities for early design changes, which are cost-effective [13]. At present, industrial robots, computerized numerical controlled (CNC) machine tools, and various automation equipment are widely utilized in the manufacturing industry. Nonetheless, these current automation tools frequently lack the capability to handle a wide range of complex tasks with flexibility. As a result, manual labor remains predominant in the majority of tasks within the manufacturing sector. Human factors play a core role in transitioning to sustainable manufacturing processes and consumption in Industry 4.0. Assembly simulation is one of the most important application fields of DHMs. Considering DHMs for assembly process simulation helps identify operational risks and judge assembly feasibility and perception, emotion, psychology, sociality, etc. [14].

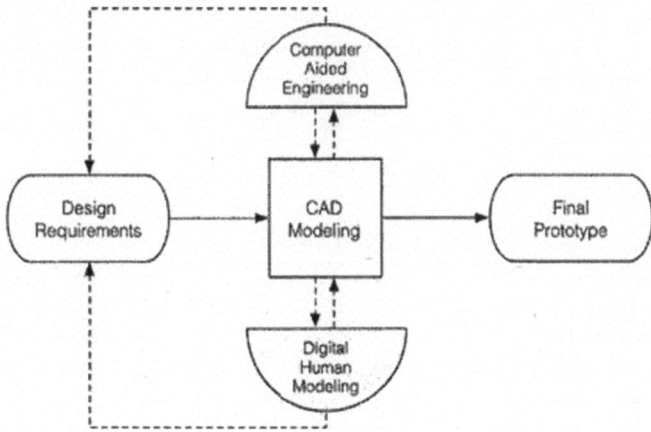

Fig. 9. Concurrent design workflow where human aspects of the design process are integrated early into the design process through the introduction of DHM [13].

3.1.1   Application of Digital Human Modeling [DHM]

DHM technology is applied in a diverse range of domains which include manufacturing, automobile, aviation, healthcare, space, and consumer goods. Many publications within the manufacturing domain extensively explore the utilization of Digital Human Modeling (DHM) in the field of occupational ergonomics. These publications primarily emphasise the optimization of workstations and task designs within manufacturing and assembly environment.

3.2   Digital Twin [DT]

DT originated from aerospace engineering and manufacturing in the United States, especially in the 1969 NASA Apollo project, which reflected this concept but did not explicitly propose the term "Digital Twin". At that time, two identical spacecraft were created, one of which was sent to space for missions while the other was kept in a simulated environment on the ground to reflect the actual situation of the spacecraft in space [15]. A Digital Twin acts as a software-generated duplicate of a physical entity, capturing its unique features and core attributes. It presents a digital model of concrete objects like automotive engines, building structures, solar farms, or even entire urban environments. These applications harness technologies such as the Internet of Things (IoT), Artificial Intelligence (AI), and data analytics to optimize operational results. Additionally utilizing 3D simulations enhanced with augmented and virtual reality, engineers can accelerate the design process and bypass several labor-intensive phases usually associated with creating a new product. Before investing in physical materials, virtual assessments can be made regarding product specifications, material selections, and adherence to crucial regulations and standards. By implementing a digital twin, engineers can preemptively identify potential quality and viability concerns, resulting in significant cost savings. Digital Twin aims to create a digital version of an organization's or a manufacturing plant's physical assets. Figure 10 shows the process used by DT in Industry 4.0 [3].

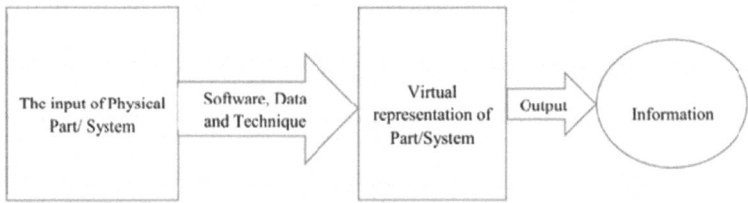

Fig. 10. Process used in Digital Twin for Industry 4.0 [3].

3.2.1   Application of Digital Twin [DT]

DT technology is applied in a diverse range of domains which include manufacturing operations, the automobile industry, healthcare services, power generation equipment, and urban planning. From a manufacturing perspective, it provides engineers with virtual tools for inspecting, exploring, and evaluating existing assets, processes, and systems. Digital twin technology has become necessary for Industry 4.0 journey to digitalize, optimize, and manage their factories more smartly and efficiently. Digital Twin enables producers to understand their operations better by considering different production aspects. These include equipment monitoring, process optimization, and digital maintenance [3]. In the initial lifecycle, a Digital Twin (DT) emerges during the design phase of its physical counterpart, which is yet to be realized. Once the physical twin is constructed, the DT and its counterpart coexist in continuous communication and interaction. In the second scenario, a DT is formed after the physical twin has already been in operation for some time, such as when a manufacturing device transitions into a connected device through Industry 4.0 solutions. Here, the DT requires linkage to the physical twin, and both entities proceed to interact seamlessly in their ongoing operation.

4   Procedure for Ergonomic Analysis Using RAMSIS

RAMSIS 3D software was used to perform the ergonomic analysis of a 5th percentile Female Manikin in a heavy truck environment. Multiple steps were performed to carry out this analysis as listed below. The details of the steps and the relevant images are shown.

4.1   Steps Followed for the Ergonomic Analysis

Step 1

1. Open RAMSIS Software-'launchNextGenAutomotive' design environment.
2. Execute the following plug-ins:
   - Anthropometric
   - Ergonomics
   - Project
   - Cognitive

Step 2

1. Create a female Manikin using 'NextGen body builder' from the Start menu.
2. Select the 'Anthropometric Database' and 'Typology' from the drop-down and then add manikin details - gender, age, nation, and body measurements [height, waist circumference, and sitting height]. In our project, the 5th percentile female human manikin is created.
3. Add Body Measure list to structure tree.
4. Assign a role using the 'role definition' icon to the female manikin as 'Driver'.
5. Figure 11 shows 5th percentile female manikin positioned near heavy truck.

Fig. 11. 5th percentile female manikin positioned near heavy truck.

Step 3

1. Load the 3D heavy truck geometry file '$truck_cab.sat$' into the design environment.
2. Manikin H-Point is aligned with the floor level. Using the 'Translate Object' icon, position the manikin for easy accessibility of all the body parts near the heavy truck.
3. Hide all the exterior portion on the heavy truck, where the manikin will be placed to drive the truck. Go to the structure tree 'Geometry' section and click on the geometry to execute the command accordingly.

Step 4

1. Add shoes to the female manikin. Double-click on the manikin, "NextGen-EdiManikin" window pops up.
2. Click 'Additional options' and then from the drop-down shoe model, select 'Workshoe'.
3. Hide the Skin of the Manikin and switch on the 'Wire Frame' icon to apply constraints.

Step 5

1. To place the female manikin onto the seat of the truck, the constraint process is carried out using the 'Define Restriction' in the operations drop-down icon.
2. Select the 'Restriction Type' as the target.
3. In the 'Manikin Comp' box, an H-point is selected on the manikin physically.
4. In the 'Env. Object' Box select seat surface plane for position adjustment.
5. Click "create" for the constraint to be executed on H-Point and seat surface plane.

Step 6

Similar to Step 5, target constraint is executed between -

1. Skin points on the shoe heel and floor surface. Right Heel / Floor and Left Heel /Floor.
2. The points on the shoe bottom and the Accelerator / Footrest. RightBall / Accelerator and LeftBall /Footrest.
3. The points on the shoe bottom and Accelerator / Footrest. RightBall / Accelerator and LeftBall /Footrest.
4. The points on the shoe bottom and Accelerator / Footrest. RightBall / Accelerator and LeftBall /Footrest.
5. Skin points on the hand and the steering wheel. $HAL2_1/STW_{Left}$ and $HAR2_1/STW_{Right}$.
6. Figure 12 shows application of Manikin Target Constraint

Fig. 12. Manikin Target Constraint application.

Step 7

1. After all the target constraints are established, click on the 'Posture Calculation' icon in the 'Define Restriction' window. A NextGen-Posture Calculation window appears, showing several Target 'Active', what is 'Accomplished', 'Not Accomplished', and any 'Inconsistent'.
2. Click on the "Start" icon and the status will show if the posture calculation is completed. In this analysis, the posture calculation was completed.
3. Figure 13 shows Manikin seated in truck and completed posture calculation.

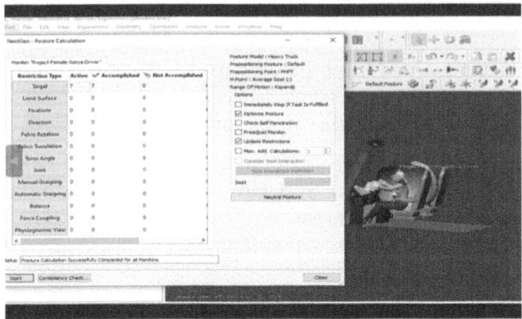

Fig. 13. Manikin seated in truck and completed posture calculation.

Step 8

1. To do 'Reachability Analysis' from the 'Analysis' drop-down icon select 'Reach Definition'. A NextGen-Define Reach window pops up. Click on the Start Joint and select from the dropdown using the right-click 'Shoulder Joint'
2. Click on body point and select the skin point of an index finger for the right hand. This will create a maximum reachability envelope on the right-hand side of the Driver.
3. Figure 14 shows completed reachability analysis.

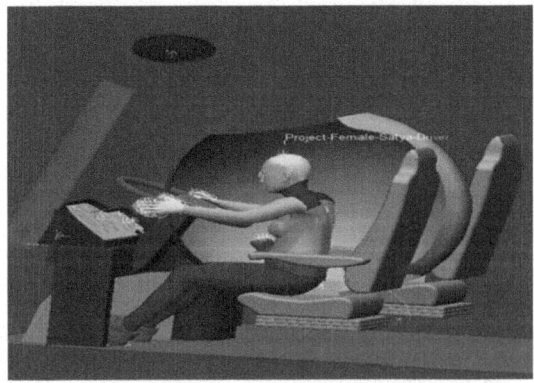

Fig. 14. Reachability analysis of the 5th Percentile female manikin.

Step 9

1. Create a Point and Plane on the Steering Wheel and rotate the plane by -8°C.
2. Plane created on the steering wheel is moved in the z-axis 50mm.

3. Apply the 'Limit Surface' constraint between the mid-eye of the 5th percentile female manikin.
4. Click on the Start icon and Status will show if the Posture Calculation is completed. In this analysis, the Posture Calculation was successfully completed.
5. Figure 15 shows completed posture calculation after creating point and plane on steering wheel.

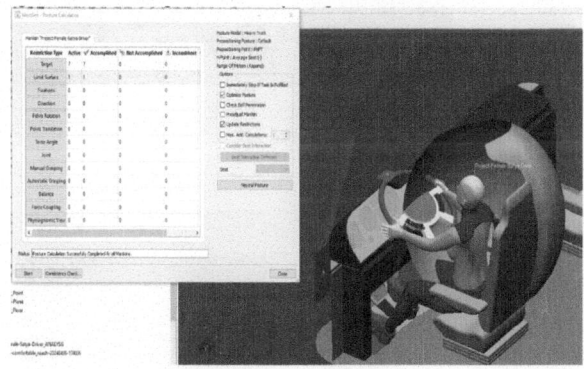

Fig. 15. Posture calculation completed after translation of the plane.

Step 10

1. To do the 'Comfort Feeling' analysis, select 'Comfort Feeling' from the Analysis drop-down. A discomfort assessment window pops up showing the posture values. Initial comfort analysis of the Female Manikin shows a high Posture value (>3.5) for the body parts -Neck and Shoulder, Discomfort feeling, Fatigue, and Health.
2. The posture value is set as 'Reference' and added to structure tree.
3. Figure 16 shows initial comfort analysis.

Step 11

To reduce the discomfort level from the initial analysis [Step10], the following adjustments were done

1. Head adjustment on Z-axis to make it straight.
2. Seat height is raised in the z-axis by 30mm.
3. Comfort feeling assessment is carried out and their is marginal improvement in the posture value as shown in Fig. 17. Even after this adjustment, the values are greater than 3.5.

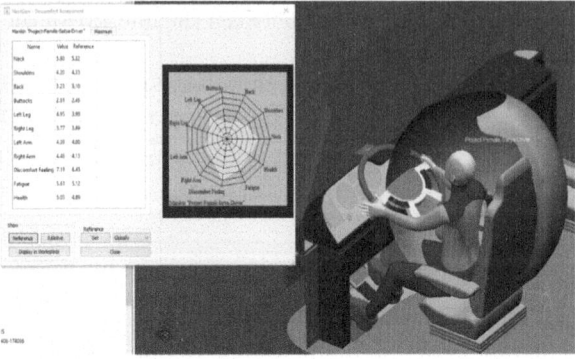

Fig. 16. Initial comfort analysis after mid-eye adjustment to the plane on the steering wheel.

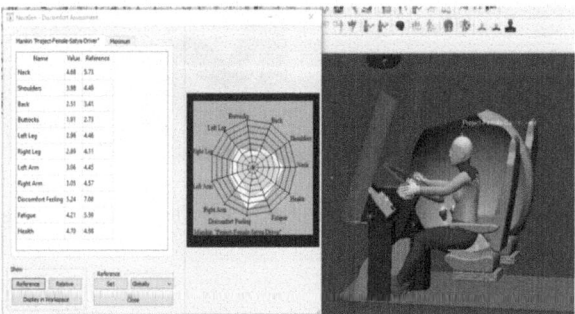

Fig. 17. Comfort assessment after head adjustment and seat raise by 30mm.

Step 12

1. Raise the seat level up to 50mm.
2. Comfort feeling analysis is carried out and results show a good improvement in posture values of neck and shoulders. However, values are still greater than 3.5.

Step 13

1. Select the Steering wheel in the structure tree and copy and rename it as 'Steering wheel-Original'.
2. Translate the steering wheel in the X-axis towards the manikin by 50mm and 70mm.
3. Click on posture calculation to determine the successful completion.
4. Perform comfort feeling analysis from the 'Analyze' drop-down.
5. The results showed a slight improvement in the posture values after a movement of the steering wheel by 50mm and 70mm respectively. The same was

translated relatively up to 70mm and the results indicate a significant reduction in the neck and shoulder posture values. Figure 18 shows all the Posture values after this adjustment are less than 3.5.

Step 14

1. To find out if there is any obstruction on the manikin sight limit after the steering wheel adjustment, on the IP glass in the control panel, a visibility assessment was carried out.
   a. From the 'Analyze' drop-down menu, 'Sightlimit' is selected.
   b. Select Steering wheel and IP Glass and click OK. Refer Fig. 19.

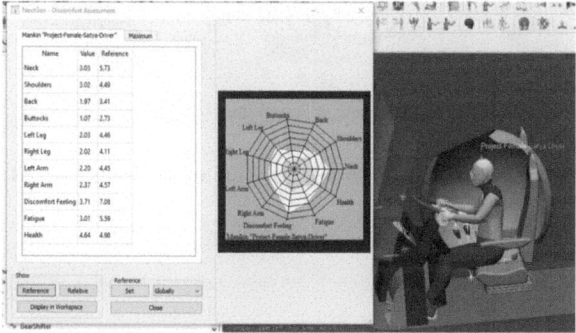

Fig. 18. Comfort assessment completed after steering wheel linear X axis - 70mm.

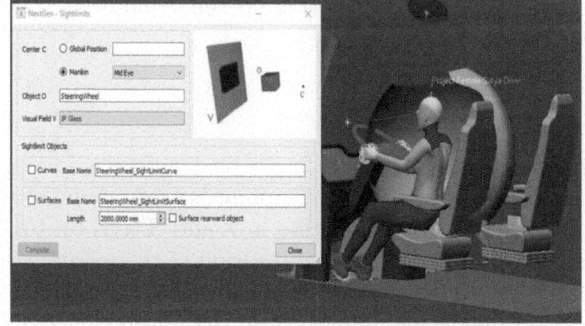

Fig. 19. Visibility assessment - steering wheel and IP glass control panel.

Step 15

Look for any obstruction lines on the IP glass panel. Figure 20 shows that for this particular 5th percentile manikin, there is no line on the IP Glass control panel indicating no obstruction on the sight limit.

Fig. 20. Visibility Assessment - No Obstruction of Steering noticed on IP Glass

Step 16

1. To find out any nighttime reflection, 'Reflection Assessment' is carried out by selecting the 'Cognitive' plugin.
2. Select the Windshield and IP Glass Control Panel.
3. Update the accuracy resolution to 1000. Click "OK".
4. Click "Compute".
5. Figure 21 shows that there is no particular reflection of the control panel on the windshield.

Step 17

1. To improve the comfort level further, a point is created on the steering wheel handle, and it is rotated by translating in Z and X-axis by 10mm each.
2. Final Comfort feeling analysis at this position of the manikin is determined.
3. The results indicate a significant improvement in comfort level. The neck and shoulder posture values have reduced from the initial values of 5.73 and 4.49 to 2.27 and 2.62 respectively as shown in Fig. 22.

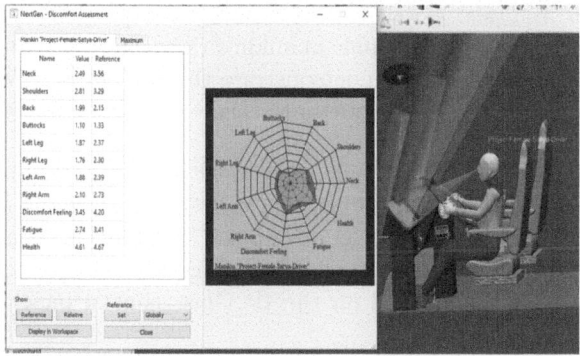

Fig. 21. Reflection assessment [Nighttime] - no reflection on the windshield.

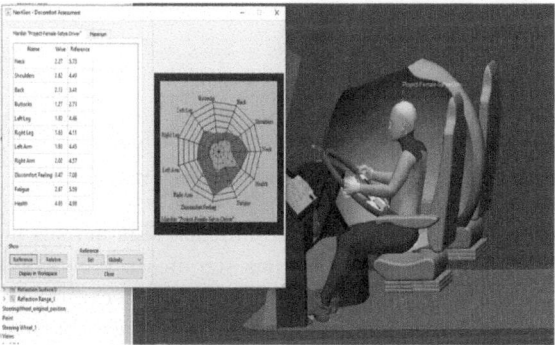

Fig. 22. Final posture for the 5th Percentile female manikin - final comfort assessment.

5   Results

The RAMSIS 3D software was used to perform an ergonomic analysis of a heavy truck driver considered to be a 5th-percentile female manikin. Four analyses were carried out - Comfort, Reachability, Visibility, and Reflection. There were 7 target constraints applied to the manikin initially to place the manikin into the truck environment and the initial posture calculation was completed.

Comfort Analysis. The first comfort analysis statistics show higher posture values (>3.5) indicating high discomfort levels in the neck and shoulder. The same analysis was carried out at a neutral position and the posture values were determined. To reduce the discomfort level, several adjustments were made to the seat height. Figure 17 shows the reduction in the discomfort level after these adjustments. To further improve the posture values, steering wheel adjustments were carried out. The steering wheel is moved linearly in the x-direction towards the manikin. Multiple iterations were carried out and a significant improvement in the posture values of body parts was noticed. Figure 22 shows the final posture value results.

Reachability Analysis. A reachability analysis was performed to understand the reach of the 5th percentile female manikin's right hand to the steering wheel, control panel, and gear levers. To demonstrate this, an envelope was created by selecting the appropriate skin points on the right-hand shoulder joint and index finger.

Visibility Assessment. A visibility assessment was conducted to determine if there was any obstruction on the manikin sight limit after the steering wheel adjustment, on the IP glass in the control panel. A visibility cone appears after the computation and for this particular 5th percentile manikin, there seems to be no line of the steering wheel on the IP Glass control panel indicating no obstruction on the sight limit.

Reflection Assessment. A reflection assessment was conducted to find if there was any nighttime reflection. The result shows there is no reflection of the control panel on the windshield. Hence, in this case, there was no need to adjust the IP glass control panel position.

6   Conclusion

The effective use of software modeling and simulation tools early in the design process is arguably becoming a gold standard for modern product development. Digital human modeling using RAMSIS 3D software enables modeling and simulation of humans within a virtual environment. This human modeling carried out using the anthropometric database has significantly benefited the engineers in designing products and processes that are human-centric through effective ergonomics analysis and improvements in the early stage. In this project, RAMSIS software was used to model a 5th percentile female manikin from the anthropometric database and perform ergonomics analysis to determine the best comfortable position having lower stress values on body parts like neck, shoulders etc. The paper also focused on a brief literature review on Digital Human Modeling and emerging technology Digital Twin and their applications in manufacturing.

7   Future Work

The application of DHM has gained attention in the design process of the manufacturing industry, agriculture, healthcare sectors, transportation and aviation sectors, etc. However, the use of DHM for designing ergonomic products and work environments for the specially-abled and elderly is quite limited [1]. Furthermore, DHMS technology needs to be developed to function in digital twin solutions. This means that DHMS technology needs functionality for simulations in the virtual world to feed reality with information but also have the functionality to work the other way around, i.e. to be fed with information from the real world to continuously learn and improve, and thereby gain future designs and simulations made in the virtual world [16]. Human beings are more complex systems than any machines or manufacturing processes and hence, full lifecycle management of humans is far more difficult. Digital Twin has the potential to solve this problem effectively [17].

References

1. Maurya, C.M., Karmakar, S., Das, A.K.: Digital human modeling (DHM) for improving work environment for specially-abled and elderly. SN Appl. Sci. **1**(11), 1326 (2019)
2. Breese, J.T., Fuhrmann, A.M., Duffy, V.G., Luebke, A.: Developing ergonomic design recommendations using human-centric RAMSIS analysis. In: Duffy, V.G., Rau, P.-L.P. (eds.) HCI International 2022 – Late Breaking Papers: Ergonomics and Product Design: 24th International Conference on Human-Computer Interaction, HCII 2022, Virtual Event, June 26–July 1, 2022, Proceedings, pp. 96–112. Springer Nature Switzerland, Cham (2022). https://doi.org/10.1007/978-3-031-21704-3_7
3. Javaid, M., Haleem, A., Suman, R.: Digital Twin applications toward Industry 4.0: a review. Cogn. Robot. **3**, 71–92 (2023). https://doi.org/10.1016/j.cogr.2023.04.003
4. Google Ngram. https://books.google.com/ngrams/
5. Kanade, S.G., Duffy, V.G.: Exploring the effectiveness of virtual reality as a learning tool in the context of task interruption: a systematic review. Int. J. Ind. Ergon. **99**, 103548 (2024)
6. Scopus. https://www.scopus.com/search/form.uri?display=basic&zone=header&origin=searchbasic#basic
7. VOSviewer. https://www.vosviewer.com/
8. Kanade, S.G., Duffy, V.G.: A systematic literature review of game-based learning and safety management. In: Duffy, V.G. (ed.) HCII 2020. LNCS, vol. 12199, pp. 365–377. Springer, Cham (2020). https://doi.org/10.1007/978-3-030-49907-5_26
9. Kanade, S.G., Duffy, V.G.: Use of virtual reality for safety training: a systematic review. In: Duffy, V.G. (ed.) Digital Human Modeling and Applications in Health, Safety, Ergonomics and Risk Management. Health, Operations Management, and Design: 13th International Conference, DHM 2022, Held as Part of the 24th HCI International Conference, HCII 2022, Virtual Event, June 26 – July 1, 2022, Proceedings, Part II, pp. 364–375. Springer International Publishing, Cham (2022). https://doi.org/10.1007/978-3-031-06018-2_25
10. CiteSpace. https://citespace.podia.com/
11. Web of Science. https://clarivate.com/products/scientific-and-academic-research/research-discovery-and-workflow-solutions/webofscience-platform/
12. Islam, M.T., Sepanloo, K., Velluvakkandy, R., Luebke, A., Duffy, V.G.: Enhancing ergonomic design process with digital human models for improved driver comfort in space environment. In: Duffy, V.G. (ed.) Digital Human Modeling and Applications in Health, Safety, Ergonomics and Risk Management: 14th International Conference, DHM 2023, Held as Part of the 25th HCI International Conference, HCII 2023, Copenhagen, Denmark, July 23–28, 2023, Proceedings, Part I, pp. 87–101. Springer Nature Switzerland, Cham (2023). https://doi.org/10.1007/978-3-031-35741-1_8
13. Demirel, H.O., Duffy, V.G.: Building quality into design process through digital human modelling. Int. J. Digit. Hum. **1**(2), 153–168 (2016)
14. Yin, M.-Y., Li, J.-G.: A systematic review on digital human models in assembly process planning. Int. J. Adv. Manuf. Technol. **125**(3), 1037–1059 (2023)
15. Sun, Z., Zhang, R., Zhu, X.: The progress and trend of digital twin research over the last 20 years: a bibliometrics-based visualization analysis. J. Manuf. Syst. **74**, 1–15 (2024)

16. Lämkull, D., Zdrodowski, M.: The need for faster and more consistent digital human modeling software tools. In: DHM2020, pp. 299–310. IOS Press (2020)
17. Shengli, W.: Is human digital twin possible? Comput. Methods Programs Biomedicine Update **1**, 100014 (2021)

A Wearable and Semi-automated *Timed-Up and Go* Test: Implementation and Accuracy Validation

Paolo Perego[1]([✉]) [iD], Marcello Cono Fusca[1] [iD], Nicola Francesco Lopomo[1] [iD], and Giuseppe Andreoni[1,2] [iD]

[1] Dipartimento di Design, Politecnico di Milano, Milano, Italy
{paolo.perego,marcello.fusca,nicola.lopomo,
giuseppe.andreoni}@polimi.it
[2] Bioengineering Laboratory, Scientific Institute IRCCS "E. Medea", Bosisio Parini, Italy

Abstract. In the last decade the introduction of wearable technologies supported the implementation of reliable quantification tools for clinical functional assessment. Within this frame, this work was focused on the development and validation of a wearable system for analyzing motor function, particularly using the *Timed-Up and Go* (TUG) test. This study specifically aimed to create a wearable device that could quantify and automate the TUG test, collecting not only the time taken but also various kinematic parameters like accelerations, velocity, and number of steps. The wearable actigraph, fixed at the pelvis by means of an elastic band, measured and stored 3D inertial parameters for processing and analysis. The validation involved comparing manual TUG test times with those obtained using the actigraph, showing a high level of agreement and accuracy. The study included healthy subjects and individuals with different pathologies like post-stroke, multiple sclerosis, and Parkinson's, demonstrating the system's feasibility in clinical settings. Overall, the wearable system proved effective in quantifying and automating the TUG test, offering a possible remote, self, and unsupervised method for functional evaluation and tele-rehabilitation programs.

Keywords: Functional evaluation · rehabilitation · wearable actigraph · wearable motion monitoring · timed-up and go · TUG test

1 Introduction

The *Timed-Up and Go* (TUG) test has been widely reported to be an assessment tool used in the context of functional assessment, particularly for evaluating functional mobility, balance, and locomotor performance in various populations, including older adults and subjects presenting mobility impairments. In its simplest declination, the TUG test represents a standardized and widely accepted assessment test that measures the time taken by an individual to complete a series of tasks that simulate daily activities, such as rising from a seated position, walking a short distance, turning, and returning to the starting position [1]. Indeed, the TUG test has been shown to be a reliable and valid measure of functional mobility in different contexts, with high inter/intra-tester reliability [2–6].

The TUG test is part of a broader framework of functional assessment approaches that aim to evaluate an individual's ability to perform daily activities and maintain independence in their daily lives. Functional assessments are essential in healthcare as they help identify individuals who may be at risk of falls, mobility impairments, or other health issues related to decreased functional capacity [1]. Indeed, functional assessments addresses a range of tests and measures that evaluate various aspects of an individual's functional abilities, including mobility and locomotion, balance and postural control, daily living activities, cognitive function and sensory and motor function. Within this frame, different assessment tools have been proposed and validated including, among the others, TUG, 6-min walk test, Short Physical Performance Battery (SPPB), Berg Balance Scale, Balance Evaluation System Test (BESTest), Instrumental Activities of Daily Living (IADL), Basic Activities of Daily Living (BADL), Mini-Mental State Examination (MMSE), Montreal Cognitive Assessment (MoCA), Sensory Organization Test (SOT), Motor Function Measure (MFM), etc. As previously stated, all these functional assessment approaches are crucial in healthcare as they help identify individuals who may be at risk of falls, present mobility impairments, or other health issues related to decreased functional capacity; they also provide valuable information for healthcare professionals to develop targeted interventions and rehabilitation strategies tailored to an individual's specific needs.

Focusing on the TUG test, usually, the time required to complete the whole sequence of tasks is acquired (i.e., shorter completion time indicate better performance); a time of 10 s or less is generally considered normal, while times between 11 s and 20 s may indicate some degree of mobility impairment, and times above 20 s often suggest a higher risk of falls and the need for further evaluation and intervention. Besides times, during the execution of the TUG test, usually clinicians pay attention also to the identification of any issue related to the standing/sitting, walking and turning phases; in fact, several key functional abilities, including lower extremity strength and function, gait speed stride length, arm swing, and rhythm during the walk, dynamic balance, postural stability, can provide insights into potential neurological or musculoskeletal impairments that may contribute to mobility limitations and fall risk.

While the standard implementation of the TUG test can use a simple stopwatch to time the patient, more advanced technologies have been explored to enhance reliability and provide quantitative information. Besides the use of complex and bulky technologies, which can constrain the overall ecology of the movement (e.g., optoelectronic stereophotogrammetric systems, pressure-sensitive mats, etc.), during the last decade the use of inertial measurement units (IMUs) supported the possibility of having detailed kinematic data on the patient's movements during the TUG, such as velocity, acceleration, and angular velocity [7, 8]. Indeed, IMUs can be easily integrated within wearable solutions, that can be attached to various body locations, such as the trunk, limbs, or feet, to capture detailed kinematic data during the execution of the TUG test [5]. In fact, by incorporating wearable technology, the TUG test can provide a more comprehensive, quantitative and reliable assessment of an individual's functional abilities, potentially leading to earlier identification of mobility issues and more targeted interventions.

Within this frame, the main goal of this work was to design and validate a prototypical wearable solution able to answer the need for remote monitoring of subjects with functional limitations due to specific pathologies (e.g., post-stroke patients) or for the prevention of the risk of falling in the elderly; particular attention was thence given to the need for a reliable quantification of the TUG test.

2 Materials and Methods

2.1 Requirements Definition

Considering the literature, the "best" features of the technologies reported in each identified and analyzed studies were extracted and systematically summarized in order to support the design of a miniaturized wearable actigraph prototype/demonstrator, mainly addressing remote monitoring of subjects with stroke outcomes and elderly individuals at risk of falling. Eventually, we specifically hypothesized that the device should have matched the following technical requirements:

- *Wearability* – In fact, it is crucial that the wearable device did not cause obstruction and remains imperceptible, ensuring that the TUG test was conducted naturally and in the most ecological way, thus most accurately representing the subject's actual motor conditions.
- *Physical proximity to the body center of mass (CoM)* - The wearable device should have placed as close as possible to the CoM, so as to describe its overall kinematic characteristics during the execution of the TUG test.
- *Detection of 3D kinematics* - The device should have been able to acquire both accelerations but also estimation of pelvis orientation angles.
- *On-board recording* – The device should have been able to save the acquired data in a common format (e.g.,.csv) directly on the device flash memory; this approach should have facilitated downloading the data to a PC via USB cable once the test was completed. The maximum recording duration should have been about 3 min per patient with a sampling frequency coherent with the CoM dynamics associated to the TUG test (i.e., above 50 Hz). Further development would have included data transmission.
- *Power Battery* – The device should have integrated a power battery for power supply so as to ensure device wearability and overall autonomy during the execution of several in/outpatient assessment sessions.

In accordance with the above requirements and by studying various prototyping electronic board models available on the technological market, we decided to consider as backbone for developing our wearable solution the tinyTILE device, a miniaturized device of the Arduino/Genuino 101 board associated with the Intel Curie module. The overall characteristics of the designed and implemented prototypes are hereinafter presented.

2.2 Electronic Board Prototype

As previously reported, among all the prototyping electronic boards available on the market, we chose to use the tinyTILE device (Fig. 2 - left), which provided relevant characteristics for the development of our wearable device. In particular, this miniaturized board retained many features of the Arduino/Genuino 101 series, including Bluetooth Low Energy (BLE) capabilities and an integrated 6-axis accelerometer/gyroscope and a magnetometer, and possibility of programming by using the Arduino IDE or Intel Curie Open Developer Kit (CODK); furthermore, the tinyTILE device was ideal for continuous motion monitoring and wireless applications that require minimal power consumption; it housed two small cores, an x86 (Quark) and a 32-bit ARC architecture core, both operating at 32 MHz and includes 14 digital I/O pins with, six analog inputs with 12-bit ADC, 384 kB of flash memory, 80 kB of SRAM, and a microUSB port for serial communication and uploading sketches. The board operated at a voltage of 3.3 V, with built-in protection for all pins against overvoltage. It is worth noting also its CE/FCC certification and the overall reduced dimensions (35 × 26 mm), which enabled its wearability.

A double buffer for writing and reading operations was implemented on the micro-controller, in order to reduce the loss of data acquired during performances; acceleration, angular velocity and orientation information was saved in a separate file for each test in *csv* format considering a sampling rate of 64 Hz. Furthermore, when designing the wearable actigraph, we structured the flash memory as a file system, so as to easily read and download the acquired data.

The power supply was provided to the board by means of a Li-Po battery (600 mAh), which was directly connected to the V_{in} pin of the board itself; furthermore, a battery charger module was connected to the board in order to allow recharging of the battery by means of USB connection. By considering the average duration of the writing/reading phases and the corresponding power consumption, we obtained an overall battery autonomy of about 22 h, which was indeed enough to cover a whole day of TUG test assessment (Fig. 1).

An 3d-printed enclosure was finally realized to contain the prototype so that it can be secured to the patient's waist (i.e., at L5-S1 spine level) by using an elastic band (Fig. 2 - right).

Fig. 1. On the left the *tinyTILE* electronic board; on the right, an example of the placement of the wearable device on the patient's waist by means of an elastic band.

2.3 Experimental Validation and Pilot Testing

The developed prototype was validated and tested in different phases and including 2 different clinical contexts (i.e., San Gerardo Hospital - Monza (MI), Italy and Villa Beretta Hospital - Costa Masnaga (LC), Italy), specifically recruiting healthy subjects and patients with different pathologies (e.g., post stroke, multiple sclerosis, and Parkinson disease, etc.). The protocols for preparing the subject and carrying out the test were kept as simple and non-invasive as possible. In particular, the subject was asked to wear the elastic band containing the device in a special opening; as previously reported, the device was positioned in correspondence with the body's CoM, precisely in the L5/S1 area. The subject started the test sitting on the chair with armrests, in agreement to standard specifications (i.e., seat height approximately 44–47 cm, armrest height approximately 64 cm). After having turned on the device, the subject was asked to realize the test, which – as previously underlined - included getting up, walking for 3 m on a straight path, turning back and sitting down again

All the subjects were instructed about the experimental tests, and they gave their informed consent to the experimentation.

2.4 Data and Statistical Analysis

In all the considered conditions, the test execution time was considered as a comparison parameter; more in detail, the times obtained from the prototype were compared with those obtained manually using the classic digital stopwatch. In particular, after carrying out the three tests for each subject, the device was connected to a PC and the *cvs* files download and saved. A custom routine (Matlab, The Mathworks Inc) was specifically realized to get the information concerning the accelerometer, gyroscope and magnetometer (Fig. 3).

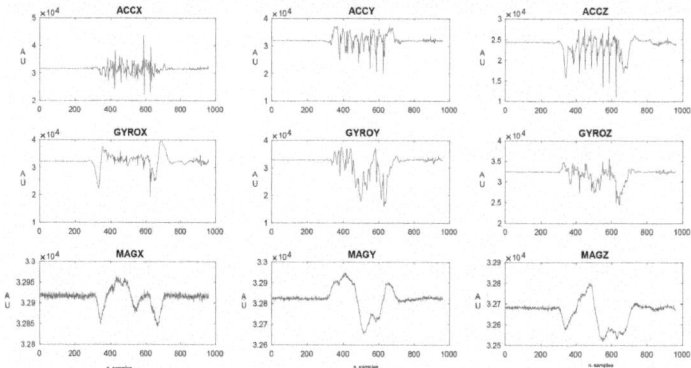

Fig. 2. Example of acceleration (ACC-X,-Y,-Z), angular velocity (GYRO-X,-Y,-Z) and orientation (MAG-X,-Y,-Z) data during the execution of the TUG test.

For the identification of the test start and end events, we specifically focused on Y and Z components of the acceleration and magnetometer data; in fact, the acceleration data allowed to identify each step performed during the test, whereas the magnetometer data allowed to highlight the rotational phases (Fig. 4).

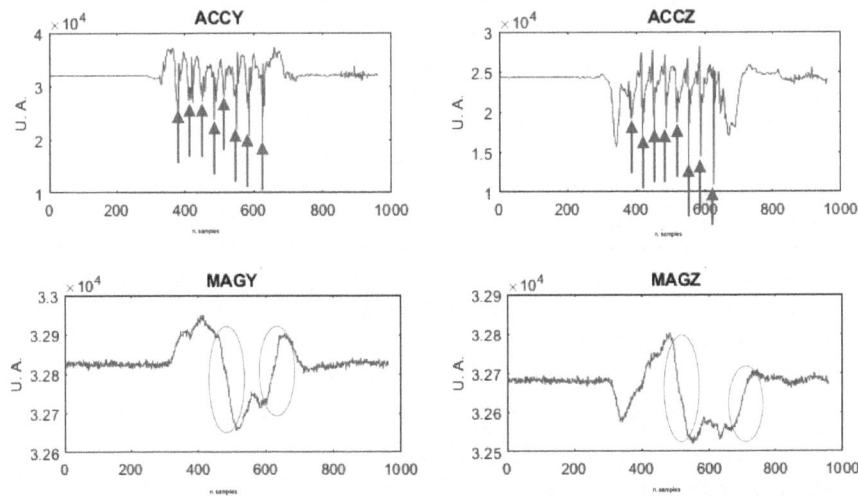

Fig. 3. Example of acceleration (ACC-Y,-Z) and orientation (MAG-Y,-Z) data used to identify the steps performed the TUG test and the corresponding turning phased.

To evaluate the accuracy of the measurements, the relative, absolute and percentage error between the times obtained from the two measurement systems was calculated, taking the stopwatch value as the true measurement. Furthermore, to assess their reliability, the Intraclass Correlation Coefficient (ICC) was used; ICC specifically allowed to establish an existing correlation between two measures belonging to the same group or, in this particular case, an absolute agreement between two different evaluation methods.

3   Results and Discussion

3.1   Validation on Healthy Subjects

The experimental tests were carried out by recruiting 10 healthy subjects with a range of ages between 18 and 63 years old; each of them was asked to take the TUG test 3 times. In Table 1, we reported the times acquired by using the manual stopwatch and the corresponding times estimated by using the proposed wearable device.

The accuracy of the measurement is summarized in Table 2, where, for each subject, we reported the relative, absolute and percentage error related to the differences in the 2 evaluation methods for each one of the three tests.

Focusing on the reliability evaluation, we compared the two evaluation methods by using the Intraclass Correlation Coefficient with a 95% confidence interval; in particular, we noted an excellent agreement in all three tests carried out (Table 3).

Table 1. Times (in s) required to complete the TUG tests acquired by means of a digital stopwatch and estimated by using the proposed wearable device.

Subject ID	Test 1		Test 2		Test 3	
	Stopwatch	Wearable Device	Stopwatch	Wearable Device	Stopwatch	Wearable Device
1	8.48	8.40	7.99	7.85	8.58	8.29
2	7.36	7.33	7.63	7.28	7.95	8.1
3	6.05	5.95	6.95	6.67	6.49	6.53
4	7.22	6.94	6.76	6.64	6.78	6.93
5	7.43	7.92	6.58	6.82	6.76	6.39
6	7.32	7.46	7.42	7.37	7.25	7.11
7	8.25	8.21	7.43	7.57	7.18	7.23
8	7.20	7.24	6.36	6.16	6.10	6.23
9	7.05	6.88	6.90	7.00	6.64	6.55
10	7.85	7.63	7.00	6.96	6.76	6.42

Table 2. Relative, absolute and percentage error between the stopwatch time and the time estimated by using the proposed wearable device for the TUG test; relative and absolute error are reported in s, whereas absolute percentage error in %.

Subject ID	Test 1			Test 2			Test 3		
	Rel. Err	Abs. Err	Abs. Err. %	Rel. Err	Abs. Err	Abs. Err. %	Rel. Err	Abs. Err	Abs. Err. %
1	−0.08	0.08	0.94	−0.14	0.14	1.75	−0.3	0.3	3.49
2	0.37	0.37	5.03	−0.35	0.35	4.59	0.15	0.15	1.89
3	−0.1	0.1	1.65	−0.28	0.28	4.03	0.04	0.04	0.62
4	−0.28	0.28	3.88	−0.12	0.12	1.78	0.15	0.15	2.21
5	0.49	0.49	6.59	0.24	0.24	3.65	−0.37	0.37	5.47
6	0.14	0.14	1.91	−0.05	0.05	0.67	−0.14	0.14	1.93
7	−0.04	0.04	0.48	0.14	0.14	1.88	0.05	0.05	0.70
8	0.04	0.04	0.56	−0.20	0.20	3.14	0.13	0.13	2.13
9	−0.17	0.17	2.41	0.10	0.10	1.45	−0.09	0.09	1.36
10	−0.22	0.22	2.80	−0.04	0.04	0.57	−0.34	0.34	5.03
Mean	0.02	0.19	2.63	−0.07	0.17	2.35	−0.07	0.18	2.48
Std Dev	0.25	0.15	2.01	0.19	0.10	1.41	0.21	0.12	1.68

Table 3. Comparison between stopwatch times and times estimated by using the wearable device, with indication of the Intraclass Correlation Coefficient (ICC).

Test ID	Stopwatch		Wearable Device		ICC
	Mean	Std Dev	Mean	Std Dev	
1	7.42	0.68	7.44	0.72	0.97
2	7.10	0.50	7.03	0.50	0.96
3	7.05	0.74	6.98	0.72	0.98

3.2   Pilot Tests on Patients

The pilot testing of the wearable system was tested on 2 different clinical settings in 2 different days.

First Clinical Setting. In the first setting (San Gerardo Hospital - Monza - MI, Italy), 10 subjects were recruited (7 males and 3 females) with an average age of 61.7 ± 10.4 years old. All the subjects presented different kind of neuropathologies that involved their ability to properly walk; in fact, two patients used their mobility aids (e.g., crutches or a cane) which they were used to use in the everyday life. As highlighted in Fig. 5, the time values estimated by the wearable device are greater than the ones measured by using the stopwatch for every subject, although the differences between the two times are quite small (less than 0.75 s).

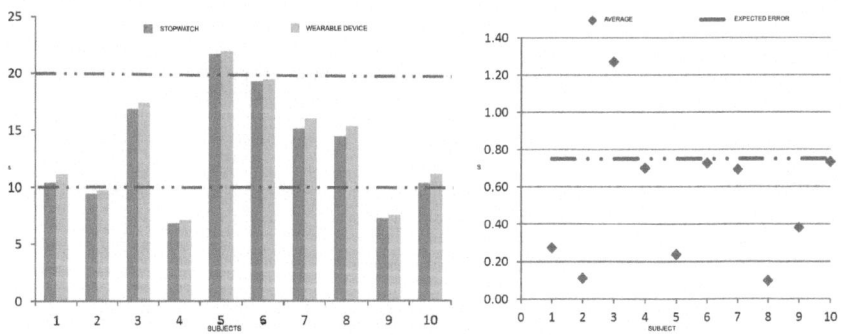

Fig. 4. On left side, the differences between the values acquired by using the stopwatch and that estimated by using the wearable device (dashed red lines highlight the thresholds for healthy subjects [<10 s], frail but autonomous subjects [10 s–20 s] and at high risk of falling [>20 s]); on the right side the average errors for each subject and the expected error.

Analyzing the differences between the two approaches by using Student's t-test for paired data, it resulted to be quite evident that those underestimates were not stochastic but indeed systematic, likely due to the operator's reaction time. The dashed red lines delimit the cut off scores for healthy subjects (<10 s), frail but autonomous subjects (between 10 and 20 s), a high risk of falling (>20 s).

Furthermore, we also analyzed the deviation of the average of the three absolute errors obtained subtracting the time estimated by using the wearable device from the stopwatch time and taking the absolute value, considering it for each subject with respect to the expected error in performing the measurement; this latter was hypothesized to be about 0.25 s, considering the reaction time, on average, for a healthy subject; then, counting this amount for both the beginning and the end of the trial and considering an additional overall 50% of tolerance, we obtained 0.75 s, i.e., the expected error in performing the measurement. As reported in in Fig. 5, all the reported values were within the limits of this error, except for *Subject 3*; in fact, in this particular case the average of the three errors deviates considerably from the expected error, probably due to the presence of tremors during walking due to his specific pathologies (i.e. Parkinson disease). In Table 4, we reported the absolute percentage errors for each of the three tests carried out.

Table 4. Percentage error between the stopwatch time and the time estimated by using the proposed wearable device for the TUG test for the subjects tested in the first clinical pilot.

Subject ID	Test 1	Test 2	Test 3
1	0.08	7.43	0.60
2	2.02	1.87	3.30
3	10.99	1.95	3.09
4	2.09	8.43	4.26
5	0.60	2.57	0.88
6	6.36	1.79	1.04
7	6.27	0.58	5.90
8	2.04	1.62	6.32
9	4.44	3.11	4.76
10	4.72	8.37	7.57

Second Clinical Setting. In the second clinical setting (Villa Beretta - Costa Masnaga – LC, Italy), 12 subjects (4 females and 8 males) with an average age of 60.67 ± 14.27 years old were recruited to test the proposed wearable device. In a different way with respect to the first setting where the patients presented heterogeneous pathologies, in this case all the subjects were reduced by an ischemic event that caused paralysis either of the right or left side of the body; *Subject 6* used his cane during the execution of the TUG test, as it is also used in everyday life as an aid. The times obtained from the two evaluation methods are reported in Fig. 6, as well as the average of the absolute errors compared to the expected error in the measurement, as previously defined.

Analyzing the data, there was an excellent correspondence between the times obtained by the two different procedures; unlike the tests carried out in the first clinical setting, in which the actigraphic times were always greater than the stopwatch ones, in this setting there was no systematic under/overestimation. It is worth noting the values

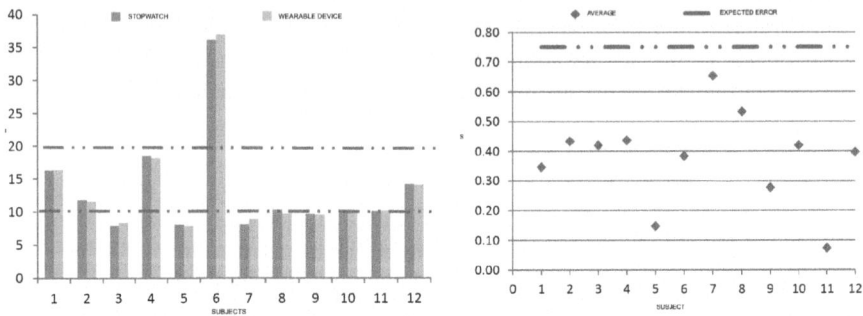

Fig. 5. On left side, the differences between the values acquired by using the stopwatch and that estimated by using the wearable device (dashed red lines highlight the thresholds for healthy subjects [<10 s], frail but autonomous subjects [10 s–20 s] and at high risk of falling [>20 s]); on the right side the average errors for each subject and the expected error.

corresponding to the *Subject 8*, for whom the difference between the time measured with the stopwatch (10.26 s) and that measured with the wearable actigraph (9.71 s) would ideally shift the evaluation from a fragile subject to a healthy subject. Table 5 shows the percentage of the absolute error calculated for each subject in each of the three tests performed.

Table 5. Percentage error between the stopwatch time and the time estimated by using the proposed wearable device for the TUG test for the subjects tested in the first clinical pilot.

Subject ID	Test 1	Test 2	Test 3
1	2.25	1.56	2.15
2	5.66	1.78	2.85
3	6.46	6.60	2.44
4	1.73	2.39	2.82
5	2.21	0.11	2.48
6	0.48	0.31	2.22
7	7.59	4.47	1.30
8	7.52	4.48	3.14
9	0.76	7.28	0.00
10	0.20	7.53	4.14
11	0.69	0.39	1.05
12	0.71	2.41	5.08

4   Conclusions

In the last twenty years, thanks to better socio-economic conditions, a more sustainable lifestyle, and continuous progress in the medical field, we are witnessing a demographic transformation that has been leading to an overall aging of the general population. At the same time, we have made giant strides in the technological field, with the miniaturization of electronic components, the introduction of nanotechnologies, and the cost-effective production of innovative materials. All these technological improvements have been enabling the introduction of reliable tools capable of supporting the evaluation of the functional conditions, even in elderly subjects or those with specific pathologies.

Within this context, this preliminary work aimed to promote the use of wearable technologies to reliably support the diagnosis of pathologies that impact motor function and support their use of remote rehabilitation strategies. The work, specifically focusing on the quantification of the TUG test and exploiting the close relationship with clinical personnel, led to the development of a miniaturized wearable *actigraph* prototype. This device proved to be reliable and in perfect agreement with conventional methods (i.e., stopwatch) in defining the overall TUG duration, with an average percentage absolute error of 3.82%. Furthermore, the average errors were within the error range expected in performing the measurement. Indeed, the presented device was small, not bulky, and easy to use, meeting all the defined requirements.

Possible future steps will involve the introduction of wireless communication interfaces (i.e., Bluetooth) and the development of a mobile app to manage both the acquisition and transmission of the data and patients/sessions management.

References

1. Shumway-Cook, A., Brauer, S., Woollacott, M.: Predicting the probability for falls in community-dwelling older adults using the timed up & go test. Phys. Ther. **80**, 896–903 (2000). https://doi.org/10.1093/ptj/80.9.896
2. Cimolin, V., et al.: Do wearable sensors add meaningful information to the Timed Up and Go test? a study on obese women. J. Electromyogr. Kinesiol. **44**, 78–85 (2019). https://doi.org/10.1016/j.jelekin.2018.12.001
3. Buisseret, F., et al.: Timed up and go and six-minute walking tests with wearable inertial sensor: one step further for the prediction of the risk of fall in elderly nursing home people. Sensors **20**, 3207 (2020). https://doi.org/10.3390/s20113207
4. Hall, M., Perraton, L.G., Stevermer, C.A., Gillette, J.C.: Alterations in medial-lateral postural control after anterior cruciate ligament reconstruction during stair use. Gait Posture **77**, 283–287 (2020). https://doi.org/10.1016/j.gaitpost.2020.02.011
5. Iovanel, G., Ayers, D., Zheng, H.: The role of wearable technology in measuring and supporting patient outcomes following total joint replacement: review of the literature. JMIR Perioper Med. **6**, e39396 (2023). https://doi.org/10.2196/39396
6. Friedrich, B., Lau, S., Elgert, L., Bauer, J.M., Hein, A.: A deep learning approach for TUG and SPPB score prediction of (Pre-) frail older adults on real-life IMU data. Healthcare **9**, 149 (2021). https://doi.org/10.3390/healthcare9020149

7. Kleiner, A.F.R., et al.: Timed Up and Go evaluation with wearable devices: validation in Parkinson's disease. J. Bodyw. Mov. Ther. **22**, 390–395 (2018). https://doi.org/10.1016/j.jbmt.2017.07.006

8. Choi, J., Parker, S.M., Knarr, B.A., Gwon, Y., Youn, J.-H.: Wearable sensor-based prediction model of timed up and go test in older adults. Sensors **21**, 6831 (2021). https://doi.org/10.3390/s21206831

The Effects of the Use of Exoskeletons for Manual Handling on Cognitive Abilities: A Mixed Reality Approach

Alessandro Piol[1]([✉]) [iD], Emilia Scalona[2], Maria Lucia Cavallo[3], Martina Mosso[1], Fatehia Bushara Garma Bushara[1], Gianluca Rossetto[1], Giacomo Valli[3], Noemi Pintori[3], Luca Falciati[3], Debora Brignani[3], Francesco Negro[3], and Nicola Francesco Lopomo[4]

[1] Dipartimento di Ingegneria dell'Informazione, Università degli studi di Brescia, Brescia, Italy
alessandro.piol@unibs.it
[2] Dipartimento di Specialità Medico-Chirurgiche, Scienze Radiologiche e Sanità Pubblica, Università degli Studi di Brescia, Brescia, Italy
[3] Dipartimento di Scienze Cliniche e Sperimentali, Università degli studi di Brescia, Brescia, Italy
[4] Dipartimento di Design, Politecnico di Milano, Milan, Italy

Abstract. Recently, the "Industry 5.0" paradigm has been proposed, thus underlining the need for a "human-centric" approach within the industries and a shift in focus from welfare to the wellbeing of the operator by exploiting enabling technologies, such as exoskeletons. However, the impact of these technologies on cognitive load and motor control – and their interaction - during the execution of working tasks, has not yet been thoroughly analyzed. The present study aims to develop and preliminarily present an integrated tool for the evaluation of the effects induced using exoskeletons on cognitive load. A single participant performed a free-hand cognitive task implemented in a mixed reality (MR) environment and under three different conditions: (1) static condition, (2) while performing a whole-body motor task (i.e., lifting), and (3) while performing the same motor task but with the assistance of a hybrid upper-body exoskeleton. Accuracy data and reaction times were collected for the cognitive task, while whole-body kinematics and kinetics were acquired to assess the motor performance by using wearable inertial measurement unit-based and surface EMG systems. The obtained results highlighted differences in cognitive effort for the realized motor task when performed with or without the exoskeleton; in fact, accuracy decreased and reaction times increased when performing the motor task while using the exoskeleton. This preliminary study resulted promising and allowed to obtain useful hints for gathering multifactorial, quantitative, and reliable information concerning the motor-cognitive interactions while using exoskeletons within specific working environments.

Keywords: Mixed Reality · Exoskeletons · Cognitive Load · Motor Task · Working Environment · Industry 5.0

1 Introduction

In the area of worker health protection, a key consideration concerns the promotion of initiatives to mitigate the risks of injuries and technopathologies. In *Industry 4.0*, and furthermore, in the *Industry 5.0* scenarios, where automation and digitization permeate industrial processes, the topic of preventive measures has seen the emergence of exoskeletons as a key technological intervention [1–4]. Whether active or passive, these exoskeletons are among the most studied solutions to limit the occurrence of disorders or diseases affecting the musculoskeletal system in work environments (WMSD) [5]. Especially in industries where workers are frequently exposed to biomechanical overloads, such as those involving manual handling, exoskeletons have received considerable attention [6].

Although the use of exoskeletons is supposedly aimed at relieving the load on the musculoskeletal system, the body of scientific evidence regarding their biomechanical benefits remains incomplete. In particular, in several occupational tasks - such as those involving the handling of asymmetrical loads - these technological aids may inadvertently amplify the risks associated with WMSDs. This phenomenon could be attributed, at least in part, to their inability to adapt dynamically to the user, task demands, and environmental factors. As a result, such aids may contribute to increased biomechanical strain [7], muscle activation [8], or metabolic expenditure [9]. Moreover, these challenges extend into the cognitive domain, where the employment of exoskeletons can lead to cognitive overload resulting from the alterations introduced by the device at motor control level. This, in turn, could impede the user's proficiency in executing complex movements, potentially increasing the risk to the worker's health [10].

This complex interplay among biomechanical, physiological, and cognitive factors underscores the need for comprehensive investigations. However, existing research often is limited to short-term studies ranging from minutes to hours. Longitudinal examinations spanning weeks or months, crucial for comprehensively understanding the sustainability of exoskeleton benefits and potential drawbacks, are scarce and sporadic. Moreover, such inquiries tend to focus narrowly on aspects related to usability and user acceptance [11].

Considering these gaps, the present study endeavored to fill this void through the proposal of an integrated technological solution (with particular attention to the mixed reality approach) able to delineate the multifaceted effects induced by exoskeleton utilization, with particular interest in the cognitive aspects. Without loss of generality, this study aimed to assess the impact of upper body exoskeletons - designed to augment support for upper limbs and the spine - during manual handling tasks. By examining variables spanning neuromuscular control, kinematics, cognitive performance, and device usability/discomfort, this research seeks to provide a focused understanding of the implications associated with exoskeleton integration in occupational settings.

2 Materials and Methods

2.1 Participants

This preliminary and descriptive analysis included the enrollment of a single healthy volunteer. The subject reported no previous history of neurological disorders or recent orthopedic injuries. The subject was right-handed according to the Edinburgh Handedness Inventory [12]. The subject was instructed about the experimental session and gave his explicit consent to participate in the pilot study.

2.2 Experimental Approach

To assess the impact of an upper body hybrid exoskeleton on both cognitive and motor domains, a cognitive-motor dual task was implemented. Considering the cognitive task, the subject was instructed to perform, while performing the hereinafter-described lifting task, a hands-free cognitive task administered with a commercial mixed reality headset (Hololens 2, Microsoft) and relied on its eye tracking as an assessment tool. On the other side, the participant was directed to execute a motor task, which involved lifting and relocating a box from a designated starting point to a final point. Initially, the task was completed without any assistance and then repeated while wearing a hybrid upper-body exoskeleton (LBE 30, Wearable Robotics).

2.3 Cognitive Task Setup

The cognitive task routine was developed using Unity software for deployment on the Microsoft Hololens 2 (HL) headset. The Microsoft Hololens is a mixed reality device that enables the creation of holograms with which the user can interact. As previously noted, the protocol was designed to assess cognitive performance exclusively utilizing the eye gaze tracking functionality of the HL. The Unity Editor version utilized was 2022.3.9f1, while the third-generation Microsoft Mixed Reality Toolkit (MRTK3) was employed for integration with the HL. A dedicated app enabled wireless connection between the HL and the Unity software, using a local network; the system worked at a frequency of 60 Hz.

The implemented routine comprises multiple trials, each featuring two machine-user interaction scenarios:

1. The first scenario involves a basic attention recall task, requiring the participant to fixate their gaze at the center of the field of view, marked with a cross, within a specified timeframe.
2. The second scenario is cognitively more complex and is performed only if the first one has been successfully completed. It requires the participant to identify a specific target among distractors within a limited timeframe.

Target and distractors appear within 8 fixed, equally spaced placeholders arranged in a circle (5 cm radius) around the fixation cross. The target's position is random and changes with each trial. The target is in the shape of an empty diamond, while the distractors are in the shape of empty squares.

The panel containing the fixation cross and the placeholders, which remain fixed and visible to the user throughout the entire duration of the task, was set at a distance of 70 cm from the physical origin of the HL. The physical origin of the HL was identified as the center of the user's eyes.

Figure 1 depicts the holographic panel as observed by the user during various stages constituting a trial, which was repeated 80 times. More in detail, Fig. 1a represents the rest configuration (RC), which persists for a random duration ranging from 3.5 to 5 s, thereby introducing unpredictability in the initiation time of subsequent stages. Figure 1b and 1c, defined respectively as Yellow Cross Triggerable (YCT) and Rest Cross Triggerable (RCT), depict the phases wherein the fixation cross can be activated by the user; namely, these represent the stages where the participant is required to direct their gaze to the cross within 1.3 s. The cross changes color to yellow and doubles its size for a duration of 0.2 s (YCT) to capture the participant's attention. Upon successfully activating the fixation cross, the target and distractors appear (Fig. 1d) following a random interval ranging from 0.5 to 0.8 s. The target and placeholders are visible for a duration of 0.1 s (Target Appears, TA); subsequently, to successfully conclude the trial, the participant has 2 s to fixate their gaze on the placeholder (Fig. 1e) where the target object was previously located (Target Triggerable, TT). The blank screen (BS) depicted in Fig. 1f indicates the end of the trial to the participant and can be displayed, in any case for a duration of 0.1 s, at two temporal instances: (1) if the participant fails to reach the fixation cross with their gaze within the predetermined time; (2) when the time to reach the placeholder where the target appeared expires. When all 80 trials have been completed, the task stop (TS) panel appears, in which the fixation cross and placeholders turn red.

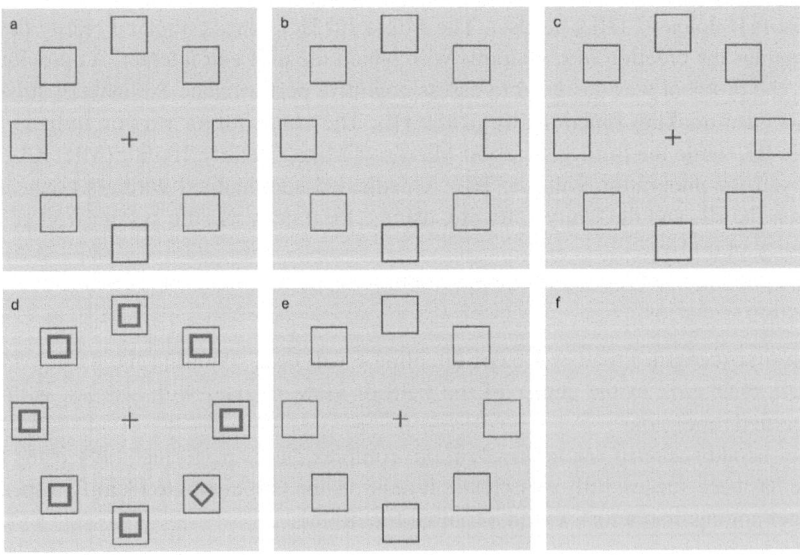

Fig. 1. Holographic panel as observed by the user during various stages of a trial.

Unity employs an object-oriented system in a three-dimensional space and the C# programming language. Figures 2 and 3 illustrate a summary block diagram of the created program, referring to periods and abbreviations defined above.

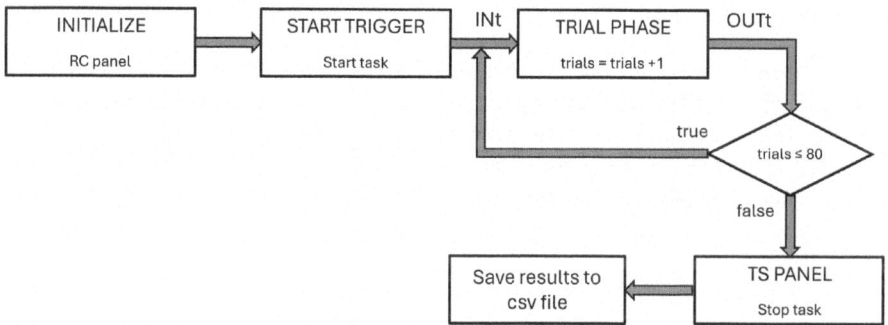

Fig. 2. General flowchart of the Unity program, from the initialization to the results saving. "INt" and "OUTt" labels indicate respectively the input and the output for the "TRIAL PHASE" flowchart block.

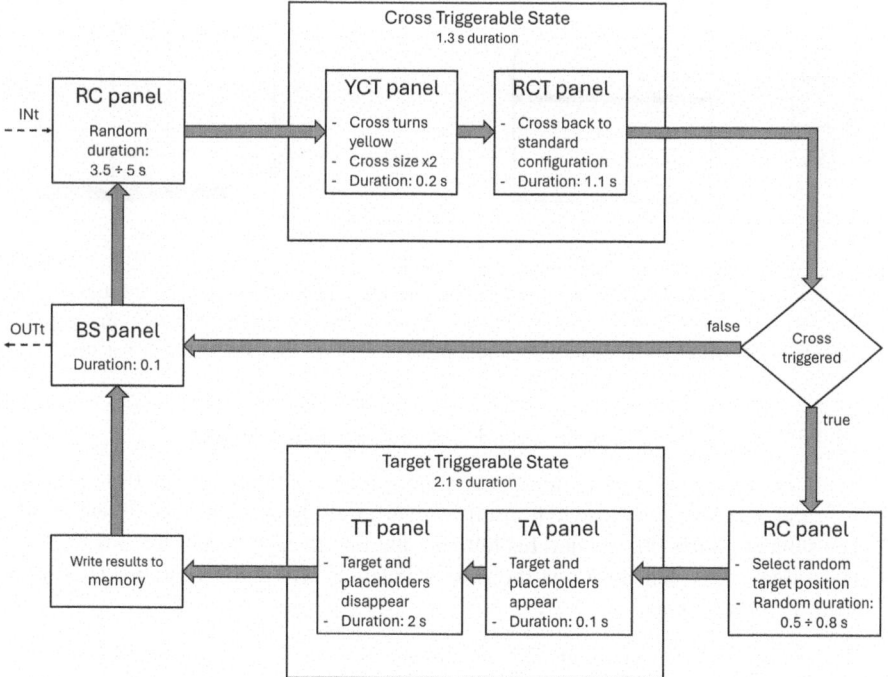

Fig. 3. Specific flowchart for the "TRIAL PHASE" of the Unity program; this step is done in loop for a total of 80 times. Abbreviations refer to those mentioned above. "INt" and "OUTt" labels indicate respectively input and output for the "TRIAL PHASE" flowchart block, as shown in Fig. 2.

Through this method, it was possible to conduct a quantitative and qualitative analysis of the subject's performance, with reference to the completion or non-completion of the aforementioned tasks.

2.4 Motor Task Setup

Starting point "A" was positioned at a height of 95.5 cm above the ground, while endpoint "B" was aligned with the subject's acromion (152 cm) and positioned 90° from point "A" (see Fig. 4). Furthermore, endpoint "B" was set at 86 cm from the subject's acromion, calculated to be 80% of the participant's upper limb length. The box measured 50 × 30 × 30 cm and weighed a constant 5 kg.

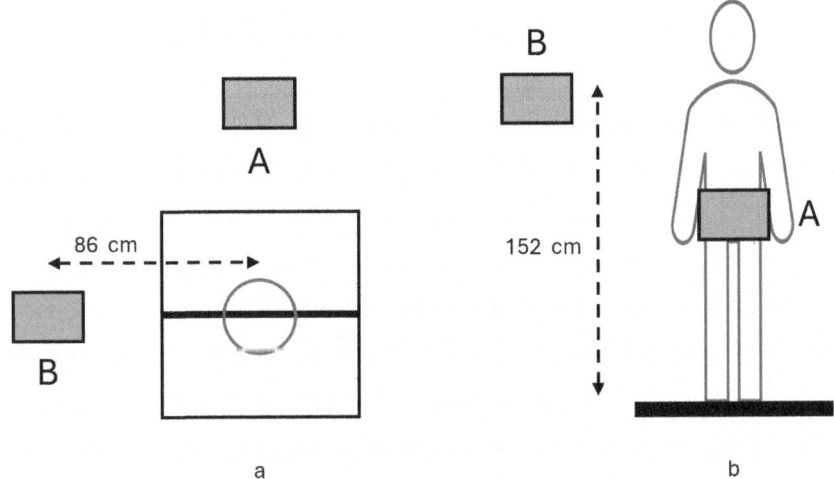

a   b

Fig. 4. Diagram illustrating the positions of the starting and ending points of the motor task, shown from top (a) and lateral (b) perspectives. "A" indicates the starting point, from which the box is picked up, while "B" indicates the endpoint of the movement, where the box is placed.

The motor task resulted in the completion of 3 movement steps:

1. From the resting position (neutral pose), the subject picks up the box from position "A", and then brings it close to himself, with arms along the sides and elbows at 90°.
2. The subject rotates 90°, toward his left, maintaining the position of the box.
3. The subject lifts and positions the box at location "B" and returns to the resting position (neutral pose).

The motor task was conducted in 20-s intervals until the conclusion of the cognitive task. This temporal framework provided the subject with abundant opportunity to complete all steps of the task. Meanwhile, an external operator was relocating the box from position "B" to position "A". This coordinated approach ensured task continuity and facilitated box relocation as required.

2.5 Instrumentation

Motion Tracking. Whole-body kinematics was acquired by using a full-body motion tracking system based on inertial measurement units - IMUs (MVN Link and Biomech Awinda, XSens, The Netherlands). The motion trackers were positioned within the suit according to the protocol required by the manufacturer; in particular, 17 sensors were positioned on the subject to capture the movement of the following 23 body segments, which included the head, neck, eighth and tenth thoracic vertebra, third and fifth lumbar vertebra, right and left shoulder, right and left arm, right and left forearm, right and left hand, pelvis, right and left thigh, right and left shank, right and left foot, and right and left forefoot. Before starting the recording session, a calibration procedure was performed to align the motion trackers to the anatomical segments of the subject. The movement was acquired by using a sampling frequency of 60 Hz. Joint kinematics in terms of joint angles was exported for custom analysis.

In order to synchronize HL and Xsens systems, a cable connection was established; specifically, a trigger signal was configured in Xsens and transmitted to Unity to initiate the routine.

Electromyography. A total of 16 upper-body muscles were selected for EMG acquisition. The acquisition system used is the Cometa MiniWave (Cometa srl, Bareggio - MI, Italy), which employs bipolar sensors with a sampling frequency of 2000 Hz.

To ensure a more precise analysis of the motor task movement, the 16 sensors were strategically positioned on the muscles: right and left anterior deltoid (DA), right and left upper trapezius (UT), right and left posterior deltoid (DP), right and left medial triceps (MT), right and left pectoralis major (PM), right and left biceps brachii (BB), right and left flexor carpi radialis (CR), right and left longissimus dorsi (LD).

Exoskeleton. The exoskeleton utilized in this research was the Wearable Robotics LBE 30 (Wearable Robotics srl, Ghezzano, San Giuliano Terme - PI, Italy). This device is an upper limb hybrid exoskeleton designed to assist the user in shoulder flexion movements. Activation of the force, applied at the wrist level, is initiated by the user through two pressure sensors located on the thumbs. The applied force can be wirelessly adjusted via a smartphone and ranges from 0 to 25 kg. The exoskeleton is programmed to distribute the force evenly between the two upper limbs. For this study, a total force of 5 kg was selected for the task.

2.6 Experimental Protocol

The Experimental Protocol Comprised Three Distinct Tests. During the initial phase, participants were instructed to solely engage in the cognitive task while maintaining a neutral position with their head still (STEADY). This phase aimed to establish a baseline under resting conditions, allowing participants to focus exclusively on the cognitive task. The phase concluded upon the appearance of the TS panel.

In the second phase, participants simultaneously performed both the cognitive and motor tasks with no exoskeleton (NO EXO). Upon the TS panel's appearance, participants completed the ongoing motor task and, upon returning to the neutral position, this phase was deemed complete.

In the third phase, participants simultaneously engaged in cognitive and motor tasks while utilizing the WR exoskeleton (WR). The exoskeleton was activated prior to retrieving the box from position A and deactivated after depositing the box at position B. Like the previous phases, participants concluded the current motor task upon the TS panel's appearance, and, upon returning to the neutral position, this phase was considered concluded.

Figure 5 illustrates the experimental setup (phase with exoskeleton) across three stages of the motor task, namely: the pick-up phase (Fig. 5a), the intermediate phase of moving and lifting the box (Fig. 5b), and the phase of releasing the box to its final position (Fig. 5c).

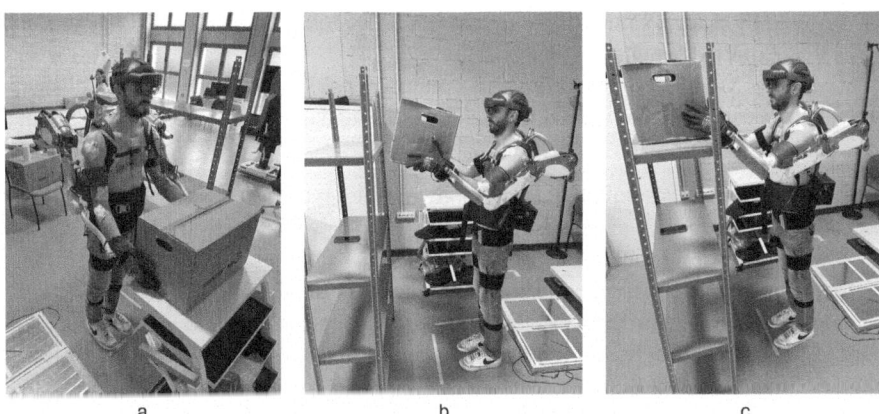

a   b   c

Fig. 5. Motor task executed with exoskeleton in the phases of: picking up (a), lifting (b) and releasing the box (c).

2.7 Data Analysis

The data extracted from the cognitive task indicate the achievement or non-achievement of the goals in the two triggering phases, namely, the fixation cross and target eye gaze positioning within the time limits. Furthermore, in the event of successful triggering, the time taken to activate the trigger event is also recorded. All the aforementioned data were stored in a CSV file, for each of the 80 trials.

Three-dimensional joint angles were extracted from exported files via custom processing and analysis pipeline (Matlab2023a; MathWorks Inc.). The angles of the shoulder joint, elbow joint, wrist joint, and pelvis-T8 were chosen for analysis based on the characteristics of the motor task. The selected temporal period for data analysis extends from the initiation of the cognitive task, triggered by Xsens, to the completion of the final motor task trial.

The acquired raw EMG data were post-processed using Matlab2023a. Specifically, the signal has been filtered (band-pass and notch) in order to suppress undesired noise and interferences, and then rectified. Finally, after obtaining its envelope, the signal was normalized using the maximal voluntary contractions (MVCs), which were acquired prior to the beginning of the motor tasks.

3 Results and Discussion

Table 1 shows the accuracy results obtained for the cognitive task, for the 3 tests, indicating whether the subject successfully hit or missed both the fixation cross and/or the target. Hit/missing percentages are calculated for the cross and the target trigger status; moreover, percentages are calculated for the target hit considering only the trials where they effectively appeared.

Table 1. Accuracy results for the cognitive task, for the 3 tests performed.

	Trigger	Missed (Missed %)	Hit (Hit %)
STEADY	Cross	0 (0%)	80 (100%)
	Target	5 (6.3%)	75 (93.7%)
	Target/Presented	5 (6.3%)	75 (93.7%)
NO EXO	Cross	8 (10%)	72 (90%)
	Target	24 (30%)	56 (70%)
	Target/Presented	16 (22.2%)	56 (77.8%)
WR	Cross	4 (5%)	76 (95%)
	Target	23 (28.8%)	57 (71.2%)
	Target/Presented	19 (25%)	57 (75%)

In the STEADY test, the subject consistently hit the fixation cross without any misses and successfully completed the cognitive trial 93.7% of the time, hitting the final target 75 times out of 80.

During the motor task test with no exoskeleton, the fixation cross was missed 10% of the time, and the cognitive task was successfully completed 70% of the time (56 out of 80 attempts). When considering the accuracy in hitting the target only when it appeared (72 out of 80 times), the completion rate of the cognitive task increased to 77.8%.

In the motor task test with the exoskeleton, there was a 5% miss rate for the fixation cross (4 out of 80), with the cognitive task successfully completed 71.2% of the time. However, when analyzing the percentage of targets hit only when they actually appeared (76 out of 80 times), the percentage of missed targets decreased by 3.3 percentage points (75% hit rate).

These results were as expected; in the STEADY test, the subject had no incentive to miss the fixation cross, as they could maintain focus on it without distraction.

When performing the motor task, the lower error rate for triggering the cross (turquoise color in Table 1) may indicate learning of the cognitive task, as that phase of the task was not overly challenging. Furthermore, comparing the accuracy of hitting the target only when it effectively appeared, it was observed that the success rate decreased by almost 3 percentage points when using the exoskeleton (green color in Table 1).

The average reaction time taken to hit the target was 0.671 s for the STEADY test, 0.691 s for the NO EXO test, and 0.745 s for the WR test.

The results reveal an increase in reaction times with the increase in cognitive difficulty of the tasks. Specifically, there is an observed rise in reaction times in the test with the exoskeleton, indicating a greater cognitive effort exerted during the motor task.

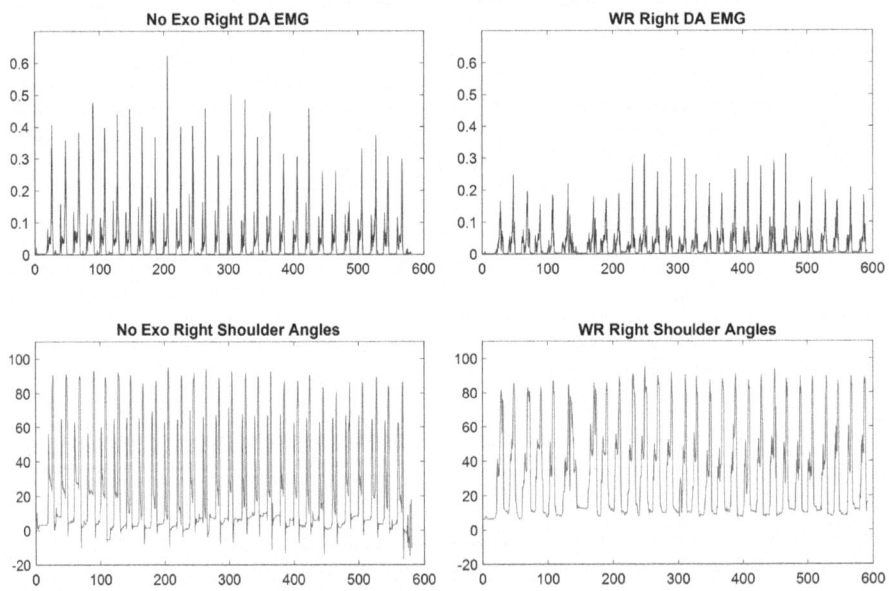

Fig. 6. Muscle activation of the right anterior deltoid (top) and right shoulder flexion-extension angles (bottom) during acquisitions without exoskeleton (left) and with exoskeleton (right).

Figure 6 shows plots for EMG measurements (top) and joint angles (bottom) during acquisitions without exoskeleton (left) and with exoskeleton (right). For simplicity, only the muscle activations of the right DA and the flexion/extension angle of the right shoulder are shown in the figure. For both tests, 28 motor tasks were performed, which is consistent with what was expected. In fact, by observing the signals, the instants of beginning and ending of individual movements can be clearly distinguished. From the perspective of force employed, we observe that the amplitude of the EMG signals is lower in the test using the exoskeleton, indicating reduced force exertion at the shoulder.

Figure 7 provides a detailed view of the DA EMG signals (top) and right shoulder flexion-extension angle (bottom) corresponding to two specific time windows. Specifically, the signals pertain to the 18th motor task for the free-body acquisition and the 16th motor task for the exoskeleton test. The dashed green vertical lines indicate the temporal moment when the fixation cross becomes triggerable by the subject, corresponding to the YCT panel described in the preceding paragraph. On the other hand, the dashed magenta vertical lines indicate the temporal moment when the target and distractors appear (TA panel). The absence of the magenta line in the second cognitive task indicates that the subject failed to trigger the fixation cross within the predetermined time, resulting in the target not appearing.

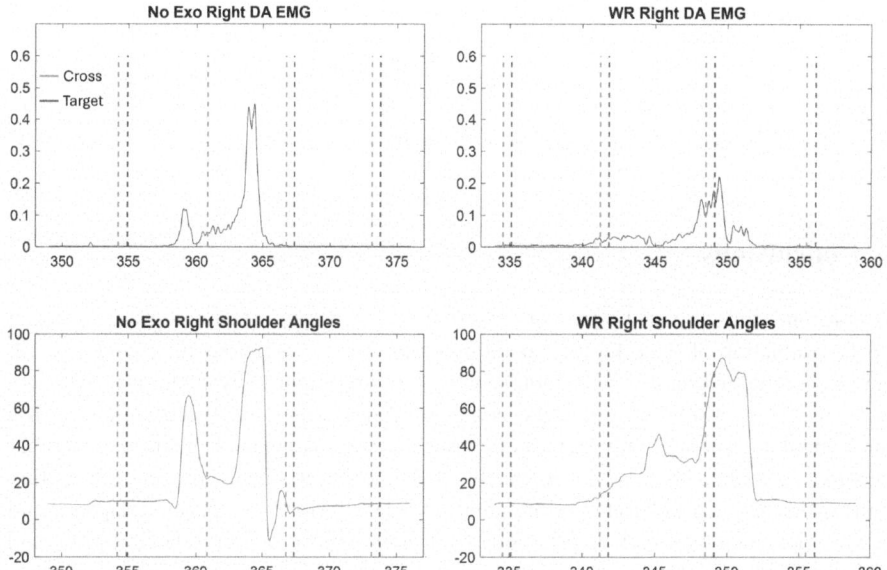

Fig. 7. Diagram illustrating the positions of the starting and ending points of the motor task, shown from top (a) and side (b) perspectives.

Figure 8 displays the same time windows and measurements as Fig. 7, but for the right BB muscle and the right elbow joint.

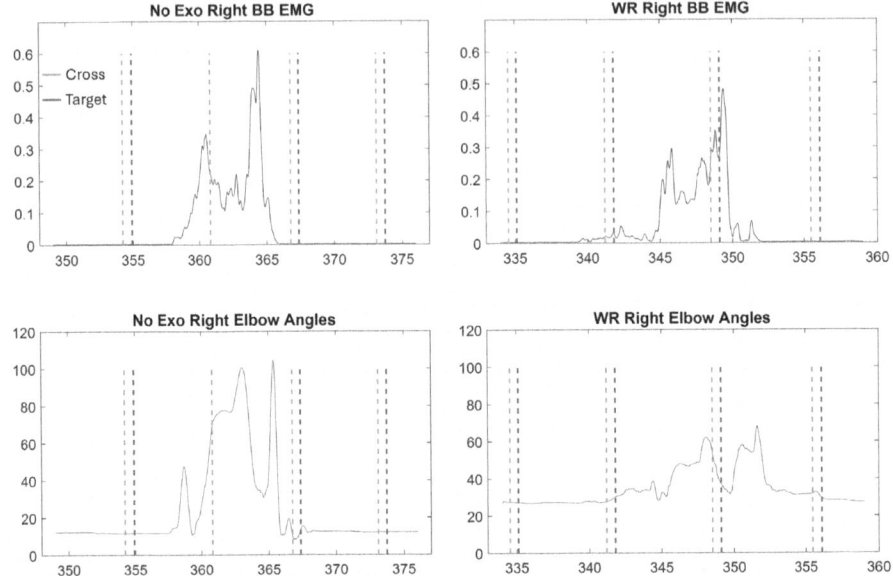

Fig. 8. Diagram illustrating the positions of the starting and ending points of the motor task, shown from top (a) and side (b) perspectives.

4   Conclusions

The present study aimed to present, describe and integrate a technological approach for the evaluation of the effects induced by the use of exoskeletons on cognitive load, and its possible interaction with motor skills. It is important to evaluate how exposure to the use of exoskeletons alters the cognitive abilities of the subject/worker, with a focus on whether this mainly impacts the motor system-dependent functions and other cognitive functions. Moreover, it is possible to define a user-specific process of adapting to the use of the exoskeleton (e.g. the identification of "slow" or "faster" adapters) and then promote an individualized program of learning to prevent work-related injuries and diseases.

From the main findings obtained in this study, learning emerged in one of the components of the cognitive task during the trials conducted while also performing the motor task; specifically, the learning was more pronounced in the less demanding phase of the cognitive task. However, in the more cognitively demanding phase, worse accuracy and reaction times were obtained. This implies that the use of the exoskeleton affects cognitive effort, at least in a short-term period.

Future work will involve extending the experiment to a more significant number of subjects, to obtain statistically valid data.

Acknowledgments. This study was funded by INAIL (Istituto Nazionale per l'Assicurazione contro gli Infortuni sul Lavoro), grant number BRIC 2022, ID-58.

Disclosure of Interests. The authors have no competing interests to declare that are relevant to the content of this article.

References

1. Scalona, E., et al.: Human ergonomic assessment within "industry 5.0" workplace: do standard observational methods correlate with kinematic-based index in reaching tasks? In: Duffy, V.G. (eds.) Digital Human Modeling and Applications in Health, Safety, Ergonomics and Risk Management. HCII 2023. LNCS, vol. 14028. Springer, Cham (2023). https://doi.org/10.1007/978-3-031-35741-1_17
2. Xu, X., Lu, Y., Vogel-Heuser, B., Wang, L.: Industry 4.0 and industry 5.0—inception, conception and perception. J. Manuf. Syst. **61**, 530–535 (2021)
3. Leng, J., et al.: Industry 5.0: prospect and retrospect. J. Manuf. Syst. **65**, 279–295 (2022). https://doi.org/10.1016/j.jmsy.2022.09.017
4. Maddikunta, P.K.R., et al.: Industry 5.0: a survey on enabling technologies and potential applications. J. Ind. Inf. Integr. **26**, 100257 (2022). https://doi.org/10.1016/j.jii.2021.100257
5. Bortolini, M., et al.: Procedia CIRP **72**, 81–86 (2018)
6. Landau, K., et al.: International journal of industrial ergonomics , pp. 561–576 (2008)
7. Weston, E., et al.: Appl. Ergon. **68**, 101–108 (2018)
8. Theurel, J., et al.: Physiological consequences of using an upper limb exoskeleton during manual handling tasks. Appl. Ergon. **67**, 211–217 (2018)
9. Gregorczyk, K.N., et al.: Effects of a lower-body exoskeleton device on metabolic cost and gait biomechanics during load carriage. Ergonomics **53.10**, 1263–1275 (2010)
10. Mudie, K., et al.: Eur. J. Sport Sci. 35–42 (2022)
11. Bar, M., et al.: Appl. Ergon. 103385 (2021). https://doi.org/10.1016/j.apergo.2021.103385
12. Oldfield, R.C.: The assessment and analysis of handedness: the Edinburgh inventory. Neuropsychologia **9**(1), 97–113 (1971)

Systematic Review on Work-Related Musculoskeletal Health Risks in Haemodialysis Nurses

Yu-Chung Tsao[1], Yu-Cheng Pei[2], Kai-Fen Liu[3,4], and Kevin C. Tseng[3,4](✉) iD

[1] Department of Occupational Medicine, Chang Gung Memorial Hospital, Taoyuan, Taiwan, ROC
[2] Department of Physical Medicine and Rehabilitation, Chang Gung Memorial Hospital, Taoyuan, Taiwan, ROC
[3] Department of Industrial Design and Master Program of Innovation and Design, National Taipei University of Technology, Taipei, Taiwan, ROC
ktseng@pddlab.org
[4] Product Design and Development Laboratory, Taoyuan, Taiwan, ROC

Abstract. In Taiwan, there are 364,000 patients suffering from chronic kidney disease, with over 90% of them requiring haemodialysis to sustain their lives due to kidney function failure. However, the substantial demand for haemodialysis care has often resulted in nurses' overwork. The nature of their work, which requires high concentration and puts them under constant high pressure for prolonged periods, significantly impacts the physical and psychological well-being of haemodialysis nurses. Despite this, only a limited number of studies have addressed the health problems caused by their work. Therefore, this study attempts to conduct a systematic literature review to investigate and summarise health problems and risk factors related to musculoskeletal disorders caused by the work of haemodialysis nurses. The study conducted a systematic literature search in PubMed and Web of Science databases, eventually including ten articles for discussion. The systematic review covers topics that may contribute to haemodialysis nurses' health problems and musculoskeletal disorders. Furthermore, the study aims to analyse whether musculoskeletal symptoms among haemodialysis nurses are due to the specific nature of haemodialysis tasks, work intensity, stress, fatigue, and other factors. The research findings indicate that haemodialysis nurses experience significant work-related stress due to their unique responsibilities, labour-intensive and skill-intensive tasks, repetitive nature of their tasks, and improper posture. These factors may lead to musculoskeletal problems, with hand-related musculoskeletal discomfort twice as prevalent in haemodialysis nurses as in other specialities. Musculoskeletal disorders are one of the leading causes of absenteeism among haemodialysis nurses.

Keywords: ergonomics · haemodialysis nurse · musculoskeletal disorders · work-related health problems

V. G. Duffy (Ed.): HCII 2024, LNCS 15376, pp. 308–325, 2025.
https://doi.org/10.1007/978-3-031-76809-5_22

1 Introduction

With medical technology's continuous development and advancement, the average human lifespan has increased significantly. At the same time, as the population ages, the incidence of kidney disease has risen correspondingly [1]. For the majority of patients with end-stage renal disease (ESRD), haemodialysis has become a critical life-sustaining treatment. Due to the availability of appropriate care for these patients, the global number of people undergoing haemodialysis has shown a year-over-year increase. According to statistics, in 2010, 2.62 million people were receiving renal replacement therapy worldwide, and it is projected that by 2030 the demand for dialysis treatment will double [2]. As the global population receiving haemodialysis continues to grow, haemodialysis nurses face increasing professional risks and challenges.

Haemodialysis nurses in their professional careers face multiple risks, one of the most significant being musculoskeletal disorders (MSDs). These risks primarily arise from repetitive hand activities, especially during the priming and dismantling of disposable items and the manipulation of haemodialysis tubing clamps. Prolonged repetitive motions and improper force postures may lead to health conditions such as tendinitis [3] and tendon sheath inflammation [4]. Furthermore, the high technical complexity and intricacy of haemodialysis nursing demand nurses to efficiently perform treatment within specified timeframes. Their primary responsibilities include but are not limited to assisting patients with treatment completion, day-to-day dialysis management, executing safe and evidence-based haemodialysis treatment, dismantling used disposable equipment, and cleaning and disinfecting dialysis machines, other equipment, and surfaces [2]. During haemodialysis sessions, one of the most severe complications is sudden cardiac arrest, requiring nurses to provide continuous care and monitoring for patients. They must adjust treatment lines based on patient conditions to ensure the safe progression of the treatment. Thus, haemodialysis nursing is a highly alert and challenging profession. It poses not only physical health threats to nursing personnel but also the potential accumulation of psychological stress.

Compared to other nursing specialities, haemodialysis patients often face the pain of illness and treatment and even the fear of death. Haemodialysis nurses are constantly exposed to such almost incurably despondent patients and their working environment (such as in enclosed spaces, machine noise, infection risks, etc.), which is believed to lead to long-term stress and tension [1]. Additionally, studies have shown that the repetitive priming and dismantling disposable equipment used for haemodialysis treatment may be a significant factor leading to musculoskeletal disorders in the hands [2]. Haemodialysis nurses repeatedly control treatment tubing clamps during sessions and continuously perform opening and closing actions to facilitate blood circulation and occlusion. Generally, there are four clamps (one large, three small) on the arterial end and three clamps (one large, two small) on the venous end, all requiring long-term repetitive manual manipulation, which may result in tendinitis [3], tenosynovitis [4], and other hazards due to improper force posture or excessive force application.

This study addresses a notable gap in the existing research on the health of haemodialysis nurses, with a particular focus on musculoskeletal disorders (MSDs). While the bulk of previous studies have concentrated on the psychological well-being of nurses, including stress, fatigue, job satisfaction, and their intentions to leave their positions, there is a relative scarcity of research specifically targeting work-related MSDs among haemodialysis nurses [1]. This study sets out to fill this gap by conducting a systematic literature review to identify and analyse various occupational health risk factors that haemodialysis nurses face, especially those that could lead to musculoskeletal disorders. The ultimate goal of this research is to provide a comprehensive summary of these risk factors, which will not only contribute to a better understanding of the occupational health challenges faced by haemodialysis nurses but also support further studies into the psychological risks and work-related musculoskeletal disorders within this profession.

Moreover, future research should consider shifting the focus towards improving medical devices and equipment to reduce the musculoskeletal burden on haemodialysis nurses while performing their duties. For example, developing haemodialysis machine designs that are more ergonomic to reduce the physical strain on nursing staff during operations or researching innovative assistive technologies to help nurses perform haemodialysis treatments more efficiently, thereby reducing the occurrence of work-related MSDs. Implementing these improvement measures can enhance nurses' work efficiency and the quality of patient care and improve nurses' occupational health and overall job satisfaction.

2 Methods

This review was based on the Preferred Reporting Items for Systematic Reviews and Meta-Analyses (PRISMA).

2.1 Search Strategy

The research question, formulated using the PICOS framework (population, intervention, comparison, outcomes, and study design), explores the relationship between haemodialysis nursing staff and work-related musculoskeletal disorders, including relevant influencing factors. The literature search was conducted in PubMed and Web of Science databases, considering studies published until 2023, and was limited to full-text English (Table 1).

2.2 Selection of Articles

In this study, we initially screened articles from designated databases available in full text, excluding duplicates, and ultimately identified 37 articles that met the criteria. We then carefully evaluated the titles and abstracts of these articles to ensure they aligned with the theme and objectives of our research. During the screening process, articles not focusing on haemodialysis nurses, those not working in medical institutions, general home care workers, nursing students, and literature pertaining to haemodialysis patients were excluded. Through this rigorous selection process, 10 articles were finally determined to meet the criteria. Subsequently, we conducted a full-text reading and detailed analysis of these 10 articles. Based on the differences in research content, these articles were divided into two categories: six studies exploring the psychological stress and physiological issues of haemodialysis nurses and four studies focusing solely on physiological aspects (Fig. 1). We provided an overview of these studies presented a detailed organisation and review in Sect. 3.

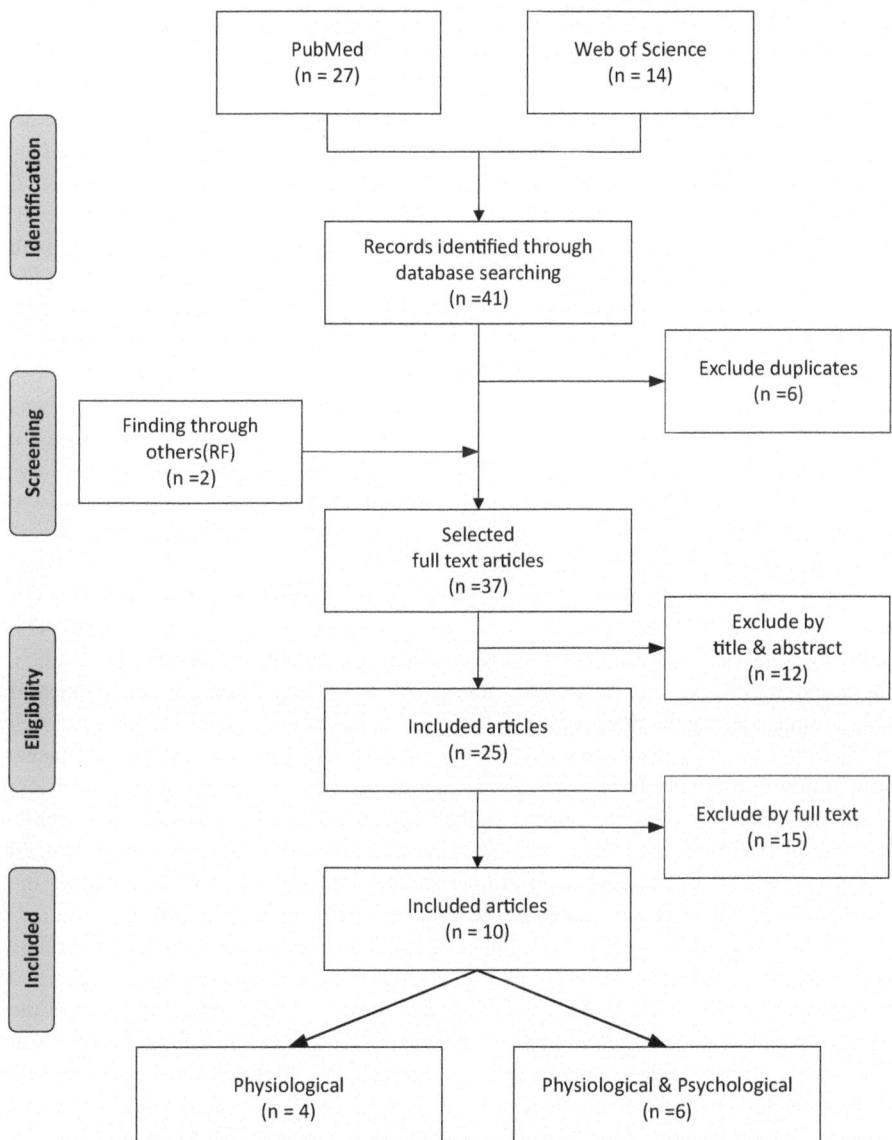

Fig. 1. Flow diagram of the process of identifying and including studies.

3   Result

This study, through a systematic literature review, investigates the psychological and physiological health issues of haemodialysis nursing personnel, ultimately incorporating 10 relevant articles for in-depth analysis. These articles were divided into two main categories: one focusing on physiological factors, and the other involving studies on both physiological and psychological factors. These two categories of research are detailed and summarised in Tables 2 and 3, respectively.

In the physiological factor category, four studies were included (see Table 2). These studies were conducted in Brazil, Sweden, and Denmark, covering research populations of various sizes, ranging from 46 to 545 participants, all of whom were nurses working in haemodialysis units. The research methodologies included cross-sectional, qualitative, and descriptive quantitative studies. Several scholars, including Dissen et al. [5] and Prestes et al. [1], believe that musculoskeletal disorders are the primary reason for absenteeism among haemodialysis nursing staff, mainly due to severe back and leg pain. Westergren et al. [2] found that the incidence of musculoskeletal disorders among haemodialysis nursing staff appears to be higher than that of other nurses, especially concerning hand issues, which directly impacts their absenteeism rate. Notably, these studies discovered that the rate of hand musculoskeletal discomfort among haemodialysis nurses, due to repetitive hand movements in their work, is twice as high as that of hospital nurses and primary health care nurses. This highlights the uniqueness of haemodialysis nursing work and the urgent need for improvements in dialysis equipment and the working environment.

Six articles were identified in the category of studies involving both physiological and psychological factors (see Table 3). These studies originated from China, Germany, France, Serbia, and Australia, with participants ranging from 23 to 10,570. The methodologies primarily included cross-sectional and qualitative descriptive studies. The research indicates that the primary sources of stress for haemodialysis nursing staff include time management, emergency response, and technical tasks, which can often be mitigated through peer support [6]. One study noted that for experienced nurses, compassion or empathy fatigue is a significant cause of occupational burnout; for less experienced nurses, work stress becomes the main issue [7]. Guo et al. [8] found significant regional differences in occupational burnout among haemodialysis nurses, linked to various factors. Burnout was closely associated with several factors, including the atmosphere of the work environment, the stress of night shifts, relationships with colleagues, family burdens such as the number of children, marital status, and whether they had received specialised nurse training [9]. Furthermore, Cao and Chen [10] identified compassion fatigue as the most significant factor leading to the intention to leave the profession among haemodialysis nurses. The level of job engagement and resilience also significantly impacted the tendency to leave. Specifically, higher levels of compassion fatigue and lower levels of resilience and job engagement increased the tendency of haemodialysis nurses to leave their jobs. Additionally, the research found a significant relationship between burnout, depersonalisation among nurses, and their intention to leave. Hayes et al. [11] elucidated that occupational burnout is a significant issue for haemodialysis nurses in Serbia. Despite often being affected by emotional exhaustion, they maintain a high level of empathy and personal achievement. These findings suggest that to improve the working conditions of haemodialysis nurses and reduce occupational burnout, targeted improvements in the work environment, support systems, training opportunities, and adequate attention and support for nurses' mental health are necessary. Moreover, Guo et al. [8] recommend improving the work atmosphere and interpersonal relationships or providing more training opportunities to alleviate occupational burnout. Trbojević-Stanković et al. [7] emphasise the need for targeted strategies to prevent young and inexperienced nurses from feeling burnt out in this highly specialised nursing field.

This study conducted a systematic review in a descriptive manner. Due to the scarcity and difficulty in collecting relevant literature and the inconsistency in research designs and scales used, it was challenging to integrate the data uniformly. Therefore, this study did not adopt a meta-analysis approach. The results of this systematic review underscore the need for future research to focus on the occupational health issues of haemodialysis nursing staff, especially regarding work-related musculoskeletal disorders and psychological stress.

Table 1. PICOS Search Strategy and Keywords

PICOS	Search keywords
P (Patient or Population)	haemodialysis, (OR) haemodialysis, (OR) (dialysis) nurses, (OR) nursing workers
I (Intervention)	musculoskeletal disorders (MSDs), (OR) work-related musculoskeletal disorders (WMSDs), (OR) disease, (OR) discomfort, (OR) complaint, (OR) health problem
C (Comparison)	non-haemodialysis/haemodialysis nurses
O (Outcome)	conditions, (OR) factors
S (Study)	Any primary studies (not set)

Measuring instrument: B-PEM, the Brisbane practice environment measure; CDRS, Connor-Davidson resilience scale; CFS, compassion fatigue scale; COPSOQ, Cross-sectional study with Copenhagen psychosocial questionnaire; JSE, Jefferson scale of empathy; LLP, low level of personal accomplishment background information questionnaire; MBI, Maslach Burnout Inventory; NNS, Nursing Stress Scale; UWES, Utrecht work engagement scale and turnover intention scale.

4 Discussion

This study conducted a systematic review to explore factors that may lead to health problems among haemodialysis nurses, with a focus on both physiological and psychological aspects and their interplay. In Taiwan, nearly 94.3% of nurses believe that incorrect working postures, psychological issues, and shift work or insufficient rest are the main causes of MSDs [14]. The study by Soylar and Ozer [15] also indicates that work-related MSDs are often associated with cumulative trauma and repetitive tasks, such as lifting, transferring or repositioning, prolonged standing, and awkward postures.

The goal of this study was to evaluate work-related health problems and MSDs among haemodialysis nurses. Given the specific and highly specialized nature of haemodialysis

Table 2. Overview of the studies included in the category 'Physiological Factors' (sorted by publication year; abbreviation: HD – haemodialysis)

Year	Title	Author/Country	Study question	Study population/ Return rate/ Sample	Study design/ Instrument	Results and Conclusions
2020	Associations between materials used and work-related musculoskeletal hand complaints among haemodialysis nurses	Westergren et al./Sweden and Denmark [12]	To examine the association between the type of dialysis machine and disposables used with the occurrence of hand complaints among haemodialysis nurses	Haemodialysis nurses 63.4% (282/445)	Cross-sectional study/Nordic musculoskeletal questionnaire	• This study did not reveal any association between the use of disposable materials and the occurrence of hand complaints among HD nurses • A deeper ergonomic analysis of the work environment is needed to understand the prevalence of hand complaints among nurses working in HD settings
2019	Prevalence of musculoskeletal complaints among haemodialysis nurses - a comparison between Danish and Swedish samples	Westergren et al./Sweden and Denmark [2]	To compare the prevalence of musculoskeletal complaints among haemodialysis nurses in Denmark and Sweden	Haemodialysis nurses 545 Denmark 40.2% (194/482) Sweden 64.9% (351/541)	Cross-sectional study/Nordic musculoskeletal questionnaire	• The prevalence of musculoskeletal complaints is higher among HD nurses than among nurses in general. Complaints about the hands are common and are also related to absenteeism from work • Manufacturers of dialysis equipment and nurse managers must recognise these occupational health and safety hazards in their efforts to create a good work environment

(continued)

Table 2. (*continued*)

Year	Title	Author/Country	Study question	Study population/ Return rate/ Sample	Study design/ Instrument	Results and Conclusions
2016	Health problems among nursing workers in a haemodialysis service	Prestes et al./Brazil [1]	To measure work-related health problems among nursing workers at a haemodialysis unit in southern Brazil and associate these issues with the socio-occupational characteristics of the workers	Haemodialysis nurses (haemodialysis unit in southern Brazil) 100% (46/46)	Qualitative study/EADRT (Work-Related Damage Assessment Scale)	• Physical, psychological, and social problems were considered bearable and job satisfaction was associated with current income and work absenteeism for health treatment • Back pain and leg pain were considered severe • There was a direct correlation between health issues • Despite the positive results of the work-related health assessment among the population studied, the results confirm the need to promote the health of nursing workers

(*continued*)

Table 2. (*continued*)

Year	Title	Author/Country	Study question	Study population/ Return rate/ Sample	Study design/ Instrument	Results and Conclusions
2014	Characterisation of absenteeism-disease in nursing workers of a haemodialysis service	Dissen et al./ Brazil [5]	Characterising the absenteeism-disease of nursing staff of a haemodialysis service	Haemodialysis nurses, technicians and nursing assistants 141 medical certificates	Descriptive, retrospective and documental study with a quantitative approach/Self-developed questionnaire	• The predominant causes of absenteeism illness were musculoskeletal disorders, dental and eye care, and mental disorders • Need to evaluate unplanned absences of the nursing staff, as well as the working conditions of this working class, as a resource for relocation or for relocation of workers and consequent improvement of working conditions of the nursing team

Abbreviations: HD, haemodialysis

Table 3. Overview of the studies included in the category 'Physiological & Psychological Factors' (sorted by publication year; abbreviation: HD – haemodialysis).

Year	Title	Author/Country	Study question	Study population/ Return rate/ Sample	Study design/ Instrument	Results and Conclusions
2021	Haemodialysis nurse burnout in 31 provinces in mainland China: A cross-sectional survey	Guo et al./China [8]	To investigate the prevalence and level of job burnout among HD nurses in China and explore the potential factors associated with burnout among HD nurses	Haemodialysis nurses 10,570 surveys	• Cross-sectional survey • Chinese version of the MBI	• There were noticeable regional differences in the burnout of HD nurses • The emotional exhaustion and depersonalisation scores of HD nurses in Northeast China were significantly higher than those of the other three regions • Burnout was substantially and consistently related to the work environment, night shift, relationships with colleagues, number of children, marital status, and specialist nurse training • There is a significant association between depersonalisation and the intention of leaving the HD nurses • These data highlight the importance of the working environment, relationships with colleagues, and specialist nurse training for nurse burnout and have particular implications for recommendations on nurse management

(continued)

Table 3 (*continued*)

Year	Title	Author/Country	Study question	Study population/ Return rate/ Sample	Study design/ Instrument	Results and Conclusions
2021	Relationships between resilience, empathy, compassion fatigue, work engagement and turnover intention in haemodialysis nurses: A cross-sectional study	Cao et al./China [10]	To explore the relationships between resilience, empathy, compassion fatigue, work engagement and turnover intention in Chinese HD nurses	Haemodialysis nurses 90.1% (528/586) Female 480, Male 48	• Cross-sectional study • Two-stage sampling method to recruit • CDRS, JSE, CFS, UWES	• Compassion fatigue is the strongest contributor to intention to leave, followed by work engagement and resilience • HD nurses in tertiary hospitals have higher levels of intention to leave compared to those in secondary hospitals. Higher levels of compassion fatigue and lower levels of resilience and work engagement can result in a higher tendency of intention to leave in HD nurses • It is recommended to develop nursing policies in clinical practice settings, which support the training and continuing education of psychological resilience, stress reduction ability, and clinical competencies in order to alleviate the intention of turnover perceived by HD nurses

(continued)

Table 3. (continued)

Year	Title	Author/Country	Study question	Study population/ Return rate/ Sample	Study design/ Instrument	Results and Conclusions
2016	Empathy and stress in nurses working in haemodialysis: a qualitative Study	Vioulac et al./France [6]	To explore the concepts of empathy and stress in nurses working in HD units in France and their possible interactions	Haemodialysis nurses 23	• A qualitative descriptive study • Semi-structured interviews, investigated, through nurses' discourse	• The special features of nurses' work in HD and the need for further studies • Investigate these concepts. The influence of stress on empathy needs to be explored more precisely, especially with respect to the experience of nurses and its impact on patients • This could provide us with cues to better prepare nurses to work in HD and improve their training. The main stressors that emerged from their speech were time management, emergencies and technical work, which could be modulated by peer support • Empathy prevailed in more experienced HD nurses, while stress prevailed in less experienced nurses

(continued)

Table 3. (*continued*)

Year	Title	Author/Country	Study question	Study population/ Return rate/ Sample	Study design/ Instrument	Results and Conclusions
2015	Work-related factors as predictors of burnout in Serbian nurses working in haemodialysis	Trbojevic´-Stankovic et al./Serbia [7]	To provide an overview of burnout in nurses working in haemodialysis settings in Serbia	Haemodialysis nurses 210	• Cross-sectional descriptive study/ primarily quantitative with a qualitative component • Background information questionnaire/ MBI, Health Services Survey, 7-point Likert scale	• Burnout is a significant issue for nurses who work in HD in Serbia • The HD nurses were highly affected by emotional exhaustion, but still maintained a high level of empathy and a feeling of personal accomplishment • The number of children, the involuntary choice of current position, and the unwillingness to choose the same type of job again were identified as significant predictors of burnout in this population • Identifying and assessment of burnout would allow the implementation of adequate means to reduce it

(*continued*)

Table 3. (*continued*)

Year	Title	Author/Country	Study question	Study population/ Return rate/ Sample	Study design/ Instrument	Results and Conclusions
2015	Work environment, job satisfaction, stress and burnout among haemodialysis nurses	Hayes et al./Australia [11]	To examine the relationships among nurse and work characteristics, job satisfaction, stress, burnout and the work environment of HD nurses	Haemodialysis nurses 417(Australia 396, New Zealand 21)	Cross-sectional online survey/ B-PEM, Index of Work Satisfaction, NNS, MBI, 5-point Likert scale	• HD nurses experienced high levels of burnout even though their work environment was favourable and they had acceptable levels of job satisfaction • Nurses who were older and had worked in HD the longest had higher satisfaction levels, experienced less stress, and lower levels of burnout than younger nurses • Implications for nursing management Targeted strategies are required to retain and avoid burnout in younger and less experienced nurses in this highly specialised field of nursing

(*continued*)

Table 3 (*continued*)

Year	Title	Author/Country	Study question	Study population/ Return rate/ Sample	Study design/ Instrument	Results and Conclusions
2014	Psychological stress and strain on employees in dialysis facilities: a cross-sectional study with the Copenhagen Psychosocial Questionnaire	Kersten et al./Germany [13]	The present study examines the stress and strain currently experienced by the staff of German dialysis facilities	Dialysis staff 55% (367)	COPSOQ • By comparison with other professions in medical care • Nurses and geriatric nurses • Using data recorded in the German COPSOQ database	• For almost all psychosocial aspects, the dialysis staff regarded stress and strain as being more critical than the geriatric nurses • There were some positive differences compared to hospital nursing, including fewer conflicts between work and private life. However, there were also negative differences, such as fewer possibilities to influence the work • Improvement in feedback culture and the emphasis of the superior on greater employee participation and involvement could reduce the stress suffered by dialysis employees, as differences from hospital and geriatric nursing are greater in these areas

Abbreviations: EE, emotional exhaustion; HD, high depersonalization; HEE, high emotional exhaustion.

nursing tasks, nurses need to remain highly vigilant at all times, often interacting with depressed patients and dealing with the negative emotions of family members. Occupational stress, work intensity, burnout, and the unique responsibilities of the haemodialysis unit are major factors influencing musculoskeletal symptoms; and musculoskeletal discomfort directly affects the absenteeism rate of haemodialysis nurses. Ando et al. [16] noted that in a high-pressure and socially unsupported work environment, repetitive motions and improper postures can easily lead to muscle strains, thereby triggering or exacerbating pain. The work of haemodialysis nurses involves operating all equipment related to the dialysis procedure. The study by Westergren et al. [2] found that the infusion and disassembly of disposable items could be an important factor causing MSDs. These operations involve repetitive tasks and improper postures, which may cause acute or cumulative trauma, especially related to hand problems. Indeed, the most common musculoskeletal problems among haemodialysis nurses' absences are related to hand discomfort. This phenomenon is also reflected in clinical observations in hospitals, where nursing staff often complain about the disposable materials used during treatment, such as tubing clamps, which require constant repetitive force, not only increasing the burden on the hands but also potentially leading to long-term discomfort and pain.

These findings highlight the importance of ergonomic design of working conditions and equipment in haemodialysis nursing and suggest the need for further research and improvement measures to reduce the physical burden on nursing staff, enhance work efficiency, and comfort. Studies show that ergonomic interventions can significantly improve the hospital work environment [15]. By establishing ergonomically designed equipment and service processes, reducing musculoskeletal discomfort caused by work, and combining regular and continuous education programs and relevant nursing policies, the clinical skills, psychological resilience, and stress reduction capabilities of haemodialysis nurses can be enhanced.

This study encountered several limitations. Most of the included studies were cross-sectional, which does not allow for a detailed analysis of the causal relationships between different factors. The lack of longitudinal studies limits a deeper understanding of the severity of musculoskeletal symptoms, psychosocial factors, exposure to harmful elements, and the analysis of the work environment. Furthermore, there is a relative scarcity of research globally focused on the health issues of haemodialysis nursing staff, reflecting an urgent need for more studies to address the health issues of nurses amidst the growing demand for haemodialysis services. This gap highlights the importance of not only increasing research in this area but also the necessity of employing diverse study designs, including longitudinal research, to better understand the dynamics and causality of health issues among haemodialysis nurses. Such efforts could contribute significantly to developing targeted interventions and policies aimed at improving the working conditions and health outcomes for these essential healthcare professionals.

5   Conclusion

This study comprehensively reviewed the health challenges faced by haemodialysis nursing staff in the course of their professional duties, particularly at the physiological and psychological levels. This high-tech and labour-intensive job requires nurses to maintain constant vigilance and often comes with significant physiological and psychological stress. Physiologically, MSDs are the main reason for absenteeism among haemodialysis nurses, with hand problems being particularly prominent, closely related to repetitive hand movements in their work. These issues not only exceed those of the general hospital nursing staff, but also directly affect the absenteeism rate of nurses. Psychologically, the main sources of stress for nursing staff include time management, emergency response, and technical operations. Due to the specificity of haemodialysis tasks, nurses need to maintain a high level of empathy in their interactions with depressed patients and their families, which imposes additional psychological stress on them. Studies have indicated that improving the work environment and implementing ergonomic interventions are crucial to reducing the risk of MSDs among nursing staff and improving their mental health. This includes establishing ergonomically designed equipment, improving service processes, providing continuous education, and formulating relevant nursing policies, among other multidimensional measures. These efforts will help enhance the clinical capabilities, psychological resilience and stress reduction abilities of the haemodialysis nursing staff, thereby improving their overall work environment and health status.

Acknowledgements. The author(s) disclosed receipt of the following financial support for the research, authorship, and/or publication of this article: This work was supported in part by the National Science and Technology Council under grant number NSTC 112-2410-H-027-017-MY2 and NSTC 111-2410-H-027-021-MY3, by the Ministry of Science and Technology under grant numbers MOST 109-2410-H-027-003-MY2, MOST 108-2410-H-027-024-MY3, and by Chang Gung Memorial Hospital and the National Taipei University of Technology joint research programme under grant number NTUT-CGMH-110-05, NTUT-CGMH-112-02 and CORPG3I,0141. The funders had no role in the study design, data collection and analysis, decision to publish, or the preparation of the manuscript.

Disclosure of Interests. The authors have no competing interests to declare that are relevant to the content of this article.

References

1. Prestes, F.C., Beck, C.L., Magnago, T.S., Silva, R.M., Coelho, A.P.: Health problems among nursing workers in a haemodialysis service. Rev. Gaucha Enferm. **37**, e50759 (2016)
2. Westergren, E., Ludvigsen, M.S., Lindberg, M.: Prevalence of musculoskeletal complaints among haemodialysis nurses – a comparison between Danish and Swedish samples. Int. J. Occupat. Safety Ergon. 896–901 (2019)
3. Liu, C.-S.: Occupational tendinitis recognition reference guidelines. In: Ministry of Labor and Occupational Safety and Health Administration (ed.), pp. 1–24. Ministry of Labor and Occupational Safety and Health Administration, Taipei (2017)
4. Liu, C.-S.: Occupational tenosynovitis recognition reference guidelines. In: Ministry of Labor and Occupational Safety and Health Administration (ed.). Ministry of Labor and Occupational Safety and Health Administration,, Taipei (2017)
5. Dissen, C.M., Beck, C.L.C., Prestes, F.C., Freitas, N.Q., Coelho, A.P.F., Sangoi, T.P.: Characterization of absenteeism-disease in nursing workers of a hemodialysis service. J. Nurs. UFPE Online **8**, 272–278 (2014)
6. Vioulac, C., Aubree, C., Massy, Z.A., Untas, A.: Empathy and stress in nurses working in haemodialysis: a qualitative study. J. Adv. Nurs. **72**, 1075–1085 (2016)

7. Trbojević-Stanković, J., Stojimirović, B., Soldatović, I., Petrović, D., Nešić, D., Simić, S.: Work-related factors as predictors of burnout in Serbian nurses working in hemodialysis. Nephrol. Nurs. J. **42**, 553–562 (2015)
8. Guo, W., et al.: Hemodialysis nurse burnout in 31 provinces in mainland China: a cross-sectional survey. Hemodial. Int. **25**, 348–360 (2021)
9. EunJin, R., Eun, C.S.: Effects of emotional labor, compassion fatigue and occupational stress on the somatization of nurses in hemodialysis units. Korean J. Occupat. Health Nurs. **26**, 65–73 (2017)
10. Cao, X., Chen, L.: Relationships between resilience, empathy, compassion fatigue, work engagement and turnover intention in haemodialysis nurses: a cross-sectional study. J. Nurs. Manag. **29**, 1054–1063 (2021)
11. Hayes, B., Douglas, C., Bonner, A.: Work environment, job satisfaction, stress and burnout among haemodialysis nurses. J. Nurs. Manag. **23**, 588–598 (2015)
12. Westergren, E., Ludvigsen, M.S., Lindberg, M.: Associations between materials used and work-related musculoskeletal hand complaints among haemodialysis nurses. J. Ren. Care **46**, 185–192 (2020)
13. Kersten, M., Kozak, A., Wendeler, D., Paderow, L., Nübling, M., Nienhaus, A.: Psychological stress and strain on employees in dialysis facilities: a cross-sectional study with the Copenhagen Psychosocial Questionnaire. J. Occupat. Med. Toxicol. **9** (2014)
14. Chung, Y.-C., et al.: Risk of musculoskeletal disorder among Taiwanese nurses cohort: a nationwide population-based study. BMC Musculoskelet. Disord. **14**, 144 (2013)
15. Soylar, P., Ozer, A.: Evaluation of the prevalence of musculoskeletal disorders in nurses: a systematic review. Med. Sci. **7**, 479–485 (2018)
16. Ando, S., et al.: Associations of self estimated workloads with musculoskeletal symptoms among hospital nurses. Occup. Environ. Med. **57**, 211–216 (2000)

Evaluation of Operating Comfort of Biological Microscopes

Yong Wang[1], Tianmei Zhang[1], and Jiubin Tan[2(✉)]

[1] School of Architecture and Design, Harbin Institute of Technology, Harbin 150001, China
{wangyong77,zhangtianmei}@hit.edu.cn
[2] School of Instrumentation Science and Engineering, Harbin Institute of Technology, Harbin 150001, China
jbtan@hit.edu.cn

Abstract. The operating comfort of biological microscopes is directly related to the operators' health and the accuracy of observation results. In this paper, the neck and arm comfort of biological microscope operators was researched. Firstly, the evaluation experiments included two parts: one was the evaluation of operating comfort for the neck and shoulder, the other was for the arm. The surface electromyography (sEMG) data of the measured muscles such as the splenius capitis, sternocleidomastoid, trapezius, flexor carpi and brachioradialis were acquired within the range of 0–40° neck angle and 90–150° elbow angle. In addition, the rating of perceived exertion (RPE) of operators was taken as the subjective evaluation results for different operating postures. Secondly, the root mean square (RMS) data of different subjects' sEMG were normalized to the corresponding RMS of 20%MVC. It can be seen that the load of the splenius capitis, sternocleidomastoid and trapezius all increased with the increase of the head bow angle, and the load of measured muscles reached the maximum in 35–45°. And when the angle between the forearm and the upper arm was 115–125°, the load on the flexor carpi radialis, brachioradialis and trapezius was minimal. Finally, the ANOVA statistical analysis was proceeded to the RMS data of the measured muscles. It was found that the load of the splenius capitis and sternocleidomastoid was positively correlated with the bow angle, and the load range was 4%–30%MVC.

Keywords: Biological Microscope · Operating Comfort · Operating Posture

1 Introduction

The long-time operation, uncomfortable sitting position and complex operation process bring the operators of professional biological microscopes excessive load on the neck, shoulder and arm muscles, resulting in a certain musculoskeletal fatigue, pain and even injury [1–3]. Furthermore, the observation results are easily biased due to the operating discomfort. Therefore, the operating comfort of biological microscopes is directly related to the operators' health and the accuracy of the observation results. The microscope designers in China tend to focus more on improving the performance of the instrument, while neglecting the comfort, efficiency and amenity of the instruments.

Although many scholars have done the corresponding research on the human-machine interaction relationship about microscopes, the research on the operating comfort of microscopes is still not clear.

Since the 1990s, some scholars have done the ergonomics research on the microscope and workstation. James of Duke University conducted a survey on the comfort of cytopathology employees in microscope operation, and finally determined the uncomfortable aspects of microscope and workstation [4]. Therefore, he proposed the improvement methods of human-machine microscope, that is the height and angle of eyepiece can be adjusted, and the arm bracket can be added. James subsequently conducted a comparative study between ordinary microscope and ergonomics microscope. Results show that the ergonomics microscope was significantly more comfortable than ordinary microscope [5].

J. Sillanpaa et al. of the University of Tampere in Finland proposed that a microscope with head support was in line with ergonomics. The support can balance the head weight when operator was observing the eyepiece, and keep the head in the proper position, thus the pressure of neck muscles was alleviated [6, 7]. Kreczy designed forearm support, microscope accessory, and the ergonomics lift chair to reach the ideal man-machine model [8]. Ananth Vijendren et al. designed a pose support chair which was used to match the microscope of otolaryngology surgery to delay the fatigue feeling of the neck [9].

The famous designers and manufacturers of optical product such as Zeiss, Leica, and Olympus have carried out ergonomic research on the efficiency and comfort of microscope operation. In 2007, Zeiss began to develop the most ergonomic laboratory microscope. The ergonomics criteria for microscopes were screened by evaluating several categories of products. Based on these, an ergonomic microscope with adjustable eyepiece height and angle was developed to ensure that the user could work comfortably in a reasonable posture [10]. To the laser scanning confocal microscope and other advanced instrument products, Leica designed the novel handwheel to realize remote control, and satisfy the operators' collaborative demand about microscope usage and control software. In order to meet the needs of relieving the daily fatigue of microscope operation, Olympus BX46 ergonomic microscope series took the double-side eyepiece with lifting, stretching, tilt and other adjustment functions, which can help operators reduce the operating fatigue in more comfortable posture.

In conclusion, United States and Europe pay more attention to the study of microscope ergonomics. Relevant scholars and institutions conducted human-machine relationship research on the operating comfort and efficiency of microscope users, and improve the operating comfort by adjusting the height and angle of eyepieces, knobs position, liftable chair, and adding supporting accessories. Zeiss proposed the corresponding design principles for human-machine microscopes. However, It can't be found that the methods and details were used to evaluate comfort of operating microscope, there were no corresponding evaluation standard and theory for the design of human-machine microscope. In China, the research of microscopic instruments did not focus on the study of ergonomics, and the research framework of ergonomics system of microscopic instruments has not been established. So, the neck and arm comfort evaluation of operating the biological microscope is researched including evaluation method and measurement data analysis in this paper.

2 Experiment

2.1 Design

Experiment 1. Comfort evaluation experiment for the neck and shoulder.
The main purpose of the first experiment was to find out the relationship between the load of the measured muscle of neck and shoulder and operating posture angle by the measurement and analysis of sEMG signal, and propose the objective and subjective evaluation method of the operation comfort, and provide the evaluation results. When the human operated the microscope, the neck mainly did flexion and extension. Considering the neck motion range of the microscope operator from -5–$45°$ and the difference of individual posture, the head bow angle was set to three levels: -5–$5°$, 15–$25°$ and 35–$45°$, as shown in Fig. 1.

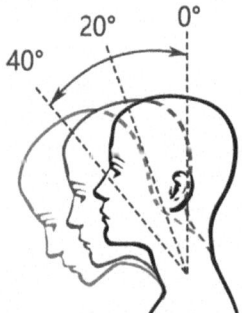

Fig. 1. Head bow angle in neck comfort evaluation experiment

Due to the change of neck joint angle, the different measured postures had distinct effects on the load of the measured muscles. The measured muscles included splenius, sternocleidomastoid and trapezius, the experimental period was 5 min. After the experiment, the subjects evaluated the comfort of neck and shoulder in each operating posture, and scored RPE.

Experiment 2. Comfort evaluation experiment for the arm.
This main purpose of the second experiment was find out the relationship between the load of the measured arm muscle and elbow joint angle by the measurement and analysis of sEMG signal, and combined with the operators' subjective evaluation RPE, evaluation results of arm operation comfort were acquired.

When human operated the microscope, the arm movement was mainly reflected in the angle change of the operator's elbow joint and the support position change on the operating table. The angle between the elbow joint and the operating microscope was 90–$150°$, the angle of the elbow joint was set to three levels: 85–$95°$, 115–$125°$, and

145–155°. The support parts are forearm (point), forearm (full), and wrist, as shown in Fig. 2. The load of the measured muscles was distinct in different arm postures. The measured muscle included the flexor carpi, brachioradialis and trapezius, and the experiment period was 5 min. After the experiment, the subjects were asked to score RPE to evaluate the arm comfort in each operating posture.

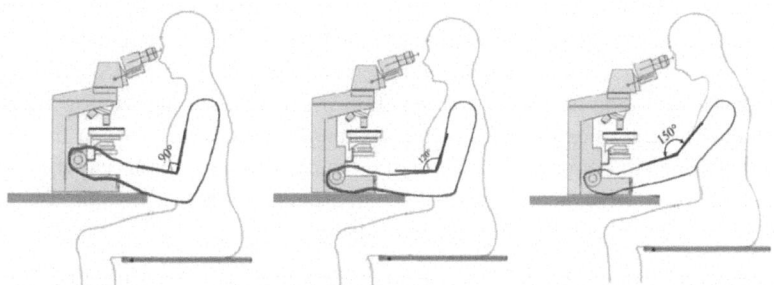

Fig. 2. Elbow joint angle in arm comfort evaluation experiment

2.2 Subjects

Experiment 1 consisted of 18 persons and experiment 2 consisted of 12 persons. Each experiment respectively chose P_5 percentile of women height as lower limit, P_{95} percentile of man height as upper limit, so that the test data for the microscope eyepiece height and location design of adjusting knob. The informed consent was obtained from all subjects. The subjects had no musculoskeletal diseases and sensitive skin. The subjects did not do excessive exercise for 24 h before the experiment, and the relevant experiment manipulations were carried out after they were familiar with the experiment requirements and methods.

2.3 Measurement

SEMG of Measured Muscles

Measured Muscle of Neck and Should. Human neck muscles are complicatedly distributed, and splenius capitis, sternocleidomastoid and trapezius were selected as the main research objects. Because the action of operating microscope was bilateral and symmetry, so the unilateral three muscles of measured subjects were sampled.

Measured Muscle of Arm. The arm muscles played a major role in the microscope operation including flexor carpi radialis, brachioradialis, and trapezius. The flexor carpi radialis is responsible for elbow flexion and internal rotation of the upper arm. The brachioradialis muscle is located in the most lateral subcutaneous of the forearm, and to bring the upper arm forward. The flexor carpi, brachioradialis and trapezius were choosing as measured muscle.

SEMG Signal Processing. A 16-channel multichannel physiological recorder (MP150, Biopac Systems) was used for data acquisition. A DA100C universal amplifier was used for gain setting and offset adjustment.

The frequency range of sEMG signals of human muscles was 8–500 Hz. Due to the influence of noise, the collected sEMG signals need to be filtered. In this paper, the filtering was carried out in the AcqKnowledge 4.2 of Biopac multi-channel physiological instrument. The FIR filter was used with low-pass cut-off frequency of 450 Hz and high-pass cut-off frequency of 10 Hz. The IIR band stop filter with a cutoff frequency of 50 Hz was used to remove the power frequency interference signal. For the RMS of sEMG data processing, the sampling frequency was set 1000 Hz, and the sliding window was taken 10 s to move average. For the sake of the comparative analysis between the groups, sEMG signals need to be further standardizing (Normalization). In this experiment, the individual measured RMS need to normalized to the corresponding RMS of 20% MVC, and EMG% was calculated for subsequent analysis.

Neck Angle and Elbow Angle. The operating postures were measured by Qualisys motion capture system from Sweden. The feature points were arranged on the body of the microscope operators such as head, shoulder, upper arm, forearm decorate, used to provide location information.

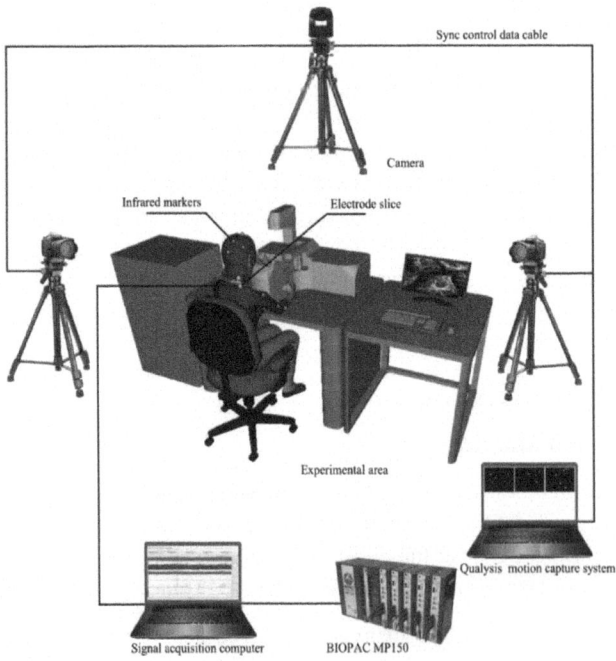

Fig. 3. sEMG system of Biopac and motion capture system of Qualysis

The location information was collected by cameras, and at least two cameras should be used to capture each feature point at the same time during the experiment. When operating the microscope, the head movement of the operator is mainly flexion and extension movement, and the motion range is limited. In the experiments, three cameras were selected to be arranged around the operator, as shown in Fig. 3. The coordinates of the feature points were used to finally obtain the attitude angles which were calculated by the angle algorithm of neck and elbow joint.

MVC of Measured Muscle. Zhiqu HP-100 digital push-pull dynamometer was used, range 100N, accuracy ±1%, real-time display test curve, and record data for detailed analysis. The rigid support is fixed horizontally on the wall surface, and the dynamometer and support are connected by screws.

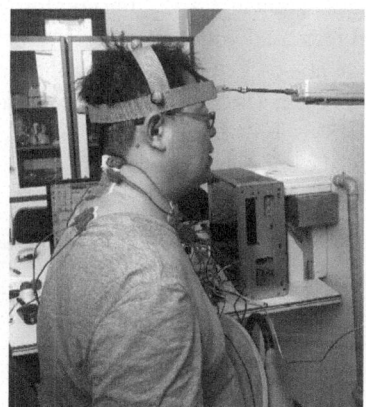

Fig. 4. MVC measurement of neck muscles

The maximal voluntary contraction (MVC) was defined as the peak value of the amplitude of the electromyography signal corresponding to the maximum peak contraction force of the measured muscle [11, 12]. Human electromyographic signal was not stable, influenced by multiple factors such as the quality of electrode, muscle state, and different subjects will produce certain difference, the results need to be standardized.

First, the maximum voluntary contraction force MVC of each part of the neck and arm muscles of the subjects was measured. Each action lasted 10s and was repeated for 3 times, with a rest of 5 min each time. Then, the EMG signal of the measured muscle at 20%MVC was tested, and the subjects were instructed to exert force according to different measurement actions. After reaching the value of 20%MVC, the EMG signal was maintained for 10s, and the EMG signal was recorded at this time. EMG% is used to represent the ratio of measured data. The test method is as described previously, and the test experiments are shown in Fig. 4.

3 Results and Discussion

3.1 Statistical Analysis of Neck-Shoulder Comfort Evaluation

EMG% of Neck Muscles. Firstly, the load of the measured muscles of 18 subjects in the neck comfort of experiment 1 was analyzed. The collected EMG data including the maximum muscle force MVC data were preprocessed and then the RMS data in the time domain were processed. The feature points of data were collected to calculate the head bow angle.

Figure 5 shows the histogram of the mean load of the neck and shoulder muscles. The mean load of the splenius capitis increased with the increase of the angle of head bow. EMG% at 15–25° increased by 9.4% compared with that at −5–5°, EMG% at 35–45° increased by 17.8% compared with that at 15–25°, indicating that the load of the splenius capitis changed significantly at 35–45°, the comfort is decreased; The average load of sternocleidomastoid increased with the increase of head bow angle. EMG% at 15–25° was 4.2% higher than at −5–5°, EMG% at 35–45° was 12.9% higher than that at 15–25°, the comfort is decreased; The EMG% of trapezius at 15–25° and −5−5° was nearly equal, EMG% at 35–45° is 4.3% larger than at 15–25°, indicating trapezius load in 35–45°changes obviously, the comfort is decreased.

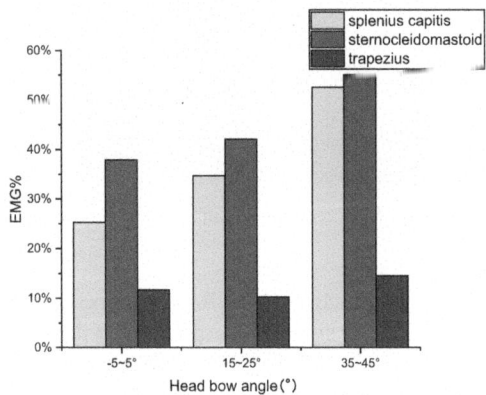

Fig. 5. EMG% of neck muscles

ANOVA of EMG% for Neck-Shoulder Muscles. Table 1 shows the results of one-way ANOVA and trend test. The results show that under different posture levels, the splenius capitis muscle $p = 0.0001 < 0.01$, the difference is extremely significant. Trapezius $p = 0.092, 0.05 < p < 0.10$, there was a trend of difference; Sternocleidomastoid muscle $p = 0.014 < 0.05$, the difference was significant. It can be considered that the EMG amplitudes of neck and shoulder muscles are different under different microscope operating postures. Statistical significance: $p < 0.01$, the difference was extremely significant (**); $p < 0.05$, the difference was significant (*); $0.05 < p < 0.10$, there are differences in trends (+); $p > 0.1$, no difference (++).

Table 1. ANOVA for EMG% of neck muscles measured

Measured muscles		Quadratic sum	DOF	RMS	F	significance
splenius capitis	interblock	0.691	2	0.346	25.707	0.001[**]
	intraclass	0.685	51	0.013		
	total	1.376	53			
trapezius	interblock	0.017	2	0.008	2.496	0.092[+]
	intraclass	0.173	51	0.003		
	total	0.189	53			
sternocleidomastoid	interblock	0.288	2	0.144	4.639	0.014[*]
	intraclass	1.582	51	0.031		
	total	1.870	53			

Subjective Evaluation of Neck and Shoulder Comfort. The subjective comfort questionnaire of 18 subjects was collected, and the neck comfort corresponding to the three levels of neck flexion angles was divided into the front of the neck, the back of the neck and the shoulder respectively for RPE scores. Then the scores of 18 subjects were averaged, and the evaluation results were shown in Table 2. From the average RPE value of the neck evaluation site, it can be seen that the score of the posterior neck muscle is the highest, and the score of the anterior neck and shoulder is equivalent. From the neck curved Angle of 35–45° RPE scored the highest, lowest scoring - 5 - 5°.

Table 2. RPE subjective evaluation results of neck comfort

Evaluation part	Head bow angle			
	−5~5°	15~25°	35~45°	Mean
Neck front	1.3	2.4	4.2	2.63
Neck back	1.7	3.1	5.5	3.43
Shoulder	2.1	1.9	3.8	2.6
Mean	1.7	2.46	4.5	—

3.2 Statistical Analysis of Arm Comfort Evaluation

EMG% of Arm Muscles. In experiment 2, the EMG data of 12 subjects' arm flexor carpi radialis, brachioradialis and trapezius, including the maximum muscle force MVC data, were processed.

The measured RMS data of flexor carpi radialis, brachioradialis and trapezius need to be normalized. Because the arm muscle load is unchanged during the microscope

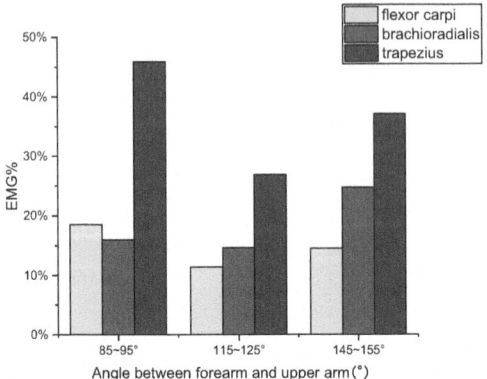

Fig. 6. EMG% of arm muscles

operation, it is a static isometric contraction, so the difference between the maximum muscle force MVC is large. In order to reduce the error, the measured RMS data are normalized to the corresponding amplitude of 20%MVC. Figure 6 shows the EMG% statistical plot of the arm muscles at the three levels at three arm postures.

ANOVA of EMG% for Arm Muscles. Table 3 shows the results of ANOVA for EMG% of arm muscle measured. The results show that the significance of the flexor carpi radialis and brachioradialis muscles in different posture levels is p < 0.01. Therefore, it is considered that the difference of EMG amplitude in different arm postures is extremely significant, while trapezius muscle is p > 0.1, and the difference is not significant.

Table 3. ANOVA for EMG% of arm muscle measured

Measured muscles		Quadratic sum	DOF	RMS	F	significance
flexor carpi	interblock	0.031	2	0.016	5.813	0.007[**]
	intraclass	0.088	33	0.003		
	total	0.119	35			
brachioradialis	interblock	0.072	2	0.036	8.799	0.001[**]
	intraclass	0.135	33	0.004		
	total	0.207	35			
trapezius	interblock	0.218	2	0.109	1.625	0.212[++]
	intraclass	2.208	33	0.067		
	total	2.426	35			

The muscle to be measured in the radial side of the forearm wrist muscle and the humerus was extremely remarkable differences between radial muscle, trapezius muscle was not significant. The forearm had the smallest mean RMS value in posture 2 (horizontal), the flexor carpi radialis and trapezius had the largest mean RMS value in posture 1(forearm upward lift), and the brachioradialis had the largest RMS value in posture 3 (cantilever wrist support). In the third horizontal cantilever wrist support, the microscope operator need to balance more arm weight, and the scapula spine need to be lifted when the horizontal forearm was raised in the first posture, that was, there was a trend of shrug. However, when the arm was placed horizontally in the second posture, the shoulder was relatively relaxed, and the trapezius muscle load RMS was small. The EMG load of the three parts of the muscles showed that the arm was in the horizontal state, and when the forearm was supported with the operating table, the muscle load of each part was the smallest and the most comfortable. Pose 1 was closer to the situation where the microscope focusses and other knob Settings were higher or the seat is lower, and pose 3 was closer to the situation when the microscope is operated without support or the seat is higher. From the perspective of human-machine design of microscope, in order to make the operator more comfortable, the position of the microscope adjustment knob should be designed, the arm support should be designed, and the height of the operating seat can be adjusted to a large range to meet the needs of most operators.

Subjective Evaluation of Arm Comfort. The subjective comfort questionnaire of 12 subjects was collected, and the arm comfort corresponding to the three levels of elbow joint angle was divided into forearm and shoulder respectively for RPE scoring. Then the scores of 12 subjects were averaged, and the evaluation results were shown in Table 4. RPE scores were the highest for forearm elevation, and the lowest for forearm horizontal placement.

Table 4. RPE Subjective Assessment of arm comfort

Evaluation part	Elbow angle			
	85~95°	115~125°	145~155°	Mean
Medial forearm	4.7	2.1	3.8	3.53
Lateral forearm	3.1	2.2	3.5	2.93
Shoulder	5.2	2.2	4.3	3.9
Mean	4.33	2.17	3.87	—

4 Conclusion

The evaluation experiment was designed for the evaluation of operating comfort of biological microscopes. The evaluation experiment of neck and shoulder comfort and the evaluation experiment of arm comfort of microscope operation were proceeded. The RMS of neck, shoulder and arm muscles' sEMG was measured in the range of neck flexion angle 0–40° and elbow joint angle 90–150° as an objective evaluation result. Based on the single factor ANOVA, the RMS of sEMG were analyzed, and it was found that muscle load and joint motion angle are related, the load was in the 4–30% MVC.

Based on the objective sEMG and subjective RPE, the operation comfort was evaluated. The most comfortable posture range of the operating microscope was concluded. This evaluation method combined the load of the measured muscle with the subjective operation habit, it can be used to estimate optimal operation posture for different operating persons, and to guide the designers on the basis of microscope operators' body parameters such as eye height, elbow height, sit height to design adjustable eyepiece, the arm support, focusing knob layout, etc.

References

1. Jain, G., Shetty, P.: Occupational concerns associated with regular use of microscope. Int. J. Occup. Med. Environ. Health **27**(4), 591–598 (2014)
2. Gupta, A., Mhaske, S., Ahmad, M., et al.: Ergonomic microscope: need of the hour. J. Clin. Diagn. Res. **9**(5), 62–65 (2015)
3. Vijendren, A., Devereux, G., Tietjen, A., et al.: The Ipswich Microbreak Technique to alleviate neck and shoulder discomfort during microscopic procedures. Appl. Ergon. **2**(83), 102679 (2020)
4. James, T.M.: An ergonomic approach to modifying microscope design for increased comfort: a case study. In: Proceedings of the Human Factors and Ergonomics Society 39th Annual Meeting, vol. 39, pp. 573–577 (1995)
5. James, T., Lamar, S., Marker, T.: An intervention study comparing traditional and ergonomic microscopes. In: Proceedings of the IEA/HFES 2000 Congress, vol. 6, pp. 31–34 (2000)
6. Sillanpää, J., Nyberg, M.: The ergonomics of microscope work. Microscopy: science, technology. Appl. Educ. 1333–1538 (2010)
7. Sillanpää, J., Nyberg, M., Laippala, P.: A new table for work with a microscope, a Solution to ergonomic problems. Appl. Ergon. **34**(6), 621–628 (2003)
8. Kreczy, A., Kofler, M., Gschwendtner, A.: Underestimated health hazard: proposal for an ergonomic microscope workstation. Lancet **354**(13), 1701–1702 (1999)
9. Vijendren, A., et al.: Effects of prolonged microscopic work on neck and back strain amongst male ENT clinicians and the benefits of a prototype postural support chair. Int. J. Occup. Saf. Ergon. **25**(3), 402–411 (2019)
10. Zenner-Gellrich, S.: Breakthrough in ergonomics for laboratory and clinical microscopes. Microscopy Today **21**(5), 18–21 (2013)
11. Sommerich, C.M., Joines, S.M.B., Hermans, V., et al.: Use of surface electromyography to estimate neck muscle activity. J. Electromyography Kinesiol. **10**, 377–398 (2000)
12. Martire, R.L., Gladh, K., Westman, A., et al.: Neck muscle EMG-force relationship and its reliability during isometric contractions. Sports Med. **3**(16), 1–10 (2017)

Author Index

V. G. Duffy (Ed.): HCII 2024, LNCS 15376, pp. 337–338, 2025.
https://doi.org/10.1007/978-3-031-76809-5

GPSR Compliance

The European Union's (EU) General Product Safety Regulation (GPSR) is a set of rules that requires consumer products to be safe and our obligations to ensure this.

If you have any concerns about our products, you can contact us on ProductSafety@springernature.com

In case Publisher is established outside the EU, the EU authorized representative is:

Springer Nature Customer Service Center GmbH
Europaplatz 3
69115 Heidelberg, Germany

The manufacturer's authorised representative in the EU is Springer
Nature Customer Service Centre GmbH, Europaplatz 3, 69115 Heidelberg,
Germany. If you have any concerns regarding our products, please
contact ProductSafety@springernature.com

Printed and bound by CPI Group (UK) Ltd, Croydon, CR0 4YY
29/04/2026
02099532-0009